# Sports

**Recent Titles in
American Popular Culture**

American Popular Illustration: A Reference Guide
*James J. Best*

Recreational Vehicles and Travel: A Resource Guide
*Bernard Mergen*

Magic: A Reference Guide
*Earle J. Coleman*

Newspapers: A Reference Guide
*Richard A. Schwarzlose*

Radio: A Reference Guide
*Thomas Allen Greenfield*

Popular American Housing: A Reference Guide
*Ruth Brent and Benyamin Schwarz, editors*

Fashion and Costume in American Popular Culture: A Reference Guide
*Valerie Burnham Oliver*

Editorial Cartooning and Caricature: A Reference Guide
*Paul P. Somers, Jr.*

American Mystery and Detective Novels: A Reference Guide
*Larry Landrum*

Self-Help and Popular Religion in Early American Culture: An Interpretive Guide
*Roy M. Anker*

Self-Help and Popular Religion in Modern American Culture: An Interpretive Guide
*Roy M. Anker*

Pornography and Sexual Representation: A Reference Guide
*Joseph W. Slade*

# Sports

## A Reference Guide and Critical Commentary, 1980–1999

Donald L. Deardorff II

American Popular Culture
M. Thomas Inge, Series Editor

**GREENWOOD PRESS**
Westport, Connecticut • London

**Library of Congress Cataloging-in-Publication Data**

Deardorff, Donald L.
    Sports : a reference guide and critical commentary, 1980–1999 / by Donald L. Deardorff II.
      p.   cm. — (American popular culture, ISSN 0193–6859)
    Includes bibliographical references and index.
    ISBN 0–313–30445–9 (alk. paper)
    1. Sports. 2. Sports—United States—History—20th century. I. Higgs, Robert J., 1932–
Sports. II. Title. III. Series.
    GV704.D42   2000
    796′.09′048—dc21      00–020466

British Library Cataloguing in Publication Data is available.

Library of Congress Catalog Card Number: 00–020466
ISBN: 0–313–30445–9
ISSN: 0193–6859

First published in 2000

Greenwood Press, 88 Post Road West, Westport, CT 06881
An imprint of Greenwood Publishing Group, Inc.
www.greenwood.com

Printed in the United States of America

The paper used in this book complies with the
Permanent Paper Standard issued by the National
Information Standards Organization (Z39.48–1984).

10 9 8 7 6 5 4 3 2 1

# Contents

# Preface

The problem with writing a book entitled *Sports: A Reference Guide and Critical Commentary, 1980–1999* is that it is hard to establish its scope and limitations. One wants to include every book and article that might be of value to any student of sport. Yet, even a discussion of the material produced within the last year could take up the entire book. It was necessary, therefore, to determine which items would be discussed in the text of the work, which ones would simply be listed in the bibliographies, and which would be left out altogether. In doing this, I have evaluated each book according to the following criteria: the substantive quality of the information presented, its timeliness and significance, whether or not it is the product of solid research and documentation, and the quality of the writing and overall presentation. Naturally, not all of the books rated highly in each category. A novel included in the sports literature chapter, for instance, might not have been the product of extensive research, but it would certainly have to be well crafted. Likewise, a book on the influence of new technologies on sport might be a bit dry, but it would have to be timely and meticulously researched.

The principal focus of this book is American sports, but I did include a chapter on sport and world history. In addition, I tried whenever possible to include works written in countries other than the United States. Because the audience for this book is thought to be predominantly English speaking, nearly all of the works profiled are written in English. Regrettably, this leaves out many of the influential works penned in other languages over the last two decades. Admittedly, this is a drawback. However, space and language limitations prevented me from including such texts. Otherwise, I believe that the twelve chapters that comprise this edition represent the most important topic areas in sport studies. In addition, while I could not include every book that might have been appropriate for each chapter, I think that the generalist, the beginning scholar, and even the specialist will find enough good information for each topic to make the book a useful research tool.

Only books are profiled in this volume. Many of the books have thorough bibliographies that list scores of the latest academic articles on sport. I have also listed the academic journals most likely to contain current articles on each topic covered in the book at the end of each chapter. There is a master list of periodicals dedicated exclusively to sport in Appendix 2.

So many people have helped with this project that I cannot possibly list all of them by name. I can only give my most heartfelt thanks to the many friends, colleagues, and professional acquaintances who brought fresh insight to the book. I would like to thank the entire Cedarville College Library staff, especially Interlibrary Services Coordinator Melinda Howard and her staff. They processed hundreds of books that I reviewed for this project, and they consistently displayed patience and good humor. I am also grateful for the Ohio academic libraries' OhioLINK system, which makes the identification and borrowing of materials located at more than sixty academic libraries statewide so easy.

I would also like to thank several people without whose emotional and intellectual support this book would never have been completed. I will always be indebted to Dr. Jack Higgs, by whose recommendation I was awarded the contract to write the book. I am equally indebted to him for the example he gave me to follow by writing the first edition of *Sports: A Reference Guide* in 1980, a contribution that changed the way academics conducted scholarly research into sport. In addition, I would like to thank series editor M. Thomas Inge, Blackwell Professor of the Humanities at Randolph-Macon College, for his timely support and encouragement, and my two editors at Greenwood Press, Alicia Merritt and Pamela St. Clair, for their guidance and consistent professionalism. I would also be remiss in not mentioning the technical expertise of Sarah Laramore, whose computer savvy and writing skills greatly aided the completion of this project. Most of all, I would like to thank my wife, Julie Deardorff, Cedarville College's Assistant Library Director for Collection Services, for her identification of new books relating to sport and her countless hours of proofreading. I was also the beneficiary of her superior listening skills and overall benevolence.

# Introduction

It is hard to believe that anyone living in our present age would question the power of sport in the contemporary world. After all, in the United States we live in a society where the antics of professional wrestling play to sell-out crowds even though the entire audience is well aware that the competition is, shall we say, less than genuine. Equally disconcerting, but no less revealing of the importance we place on sport, is that a professional athlete whose salary is a million dollars per year is so "underpaid" that one would assume that he must be an unheralded rookie or an aging veteran backup finishing out his career on the bench. Holidays are defined as much by the sporting contests traditionally staged on those dates as by the religious or historical event that gave rise to the special day in the first place. The National Football League's Super Bowl is usually the highest rated television program of the year, and at least three networks, ESPN, FOX, and CNN, boast twenty-four hour a day sports networks that do not seem to hurt for ratings. Anyone who followed the World Cricket Championships in India in 1999 or the World Cup of Soccer in France in 1998 knows that sport wields its cultural power in every country across the globe. All who know the stories of the Roman Coliseum or the Greek Olympics know that sport has from the beginning of Western society been an important political, social, religious, and economic force.

Yet, sport still gives scholars a problem in terms of definition. As Jack Higgs wrote in *Sports: A Reference Guide* back in 1980, "Sport has become as ubiquitous as the weather and is understood just about as well" (Higgs 1980, 3). Many scholars have attempted to distinguish between sports and games, or sport and play, or even sport and sports. I have not worried as much about adhering to any one definition of any of these terms in this book. Instead, I have adopted a broad, fluid definition of sports that I believe corresponds with the way many Americans view them: as physical contests, sometimes individual in nature and sometimes within a team context, in which we engage for physical, emotional, spiritual, or psychological fulfillment. Baseball, mountain climbing, golf, auto racing, running, and fishing are good examples. By contrast, cards, darts, and dice games are just that, games, not sports. I should note, however, that while I privilege sport over games, I also tend to give more coverage to competitive team sports than to individual sports, even if the individual athletic act takes place in a competitive context.

My loose definition of sport, a term that I use interchangeably with sports, and the process by which I researched this book certainly determined the material that eventually wound up in its pages. However, it did not affect the topic areas designated by the twelve chapter headings. Those were actually "chosen" by hundreds of scholars across the United States and the world, whose quality works have made it impossible not to recognize certain research areas that are clearly so important to them. Though the reader will have to read the chapters to fully discover all that they contain, I can briefly discuss the layout of the book.

Chapter 1 covers sport and American history, including the colonial period, nineteenth- century sport, the history of baseball and other sports that have defined the American experience, the sporting history of specific regions, and the effects of social and political movements on sports in the United States. Chapter 2 profiles some of the most pressing business and legal issues that continue to impact sport. I discuss sources whose authors comment on the business structure of professional and college sport, the labor history of sport, sports marketing, public relations, and important legal rulings that have changed the way sport is conducted. Chapter 3 focuses on the relationship between sport and education and explores whether or not sport is a good educational tool, the consequences of big-time college athletics, and the possibilities of using sport as a means for educational reform. Chapter 4 deals with ethnicity and race. It analyzes the importance of sport to ethnic identity in the United States and around the world and examines how sport both combats and exacerbates racial discrimination. Chapter 5 considers sports and gender and focuses on the impact that sport has on gender roles and expectations, as well as the impact of Title IX legislation on contemporary sporting practice. Chapter 6 is a discussion of sport and literature. I tried to profile some of the best fiction, short stories, drama and poetry written about sport, as well as some of the best criticism on the material. Chapter 7 profiles sport's relationship with philosophy and religion. It examines whether or not sport acts as a type of secular or civic religion, why we play, and what sport means to various athletes and spectators across the globe. Chapter 8 analyzes the power of sport in popular culture, including film, photography, pop art, architecture, the media, language, and juvenile texts. Chapter 9 covers sports psychology, including the history of the discipline; how athletes deal with pain, fear, and fatigue; the effects of aggression on athletes; and contemporary strategies used by sports psychologists on both teams and individuals to promote success. Chapter 10 examines how developments in science and technology continue to change sport. Chapter 11 covers the sociology of sport. In it, I discuss how scholars have tried to answer such questions as what sport means to various countries around the world, how sport reveals national values, what constitutes a sports hero and how his or her status is sustained, and why sports subcultures exist. Chapter 12, by far the toughest chapter to write and the topic about which I wish I could have written more, is on sports and world history. Its focus is the history of sport in the ancient world, Western Europe, and the Far East. A few other areas are given some attention as well.

Each chapter is followed by a complete bibliography that contains more works that pertain to the subject area than I actually profiled in the text. In addition, I have concluded each chapter with an alphabetical list of the academic journals that frequently contain articles on that subject. Two appendices follow at the end of the book. The first contains a list of some of the most important dates in sports history from 1980 to 2000. It is intended to help scholars gain contexts for any event they might be researching. The second appendix contains lists of web sites, databases, sports related periodicals, and research centers that would be helpful for students of sport.

As a professor and scholar, and as an athlete and fan, it is my most sincere hope that this book does justice to a topic that is so important to me and, no doubt, to millions of people all over the world. If it turns out to be half as useful to students and scholars as Jack Higgs's 1980 edition, I will be well pleased.

## REFERENCE

### Book

Higgs, Jack. *Sports: A Reference Guide*. Westport, CT: Greenwood Press, 1980.

# 1

# Sport and American History

It is not difficult to pinpoint books and articles on sport that comment on American history. There are literally hundreds if not thousands of quality works that deal with nearly any topic about which one could want information. Historical works are available on every period of American history and on every sport that has enjoyed any significant popularity at any time in the country's history. The problem is not finding good sources. It is deciding how to limit sources for chapters such as this. For nearly every work profiled in this volume is historically oriented to some degree, and most of them touch on events that are part of the story of the United States. No matter whether a book's main concern is rooted in sociology, psychology, science and technology, literature, business, law or philosophy, there is usually a decidedly historical bent to the subject matter. Of course, one cannot profile every work. Choices must be made. Accordingly, this chapter is divided into six sections, each of which profiles works dealing specifically with some aspect of American sports history, and which have been produced only after rigorous historical research. The first category involves general histories, books that focus on sport in a specific historical period, athletic participation among members of specific groups of Americans, or technological, economic, political, religious, or social changes that have impacted American sport from the colonial period to the present. The second category contains books on the history of baseball, a subject that has drawn the attention of some of the field's top scholars. Other categories include the history of boxing, the history of collegiate sports, the history of sport in specific cities, and miscellaneous works that deal with everything from African American sports history to the history of volkssporting. As always, the reader should be aware that hundreds of articles not profiled in this chapter can be found through the SPORTSDiscus CD-ROM, and any one of several excellent journals, including *American History, American History Review, American Indian Culture and Research Journal, American Jewish History, American Sports, American*

*Studies International, Hispanic American Review, International Journal of the History of Sport, Journal of American Culture, Journal of American Studies, Journal of Interdisciplinary History, Journal of Negro History, Journal of Physical Education, Journal of Popular Culture, Journal of Sport History, Journal of Sport and Social Issues, Journal of the Philosophy of Sport, Reviews in American History, Sociology of Sport Journal, Sport History,* and *Sport History Review.*

## GENERAL HISTORIES OF AMERICAN SPORT

There are so many good general histories of sport in America that it is hard to know where to start or how to separate them into different categories. Most of them cover several periods in the country's history and are careful to discuss why and how sport was played during those periods, who the key players and innovators were, and what sport meant to different Americans at different times. Still, some of the books have special strengths that distinguish them from the others. For instance, Nancy Struna's *People of Prowess: Sport, Leisure, and Labor in Early Anglo-America* focuses on the use and development of sport in colonial America. The book is painstakingly researched and covers several topics, including how Puritans played, the function of sport in precolonial days, the differences between sport in colonial Virginia as opposed to sport in Boston, the differences in athletic pursuits between social classes, the factors that led to the rise of horse racing as the first mass spectator sport late in the eighteenth century, and the relationship between labor and sport that defined athletic practices for much of the colonial period. This last aspect is particularly interesting, and Struna dedicates much of the book to explaining how work informed sport. In all, she explains why several types of workers, from rich plantation owners to small farmers to city laborers played the way they did. While large land owners in the South raced horses as a means of displaying their wealth and gaining prestige within their closed but highly influential society, urban laborers in Boston engaged in "sports" such as cock shailing as a means of resisting horrible working conditions. As Struna explains, "More than an act of resistance to ministers and other churchgoers, cock shailing may have been a form of defiance meted out by laborers against wealth and property holders. It may have even been an instance of what the dominant culture considered to be the residual leisure preference. As such, it was also an effort on the part of laborers to reestablish control of their leisure practices and, in the process, reclaim an advantage for themselves as workers" (Struna 1996, 93). Struna goes on to explain how work effected the sporting habits of many Americans, concluding that leisure sports, dictated by the amount of time a group of individuals had and the way their working habits demanded that they use sport, were "constructed by the colonial upper rank and borrowed and reframed in subtle ways by the early national urban middle class" and eventually "became the basis for modern sport" (Struna 1996, 198).

Other works that discuss the role of sport in the colonial period include David K. Wiggins's *Sport in America: From Wicked Amusement to National Obsession* and Benjamin Rader's *American Sports: From the Age of Folk Games to the Age of Spectators* and his later *American Sports: From the Age of Folk Games to the Age of Televised Sports*. Wiggins includes a chapter by Allen Guttmann entitled "Puritans at Play: Accusations and Replies" that provides a strong and convincing rebuttal to revisionist historians who have tried to frame Puritans as being catalytic agents in the development of modern sport. Guttmann demonstrates that Puritan attitudes toward sport and like physical activity were not, in fact, puritanical. He shows that many Puritan ministers favored some degree of play and physical exertion, usually in a fairly controlled setting. Still, while affirming Puritan use of sport as a way of celebrating God and keeping the holy temple of the body pure, he resists the notion advanced by some scholars that Puritans somehow paved the way for modern capitalist sport. As he concludes, "That the English and American Puritans retarded the emergence of modern sports, which 'took off' only when Puritan magistrates were replaced by more worldly rulers, seems undeniable. To argue the contrary, as the revisionists have done, is a distortion of the historical facts" (Wiggins 1995, 11). Those looking for information on the revisionist position to which Guttmann refers should also read this essay and consult its bibliography.

In *American Sports: From the Age of Folk Games to the Age of Spectators*, Rader divides the history of American sports into three parts. The first is the age of folk games, which Rader argues ran from the American Revolution through 1850 when technological advances allowed for development of organized sports with formal rules and players. He contends that colonial sport was guided by games instead of sports. These games "were far less formal than modern sports. The rules of their games were relatively simple, unwritten, legitimated by custom, and sometimes revised to fit the circumstances of the moment. The rules prevalent in one locality often differed sharply from those of another, and the significance of the game usually extended only to the immediate region. No bureaucracies or referees supervised contests, and few players trained for their performances" (Rader 1983, 2–3). In *American Sports: From the Age of Folk Games to the Age of Televised Sports*, Rader updates his first book and gives several examples of how these games were played in New England, the South, and the Middle Colonies. One of the more interesting segments is on how the southern gentry constructed their houses with informal gaming practices in mind: "The great southern planters sought to imitate the life style of the English country gentry. They built splendid mansions that often included special rooms for dancing and billiard playing" (Rader 1996, 10). Still, according to Rader, "no pastimes ignited the passions of the southern gentry more than horse racing and gambling. Wherever a few great planters gathered, someone nearly always produced a deck of cards, a backgammon board or a pair of dice" (Rader 1996, 10). Informal, loosely regulated, and highly spontaneous, such were sports in the colonial period. Other books that contain excellent chapters on the period include Donald Spivey's *Sport in America: New Historical Perspectives*, Steven Riess's *The American Sporting Experience: A Historical Anthology of Sport in America*, and Peter Levine's *American Sport: A Documentary History*.

Most historians look at the nineteenth century as the period in which modern sport took shape. Consequently, there are several quality books and essays available that explain what sport meant to various Americans as the century evolved. Steven Pope's *Patriotic Games: Sporting Traditions in the American Imagination, 1876–1926* is one of two book-length studies that focuses on what sport meant to America in general during the last half of the century. Pope argues that games evolved into cherished sports undergirded by highly bureaucratized structures because Americans viewed sport as an arena in which to display the nationalistic pride they felt in their burgeoning nation after it healed from the pain of reconstruction to develop into a formidable world power. In addition, sport became a vehicle for evincing national unity and patriotism in the face of some rather serious cultural strains, including immigration, poverty, sectionalism, and several economic and social alterations brought about by a surging industrial economy. Pope argues that "nationalism appealed to psychological needs during a time when the community, family, church, and workplace were undermined by corporate capitalism. As the working class culture itself became colonized by professionals, bureaucrats and specialists—all of whom had an interest in opposing class warfare and promoting national unity—it embraced new symbols of community, re-created on the basis of the nation—not class" (Pope 1997, 10). It is not surprising that Americans elevated baseball, a game derived from the British game of rounders, as their national sport, while also taking particular national pride in college football, derived from English rugby and soccer, and in the Olympic games, for which the ancient Greeks can be credited. Pope goes into great depth in describing the process by which this elevation took place, and his analysis of the factors that led to a growing sense of patriotism through sport in the late nineteenth century is well evidenced.

Donald Mrozek also discusses the importance of sport to the collective American psyche at the time. In *Sport and American Mentality, 1880–1910*, he reaffirms Pope's thesis about the importance of sport to the rising nationalist sentiment which gripped the country. However, Mrozek also spends several chapters arguing that two other factors were just as important in placing sport at the center of the American social scene. The first involved concerns over gender. As women became more active outside the domestic sphere, making significant inroads in the workforce as well as in the realms of politics and religion, they began to play games and even to compete in sport. Mrozek discusses the medical issues this raised, especially the concerns over the health of the supposedly weaker sex, and also shows how the desire of women to play and compete changed the way Americans approached sport. Specifically, the author shows that sport developed quickly and was embraced with such passion because men, not wanting to be outdone by women in any physical pursuit, began to view sport as a vehicle by which to prove their manliness. It is not surprising that baseball, boxing, and college football developed as the dominant sports played by men in part as a display of their own masculine worth. The second factor was the rising concern of American physicians and political leaders over the moral and physical health of Americans. Precipitated by the sedentary working environment of many urban workers and the often squalid conditions in which they lived and worked, this new anxiety over American spiritual and physical well being included both a concern over the physical stamina of the young women who would be the domestic guardians of the nation, and over the young men of the upper class who, as future leaders of state and industry, were seen by their Civil War veteran fathers as being weak, dissolute, and unmanly. Mrozek's book is thus an excellent source for those who want to understand how nationalism, gender anxiety, and moral concerns dominated the way American perceived and used sport in the last half of the nineteenth century.

## CULTURAL CHANGE AND THE DIVERSITY OF AMERICAN SPORT

Naturally, an entire century of sporting activity can not be summed up so easily. Several authors have penned works in the last few years that contribute to our understanding of how specific groups of Americans used sport within the general framework described by Pope and Mrozek. In *American Sports: From the Age of Folk Games to the Age of Televised Sports,* Rader describes the divergent approaches that Americans took toward sport in the Victorian era. He shows conclusively that the sport as moral agent movement was decidedly an invention of the middle class, whose insistence that sport be used as a weapon to combat vice was a reaction to the use of sport by both the "dissolute aristocracy" and the "unproductive rabble," both of which used sport as a means of sensual pleasure and worldly gratification (Rader 1996, 25). In addition, Pope's *The New American Sport History: Recent Approaches and Perspectives*, contains two essays on the subject. In this study, Mark Dyerson's "Regulating the Body and the Body Politic" shows how the Victorian middle class not only viewed sport as a moral agent, but also saw it as a ladder to social and political power. To that end, it attempted to articulate "a new sports ideology that reconciled their class interests with the new imperatives of corporate capitalism" in such a way that would "revitalize their ability to influence the larger body politic" (Pope 1997, 8). Another good essay in the volume is Riess's "Sport and the Redefinition of Middle-Class Masculinity in Victorian America," in which the author shows how middle-class sport for men was closely linked with attempts to bolster their masculine identities in ways that were socially acceptable and economically beneficial.

By contrast, David Wiggins and Elliott Gorn focus their attention on the antebellum South. Wiggins's essay, "Leisure Time on the Southern Plantation: The Slaves' Respite from Constant Toil, 1810–1860," is located in Donald Spivey's *Sport in America: New Historical Perspectives*. Wiggins's explanation of the various function of sport for slaves is eye-opening. These functions included pure fun, feelings of individual pride and competence, the elevation of much needed heroes and role models, and a safe arena in which black slaves could satirize their white masters while erecting their own hierarchy of authority. Gorn's "Gouge and Bite, Pull Hair and Scratch: The Social Significance of Fighting in the Southern Backcountry" is located in Wiggins's *Sport in America: From Wicked Amusement to National Obsession*. The article is quite amusing and well written, and thus not only is a fine example of what academic writing should be like, but is also a quality piece of historical scholarship that shows us how poor, southern whites used sport to make sense of the violence that ruled their everyday lives. As Gorn writes, "Violence and poverty were part of daily existence, so endurance, even callousness, became functional values" (Wiggins 1995, 49). Fighting and wrestling were part of fostering such values.

As is the case with several other books, Wiggins's volume contains several essays that show how Americans were playing in the nineteenth century. These include Roberta Park's "Embodied Selves: The Rise and Development of Concern for Physical Education, Active Games and Recreation for American Women, 1776–1865," Melvin Adelman's "The First Modern Sport in America: Harness Racing in New York City, 1825–1870," and Ronald Story's "The Country of the Young: The Meaning of Baseball in Early American Culture." Peter Levine's *American Sport: A Documentary History* also contains several interesting selections of commentaries and eye-witness accounts of sports at the time. These include sections from Robert Carver's *Book of Sports*, which laid out the social functions of sport in the 1830s, a letter from William Alcott that speaks to the role of sport for women in the 1850s, an essay on gouging from Thomas Ashe's *Travels in America*, excerpts on muscular Christianity from Thomas Wentworth Higginson's *Saints and Their Bodies,* and several other fascinating artifacts.

Riess's *The American Sporting Experience: A Historical Anthology of Sports in America* contains two good essays on how Americans viewed college football late in the nineteenth century. One is Walter Camp's "Walter Camp on Sportsmanship" and the other is J. Hammond Moore's "Football's Ugly Decades, 1893–1913." The articles provide a nice contrast with Camp, the legendary coach, championing football as a sport that teaches the best of manly virtues, while Hammond demonstrates clearly that in actual practice the game did anything but cultivate virtue in its players. Another tremendous collection is Riess's *Major Problems in American Sports History*. Chapters 3, 4 and 5 cover the nineteenth century, featuring primary documents from Thomas Wentworth Higginson, Catherine Beecher, Horace Greeley, and several newspaper and magazine accounts of sporting events, as well as quality essays from several prominent scholars. Finally, those looking for information of the effects of technology on the transition from scattered, informal games to institutionalized American sport might want to look at Rader's *American Sports: From the Age of Folk Games to the Age of Spectators* or John Richards Betts's *America's Sporting Heritage: 1850–1950*, both of which show how the Civil War and the technological advances that followed it helped move sport into the modern era.

As sport has changed shape in the twentieth century, it has meant many things to the nation and to its increasingly diverse athletic participants. In *Making the American Team: Sport, Culture and the Olympic Experience*, Mark Dyerson shows how important the modern Olympic games were to a nation that was slowly inventing itself as a "Sporting Republic" because it saw international sporting prowess as symbolic of its status as a world power. Dyerson uses newspaper and journal accounts to show how Americans responded with great pride to the 1896 games in Athens, the 1900 games in Paris, the 1904 games in St. Louis, the 1908 games in London, and the games of 1912 in Stockholm, emphasizing their importance to America as a country bent on displaying its power to the world. Dyerson argues that "from the beginning the United States sought to turn the Olympics into an American spectacle. The Athens Olympics provided the sporting republic with the perfect forum for proving to Americans that the powers of sport were at work reforming society" (Dyerson 1998, 51). When several of their athletes triumphed in the games, "the results of the Athenian athletic adventure allowed Americans to judge themselves superior to the rest of the world in everything from performing Sophocles' *Antigone* to hurling discuses" (Dyerson 1998, 50). The author goes on to examine what the next several Olympic competitions meant to the United States, whose citizens often saw the games as proving the rightness of the nation's economic, political or social policies of the time. He also includes an excellent concluding chapter on how World War I ushered in the end of America's view of itself as sporting republic.

Accompanying this rising sense of national pride was a concern for the development of youth sport, a concern that was also heightened by insistence on the part of the medical community, educators, and social philosophers that children were dangerously unhealthy. Rader's *American Sports: From the Age of Folk Games to the Age of Televised Sports* has an entire chapter that deals with these and other factors that led to the rise of organized youth sports at the dawn of the twentieth century. One of these factors was, of course, the concern of Christians that the young people who would guide a great nation be as physically and spiritually fit as possible. Rader writes that "team sport offered an unparalleled opportunity for adults to encourage in boys the healthy growth of moral and religious reflexes. Stemming from the instinct of cooperation, team sports required the highest moral principles—teamwork, self-sacrifice, obedience, self-control, and loyalty" (Rader 1996, 105). One notices that Rader makes the point to use "boys" instead of boys and girls or children. His analysis makes it quite clear that most of the impetus for the development of youth programs came from anxiety about boys and their maturation into manly men of character and vigor. Rader confirms that "to the advocates of the new sporting ideology, modern life had become too soft and effeminate" (Rader 1996, 100). Sport was seen as a way to toughen up boys and prepare them for the trials of modern existence. Riess's *Major Problems in American Sports History* confirms this desire on the part of upper class men to use sport to make sure that their sons were ready to lead their nation. Riess includes a section on sports heroes and American culture in which he shows how the *Frank Merriwell* stories, which chronicled the adventures of Yale's football captain of that name who saves every game by pulling victory from the clutches of defeat while correcting several social and political irregularities on the campus, attained best-seller status because gentlemen wanted their sons to be like him and because the sons desired to be like the virile, Ivy League hero. Riess includes an excerpt from one of the stories and several commentaries on what heroes such as Merriwell meant to boys around 1920 and why they continued to be popular until the poverty and hardships of the depression era made such idealizations difficult to swallow.

Several books examine why specific sports heroes came to prominence at different times in the twentieth century. In *Idols of the Game: A Sporting History of the American Century*, Robert Lipsyte and Peter Levine profile six different types of heroes that have emerged over the last 100 years. The authors start with a chapter on the importance of early boxing champions to various members of the American populace at the turn of the century and end with a discussion of the factors that gave rise to the current postmodern idols such as Michael Jordan and Arnold Schwarzenegger. For instance, boxer John L. Sullivan, an illiterate brawler, was held in such high esteem by working class white men in the late 1800s because, in an age of immigration, women's demands for equality and changing domestic and work structures, he stood for traditional masculine dominance. The feeling of assurance he gave these men at the time was so great that even when he eventually lost a fight to Jim Corbett, "'the grandest fighter the world had ever seen' remained for many a promise that despite the close of the frontier, 'over-civilization,' and the immigrant 'hordes,' true Americans would still rule the world. American men, that is" (Lipsyte and Levine 1995, 32). If Sullivan served this function at the beginning of the century, Marshall Smelser points out in Riess's *The American Sporting Experience: A Historical Anthology of Sport in America* that Babe Ruth would assume a similar role in what the author calls American sports' "Golden Era," the years roughly between 1900 and World War II. According to Smelser, Ruth, in the Roaring Twenties and later in the depression era, appealed to everything the average American Joe wanted to be. He was uneducated and sprang from common stock, but he made it to the top of American society and hobnobbed with the cultural elite. He was crude but was loved anyway for his transparency and humanness. He was portly and didn't look like a player, but excelled as no player ever had. He symbolized hope for all of those who started at the bottom, did not have connections or education, and did not want to play by society's rules. Riess's book contains several essays such as Smelser's and is a must read for anyone who wants to get a grip on what sport has meant to Americans in this century.

Richard Mandell's *Sport: A Cultural History* contains a chapter on American sport in the 1920s in which the author asserts that despite heroes such as Ruth, nationalistic feelings that linked sport with patriotism, or the emergence of a handful of noteworthy female or black athletes, sport in the 1920s was conducted by and for white males who attempted to sue athletics to reinforce traditional social mores complete with rigid codes for race and gender relations. Mrozek's cultural approach reminds the reader that sport, like other societal institutions, has always been and remains the product of select subjectivities with vested interest in how gender, race, and class concerns can be manipulated through athletics. He also includes a chapter entitled "Sport and Recent Times" in which he shows how religion, class warfare, feminism, gay rights, and the civil rights movement have reshaped American sports in the last few decades as white, male, middle-class control of sport has weakened. The author also features two chapters on the Olympic games, which profile the meaning each competition from 1896–1980 had for various American audiences. Levine's *American Sport: A Documentary History* is also an excellent cultural history of sport in the twentieth century. Levine features several primary writings that leap off the page and speak again about the relationship between big business and sport, politics and sport, and race and gender angst and sport over the last several decades. Excerpts include a witty and insightful column by Red Smith on the corruption of intercollegiate sports in the 1970s, a beautiful piece by Maya Angelou on what Joe Louis meant to her and other African Americans growing up in the 1940s, a Bill Bradley article on the necessity of Olympic reform prior to the 1976 summer games in Montreal, a chapter from Sandra Berenson's *Spalding's Basketball for Women* (1913) that explains why the sport was so important to women in the early years of the century, and several other illuminating writings.

Other quality works include Mark Naison's "Lefties and Righties: The Communist Party and Sports During the Great Depression," located in Spivey's *Sport in America: New Historical Perspectives*, and William J. Baker's "Muscular Marxism and the Chicago Counter-Olympics of 1932," which can be found in Pope's *The New American Sports History: Recent Approaches and Perspectives*, both of which explain how American Communists tried to reshape sport in the 1930s. Samuel Regalado's "Sport and Community in California's Japanese American 'Yamato Colony,' 1930–1945" is located in Wiggins's *Sport in America: From Wicked Amusement to National Obsession* and provides an interesting look at how Japanese Americans played in the years leading up to World War II. It also explains the function that sport had for these Americans in internment camps during the war. Also in Wiggins's book is Mrozek's "The Cult and Ritual of Toughness in Cold War America," in which the author shows how American fears of the Soviet Union led to a national obsession with sports as a way to make sure young America was in shape to combat Communist aggression. Both Wiggins's and Pope's books contain many other fine essays on a variety of subjects, including the history of anabolic steroids, Title IX legislation, immigrant sports in American cities, the role schools have played in using sports as a tool for political indoctrination, the debate over black athletic superiority, sports marketing, the history of the sporting goods industry, and the role that class and ethnicity has played in sporting practices since World War II.

Eric Leifer's *Making the Majors: The Transformation of Team Sports in America* is unique because the author dedicates the entire book to explaining how professional sports developed from tiny, struggling enterprises at the beginning of the century to multimillion-dollar businesses that define the sports scene today. Leifer takes great pains to show the reader how owners have used numerous marketing techniques while consistently cutting political deals to maintain their businesses until their teams could somehow gain a psychological foothold in their city. Close games, competitive teams, revenue sharing, star players with which people of a given region identified, publicity stunts, media coverage, quality stadiums in safe neighborhoods, lights so that games could be played after the work day ended, and many other variables had to be accounted for before a team could get a spiritual grip on its town. Leifer focuses on baseball, but his book can be seen as a blueprint for explaining the success or failure of any professional league in the United States.

Finally, Paul Zingg's *The Sporting Image: Readings in American Sports History*, Douglass Noverr's *The Games They Played: Sports in American History, 1865–1980*, and Elliott Gorn and Warren Goldstein's *A Brief History of American Sports* all offer valuable perspective on sport in the twentieth century. Zingg's work contains essays on race and ethnicity in baseball between 1900 and 1910, Jack Dempsey as the perfect athletic hero for the 1920s, the role of Joe Louis in bridging gaps between the races in the 1940s, the history of abuse of African-American athletes at major colleges and universities, and the efforts that women have made in sports to overcome historical definitions of what it means to be feminine. Noverr breaks his book up into a decade-by-decade analysis, focusing on the major figures and events that shaped American sports in each decade. Two chapters, "The Flashy Fifties: Sports in the Gray Flannel Suit Era" and "The 1960s: A Decade of Turmoil and Change" are particularly enlightening. Gorn and Goldstein's effort is quite possibly the best book available on sports history in America. With graceful prose, the two scholars expose many myths that have surrounded sports in the United States and show how taboo, the love of doing something illicit, dangerous, or out of step with societal mandate, has always been the real unspoken driving force behind games and sport in this country. The book is concise, carefully researched, and contains three entertaining sections on twentieth-century sport. These include the use of football and basketball to advance social agendas, the evolution of sport in the public sphere, and the corruption of sport in a mass market economy driven by television and an obsession with winning.

## THE HISTORY OF BASEBALL

In terms of the history of specific sports, baseball more than any other sport has captured the attention of scholars. George B. Kirsch's *The Creation of American Team Sports: Baseball and Cricket, 1838–1872* provides an in-depth look at how baseball evolved from an informal activity with no definite rules to a codified game played by teams in organized leagues that flourished across the country. Kirsch dedicates several chapters to explaining the differences between what he calls premodern and modern ball games, but the best chapters are the ones that explain in great detail the factors that led to the transformation from the spontaneous, playful games that lacked rules and organization to the codified games that would become the precursor of professional baseball. Though there is not space in this book to recount the logic of Kirsch's intricate argument, we can at least highlight a few of his words about the factors that led to modern baseball: "Industrialization, transportation and communication innovations, urbanization, and a new positive ideology of athletics—these were the preconditions for the rise of modern cricket and baseball in nineteenth century America. By the 1850s they were all present in the largest American metropolitan centers as well as in many of the lesser towns across the country" (Kirsch 1989, 16). Kirsch dedicates most of his book to explaining how all of these technological, economic, and philosophical factors worked together in specific cities and towns to move baseball to the center of America's social stage.

In many ways, Riess, in *Touching Base: Professional Baseball and American Culture in the Progressive Era*, picks up where Kirsch leaves off. Instead of concentrating on technological factors that brought baseball into its modern era, however, Riess examines the social functions that baseball had for cities and their various population groups at the turn of the century. For example, Riess contends that baseball gained popularity because "the principal values and goals of the core middle-class culture were expressed through the national pastime's history and its folklore, which consisted of legends, myths, and heroes. Implicit in the rhetoric of baseball were values associated with a traditional, bourgeois, small-town society" (Riess 1980, 221). These values included efficiency, order, social control, moral and physical hygiene, discipline, community pride, and social integration and acculturation. Baseball for America's growing middle class, then, had several utilitarian functions. It was useful in producing healthy young men who were morally fit and physically robust enough to compete in the rough and tumble world. At the same time, it allowed for newcomers, mostly immigrants, to learn about America and become part of the community. Still, for many Americans, baseball was popular because it embodied the best values of a fading American frontier. These traits included honesty, toughness, competitiveness, and rugged individualism in an age of increasingly corporate activity. Naturally, the fact that baseball was an outdoor game played on grass and dirt appealed to folks from the city who were surrounded by concrete, cramped buildings, and unsanitary conditions. For some young men with few economic alternatives, baseball was an avenue of social mobility that gave them a way to make a good living. For immigrants, it was a way of becoming American and being accepted by other Americans. For social reformers, it was a way of providing troubled youths with heroes that could potentially function as good role models. Some city officials saw the games as a way of allowing for a release of tensions built up by the pressures of urban living. Still others saw the game as part of the American dream whereby playing in or attending a game of one's favorite team validated one's status as a successful American. Riess explains how and why Americans embraced the game for all of these reasons, and since most of these reasons were quite exaggerated if not the stuff of myth, Riess includes a discussion of the importance of myths in the social function and popularity of baseball at the time. In truth, the author makes it clear that if people had not created such myths around the game, it is doubtful as to whether it would have enjoyed such a privileged status.

In *Creating the National Pastime: Baseball Transforms Itself, 1903–1953*, G. Edward White outlines the process by which baseball moved from being a popular sport that served many social functions to being a professional enterprise that was adored by most Americans, who elevated the game to its position as the country's national pastime. White shows how major league baseball embedded itself in the national culture in such a deeply significant way that it actually began to affect the everyday lives of Americans. There were, of course, several complicated and tenuous steps in this process. Ballparks had to be built in safe neighborhoods, teams had to remain competitive, teams had to have players with whom local citizens identified, tickets had to be affordable, there had to be adequate newspaper coverage, and most of all, teams had to be a source of civic pride. The people of any given city had to care about the team and gain a sense of well-being from its exploits. White describes the hoops through which owners jumped to make this psychic connection between city and team permanent, including chapters on the construction of new ballparks, the implementation of a commissioner to deal with scandal, the successful adoption of the famed reserve clause to keep players loved by cities from fleeing to other cities whose teams might make them a better offer, the integration process, the rise of radio and television, the importance of ethnicity, and the coming of night baseball. White also includes a chapter on the factors that have contributed to the demise of baseball's stature as America's national game in the last three decades. These include free agency, franchise relocation, competition from other sports, and a change in what contemporary culture demands of its sports. Another excellent book that chronicles the factors that led to the success of major league baseball is Eric Leifer's *Making the Majors: The Transformation of American Team Sports*, a well-researched and beautifully written work that complements White's book perfectly. Those looking for a case study on how this process of moving from a popular team to a professional enterprise that was deeply embedded into the fabric of a city's culture should also give some attention to James Hardy's *The New York Giants Baseball Club: The Growth of a Tea—and a Sport, 1870–1900*, which shows what the team meant to New Yorkers in the early days of professional baseball.

Several other books contain essays that would be helpful to a scholar researching the history of the grand old game. Rader's *Baseball: A History of America's Game* is a short book that focuses on the high points of baseball history. Chapters include discussions on how the first professional teams and leagues developed, how baseball combated the Black Sox scandal, why the days before television really were baseball's golden age, and why the game is currently in trouble. Gorn and Goldstein's *A Brief History of American Sports* has several sections on baseball's position and social functions throughout the twentieth century and ultimately concludes that sports such as baseball will always be important because, apart from mirroring societal values, they appeal to our love of beauty and transcendence: "Arousing deep longings for beauty, for awe, for shared community, such moments give us glimpses of a better world and nourish our hopes for much that is noble in humankind" (Gorn and Goldstein 1993, 254). Larry Moffi's *This Side of Cooperstown: An Oral History of Baseball in the 1950s* provides a look at how baseball stars from that decade perceived the game and its place in American life, while Phil Pepe's *Talkin' Baseball: An Oral History of Baseball in the 1970s* features athletes, managers, owners, and umpires talking candidly about the important issues of that decade. Both books offer colorful dialogue and some rather interesting opinions about life and baseball. Another book that is less intellectual but still highly informative and entertaining is William Mead's *Baseball: The President's Game*, which features chapters on George

Washington and Abraham Lincoln's involvement with baseball, as well as chapters that profile how most presidents through Bill Clinton have used baseball as a political tool. Riess's *Major Problems in American Sports History* features several primary documents pertaining to the history of baseball, while Lipsyte and Levine's *Idols of the Game* examines how Babe Ruth, Jackie Robinson, and Mickey Mantle effected how the American public perceived the game. Those interested in understanding how vital lights were to the success of professional baseball should consult David Pietrusza's *Lights On! The Wild Century-Long Saga of Night Baseball*, a light, entertaining, and informative look at how something we take for granted, night games, was such a source of controversy for years. Riess's *The American Sporting Experience: A Historical Anthology of Sport in America* has a fascinating article on how baseball magnates have influenced public policy, while Levine's *American Sport: A Documentary History* provides a wonderful array of commentaries about baseball from such noteworthy personages as A. G. Spaulding, Jackie Robinson, and Maya Angelou.

## THE HISTORY OF BOXING

After baseball, only boxing seems to have gripped historians of American sport. Little in the way of academic histories exist for football, soccer, basketball, tennis, golf, or auto racing, but boxing has been the subject of some tremendous works. One such book is *The Manly Art: Bareknuckle Prize Fighting in America* in which Elliott Gorn examines in colorful fashion the appeal that boxing had for the working class men that supported it in the latter half of the nineteenth century. Gorn argues that "by the 1850s boxing was arguably America's preeminent sport, but its popularity was not uniformly spread throughout the population" (Gorn 1989, 129). It was the preserve of white working class men and remained so for many years because it filled several psychological needs for that group of Americans. First, it helped men who lived in a world dominated by violence, both in the workplace and in social spheres, make sense of this violence. As Gorn writes, "The context makes sense of the ring's violence. Boxing, as well as cockfighting, bullbaiting, and ratting, did not just reflect the bloodiness of life. Rather, these and similar sports shaped violence into art, pared away its maddening arbitrariness, and thereby gave it order and meaning" (Gorn 1989, 144). Second, the boxing game gave them a sense of manhood that flew in the face of the stoic, staid, proper version of bourgeois masculinity practiced by their bosses. In the face of wealth, leisure, and gentlemanly codes of honor, working class men used boxing to celebrate their own version of masculinity based on toughness, raw energy, courage, and virility—things on which they prided themselves and saw their less masculine betters sorely lacking. As Gorn writes, "The ring at least offered cultural opposition; if not a challenge to evangelical or bourgeois authority, here at least was a denial of the values that undergirded oppressive social relationships" (Gorn 1989, 146). Finally, Gorn makes the point that although boxing was responsible for contributing to some disturbing social phenomena such as excessive drinking, gambling, bullying, extortion, and domestic violence, it also gave working class men hope that life could be better or that life's nastiness could at least be dealt with successfully. Gorn concludes that "at its best the ring dramatized a world of victory for the socially downtrodden, realistically counterposed to defeat and bloodshed" (Gorn 1989, 146).

While Gorn's work is the best general history of boxing in America, there are several other good books that take up the subject. A. J. Liebling's *A Neutral Corner: Boxing Essays* is a wonderful collection of essays written about boxing as it existed at different times in the United States. Boxers are depicted in several ways, including as heroes, villains, savage beasts, criminals, desperate survivors, scoundrels, and artists, and it gives the reader a good feel for how ambivalent American attitudes toward boxing have been in the twentieth century. Jeffrey Sammons's *Beyond the Ring: The Role of Boxing in American Society* has a more academic tone, but essentially has the same function as Liebling's work. Sammons's piece is well researched and engagingly written and shows the reader exactly what boxing has meant to different groups of Americans at different points in the nation's history. Bert Suger's *100 Years of Boxing* and Gerald Healy's *A Hurting Business* are both good general histories of the sport with Healy's work more internationally focused than Suger's book, whose subject is the evolution of boxing as a business in America over the last century and a half. In addition, Rader's *American Sports: From the Age of Folk Games to the Age of Televised Sports*, Pope's *The New American Sports History: Recent Approaches and Perspectives*, Spivey's *Sport in America: New Historical Perspectives*, and Wiggins's *Sport in America: From Wicked Amusement to National Obsession*, contain articles on the history of boxing.

Many biographies of boxers are shallow hymns that sing the athletes' praises in ways that often do not ring true. There are, however, some good biographical works that examine the lives of key figures in boxing history. The best of them is *John L. Sullivan and His America*, in which Michael Isenberg chronicles the life and career of the famous Boston bareknuckle pugilist and along the way captures how, for many men, boxing was inextricably tied to notions of masculinity in the last two decades of the nineteenth century. Isenberg's writing is as clear as his research is solid, and his book is not only a good history of boxing in the last half of the century and, of course, of Sullivan's life, but is also an excellent study of the economic, political, and technological forces that shaped America at that time, forces that forever changed the way various Americans used sport. Another fine biographical effort is Randy Roberts's *Papa Jack: Jack Johnson and the Era of White Hopes*. Roberts does an excellent job of chronicling the life of American boxing's first great black champion. Like Isenberg, Roberts is able to do much more in his book than simply tell the story of a boxer. He paints an accurate picture of life in America in the early decades of the twentieth century and is especially vivid when it comes to depicting race relations. The book, like Johnson, is often humorous and quite colorful. Roberts's prose flows nicely, and he captures the outrageous, manic, defiant demeanor that Johnson displayed his entire life. Any scholar interested in what boxing has meant to African Americans should read this book, which stands as a testament to the power of sport to both unite and divide races. Other useful biographical efforts include Lenwood Davis's *Joe Louis: A Bibliography of Articles, Books, and Pamphlets*, which includes hundreds of important references to scholarly works about the Brown Bomber, Gerald Early's *The Muhammad Ali Reader*, and Allen Bodner's *When Boxing Was a Jewish Sport*, a tremendous cultural history that examines how important boxing was to Jews in the 1920s and 1930s.

## THE HISTORY OF INTER-COLLEGIATE SPORT

Those interested in the history of college sports should start with *Sports and Freedom: The Rise of Big-Time College Athletics*, in which Ronald Smith discusses the factors that led to the formation and finally the institutionalization of collegiate athletics in the nineteenth century. Smith analyzes the debt American colleges owed to English sporting traditions, the development of the extra-curriculum and its association with student freedom, the rise of the first intercollegiate sport of crew, the development of college baseball and track, and, of course, the turbulent early history of college football. Of special interest is Smith's clear examination of how college sports evolved from a student controlled, small, informal set of activities into a highly regulated, commercial enterprise used by college presidents to garner publicity and financial support from alumni and other interested parties. Smith's argument clearly demonstrates the power that sport has had in the lives of colleges and universities for the last century and a half. What is interesting is that the professionalized, highly institutionalized, mainly commercial venture known as college sports that we know today was largely in place by the early 1900s, solidly entrenched by Harvard and Yale, the two schools that set the tone for an entire century of big-time college athletics. As Smith writes: "At Harvard and at Yale, students, alumni, presidents, governing boards, and even faculties, created, or allowed the creation of big time college athletics, which produced victories and presumably improved the public status of the two leading colleges. Financial favors to sub-freshman recruits; intensive training before, during and after the season; lack of or violation of eligibility rules; questionable ethics; payment of professional coaches well beyond faculty salaries; bowing to alumni athletic interests; and construction of stadiums for the public were all part of the Harvard and Yale athletic programs" (Smith 1988, 214).

Nowhere is the big-time nature of college sports around 1900 better revealed than in Smith's *Big-Time Football at Harvard, 1905*, in which the author examines diaries of former Harvard players, coaches, and administrators to show how the Crimson's football operation of 1905 was not that different from a Southeastern Conference (SEC) or Big Ten school today. Smith shows how players were privileged in many ways, including not having to go to class, receiving financial incentives from alumni and other sources, receiving payments for fake jobs, getting away with breaking college rules, and generally displaying low character. Smith recounts the Harvard coach's description of a key player named Preston Upham: "I appealed to Upham on every ground I could think of and at times he showed signs of getting to work, but the work never lasted long. He cut, went into town continually, and stayed in for three or four nights at a time, on occasions signing himself off as sick, got into street rows, automobile scrapes, and bad repute in money matters, into gambling, and other forms of trouble" (Smith 1994, 13). Smith goes on to chronicle the story of player after player who broke rules, womanized, gambled, drank to excess, cheated on exams and generally did anything that one might hear players of today's generation being accused of doing. What is truly amazing is to see how all of this was written off or ignored, unless an incident received too much publicity, because Harvard's administrators and alumni wanted to win, to beat Yale, and to receive the prestige, money, and bragging rights associated with such victories. Most colleges would not get away with these types of violations today in an age of much closer media and National Collegiate Athletic Association (NCAA) scrutiny. Taken together, Smith's books give the reader an excellent understanding of how the college sports of today got to be the way they are, and why, despite continual outcry from faculty and incessant attempts at reform, big-time athletic programs are likely to have the same structure and importance that they have had on college campuses for over a century. According to Smith, the main reason the structure has been held in place is not because most college administrators or alumni want it that way but because sports are so important to Americans that colleges cannot fail to excel in such a revered area: "Twentieth century big-time athletics became a ritual for nearly all major universities, symbolizing in physical form the intense competition for prestige existing among various institutions." Even in the late nineteenth century, "winning athletic teams were the most visible signs of the contests for prestige taking place in all areas of university life. With the success of Harvard and Yale as competitors in higher education and in athletics, it was not surprising that the twentieth century saw a ritualized cloning of Harvard and Yale" (Smith 1988, 218).

Another tremendous book dealing with the rise of big-time college athletics is Michael Oriard's *Reading Football: How the Popular Press Created an American Spectacle*. Oriard examines how college football evolved from a sport completely controlled by students and hated by faculty and administrators to a sport that would become not only the dominant college sport, but one of America's most popular sporting spectacles in the first two decades of the twentieth century. Oriard concludes that football had several characteristics that made it a perfect fit on college campuses. First, it appealed to the men who ran the schools, men who were concerned about the lack of vitality they perceived in the nation's boys. Football's toughness also answered a growing concern over the manliness and health of the young men who would lead the nation in the year to come. In addition, the game appealed to men from working class backgrounds, who saw the game as an expression of true manhood with all of its violent and brutal connotations, and to America's gentlemen, who wanted to be more than educated, effeminate elitists who had no backbone, no physical aptitude, no ability to inflict and take pain. Of course, gender concerns played a big part in the ascendancy of college football. The gridiron was, above all, a place where men could fashion a traditionally masculine self-definition in the face of changing gender roles in the workforce, at home, and in society in general. A woman might get the right to vote, but she could hardly be a football hero. Of course, race was another factor that must be considered. Jack Johnson might have been the first black boxing champion, and Negro baseball players might be quite good, but on the gridirons of America's universities, the gladiators were white, and the image of courageous knights fighting for the honor of their school was important to white, male identity. Naturally, the media, both in terms of newspapers and popular magazines and novels were no small part of football's rise to prominence. White men of all classes ate up football news, and young boys made Burt L. Standish's Frank Merriwell stories annual best-sellers. Oriard shows how closely linked the media and college sports have always been.

Several other anthologies contain articles that deal with the history of college sports. Levine's *American Sport: A Documentary History* has three articles on the corruption in college sports in the 1970s and the attempts at reform. Riess's *The American Sporting Experience: A Historical Anthology of Sport in America* contains two articles, James Koch's "The Economics of 'Big-Time' Intercollegiate Athletics" and "The Impact of Title IX," that discuss how Division I schools do business today and how they have coped with having to add women's programs. Riess's *Major Problems in American Sports History* has primary documents in which prominent political leaders, social reformers, and educators comment on the importance of and problems with intercollegiate sport at different times in the twentieth century. Gorn and Goldstein's *A Brief History of American Sports* has two chapters that deal with the rise of college football and the importance of college sport in the Progressive Era, and the problems that college athletic programs have faced over the last half century, including drugs, racism, gambling, sexism, athletic prostitution, and preserving fading notions of amateurism and academic integrity. Rader's *American Sports: From the Age of Folk Games to the Age of Televised Sports* has a chapter on the development of intercollegiate sport in the nineteenth century and one on the significance of intercollegiate football in the first half of the twentieth century. Wiggins's *Sport in America: From Wicked Amusement to National Obsession* has an article by Ronald Smith entitled "Prelude to the NCAA: Early Failures of Faculty Intercollegiate Athletic Control," in which the author explains the problems colleges had with intercollegiate sports that led to the creation of the NCAA in 1905, and an article entitled "The Philosophical Conflicts in Men's and Women's Collegiate Athletics," in which Joan Hult explains traditional differences in the ways that men and women have approached college sports and how Title IX enforcement has changed that. Finally, the reader should consult other chapters in Wiggins's book on education, gender, and race for more books on the history of college sport.

## URBANIZATION AND THE RISE OF CITY SPORT

One thing that becomes clear when reading books on the history of American sport is that, no matter whether one speaks of professional, college, or amateur athletics, our current athletic systems are the result of two main movements, urbanization and industrialization. Without a doubt, American sport moved from its premodern phase to its contemporary state via economic and social evolution of the city. Riess has written two books that explain how these two phenomena have influenced the development of American sport over the last 150 years. The first is *Sport in Industrial America: 1850–1950*, in which he explains how American stances toward sport changed in the 1850s because of new technological advances in communication, transportation, and mass production, all of which caused cities to expand with new industries and thousands of new citizens to work in those industries. With so many people working shift work in one place, there were suddenly plenty of folks with a significant amount of leisure time on their hands. These people wanted something physical, fun, and invigorating to do, and athletic activities of all kinds fit perfectly into their new urban lifestyle. Riess has sections that show how this process worked for the diverse populations that made up America's cities from 1850–1920, including chapters on the effect of immigration on sport, the effect of changes in gender norms on sport, the reasons behind developing sports programs within education contexts, and the unique elements of urban living that paved the way for the rise of professional sports. One of his best chapters is on how class structure determined where, when, and how people played. For instance, Riess shows how upper-class participants saw sport mainly as a way of displaying their wealth and physical, emotional, and intellectual superiority over the rest of the American populace. To that end, the upper crust formed the first country clubs late in the nineteenth century as private bastion in which they could cement ties with each other and sharpen athletic skills in such sports as golf, tennis, and swimming, sports in which most Americans could not afford to take part. Naturally, yachting was another sport of the rich, who sought to use athletics as exclusive venues that would remind every American of who was in charge. The middle class, by contrast tended to be concerned with using sport as a means of fostering good morals and physical health among children, who would lead the country in years to come, and adults, who were largely responsible for drinking, gambling, extortion, violence, corruption, and other sins that made cities dangerous places to live. It is not surprising that middle-class reformers, including educators, clergy, business owners, and a growing body of professionals, enacted legislation to promote sports in public schools, set up company teams to improve the health of workers, and established parks and public recreation programs to ensure the well-being of their citizens. Finally, the working class played for several reasons, most of which were distinct from those that motivated their middle- and upper-class counterparts. These reasons included the promotion of worker solidarity, ethnic pride, escape from the drudgery of working life, the chance to make some extra money in the ring or as part of some local athletic outfit, and the chance to be bawdy, lewd, and unruly in the face of what they perceived to be restrictive moral guidelines of middle- and upper-class people who had no other interests other than to hold them down (Riess 1995, 43–83).

In Riess's other book on the subject, *City Games: The Evolution of American Urban Society and the Rise of Sports*, Riess divides his analysis into two sections, the history of sport in the "Walking City" from 1820–1870, and the history of sport in the "Radial City" from 1870–1960. In the first section he shows how, even before the prominence of trains, automobiles, good roads, the telegraph, telephone, radio or televison, or large industries, the city was still the key to the evolution of sport in America: "The first cities were small centers of concentrated populations, which provided potential players and spectators and sporting sites close by, and in which a secular cosmopolitan culture developed that regarded sport in a positive light. Voluntary sports organizations were established to encourage sociability and social segregation. Publicans became the first entrepreneurs" (Riess 1991, 252). Riess goes into great detail about sport in the pre-industrial city but supplies an even more in-depth analysis of sport in the industrialized cities that have defined American urban settings for the last century and a half. He explains the role urbanization played in shaping the urban social structure through sport, establishing racial and gender norms via sport, facilitating health reform through sporting programs, establishing youth sports, organizing professional sports, and orchestrating public policy on any number of important issues in which sport was a vital consideration. Finally, he concludes the book with a look at how urban concerns are reshaping sport in the modern era. In the end, he concludes that "the process of urbanization was both the crucial factor in shaping the rise of organized sport and a major influence in shaping the growth of recreational sports. The principal social and cultural elements of urbanization that combined to produce organic urban communities also strongly influenced the development of American sport history. At the same time the development of American sport influenced the process of city building and helped shape the path of urban development" (Riess 1991, 252). Riess's two works on the subject combine to fully explain most of the particulars surrounding this reciprocal relationship.

For those searching for analyses of how the growth of cities and sport were inseparably linked for the last 150 years, there are three tremendous books available. Gerald Gems's *Windy City Wars: Labor, Leisure and Sport in the Making of Chicago* profiles the important role that sport has had in that city's history, while Stephen Hardy's *How Boston Played: Sport, Recreation and Community, 1865–1915* and Melvin Adelman's *A Sporting Time: New York City and the Rise of Modern Athletics, 1820–1870* both show how sport functioned in Boston and New York respectively during two distinct time periods. The latter works complement each other nicely because, chronologically, Hardy picks up where Adelman leaves off. Adelman shows how in a fifty-year period urban changes pushed sport from intense local games and activities to highly organized modern contests with audiences and prize money. He has three sections in the book. The first shows how horse racing developed as the first modern sport. Adelman is masterful as he traces the social, economic, religious, and political factors that led to the professionalization of this heretofore elite sport in which southern gentry sparred with northern businessmen for bragging rights. The second section deals with the rise of baseball from a folk game to a professional business, a process aided by the Civil War, the postwar industrial boom, and the new sporting press whose influence is not missed by Adelman. Finally, the third section profiles the diversity of sport that developed in New York City during the period because of immigration and class differences. Each ethnic group and social class promoted their own sporting practices to service their unique social, physical, psychological, and sometimes economic needs. Adelman describes these efforts with great ease, and his prose catches the spirit of the times.

Hardy's work is instrumental in showing how sport developed in Boston during the period from the Civil War to World War I as a response to quickly changing urban conditions. For instance, the enormous public parks and recreation movement was largely a middle-class response to horrible living conditions in much of the city as officials desperately sought to handle unforseen problems brought on by industrial jobs, poor working conditions, dangerous after-work occupations, poor medical care, and inadequate sanitation programs. Company teams and leagues were largely the creation of middle-class managers and upper-class owners, who wanted healthy and content workers that would give them maximum production. Sporting clubs were mostly the product of upper-class men who wanted to isolate themselves from the common folk and foster a masculinity based on notions of their own superiority. Ethnic neighborhoods developed their own athletic teams as a means of showing ethnic pride. This eventually helped fuel the fires of interscholastic competition in which teams from various parts of the city, usually representing distinct ethnic groups, engaged in heated competition for city bragging rights. Finally, professional sports developed, in part because the people of Boston, for all of their divisions, were, over the course of this period, beginning to develop a unique identity as Bostonians. They might have different backgrounds and vastly different political agendas, but they had one thing in common: They were not New Yorkers. Of course, this type of city pride continues to drive professional sport to this day, and one thing that Hardy's book makes clear is that the urbanization and social and political transformations that took place around the turn of the century created a sporting scene that is still very much what we have today. Gems's book functions in much the same manner. Like Hardy, he offers a quality research and a smooth writing style that allows the reader to see how sport was crucial to the development of Chicago as a modern city in the late nineteenth and early twentieth centuries. Again, one will constantly feel as if he or she is reading about a present city, most of which continue to see sport as not only a source of big business and town pride, but also as a venue in which class conflict, gender and ethnic issues, competing political agendas, moral and public health concerns, and divergent identities are being played out.

## OTHER HISTORICAL WORKS ON AMERICAN SPORT

There are several other works about the history of sport in America that do not fit so neatly into the categories around which I have organized this chapter. Researchers looking for information on the history of professional football, for instance, might try Robert Peterson's *Pigskin: The Early Years of Pro Football* or Edward Gruver's *The American Football League: A Year-by-Year History, 1960–1969.* Peterson outlines the conditions that led to the birth of the professional game, and discusses with some colorful prose the many tactics that owners used to stay in business before the days of television. He does a good job of filling some of the gaps that have existed regarding the birth of the National Football League (NFL) and the various watershed moments that have ensured its amazing success over the last half of the century. Gruver's account is less academic in nature than some might like, but it is still quite useful because he provides a fairly detailed analysis of what the American Football League (AFL) did to force the National Football League into a merger. Perhaps because the AFL and it players were such a bawdy, fun-loving crew that played a swashbuckling style both on and off the field, the book is simply fun to read because it gives one a good feel for what the 1960s were really about in America. For, more than anything else, Gruver shows that the AFL's success lay in the fact that it appealed to a new generation of fans that loved the Beatles, was suspicious of the establishment, and knew how to let its hair down and have a good time.

Other informative works include Todd Gould's *Pioneers of the Hardwood: Indiana and the Birth of Professional Basketball*, which is a fascinating account of the early years of the pro game in the heartland. Gould shows how the early pro leagues in the Midwest, especially in Indiana, paved the way for the inception of the National Basketball Association in the 1940s. Another basketball history is Mac Kirkpatrick's *The Southern Textile Basketball Tournament: A History, 1921–1996,* in which the author examines the history of one of the country's oldest basketball tournaments located in Greenville, South Carolina. Kirkpatrick looks at the significance that the tournament has held for the region in each decade and profiles some of the famous players that have participated in the games. More than anything, the book is a good example of how a sport can become deeply rooted in any given area based on a number of complex factors.

Two other books of interest are Paula Welch's *The History of American Physical Education and Sport* and a rather singular work by Charlene Agne-Traub entitled *The History of Volkssporting in the U.S.A., 1976–1989.* The former is one of the most complete histories of physical education in America on bookshelves today. Welch is careful to meticulously cover every period of physical education in American schools from the colonial period to the present. Agne-Traub, on the other hand, focuses her analysis on the last twenty-five years, in which volks-sporting, games and sports that are by nature noncompetitive and that exist outside of firmly entrenched institutional structures, has taken root in America. She covers the birth of the American Volkssporting Association and charts the growth of this type of sporting activity in the United States. Of course, Agne-Traub's book is not the only scholarly research that exists for those seeking information on topics that have not received their fair share of coverage. For example, Wiggins's *Sport In America: From Wicked Amusement to National Obsession* contains an article by Gerald Early entitled "Hot Spicks Versus Cool Spades: Three Notes Toward a Cultural Definition of Prizefighting," in which the author provides much needed commentary on the history of Hispanic-American and African-American boxers. Another fine book is Richard Mandell's *Sport: A Cultural History* in which he dedicates the last four chapters to the history of American participation in the Olympics. Naturally, *The Journal of Sports History* and *Sports History Review* are two periodicals that consistently carry the latest information on every aspect of

American sports history. Other important periodicals are listed at the beginning of this chapter.

## REFERENCES

### Books

Adelman, Melvin. *A Sporting Time: New York City and the Rise of Modern Athletics, 1820–1870.* Urbana, IL: University of Illinois Press, 1990.

Agne-Traub, Charlene. *History of Volkssporting in the United States, 1976–1989.* Dubuque, IA: Kendall/Hunt, 1991.

Altherr, Thomas, ed. *Sports in North America: A Documentary History.* New York: Academic International, 1997.

Axthelm, Peter. *The City Game.* Lincoln, NE: University of Nebraska Press, 1999.

Berkow, Ira. *To the Hoop: The Seasons of a Basketball Life.* New York: Basic Books, 1997.

Betts, John Rickards. *America's Sporting Heritage, 1850–1950.* Reading, MA: Addison-Wesley, 1974.

Biscotti, M. L. *American Sporting Books History Series.* Madison, OH: Sunrise Publications, 1994.

Bodner, Allen. *When Boxing Was a Jewish Sport.* Westport, CT: Praeger, 1997.

Cox, Richard. *History of Sport: A Guide to the Literature and Sources of Information.* Forsham, Cheshire, Eng: British Society of Sports History in Association with Sport History Publishing Co., 1994.

Davidson, Judith A. *Sport on Film and Video: The North American Society for Sport History Guide.* Metuchen, NJ: Scarecrow Press, 1993.

Davis, Lenwood. *Joe Louis: A Bibliography of Articles, Books and Pamphlets.* Westport, CT: Greenwood Press, 1983.

Dyerson, Mark. *Making the Team: Sport, Culture, and the Olympic Experience.* Chicago: University of Illinois Press, 1998.

Early, Gerald, ed. *The Muhammad Ali Reader.* Hopewell, NJ: Ecco Press, 1998.

Fox, Stephen. *Big Leagues: Professional Baseball, Football and Basketball in National Memory.* Lincoln, NE: University of Nebraska Press, 1998.

Freedman, William. *More Than a Pastime: An Oral History of Baseball Fans.* Jefferson, NC: McFarland, 1998.

Gaschnitz, Michael. *Professional Sports Statistics: A North American Team-by-Team, and Major Non-Team Events, Year-by-Year Reference, 1876 Through 1996.* Jefferson, NC: McFarland, 1996.

Gems, Gerald. *Windy City Wars: Labor, Leisure, and Sport in the Making of Chicago.* Lanham, MD: Scarecrow Press, 1997.

Goldstein, Warren. *Playing for Keeps: An Early History of Baseball.* Ithaca, NY: Cornell University Press, 1989.

Gorn, Elliott. *The Manly Art: Bareknuckle Prize Fighting in America.* Ithaca, NY: Cornell University Press, 1989.

Gorn, Elliott, and Warren Goldstein. *A Brief History of American Sports.* New York: Hill and Wang, 1993.

Gould, Todd. *Pioneers of the Hardwood: Indiana and the Birth of Professional Basketball.* Bloomington, IN: Indiana University Press, 1998.

Gruver, Edward. *The American Football League: A Year-by-Year History, 1960–1969.* Jefferson, NC: McFarland, 1997.

Gutkind, Lee. *The Best Seat in Baseball, But You Have to Stand! The Game as Umpires See It!* Carbondale, IL: Southern Illinois Press, 1999.

Hardy, James. *The New York Giants Baseball Club: The Growth of a Team and a Sport, 1870–1900.* Jefferson, NC: McFarland, 1996.

Hardy, Stephen. *How Boston Played: Sport, Recreation and Community, 1865–1915.* Boston, MA: Northeastern University Press, 1982.

Healy, Gerald. *A Hurting Business.* London: Picador Press, 1996.

Heiner, Gillmeister. *Tennis: A Cultural History.* New York: New York University Press, 1998.

Herzog, Brad. *The Sports 100: The One Hundred Most Important People in American Sports History.* New York: Macmillan, 1995.

Hickok, Ralph. *The Encyclopedia of North American Sports History.* New York: Facts on File, 1992.

Ingham, Alan, and Stephen Hardy. *Sport in Social Development: Traditions, Transitions, and Transformations.* Champaign, IL: Human Kinetics Books, 1993.

Isenberg, Michael. *John L. Sullivan and His America.* Urbana, IL: University of Illinois Press, 1988.

Jose, Colin. *The U.S. and World Cup Soccer Competition.* Metuchen, NJ: Scarecrow Press, 1994.

Kirkpatrick, Mac. *The Southern Textile Basketball Tournament: A History, 1921–1996.* Jefferson, NC: McFarland, 1997.

Kirsch, George B. *The Creation of American Team Sports: Baseball and Cricket, 1838–1872.* Urbana, IL: University of Illinois, 1989.

Kuklick, Bruce. *To Every Thing a Season: Shibe Park and Urban Philadelphia.* Princeton, NJ: Princeton University Press, 1991.

Leifer, Eric. *Making the Majors: The Transformation of Team Sports in America.* Cambridge: Harvard University Press, 1995.

Levine, Peter. *American Sport: A Documentary History.* Englewood Cliffs, NJ: Prentice-Hall, 1989.

Liebling, A. J. *A Neutral Corner: Boxing Essays.* New York: North Point Press, 1996.

Light, Jonathon Fraser. *The Cultural Encyclopedia of Baseball.* Jefferson, NC: McFarland, 1997.

Lipsyte, Robert, and Peter Levine. *Idols of the Game: A Sporting History of the American Century.* Atlanta, GA: Turner Publishing, 1995.

Mandell, Richard. *Sport: A Cultural History.* New York: Columbia University Press, 1984.

McClellan, Keith. *The Sunday Game: At the Dawn of Professional Football.* Akron, OH: University of Akron Press, 1998.

Mead, William. *Baseball: The President's Game.* Washington, D.C.: Farragut Publishing, 1993.

Moffi, Larry. *This Side of Cooperstown: An Oral History of Major League Baseball in the 1950s.* Iowa City, IA: University of Iowa Press, 1996.

Mrozek, Donald. *Sport and American Mentality, 1880–1910.* Knoxville, TN: University of Tennessee Press, 1983.

Noverr, Douglas. *The Games They Played: Sports in American History, 1865–1980.* Chicago: Nelson-Hall, 1983.

Oriard, Michael. *Reading Football: How the Popular Press Created an American Spectacle.* Chapel Hill, NC: University of North Carolina Press, 1993.

Overman, Steven. *The Influence of the Protestant Work Ethic on Sport and Recreation.* Brookfield, VT: Avebury Press, 1997.

Pepe, Phil. *Talkin' Baseball: An Oral History of Baseball in the 1970s*. New York: Ballantine, 1998.

Peterson, Robert W. *Pigskin: The Early Years of Pro Football*. New York: Oxford University Press, 1997.

Pietrusza, David. *Lights On! The Wild Century-Long Saga of Night Baseball*. Lanham, MD: Scarecrow Press, 1997.

Pope, Steven. *Patriotic Games: Sporting Traditions in the American Imagination, 1876–1926*. New York: Oxford University Press, 1997.

———. *The New American Sports History: Recent Approaches and Perspectives*. Urbana, IL: University of Illinois Press, 1997.

Porter, David. *Biographical Dictionary of American Sports*. New York: Greenwood Press, 1988.

Putnam, Douglas. *Controversies of the Sports World*. Westport, CT: Greenwood Press, 1999.

Raabe, Thomas. *Sports in the Twentieth Century*. Golden, CO: Fulcrum Publications, 1995.

Rader, Benjamin. *American Sports: From the Age of Folk Games to the Age of Spectators*. Englewood Cliffs, NJ: PrenticeHall, 1983.

———. *Baseball: A History of America's Game*. Urbana, IL: University of Illinois Press, 1992.

———. *American Sports: From the Age of Folk Games to the Age of Televised Sports*. Englewood Cliffs, NJ: PrenticeHall, 1996.

Riess, Steven, ed. *The American Sporting Experience: A Historical Anthology of Sport in America*. Champaign, IL: Human Kinetics Books, 1984.

———. *City Games: The Evolution of American Urban Society and the Rise of Sports*. Urbana, IL: University of Illinois Press, 1991.

———, ed. *Major Problems in American Sports History*. Boston: Houghton-Mifflin, 1997.

———. *Sport in Industrial America, 1850–1920*. Wheeling, IL: Harlan Davidson Press, 1995.

———. *Touching Base: Professional Baseball and American Culture in the Progressive Era*. Westport, CT: Greenwood Press, 1980.

Roberts, Randy. *Papa Jack: Jack Johnson and the Era of White Hopes*. New York: Collins, 1985.

Robson, Kenneth, ed. *A Great and Glorious Game: Baseball Writings of A. Bartlett Giamatti*. New York: Algonquin Books, 1998.

Sage, George. *Power and Ideology in American Sport: A Critical Perspective*. Champaign, IL: Human Kinetics Books, 1998.

———. *Sport and American Society: Selected Readings*. Reading, MA: Addison-Wesley Publishing Co., 1980.

Sammons, Jeffrey. *Beyond the Ring: The Role of Boxing in American Society*. Urbana, IL: University of Illinois Press, 1998.

Smith, Ronald. *Big-Time Football at Harvard, 1905*. Urbana, IL: University of Illinois Press, 1994.

———. *Sports and Freedom: The Rise of Big-Time College Athletics*. New York: Oxford University Press, 1988.

Spivey, Donald. *Sport in America: New Historical Perspectives*. Westport, CT: Greenwood Press, 1985.

Standish, Burt L. *Frank Merriwell as Fullback*. New York: Street & Smith, 1897.

Struna, Nancy. *People of Prowess: Sport, Leisure and Labor in Early Anglo-America*. Urbana, IL: University of Illinois Press, 1996.

Suger, Bert. *100 Years of Boxing*. New York: Galley Press, 1992.

Sullivan, Dean A. *Middle Innings: A Documentary History of Baseball, 1900–1948.* Lincoln, NE: University of Nebraska Press, 1998.

Umphlett, Wiley. *Creating the Big Game: John W. Heisman and the Invention of American Football.* Westport, CT: Greenwood Press, 1992.

Vincent, Ted. *Mudville's Revenge: The Rise and Fall of American Sport.* New York: Seaview Books, 1994.

Voigt, David. *The League That Failed.* Lanham, MD: Scarecrow Press, 1998.

Welch, Paula. *The History of American Physical Education and Sport.* Springfield, IL: C. C. Thomas, 1996.

White, G. Edward. *Creating the National Pastime: Baseball Transforms Itself, 1903–1953.* Princeton, NJ: Princeton University Press, 1996.

Wiggins, David K. *Sport in America: From Wicked Amusement to National Obsession.* Champaign, IL: Human Kinetics Books, 1995.

Zingg, Paul. *The Sporting Image: Readings in American Sports History.* Lanham, MD: University Press of America, 1988.

## Journals

*American History* (Harrisburg, PA)
*American History Review* (Bloomington, IN)
*American Indian Culture and Research Journal* (Los Angeles, CA)
*American Jewish History* (Waltham, MA)
*American Sports* (Rosemead, CA)
*American Studies International* (Washington, D.C.)
*Hispanic American History Review* (Miami, FL)
*International Journal of the History of Sport* (Washington, D.C.)
*Journal of American Culture* (Bowling Green, OH)
*Journal of American Studies* (New York, NY)
*Journal of Interdisciplinary History* (Cambridge, MA)
*Journal of Negro History* (Atlanta, GA)
*Journal of Physical Education* (Reston, VA)
*Journal of Popular Culture* (Bowling Green, OH)
*Journal of Sport and Social Issues* (Thousand Oaks, CA)
*Journal of Sport History* (University Park, PA)
*Journal of the Philosophy of Sport* (Champaign, IL)
*Reviews in American History* (Madison, WI)
*Sociology of Sport Journal* (Champaign, IL)
*Sport History* (Leesburg, VA)
*Sport History Review* (Champaign, IL)

# 2

# Sport: Business and Law

Over the last ten years, scholars and practitioners have written a plethora of informative books and articles that provide students with both knowledge and methods of analysis with which to navigate their way through the often murky waters of sport business and law. One of the first things that one notices when researching the issues pertinent to either area of study is that neither exists independently of the other. Whether one investigates the underlying structures of the professional sports business, sports marketing, sports management, the relationship between municipalities and their teams, or the immensely complicated field of labor relations, one is confronted with the fact that these two disciplines are inextricably tied. It is impossible, for instance, to understand the financial bickering between players and owners that so dominates the business news of sport without coming to grips with a long string of legal rulings in the area of labor law dating from the early 1950s that eventually gave rise to collective bargaining, arbitration, and free agency. Similarly, an understanding of antitrust law is indispensable if one is to fully comprehend the historical circumstances that resulted in the current business structures of the four major professional sports leagues. Likewise, liability law informs much of the planning of a sports manager; copyright law and media law impact almost all segments of sports marketing; and tax laws and zoning codes greatly influence whether a team can make a profit in a city and, hence, whether it will stay or relocate. This chapter will highlight some of the most thoughtful, comprehensive sources that tackle sports law and business to shed light on the most pressing issues facing sports leagues; those who own, manage, and play for the franchises in those leagues; and the media, sports lawyers, merchandisers, and all those who make their living within the two billion dollar-a-year monolith that is the sports industry.

## THE STRUCTURE OF PROFESSIONAL SPORTS

Before tackling specific legal concerns that impact the business of professional sports, it is useful to survey the current market structure of the leagues in order to understand just who is involved in staging the events and what hot-button issues are currently affecting their ability to make a profit from the production of league games. Jerry Gorman's *The Name of the Game: The Business of Sports* gives the undergraduate student a highly readable introduction to the world of professional sport. Though the book lacks detail, its flowing narrative pattern allows the novice to become quickly acquainted with the fundamental structure of the sport business. For instance, the book discusses in somewhat general terms the diverse roles and concerns of the three major participants in the sport business—owners, managers, and players—and also provides a cursory glimpse of several factors, including ticket pricing, radio and television, public relations, concessions, product licensing, the use and expense of maintaining minor league developmental programs, and the effect of expansion on leagues and franchises, that influence a team's ability to operate successfully in the sports marketplace.

Perhaps the most essential point on which nearly all scholars seem to agree is that, while professional sports perform cultural work at several levels, they primarily exist for one all-encompassing reason: for owners to make money. The best way to learn about the sports industry is by examining the various factors that contribute to owner profits and losses. Most importantly, each major sports league enjoys a preciously guarded monopoly status by which it controls the market in its sport by suffocating all competing leagues. Interestingly, only Major League Baseball (MLB) can actually claim legal rights to its monopoly of American baseball courtesy of the 1922 Supreme Court decision *Federal Baseball Club of Baltimore, Inc. vs. National League of Professional Baseball Clubs*. Speaking for the court, Chief Justice Oliver Wendell Holmes, Jr., said that the Sherman Antitrust Act of 1890, which prohibited monopoly control of any interstate business, did not to apply to the National League because "the business is giving exhibitions of baseball, which are purely state affairs"(Quirk and Fort 1992, 185). Robert Burk's *Never Just a Game: Players, Owners and American Baseball to 1920*, Paul Sommers's *Diamonds Are Forever: The Business of Baseball*, Gerald Sculley's *The Business of Major League Baseball* and Andrew Zimbalist's *Baseball and Billions* all provide solid discussions of how MLB's monopoly status has worked to its advantage throughout the century. Of course, the National Basketball Association (NBA), National Hockey League (NHL), and National Football League (NFL) all exist as unsanctioned monopolies. The idea is simple enough. If there is no rival football league for fans to patronize, the NFL can charge higher prices for tickets, parking, beer, and peanuts because there is nowhere else for a football loving public to turn for professional gridiron excitement. In addition, the absence of a vibrant World Football League or United States Football League (USFL) prevents bidding wars for star athletes, holding down player salaries. In *Money Games: The Business of Sport*, Ann Weiss comments that "the owner's monopolistic practices gave them almost total control of their product: its quality, its availability, its cost." All of the competition is on the field because the leagues' absolute control effectively strips the business "of just about every scrap of commercial competitiveness"(Weiss 1993, 29). The fact that the league strictly limits the number of teams in the cartel also gives the average NFL franchise great leverage when negotiating with its city for tax breaks, stadium improvements, or new venues equipped with greater amenities designed to maximize profit. After all, there is always a city devoid of football that is looking for a team, and as of yet, there has been no congressional action to stop a franchise from whimsically moving from one place to another. As Baltimore Colts fans found out in 1984, any hometown that does not give into its team's demands might well see the owner abscond for greener pastures in the dark of night. For a good discussion of failed legislative attempts to keep teams from moving from one city to another, one might consult Steven R. Lowe's The Kid on the Sandlot: Congress and Professional Sports, 1910–1992, a short, concise account of how Congress has impacted sport throughout the twentieth century.

Several scholars have pointed out that the monopoly power of the leagues has always been challenged but has remained strong. In recent years, fledgling sports leagues such as Major League Soccer, the Women's National Basketball Association, and the Major Indoor Lacrosse League have combined with professional golf, tennis, auto racing, boxing, ice skating, events such as the Extreme Games, college sports (especially newly funded women's sports), and the biannual Olympic games to provide the four giants with some stiff competition for shares of the sports spectatorship market. Still, for the most part, all four leagues have been able to either absorb or financially destroy competing leagues that have tried to horn in on the action. The National League, for instance, ran the Federal League (1913–1914) out of business but absorbed the financially stronger American League to give us Major League Baseball as we know it. The NFL merged with the American Football League in the late 1960s but effectively drove the USFL (1983–1986) into oblivion. Both the NHL and NBA continue to expand so that leagues such as the International Hockey League (IHL) and Continental Basketball Association (CBA) are restricted only to small markets that would not interest the dominant leagues. Burks, Sommers, Zimbalist, and Scully offer discussions on baseball's history of dealing with rival leagues, while journalist Peter King's Football: A History of the Professional Game is a quick read, replete with interviews and newspaper articles covering the AFL-NFL merger. Though few academic histories of hockey or basketball exist, three books written by Paul Staudohar stand together as a meticulously researched triumvirate that details the labor history, including all challenges by rival leagues, of all four major sports leagues from their inceptions until 1996. These include Labor Relations in Professional Sports, written with Robert Berry and William Gould, The Sports Industry and Collective Bargaining, which covers in great detail the labor strife in all four leagues from 1985–1989, and Playing for Dollars, which chronicles labor issues from 1989 to 1996.

Despite the endless string of legal challenges to its monopoly status, it is evident that each league has emerged from the dust relatively unscathed. Thus, at least two questions still confront scholars: (1) Are monopolies beneficial or detrimental, and (2) what challenges to market dominance will owners receive in the next century? Several academics have argued that these monopolies will continue to be confronted not only in courts by players suing on the grounds that the leagues unfairly restrict the market for their services and on the field by other leagues, but will be challenged by the general public, the fans, who are allegedly shortchanged by monopolies. As Stephen F. Ross concludes in "Break Up Sport League Monopolies":

Monopoly sports league owners take advantage of their economic power to secure massive subsidies from local taxpayers, yet still deprive fans in many cities of expansion teams that they could economically support and emotionally cherish. Owners conspire to limit player salaries by schemes that inefficiently allocate players among teams denying individual franchises the opportunity to obtain the players they may need to develop winning or championship teams. Both major league baseball and football owe their current success and popularity to the broadcasting of their games over free television, yet the monopoly leagues are well positioned to force fans to pay millions of dollars to view these contests on cable television. Inefficient and incompetent sports executives, free from the rigors of economic competition, annually subject many fans to losing seasons for the fans' favorite franchises. (Mangan and Staudohar 1991, 167)

Ross urges fans to push Congress to "act to benefit sports fans with the same free enterprise that we expect from other business endeavors," insisting that increased competition would "limit a team's ability to extort tax subsidies" by playing one city against another, "produce the most exciting pennant and championship races" for the fans, curb mismanagement because fans of poorly run teams might switch their loyalty to a team from the other league, cause leagues to avoid work stoppages for fear of relinquishing the market to a rival league, and keep games on free television (Mangan and Staudohar 1991, 167–168). Thus far, Congress has not curtailed monopolistic practices. There are no rival leagues that truly threaten the old guard, and teams can move from city to city without fear of legal repercussions (Lowe 1995, 123–129). Still, for many fans these arguments will be convincing. The owners' dilemma will be to expand enough to continue to dominate all major markets without filling up all the markets so that they can no longer play one city against the other, and to keep the games affordable so that the average fan does not switch allegiance to less expensive leagues such as the hockey's IHL.

Part of the reason that the leagues so desperately want to preserve their competitionless existence is that they do not want to share any of the annual treasure they receive from the television and radio networks that own broadcast rights to league games. In the last two decades, all four leagues have become increasingly dependent on media money. In 1976, for instance, the NBA inked a national television agreement that netted each team slightly more than $450,000 per season. By 1985, that annual figure was at one million dollars per team. Clearly, television money was important to the league, but not as pivotal as ticket sales. In the mid 1980s, however, the league began to take flight and grab hold of the national consciousness on the strength of magnetic superstars such as Larry Bird, Ervin Johnson, and Julius Erving, and through the tremendous marketing wizardry of commissioner David Stern. At the same time, NBA players won several victories at the collective bargaining table. These included vastly expanded free agency (1988), a rising salary cap that will inflate total player salaries from $15.9 million per team in 1994 to $32 million per squad in 2001 (1995), and an expansion of the total revenue claimed by players from team coffers from 53 percent to 57.3 percent by 2001 (1995). As the players claimed more league revenue, owners sought new financial resources. Television, looking to capitalize on the NBA's new-found popularity, was ready to ante up huge payments in order to secure league broadcast rights. The savvy Stern managed to maximize profits by selling select packages of league games to the highest network bidders. The results have been staggering. In 1993, for example, the NBA signed four year agreements with television network NBC for $750 million and cable station TNT for $352 million, while still preserving a large number of games for individual franchises to sell to local stations. Of course, this does not even count the radio rights. This financial windfall has allowed owners to cope with rising costs of business, especially player contracts, while at the same time ensuring most teams a position in the black at year's end. This magic triangle linking league popularity, the newly won power of players over owners, and network competition for market shares now dominates all four major professional leagues, forcing each to rely on media revenue to stabilize its business. For instance, in 1994, the NFL signed deals with ABC, NBC, ESPN, and Fox that totaled $4.4 billion or $39.2 million annually per team. Although its teams sell most of their games to local television, Major League Baseball will take in $1.7 billion over the next five years on national contracts. Even the National Hockey League has modest, long-term contracts with ESPN and Fox. To a large extent, then, teams have become dependent on media money for both profit and survival. As Staudohar writes in *Playing for Dollars*, "The economic health of professional sport is closely linked to television. It will be even more so in the future" (1996, 176).

## PROFESSIONAL SPORTS AND THE MEDIA

Scholars have pointed out that more than an American obsession with sports lies at the center of league power to negotiate such lucrative deals. As in most segments of sport business, legal concerns come into play. All four leagues have traditionally guarded against competition by pooling their broadcast rights. Instead of each franchise selling local rights to local stations, the league sells its games in blocks to national networks and now cable networks, often parcelling out games to several networks so as to make sure that as many markets as possible are filled with its games and to ensure that no network is left out in the cold. After all, a snubbed network might buy games from a rival league, instantly giving that league visibility, credibility, and an injection of financial vitality. This is what Stern and the other league bosses continue to do, and to a large extent, this strategy of collectively auctioning off rights to the highest bidder while seeing that no significant bidder is left high and dry is what keeps the leagues swimming in money. As Gerald Scully makes clear in *The Market Structure of Sports*, this procedure is only possible because of a congressional reaction to the 1961 court decision *U.S. v. National Football League* in which the practice was deemed anticompetitive and a violation of the Sherman Antitrust Act: "What the courts undid, however, Congress permitted," passing the "Sports Broadcasting Act, which permitted leagues to act as cartels in the negotiation and sale of their broadcasting rights, and to be free of any antitrust sanction" (Scully 1995, 27). Those interested in pursuing the subject might try David Klatell's *Sports for Sale: Television, Money and the Fans*, a well-written analysis of just how much television has changed the sporting experience of the American sports fan.

Owners hungry for television dollars are not out of the woods yet, however. Scholars point out that they face at least two problems. The first is the influence that television networks can now exert over league games. Some fans blame television for the violence they see as occupying a more central place on the sporting stage. Weiss argues that "it is certainly true that many sports are more violent now than in the past" and suggests that players see television as a means of exhibiting their toughness to other teams to improve their market value, or as a way of manufacturing a bad boy, rebel image that might secure an endorsement contract. She goes on to suggest that television replays, often visible on stadium big screen scoreboards after each play, have made players more conservative and individualistic, not willing to take chances to benefit the team. For Weiss, television "is clearly responsible for another change: growing specialization." Specifically, she charges that players no longer play to their full potential because "television encourages athletes to concentrate in one small area instead of working to develop overall ability" (Weiss 1993, 54–55). Certainly, commercial television has occasioned several rule changes over the last two decades. The two-minute warning in football, a reduction of overall plays in a football game to make sure the contest stays within its allotted time period and does not interfere with prime time programming, a twelve-minute halftime instead of fifteen, overtimes in hockey, and marathon baseball games caused by lengthened commercial time between innings are only a few of the questionable changes that have been wrought by the power of television. Some contend that soccer, arguably the nation's most played sport at the grassroots level, has failed to produce a thriving professional league because it will not change its rules to allow for commercial time-outs needed by television to court advertisers.

Yet, while leagues must battle the public's skepticism over television's control over American sports, they must also grapple with a rather perplexing condition: They must look toward the media for new revenues to meet rising costs at a time when television networks are losing money on sports and seem to have maxed out their investment potential. Weiss, among others, has shown that many networks have lost millions on their broadcast agreements with leagues in the 1990s. Both NBC and CBS absorbed losses neighboring in the $200–$300 million range on the

NFL television agreement that ran out in 1994. Cable giant ESPN lost millions in its deal with Major League Baseball that expired that same year. Perhaps no network has felt the sting of overspending for sports as much as CBS, which lost a fortune on both the 1992 Winter Olympics and its $1.06 billion deal to broadcast Major League Baseball from 1990–1994. According to Weiss, increased competition from other sports and entertainment sectors, along with a struggling economy, has contributed to the shortfall experienced by networks, which rely on advertisers forking over large sums of money for the right to market their products during sporting events: "The network lost $55 million on its 1990 Major League Baseball schedule. The next year, CBS reported losses of $400 million—most of that attributable to its mammoth sports splurge" (Weiss 1993, 161). Not surprisingly, CBS did not retain its rights to the Olympics, the NFL, or Major League Baseball. In addition, both NBC and ESPN paid far less for baseball broadcasting rights in 1995. In fact, Major League Baseball became the first league to take a television pay cut, regressing from $14 million per team in 1990 to $6.8 million under the new agreement in 1995. Staudohar's *The Sports Industry and Collective Bargaining* and *Playing for Dollars* and Klatell's *Sports for Sale: Television, Money and the Fans* contain excellent discussions of the impact of recent network deficits on the sports leagues, complete with calculations as to how much money the leagues will get from free television early in the next century. It seems likely that it will be less because the networks, while content to lose some money on sports because events such as the Super Bowl contribute to the overall prestige and value of a network, do not have bottomless pockets.

Still, players' salaries and overall operating expenses continue to rise, and owners contend that they need more revenue. Staudohar argues that at least some of this new money must come from the media: "But the common denominators of success in sports ventures are the extent of their television broadcasts and the ratings those broadcasts receive. Nearly all the other important economic elements of sport—player salaries, pensions and other fringe benefits, profitability of enterprises, profit sharing—depend in large part on television revenues" (Staudohar 1996, 177). Owners are hoping that pay-per-view television will create new, greater sources of revenue to maintain their profit margins. In "Break Up the Sports Monopolies," Stephen Ross quotes Atlanta Braves owner Ted Turner's admission that "there is going to be more and more movement from over the air, free telecasts to pay television for sports events. The only thing left to go on pay television will be the World Series and the Super Bowl" (Mangan and Staudohar 1993, 159). Of course, while the overall potential of the medium is intriguing, early experiments with pay-per-view have had mixed results. To be sure, there have been disasters. For example, NBC's ambitious 1992 Olympic Triplecast flopped, netting only between 165,000–300,000 of the 2.4 million subscribers needed to break even. Likewise, college football and professional tennis have not fared well. Still, as Howard Schlossberg writes in *Sports Marketing*, "the big events flopped because they were just that—the big events, not pay-per-view events" (Schlossberg 1996, 92). Overall, pay-per-view has been successful as long as it does not alienate viewers by wresting the big events from public view. Subscriptions to regular season baseball, basketball, and hockey games packaged on a seasonal basis have sold well on networks such as Sportschannel America, and boxing and wrestling have been successful. The 1993 Evander Holyfield/ Riddick Bowe fight garnered $33 million. Of course, while owners will probably try to exploit pay-per-view to keep up with rising production costs, they will certainly face at least two problems. The first is fan alienation. Fans already being squeezed by high ticket prices will be hard pressed to maintain loyalty to teams that make them pay for what used to be free. The second involves legal challenges already being waged in Congress on behalf of fans who want to keep games on free television. Schlossberg covers some attempts to legislate away pay-per-view, focusing on Illinois Congressman William Lipinski's "idea to prohibit pay-per-view events from facilities that are taxpayer subsidized and to prohibit nonprofit and public organizations from telecasting events on a pay-per-view basis" (Schlossberg 1996, 85). Schlossberg points out that no laws have as yet been enacted but that fan anger and congressional zeal to gain votes by placating that anger will provide sturdy resistance to owners who see pay-per-view as the new wave of television revenue. Scholars interested in accessing legal discussions about pay-per-view television may want to consult Theresa A. Lee's *Legal Research Guide to Television Broadcasting and Program Syndication* or Lowe's *The Kid on the Sandlot: Congress and Professional Sports, 1910-1992.*

## LUXURY BOXES, CLUB SEATS, AND NEW STADIUMS

With networks losing money on sports and pay-per-view still a distant hope, owners will likely rely on new stadiums designed specifically to maximize revenue in order to improve their cash flow. If anything, sports business in the 1990s has been defined as much by new architecture aimed at corporate vanity and fan nostalgia as by events on the field or in the boardroom. Specifically, owners have insisted on palatial ballparks that include every possible amenity. Luxury boxes that often annually rent for between $75,000 and $300,000 and pricey "premium" seats located adjacent to an upscale, private club cater to corporate interests. In addition, nearly all of the seats in new stadiums are not directly available to the public without the purchase of permanent seat licenses (PSLs) that are often far out of the range of even the most dedicated fan. This means that in order for a fan to buy game tickets valued at $40 per ticket, he must first pay a rental fee, usually between $250 and $4,500 per seat, for the right to plunk down the $40. Finally, new stadiums are specially constructed to maximize advertising space. Included here would be the rotating signs positioned at center court of basketball arenas or behind home plate in baseball, huge scoreboards on which companies or individuals can bombard fans with messages, or extra wide concourses that feature promotional displays and presentations from area businesses as well as a wide range of restaurants peddling their wares to hungry consumers. The bottom line is that owners have hiked ticket prices up so high in recent years that many fans simply can not comfortably afford to attend games. With the average fan unable to lay out more money, owners are making an overt appeal to corporate America to choose the stadium as its place of business and entertainment. Mark Rosentraub's *Major League Losers: The Real Cost of Sport and Who's Paying for It* is one of the best books to examine the financial reasons behind the collective rush to build new playing facilities as well as the effects of this process on fans and city officials. Rosentraub concludes that in the 1980s "new and different revenue sources were needed, and luxury seats and club seating, together with expanded restaurants, became the routes to financial success. What all team owners needed and wanted were playing facilities with luxury seating and restaurants that would create additional revenue streams and additional revenues from which players could be paid and profit levels maintained" (Rosentraub 1997, 6).

In terms of raising revenue and sparking fan interest, there can be little doubt that new stadiums such as Jacobs Field in Cleveland or Coors Field in Denver have been wildly successful for owners. Nearly every game has sold out and the majority of luxury suites and club seats have been leased. Still, perhaps no new ballpark explains why every owner wants a new facility more than Oriole Park at Camden Yards. Erected on the waterfront in Baltimore in 1992, the park has been a field of dreams for club owner Peter Angelos. Not only is the park equipped with all the corporate lures, it was deliberately constructed as a "retro" ballpark, one that resonates the aura of a mythical 1920s stadium. This illustrates the second level of appeal of the modern stadium; it must make the fan feel good. Evidently, owners have decided that feeling good for the average fan might mean remembering a more innocent version of the past when the game was still on the field and not in a boardroom, when tickets were affordable, and when the old town team really represented the town. It has appealed to patrons on a deeply emotional level and has resulted in consistent sell-outs, an influx of tourist activity for local businesses, and an enhanced sense of civic pride. In short, if it has not meant a financial profit for the city, it has been a boon for the community spiritually. Peter Richmond's *Ballpark: Camden Yards and the Building of an American Dream* provides an excellent account of what the park has meant to the city's soul. He describes opening day at the Yards in 1993:

In that infant moment, tens of thousands of Baltimoreans leaned back to savor, at last, the overwhelming rightness of their new palace: the crook of the stands down the right-field line, as if the upper deck were cradling the outfield; the warehouse long and thick and chthonic, the oldest wall of any major league stadium dominating the newest playing field; the open wedge of downtown office buildings representing ninety years of urban architecture peeking in; the left-center-field seats slicing across the outfield, those fans seeming right atop the field. Nothing shouted for attention—not the warehouse, not the steel, not the comfortable slant of the grandstand. It fit. The outfield had been mowed neatly, so that the nap looked like a new haircut. The infield grass had been mowed in concentric rings. It looked like crop circles viewed from an airplane. Nothing was amiss. (Richmond 1993, 257)

Still, despite the aesthetic success and cultural significance of the Yards, Coors's Field, and Jacob's Field, the jury is out as to whether a new, publicly funded stadium is actually a good financial investment for cities or towns. In *Playing the Field: Why Sports Teams Move and Cities Fight to Keep Them,*

Charles C. Euchner uses case studies to point out that several financially strapped cities have sacrificed badly needed funds that could have been used for social programs or educational improvements to build less than successful stadiums. In addition, both Euchner and Rosentraub argue that new stadiums are so cost ineffective that it is unlikely that cities will pay them off before they are "outdated"; that financially they only benefit wealthy players, owners, and business owners; and that they stand as lonely symbols of waste because they sit unused most of the year. The problem for cities, however, is that sports is an American passion. Even casual fans love to identify themselves with a winning team. The politician who wants to be re-elected faces a tough decision. To acquiesce to owner demands and fund a modern ballpark could jeopardize a city financially. To refuse often prompts the team to move to a new city, puncturing the city's civic pride and probably costing the mayor his or her job. Euchner sums up the dilemma in *Playing the Field*, a fascinating read that provides a fairly nonjudgmental account of the financial schisms that exist nationwide between cities and their heretofore beloved teams:

Overwhelming evidence shows that sport franchises and facilities do little to revive a local economy, but states and cities continue to spend hundreds of millions of dollars to get teams. Boosters promise the revival of neighborhoods, higher tax revenues, the attraction of new firms to the city, and even the amelioration of racial and ethnic strife. Ignoring the evidence, cities accept the grandiose claims. This withdrawal from reality is understandable given the intractability of urban problems. City officials face problems such as poverty, health crises ranging from AIDS to tuberculosis, violence, housing dilapidation, racial strife, crumbling infrastructures, and bad schools. Capital and middle-class flight leave them few resources. Entrenched bureaucracies and interest groups, and sensational media, feed the sense of hopelessness. Sports offers city officials a symbolic way out. The history of American cities is the history of dramatic gestures. Bridges, highways, urban renewal, tourist malls, convention centers, and flashy subway systems are ribbon-cutting heaven. They show a city *on the move*, brazen against the odds, unwilling to settle for mediocrity. The projects might not help the city in the long run—they might even hurt it—but they do show a can-do spirit. (Euchner 1994, 185)

There are several good books that discuss just what a city or town should do to assess the feasibility of splurging for a new ballpark. James Quirk and Rodney Fort's *Pay Dirt: The Business of Team Sports* provides comprehensive tables on the costs of all professional stadiums in the four major sports up to 1989, as well as estimates of owner subsidies on publicly owned stadiums. Dean Baim's *The Sports Stadium as a Municipal Investment* examines the financial history of sixteen professional stadiums and includes a tremendous literature review that would be helpful to anyone researching the topic. An essay by Frank Hefner entitled "Using Economic Models to Measure the Impact of Sports on the Local Economy" is part of Peter Graham's *Sport Business: Operational and Theoretical Aspects* and is valuable for those looking to mathematically prove that a stadium will be profitable or not based on a variety of complex factors. Andrew Zimbalist and Roger Nolls examine the impact of new stadiums and sports franchises in general on the local economy in *Sports, Jobs, and Taxes: The Economic Impact of Sports Teams and*

*Stadiums*. Two books, Bob Andelman's *Stadium for Rent: Tampa Bay's Quest for Major League Baseball* and David Whitford's *Playing Hardball: The High Stakes Battle for Baseball's New Franchises*, are notable because they use newspaper articles and interviews to chronicle the attempts by Tampa/St. Petersburg, Denver, and Miami to lure teams by financing new stadiums. The books are particularly useful for understanding how far some cities are willing to go to secure franchises and how, armed with this knowledge, team owners can effectively play their host city against would-be suitors to get handsome stadium deals. Finally, Arthur Johnson's *Minor League Baseball and Local Economic Development* is a first-rate analysis of the factors that must be present if a city or town is to profit from a stadium investment. In effect, Johnson sums up the conclusions of most of the books by advancing the notion that whether a city should fund a stadium depends on four factors: whether the stadium can break even over the course of the team's lease; whether it will enhance the overall economic development of the region; whether it will bolster civic pride and become a rallying point for the city; and whether it provides affordable entertainment and quality recreational opportunity for the community (Johnson 1993, 246–253). If the answer is a resounding yes to each of these queries, a new stadium would probably be a good investment for any municipality.

Of course, this does not fully simplify things for city leaders, who still must assess how these variables play out for their town. No matter how important a team is to a city, municipal funds are limited and owners are gradually running out of cities to play against each other. Still, within the burgeoning field of sports marketing, there lies another potential windfall for teams: corporate sponsorship. Increasingly, franchises are looking to large corporations with deep pockets to do more than just rent luxury boxes or club seats. Stadium advertizing has, of course, become a staple for professional teams and large signs from Budweiser to Yamaha are plastered on outfield walls and hockey boards at every league venue. But recently, corporations have stepped up their financial investment by purchasing the right to have part of the game put in their name. This might include the Schwepps instant replay or the Pepsi power play challenge in which fans receive a free soft drink if the home team scores. The relationship is simple. The team gets money, the corporation gets exposure, and the fans get a little extra entertainment in which they sometimes have a stake. This is referred to as "The Event Triangle" by Phil Schaaf in his highly readable book, *Sports Marketing: It's Not Just a Game Anymore*, in which the author argues that all three parties within the triangle must be satisfied if corporate sponsorship is to be successful: "The financial success of sporting events lies within the framework of the Event Triangle. Each participant, event audience and sponsor(s), has goals satisfied by the other groups. Because sports has maintained its audience, sponsors invest billions of dollars to communicate through them. Furthermore, the reliability of fans attending and tuning into sporting events, has brought the expansion of proved event principles into new markets" (Schaaf 1995, 71).

A few businesses have adopted grander marketing strategies. Airlines and banks, for instance, have been aggressive in their attempts to purchase rights to become the official sponsor of arenas. Thus, the new Boston Garden became the Fleet Center, the Buffalo Sabres play in the Marine Midland Arena, and the Chicago Blackhawks skate in the United Center. Corporations pay steep fees for this right, but the large, up-front expenditure translates into an advertising bargain over the long term. For instance, America West Airlines paid an initial fee of $26 million for the right to put its moniker on a new arena in Phoenix, Arizona, that would house the NHL's Coyotes and the NBA's Suns. The figure seems high, but the advertising value is worth it over the airlines's thirty-year lease. According to David Carter in *Keeping Score: An Inside Look at Sports Marketing*, America West's name is mentioned enough times in one year to equal $5 million in advertising expense. Over the thirty-year lease period, then, the airline gets $150 million in exposure for the $26 million outlay (Carter 1996, 15). Carter's book is possibly the best for understanding how different companies and teams work out marketing plans that are mutually beneficial and is a must read for those interested in how corporate giants such as Nike, McDonald's and General Motors have completely altered the ways in which professional sports do business. He discusses, for example, how businesses such as The Walt Disney Company have actually opted to bring two sides of the triangle together by owning teams outright. Disney brought financial stability to baseball's Anaheim Angels by acquiring a 25 percent share in the club and to hockey's Mighty Ducks of Anaheim, which Disney purchased outright as an expansion team in 1993. In doing so, the company procured for itself an endless medium through which to reach its chief patron, families. Disney had enough money to build a new $122 million hockey arena dubbed The Arrowhead Pond and to buy the Angels' Anaheim Stadium, securing nearly all rights to parking and in-stadium revenue. Both buildings are located adjacent to Walt Disneyland, giving the crowds that pack the theme park easy access to the games. Naturally, Disney ads and products dominate both venues. The company also released successful family movies, including *Angels in the Outfield* (1993) and *The Mighty Ducks* hockey trilogy (1992–1996), whose video rentals and television reruns continually promote both the teams and the company. In 1995 Disney purchased Cap Cities/ABC, which includes ESPN and ESPN 2, for $19 billion, practically guaranteeing its teams consistent national exposure. The Disney setup, referred to by sports marketers as cross promotional marketing, looms as the prototype for the next century because it melds the team and the company into one entity that controls where it plays, how much rent it pays, all of its advertising revenue, its own publicity, and, to a large extent, its own media coverage (Carter 1996, 247). No doubt scholars will closely watch this change in ownership patterns.

## SPORTS MARKETING AND THE SEARCH FOR NEW REVENUE

Most sports marketing books concentrate on two main cogs in the marketing relationship that exists between sports and the corporate world. The first of these is licensing. This refers to companies paying huge fees to a league in order to associate their product with the league's considerable cultural power. Often, the product being marketed may have nothing to do with sports. For instance, Schaaf chronicles the marketing marriage between the Bank of America and the NBA's Portland Trailblazers. The bank paid the team a hefty fee in order to gain new checking accounts through an offer called "Blazer Checking" that included all kinds of team merchandise, entries into free ticket giveaways and personalized checks stamped with the Trailblazers logo. The effort proved to be successful because it allowed the bank to reach the thousands of Blazer fans in the Portland area, many of whom were willing to choose a bank that aligned itself with the home team over one that did not (Schaaf 1993, 249). Most licensing arrangements involve nonsport products. For example, McDonald's sponsors the NBA to move burgers, Cadillac sponsors the PGA tour because the golf connection sells its cars, and Anheuser-Busch "spends most of its $555 million annual advertising budget in pursuit of its overall sports marketing strategy" because its sports connections translate into beer sales (Carter 1996, 53). Still, some companies will secure a licensing agreement to market products that go hand in hand with the sports. Starter, for example, has become a household name because it bought the rights to manufacture NFL team merchandise, including replica jerseys and jackets. Spalding antes up big dollars to be the NBA's official ball because it translates into increased basketball sales. Perhaps the biggest player in this regard is Nike. The footwear giant spends nearly $270 million annually to corner the $12 billion-a-year shoe market. The reason is simple. The more NBA, NFL, and Major League Baseball players that sport Nike shoes and other products bearing the famous swoosh logo, the more shoes the company will sell. According to Donald Katz, whose *Just Do It: The Nike Spirit in the Corporate World* provides an in-depth account of Nike's inner workings, the company has used its association with sports so well that it "has managed to so distinguish its nine hundred different seasonal offerings that one hundred million pairs of Nike shoes were sold during the fiscal year ending in the late spring of 1994—two hundred pairs of every minute for every day" (Katz 1994, 9–10).

The other cog is endorsements, which actually exist contractually between individual players or coaches and companies but nevertheless produce benefits for the leagues. Usually, a large company such as Nike or McDonald's will pay a star athlete like Shaquille O'Neal millions to endorse its product. Because athletic heroes occupy a hallowed place on the American cultural landscape, the company will often realize an increase in profits because of the association with that athlete's mythical greatness. In 1993, O'Neal's portfolio included Pepsi, Reebok, a series of book and movie deals, and a handful of sporting goods sponsorships that netted the seven-foot center an additional $11.7 million on top of his $3.3 million basketball salary. Both Pepsi ($2.2 million per year) and Reebok ($3.3 million per year) benefitted from their association with basketball's second most popular player (Schaaf 1995, 288–290). The endorsements also pleased fans of O'Neal and basketball in general because all of the advertisements, movies, and books kept the star and his game in the public eye. Naturally, the NBA is happy to see its players powerfully representing the league's greatness on the nation's television sets, movie screens, and newspapers because such exciting images of its dynamic athletes increase the league's cultural presence and importance. It is hard to buy that kind of exposure. The owners of the star's team, in O'Neal's case the Orlando Magic from 1993–1995 and the Los Angeles Lakers since 1996, stand to gain financially because large numbers of fans buy merchandise featuring their hero's team, buy tickets to see him play, and increase the team's television exposure via their desire to see the star perform on the road. Particularly compelling is the massive windfall from team merchandising that has fueled the mania to change uniforms and logos or to adopt multiple uniforms in hopes that fans will buy all of them complete with their star's name and number embroidered on the back. This "indirect income" garnered from player endorsements is perhaps the most attractive form of revenue for leagues and teams, and is why owners are willing to shell out millions to players with magnetic personas that mesmerize the nation. The league, the teams, the athletes, and the fans profit in different ways, and the corporate sponsors pay the bill and assume all of the risks. Every now and again a company will lose when their athlete fails to perform or runs afoul of the law, but as Schaff concludes, "As long as there are gifted athletes that capture the public's attention, companies will line up to attract their promotional services" (Schaaf 1995, 296).

Still, while corporate sponsorship and endorsements should remain promising sources of income for professional leagues into the next century, this mega marketing does present the leagues with at least two major problems. The first is expansion. Realizing that much more revenue can be earned by selling itself and its teams and players to international markets, each of the four major leagues is spending millions to weave themselves into the cultural fabric of the global marketplace. The NFL has launched the World American Football League in Europe, the NHL sponsors several professional teams in Russia, and Major League Baseball broadcasts its games to parts of Central and Latin America. All of the leagues run free clinics in countries around the world in order to win over young fans. The NBA is the most advanced of the four, achieving considerable international appeal thanks to a massive marketing effort that includes both an annual series of preseason exhibitions between the NBA's top teams and European all-star teams and a few regular season games played in international venues. Schlossberg's *Sports Marketing* provides an excellent discussion of marketing efforts made by the leagues, particularly those of the NBA. The problem is that, besides the enormous cost of marketing overseas, the leagues are having to contend with the intense marketing efforts by popular international games to secure shares of the affluent, sports hungry, American market that has always supported the four major leagues. Both Schlossberg and Schaaf make it clear that golf, tennis, and auto racing have made a great impact within the United States and will probably continue to gain in popularity as participatory sports. Major League Soccer has enjoyed an auspicious beginning, and recent endorsement trends point to the fact that other sports are gaining a wide spectator base that threatens to cut into the entertainment pie (Schaaf 1995, 280–281). According to Schaaf, "International sports give athletes greater opportunities to earn money away from their events. Tennis, auto-racing, golf and the Olympics are sports marketing standards on any continent" (Schaaf 1995, 281). The question for sports leagues in the year 2000 becomes how to pay for escalating costs of operation at home and still invest large sums in marketing efforts abroad that may or may not result in increased revenue over the long haul. Schlossberg, Carter, Schaaf, and Graham all touch on this key dilemma, but the problem has yet to be undertaken in great depth and should thus provide scholars with some fodder for debate over the next few years.

The other problem aggravated by the explosion in sports marketing is competitive balance within the leagues, something each has to have if fans are going to remain interested enough to buy tickets and to watch the games on television. As with all aspects of sport business, sports law plays a considerable role in the current instability of professional sports leagues. While owners of each league have agreed to evenly divide money earned from national television and radio contracts, the 1938 case of the *Pittsburgh Athletic Company vs. The KQV Broadcasting Company* secured the right of each club to market its own games to local television and radio outlets. Michelle Murphy's "Sports Broadcasting: Who Owns Property Rights" is part of a comprehensive book entitled *Sport and the Law: Major League Cases* edited by Charles E. Quirk. Murphy's essay entails a good discussion of the *Pittsburgh* ruling and subsequent legal decisions that have reinforced it (Quirk 1996, 215–220). Not surprisingly, these decisions have led to major differences of income for teams in each league. The New York Yankee organization, for instance, rakes in nearly $50 million a year from its local media deals, while the Seattle Mariners get less than $5 million. The Chicago Bears received $4.5 million from its 1994 radio agreement, while the Indianapolis Colts made only $800,000 (Schaaf 1995, 203). This disparity in income, exacerbated by marketing efforts that often favor teams in larger markets with big budgets and a larger metropolitan audience, can be disastrous for leagues. In baseball, small market teams like the Pittsburgh Pirates or the Minnesota Twins that were successful in the 1980s have been decimated in the 1990s partly because of their inability to compete financially with large cities such as New York or Chicago, where hundreds of corporations buy luxury boxes and club seats and where sponsors spend lavishly to reach the huge audiences that follow the Yankees or Cubs. In addition, while owners have generally shared income earned from licensing agreements, some owners have shown a willingness to move away from revenue sharing towards a type of every team for itself marketing philosophy that favors big market teams. Dallas Cowboy owner Jerry Jones, for example, challenged NFL policy by negotiating separate sponsorship deals with Nike ($17.5 million for seven years) and Pepsi ($25 million for ten years). The NFL filed suit to block the move, but Jones will likely not be the last owner to challenge what has been a healthy league socialism. Future legal decisions on the matter will no doubt have a great impact on the competitive balance and stability of the leagues (Carter 1996, 237). For if individual teams can keep the fruits of their own marketing efforts, the financial gap will likely widen between large market teams with huge fan bases and enough money to buy magnetic stars and small market teams with little marketing power. This gap has already resulted in unwanted instability. Each year, small market teams lose fans early because they simply can not stay competitive over a long season. Nowhere is this more apparent than in the NHL, where small city teams Quebec, Winnipeg, and Minnesota have all relocated to larger cites (Denver, Dallas, and Phoenix) in recent years.

Richard Sheehan's *Keeping Score: The Economics of Big-Time Sports* concentrates on this dilemma. Generally, Sheehan argues that while leagues have instituted maximum spending limits (salary caps) and maintained player drafts that benefit lesser teams, free agency and individualized marketing strategies still make for less balanced competition (and thus less overall fan interest) and more volatile franchises. He calls for strict revenue sharing to achieve both competitive balance and leaguewide stability: "Revenue sharing does have strong economic justification based on the cooperation required between teams to generate league revenues. Since the game is a joint effort, economic theory can be employed to suggest how revenues can be split to provide positive rather than negative incentives" (Sheehan 1996, 178). While the suggestion seems logical, one wonders if it will happen. After all, it does call for wealthy owners to forsake millions in the name of overall league prosperity. Such a grandiose gesture may seem unlikely, but the owners will have to find some way to deal with the negative ramifications of their own marketing blitz. While sports marketing has flourished in part because of owners' demands for greater revenue, sports management continues to be one of the most critical areas for sport franchises and has been the subject of some quality academic efforts. Joy DeSensi and Danny Rosenberg's *Ethics in Sport Management* and Graham's *Sport Business: Operational and Theoretical Aspects* not only describe several ethical theories employed by sport managers, but use highly detailed case studies that make the reader grapple with the most pressing issues faced by franchise decision makers. Most interesting is the fact that the authors tend to focus on how team officials are caught in an endless cycle of public relations trickery in which they try to maintain community support by putting a neat spin on any controversy that surrounds the club. Both books address the following questions: What do clubs do when players are arrested due to narcotics violations and how do teams implement effective substance abuse programs to combat the use of steroids and other performance-enhancing drugs when the leagues themselves are supported by beer companies such as Coors and Anheuser-Busch? How does gambling affect each league? How can managers combat "fixed" games and prevent players from betting when it is clear that each league's popularity is closely tied to a largely illegal gaming industry. Should the NFL, which relies heavily on the appeal of violence for its popularity, package its brutality in such a way that it is acceptable to mass audiences when violent crime remains a national scourge? Can leagues that often contain no female players and few women administrators combat sexism or are they doomed to reproduce it? Considering the fact that people of color are the lifeblood of the NBA, NFL, and Major League Baseball, why are there so few minorities in management in those leagues? To what extent do managers make decisions that are motivated by racial concerns, and do these decisions facilitate or complicate racial relations in any given community? Should a club use its cultural power to raise money or awareness about controversial social or political issues? For instance, if having an AIDS awareness day would help raise a large amount of money to combat the disease, should the club do it even if it alienates part of its audience? How do managers set ticket prices that are high enough to allow a team to reach a certain income level without fully exploiting fans whose long standing loyalty has allowed it to operate profitably for many years? How can management answer charges that the "average" fan is being priced out of games due to the greed of players and owners? In addition, there are several "risk management issues" that have to be considered. How can teams ensure the safety of players and fans? What responsibilities does the club have to disabled fans in terms of making sure they have a safe environment in which to watch the game? How can a club ensure the quality of its concessions or that its health care personnel are ready to handle any emergency on a daily basis?

## SPORTS AND THE COURTS

Several sports law books are helpful in understanding how jurisprudence influences the way sport managers answer these questions. Much of the legal writing on risk management centers on nonprofessional sporting activity such as recreational facilities, bowling leagues, ice skating rinks, and other venues used by the general public. However, George W. Schubert's *Sports Law* has several sections that chronicle court decisions on team liability in the case of an injured spectator or employee, as well as cases in which the team can be held partially responsible for the actions of coaches, players, or officials during a contest. Herb Appenzeller's *Sports and Law: Contemporary Issues* devotes two sections to the liability assumed by a team's medical staff and its commitment to look out for the players' best interests over the temptation to sacrifice the future well-being of athletes in favor of maximizing present performance. Robert Huizenga, a former team physician for the Oakland Raiders, has written a book entitled *You're OK, It's Just a Bruise* that is rife with disturbing anecdotes that call into question the medical ethics of team doctors. The book can be used as an eye-opening comple-ment to Appenzeller's legal discussion. DeSensi's text has a section devoted to factors that influence how teams accommodate handicapped fans. Though not a legal text per se, Graham's work hashes out several of the legal concerns surrounding the building of a new stadium, including tax laws and zoning codes that must be worked out between a team and its town if the franchise is to make a profit. Glenn M. Wong's massive *Essentials of Amateur Sport Law*, Robert C. Berry and Glenn M. Wong's *Law and Business of the Sports Industries*, and Linda Carpenter's *Legal Concepts in Sport: A Primer* are just a handful of informative texts that go light on the legalese while still acquainting the reader with the key concepts and cases that continue to shape professional sports. Quirk's *Sport and the Law* contains readable accounts of major legal cases that have shaped the decisions of sport managers in regard to gambling, drugs, violence, media deals, contracts with vendors, and workman's compensation for players and other employees. Finally, Betty Van der Smissen has compiled a huge volume entitled *Legal Liability and Risk Management for Public and Private Entities* that is helpful because it defines just what liability is and gives the reader a general idea of what conditions must exist for a team to be held accountable for any given mishap.

It is important to note that all of these management concerns and marketing efforts are the by-product of a business climate that, because of a long string of antitrust and labor law rulings, favors players over owners, who must search for more and more revenue in order to cope with spiraling salaries. The key to understanding sports business as it currently exists is to examine the legal decisions that, over the course of the last half of the twentieth century, gradually allowed players to wrest power away from management. As mentioned, Robert Berry, William Gould, and Paul Staudohar authored *Labor Relations in Professional Sports,* which, along with Staudohar's *The Sports Industry and Collective Bargaining* and *Playing for Dollars,* form a tremendous trilogy that covers the relationship between sports law and business throughout the twentieth century. Staudohar performs in-depth analyses of all four major sports. Though his work highlights the subtle differences in the changes in business practices of each league, Staudohar clearly demonstrates that most professional sports have traveled the same path of legal evolution and now face similar business problems because of this road.

The key to owner control of the sports labor market for most of the twentieth century centered around what in baseball was called "the reserve clause," which gave Major League owners full control over the present and future contracts of their players. When a player's contract ran out, the owner reserved the right to either offer that player a new contract or let the player go. If a player did not like the offer, his choices were limited. He could either sign the contract or find another line of work. Thus, player salaries were fully dictated by the clubs whose reserve clause power allowed them to hold down player salaries and snuff out rival leagues by preventing their access to top athletes. Players first challenged this situation in the realm of contract law, in which a single player would sue his team in hopes of overthrowing the reserve clause and gaining the right to market himself to any team in any league. Staudohar points out that a few players were marginally successful using this strategy. In *Metropolitan Exhibition Company vs. Ward,* a National League player named John Montgomery Ward successfully argued that he should be allowed to sign with the upstart Player's League because the reserve clause in his National League contract was "indefinite" and "lacked mutuality" (Berry, et al. 1986, 25). Though Ward won the case, his hopes of controlling his own place of business never came to fruition because the Player's League, under considerable pressure from well connected National League owners, went bankrupt. Other players had bright moments, but "when it came to the one-on-one contract the players were overmatched and undersized" (Berry, et al. 1986, 27).

Baseball players also came up empty in the area of antitrust law. Players had hoped to eliminate baseball's monopoly status by proving that it unfairly squashed all other competing leagues. The presence of other leagues would have given the players new leverage in their contract negotiations with Major League teams. However, because the National League began play in 1876, it was able to avoid the powerful antitrust legislation of the twentieth century as the result of the 1922 Supreme Court ruling in *Federal Baseball Club of Baltimore vs. National League of Professional Clubs* that held that baseball was not a business that could be regulated by the 1890 *Sherman Anti-Trust Act*. On the other hand, "football, basketball, hockey and other sports experienced the sting of antitrust scrutiny" (Berry, et al. 1986, 31). The NFL, NBA, and NHL all had to deal with rival leagues after World War II. Still, while each new league brought small bidding wars that resulted in modest financial gains for players and that sometimes, as in the case of the American Football League (1966) or World Hockey League (1979), forced the dominant league into a merger, no truly significant changes in the way the leagues did business occurred. The established leagues either outlasted their usually underfunded counterparts or absorbed them (Berry, et al. 1986, 30–31). Again, small victories had been won, but owners still ruled the labor market, depressing both player movement and salaries.

By far, the most significant venue for change in sport business would come in the arena of labor law where the National Labor Relations Act of 1935 (NLRA) and strengthened player unions would combine to turn professional sports on its head. Player unions had existed for years but had always lacked power. Usually, players controlled the unions, however, they had little legal experience and were, as players, financially dependent on the leagues, a condition that made it almost impossible for them to negotiate with any leverage. In the late 1960s and early 1970s this began to change. Marvin Miller, a skilled labor lawyer whose welfare did not depend on baseball's magnates, took the reins of baseball's player association (MLBPA) in 1966. Miller invoked the National Labor Relations Act to force baseball owners to observe two important principles of the NLRA: (1) that management has to bargain collectively with its workers' union regarding working conditions and benefits and (2) that the labor unions have the right to use pressure tactics such as strikes to gain their objectives (Staudohar 1996, 9). Miller wasted little time in forcing owners into concessions at the bargaining table. In 1968, he negotiated baseball's first collective bargaining agreement in which the players received greater insurance benefits, a guarantee that the minimum salary would rise annually, and an increase in pension payments by the owners (Berry, et al. 1986, 53). In 1970, Miller altered the baseball business forever when he used the NLRA to force baseball owners to consent that any disputes not resolved through collective bargaining would be subject to the decision of "a tripartite arbitration panel with a permanent impartial chairman" (Staudohar 1996, 28). Formerly, any issues that went to arbitration were ruled upon by the commissioner who usually sided with the owners who employed him. In 1973, Miller further empowered players by arranging for a neutral arbitrator to resolve salary disputes between players and their teams. This opened the door to player movement. In 1974, Oakland A's pitcher Jim "Catfish" Hunter claimed that he could be a free agent and sign with any team because team owner Charlie Finley had not fully honored his part of the previous contract. Hunter won the grievance arbitration and moved on to the New York Yankees. In 1975, pitchers Andy Messersmith and Dave McNally also won free agent status when the same arbiter ruled that teams could not extend player contracts indefinitely. The courts upheld the arbiter's decision, legally eliminating the reserve clause. Thus, the 1976 collective bargaining agreement marked the first time baseball owners ever granted limited free agency to its players who could now become free agents after their first six years of Major League service (Staudohar 1996, 35). Utilizing the final right secured by the NLRA, the MLBPA has gone on strike three times since the 1976 agreement to strengthen free agent and arbitration rights and to secure increases in the players' share of television money, enlarged pension funds, and raises in the minimum salary. While the latest strike, which lasted 232 days in 1994, was seen by most experts as a draw, most scholars seem to feel that the balance of power has shifted from the owners to the players as the result of the player's use of labor laws that protect the worker against the potential abuses of management. As Stoudahar writes, "These accomplishments by the MLBPA established the modern era in labor relations, which has effected all professional team sports" (Staudohar 1996, 28).

The Staudohar texts give equal time to the changes wrought by litigation in the areas of labor and antitrust law in football, basketball, and hockey. Each section reveals a pattern similar to that of baseball in the shift of power from owner to player, but each is also filled with singular legal cases and collective bargaining agreements. NFL players achieved free agency rights much later than their baseball brethren due to weak leadership in their players' association, the NFLPA. For instance, in *Mackey vs. The National Football League* (1976), the courts ruled that the NFL's version of the reserve clause, dubbed the "Rozelle rule" after commissioner Pete Rozelle, was a violation of antitrust laws. Yet, with free agency at hand, the NFLPA negotiated away Mackey's legal victory at the collective bargaining table in 1977 when it accepted a large one-time payment in order to allow NFL teams who might lose a free agent to claim hefty compensation in return, usually one or two first round draft picks depending on the value of the free agent in question. Predictably, only one player changed teams as a free agent from 1977 to 1987 (Staudohar 1996, 80). NBA players were more successful.

In 1976 star forward Oscar Robertson brought suit against the league to protest its merger with the American Basketball Association. In *Robertson vs. The National Basketball Association* (1976), the court ruled that the merger could not take place because it would "have the effect of restraining trade by eliminating competition between the two leagues for college players and preventing players from jumping leagues" (Staudohar 1996, 114). Interestingly, the players, armed with their legal victory, allowed the merger in exchange for several concessions that were part of a 1976 collective bargaining agreement. The players received several financial incentives, including limited free agency and the choice to by-pass the college draft and sign with the team of their choice as long as they sat out for one year. The courts accepted the agreement but maintained the right to monitor negotiations between the league and its players for ten years to ensure that no antitrust violations hampered player rights. The NHL has been the least eventful league in terms of legal wrangling. After securing third-party arbitration for grievances in *McCourt vs. California Sports Inc.*, the NHLPA opted for a three-tier system of free agency for its players. As the result of a 1982 collective bargaining agreement, all players over the age of thirty-three were declared unrestricted free agents who could sign with another team without that team having to compensate the player's original team with draft picks. Players under twenty-four or with fewer than five years experience remained restricted under the old reserve system. Those in the middle stage were free to sign with another team, which was required to pay compensation that depended on the overall value of the free agent (Staudohar 1996, 155–156).

To some extent, hockey players have remained the least "free" of the professional athletes in the four major sports. Still, it is clear that in each sport the players enjoy significant control over the business patterns of the leagues because of their powerful unions and court decisions over the last three decades. It is, of course, true that the owners can and have locked out players to win some concessions. In 1994, for instance, NHL owners locked out players for nearly half the season to secure a cap on rookie salaries as well as heightened compensation for players between the ages of twenty-five and thirty-one that will likely restrict free agent movement (Staudohar 1996, 153). Even so, owners continue to face rising salaries because players can, to varying degrees, market their services to their league's highest bidder. Since teams need top players to win games, sell tickets, secure large local television contracts, and sell those new uniforms with the fancy logos, they must continually stretch the salary scale by offering free agents more and more money. One might argue that the owners do not have to bid for the players, that if they collectively decided not to bid the salaries would not rise so fast. However, when baseball owners tried this strategy they were found guilty of "collusion" and forced to pay $280 million in damages to players that felt that they had been victimized by the owner's bidding freeze (Staudohar 1996, 39). Thus, it appears that owners remain stuck in an upward cost spiral, the likes of which has precipitated most of the current revenue search strategies that have been discussed thus far in this chapter.

As mentioned, one solution to this dilemma is offered by Sheehan's revenue-sharing strategy that allegedly would ensure league stability both in terms of finances and on-field competition. According to Sheehan, there is plenty of money to go around, it just needs to be divided in a more socialistic fashion so that teams have similar amounts to spend on players: "Profits are healthy but are unevenly distributed. Implication: some revenue sharing is necessary, and a tax must fall more heavily on profitable franchises" (Sheehan 1996, 164). The problem is that Sheehan's argument, which is somewhat suspect because he does not list his references, is based on the idea that owners are actually doing quite well. In Sheehan's view, the owners' desperate pleas for new revenue and an end to free agency are fabrications designed to shift fans away from their own greed. If that is true, then his solution has some merit as long as the teams have enough collective revenue to keep up with rising salaries. Of course, if what the owners say is true, then their mad dash for more cash will probably continue until the fans, the television networks, and the corporate world can no longer bear the burden of such a huge expense for entertainment. One of the biggest problems is that few owners are willing to open their books so that player unions can see whether the leagues are truly in trouble and whether it is, in fact, necessary to give in to some owner demands for restricted free agency. One thing is for sure. For the foreseeable near future, the brunt of rising expenses will continue to fall on the average sport fan.

Wildly inflated ticket prices, overpriced refreshments and souvenirs, and pay television are just a few of the consequences of the labor wars between players and owners in the last half of the twentieth century.

## EDUCATIONAL RESOURCES ON SPORTS BUSINESS AND LAW

Before finishing the chapter, it is necessary to mention some of the educational resources available both for undergraduate and graduate level classes. The first Sport Management major was established at Ohio University in 1966. By 1993, there were 201 colleges and universities offering undergraduate majors, several master's programs, and six doctoral programs (Parkhouse 1996, 10–15). Several quality texts have been written for these programs and could be quite useful for anyone trying to sharpen knowledge and practical skills in any segment of the sports business. The most comprehensive source is a ten-volume set called the Sport Management Library. Each text is co-authored by members of the two authoritative bodies that preside over Sport Management as a discipline, the National Association for Sport and Physical Education (NASPE) and North American Society for Sport Management (NASSM) and is highly organized with chapter introductions and summaries, review questions that reinforce the main concepts of the chapters, application questions that force the reader to act as a manager within the sports industry, and extensive bibliographies packed with recent scholarship. While the layout of each book is similar, the content is broadly diverse, covering nearly every aspect of the sports industry. *Fundamentals of Sports Marketing* has chapters on marketing theory, global marketing, the history of sports marketing, how to conduct market research, promotion, distribution, and pricing. The book is particularly effective because it focuses more on the business of sports in general than on professional sports. For instance, students are encouraged to develop their own marketing plan to sell a product of their choice within any branch of the multifaceted sports industry. This allows them to deal with most of the concerns faced by businesses that intersect the sports world. The text is complemented by *Case Studies in Sports Marketing*, which details several specific dilemmas faced by those in business along with potential strategies for dealing with those problems. *Management Essentials in Sport Organizations* discusses the qualities that make up a good sports manager and chronicles basic management strategies used to promote healthy organizations. *Sport Facility and Planning Management* contains five case studies designed to help students understand how to manage a variety of sports venues. The authors cover such issues as hiring practices, negotiating with local politicians, contracting with concessions and security firms, and dealing with a diverse clientele that has a variety of special needs and desires. *Sport Management Field Experiences* shows students how to gain internships in different areas of the sports industry and how to turn those jobs into permanent positions. *Legal Aspects of Sports Entrepreneurship* focuses on several legal issues and specific legal cases that confront those in the sports business, especially those operating small businesses. *Financing Sport* discusses how sport managers can fund their businesses by extracting revenue from a variety of different sources. It is particularly beneficial for small or not-for-profit outfits because it teaches the practitioner specific fund-raising strategies that do not require a large initial investment. *Communication in Sport Organizations* shows sports managers how to use communication strategies to improve the cohesiveness of their management team, how to network effectively with other businesses to better market products, and how to use multimedia technology to maximize product exposure. *Ethics in Sport Management* defines several ethical theories and shows how they can be applied to various dilemmas faced by sports managers. Finally, *Sports Governance in the Global Community* is a fascinating text that takes aspects of each of the other nine books and applies them to a global context in which those in the sports industry will have to learn to market products in different cultures with different laws, while managing an internationally diverse workforce that reflects a wide range of values and mores. Again, the best feature of all of these books is that they are not only replete with usable information, but they are interactive and force readers to think about how they would actually implement the concepts contained in the books if they were sports managers. The bibliographies in each book are quite valuable.

Several other texts that are not part of the Sports Management Library are also indispensable academic works designed for classroom use in both sports business and law. Bonnie Parkhouse's *The Management of Sport: Its Foundations and Applications* has informative chapters on group decision making, organizational theory and experiential learning, as well as highly detailed instructions on how to put together an effective marketing plan. Christine Brooks's *Sports Marketing Strategies: Competitive Business Strategies for Sports* allows students to consider how they will incorporate nine different "publics" into a marketing plan that they must develop to sell their own product. Students or practitioners must convince each "public" that their marketing plan will help it in some way. For instance, the plan would have to show how the product and its proliferation would benefit local communities and governments, marketing agencies, and distribution agencies among others. David Stotlar's *Successful Sports Marketing* is a good resource that emphasizes the importance of public relations to professional teams and to sports-related businesses. Lastly, Graham's *Sport Business: Operational and Theoretical Aspects* is a diverse book that covers a number of topics related to the sports industry. Some of the topics include marketing strategies for the Olympic games, innovative trends in sports marketing, the potential of recreational sports as a profitable industry, and the marketing potential for golf and tennis in the next century. Legal texts suitable for classroom use include Linda Carpenter's *Legal Concepts in Sports: A Primer* and Walter T. Champion's *Fundamentals of Sports Law*, both of which effectively introduce readers with little legal acumen to basic relationships between sports and the law. Those interested in the impact of recent legislation on physical education programs within schools or community recreation centers should consult either Neil J. Dougherty's *Sport, Physical Activity and the Law* or John Drowatzky's *Legal Issues in Sport and Physical Education Management,* both of which are clear, concise, thorough, and designed to educate scholars and practitioners who have little in the way of a legal background. Quirk's

*Sports and the Law: Major Legal Cases* is one of the best books dealing with the most pressing legal issues facing professional sports. Along with Appenzeller's *Sports and Law: Contemporary Issues,* Quirk's text gives the reader a better understanding of how legislation has impacted professional and collegiate sports. Gambling, drug and alcohol abuse, risk management, agents, sexual and racial discrimination, and labor disputes such as workman's compensation are all covered in some detail. In addition, several young but outstanding academic journals, including the *Journal of Legal Aspects of Sport* and publications produced by universities that offer sports law programs such as at Marquette University, Seton Hall University, the University of Miami, and Villanova University, offer insight into recent legal cases that have influenced both professional and amateur sports. Finally, John Hladczuk's *Sports Law and Legislation: An Annotated Bibliography* and Glenn M. Wong's *The Sports Lawyer's Guide to Legal Periodicals* are indispensable for researchers who want to survey all legal publications that relate to sport. Hladczuk's annotations are particularly informative because they give the reader a brief glimpse at the main line of discussion in each text that is profiled. The book is organized by subject and would certainly be a good starting point for anyone researching the impact of the legal profession on the world of sports.

In concluding this chapter, it is useful to speculate on the direction of future scholarship in the inseparable fields of sports business and law. Certainly, some similarities exist between the four major sports. As Sheehan writes, "Owners keep searching for additional revenue in an entirely futile attempt to stay one step ahead of the players" (Sheehan 1996, 328). Academics and journalists will likely focus on ownership's continual search for more money and on what will happen as more teams fail to meet the bottom line. For instance, how will leagues expand and still maintain competitive balance when some teams are already losing money? If leagues expand and the talent pool gets thinner, will fans pay to see a lesser product? Will leagues be able to get large market, high profit teams to participate in revenue-sharing plans with their small-town brethren, and will players make concessions to help facilitate this process? Will cities continue to fund luxury stadiums complete with sweetheart leases that allow teams to maximize profits when those cities suffer from a myriad of social problems whose solutions require financial investment? Will fans remain loyal to teams that cater to corporations and wealthy fans that can afford permanent seat licenses?

In addition, labor law should continue to be an important area for scholars. Each league has struggled through at least one lockout or strike since 1993. Owners contending that they can not make money under current labor agreements will have to open their records to player unions if they are to convince players to negotiate away some of the hard-won labor vacates of the past. Are owners really losing money? How will labor laws impact future negotiations? What management strategies will be used by both sides to overcome the enmity that exists between players and owners? How will future work stoppages impact the business of each sport, all of which now must contend with less expensive rival leagues and popular sports such as soccer, golf, tennis, and auto racing? In addition, player unions also face internal discord because free agency has split players into two camps:

superstars that command huge salaries and the majority of the players that receive somewhere close to the minimum as they fight to stay in the league each year. Sheehan writes that "at some point players will recognize that more for the stars means less for the journeymen. This will greatly complicate labor negotiations" (Sheehan 1996, 329). Thus, scholars will also have to look at how union infighting affects business in the next century.

Of course, scholars will have to address the unique economic problems of each sport. Baseball, which lost considerable revenue on its last television contract, must consider how to make its game more marketable for television and investigate the possibility of pay-per-view television for the playoffs and the World Series. The NHL will likely press for the type of large network television deal that the other leagues enjoy. The question is: How much will baseball and hockey have to change their games to accommodate television and will this actually turn off fans? For instance, will the Fox network's insistence that the NHL use a glowing puck attract or alienate fans? Along the same lines, Sheehan contends that the NFL may reduce, if not completely eliminate, its preseason in order to maximize television revenue (Sheehan 1996, 331). NFL teams also will plead for new stadiums, arguing that they need to make the most of every possible source of stadium income because of the league's limited schedule. But, will cities really fork over hundreds of millions of dollars for a facility that can be used ten times a year? If cities agree to build all-purpose domes that can accommodate more events, will fans respond to a dome-oriented NFL? Finally, the NBA will probably be the first league to tap into international markets, perhaps with a European division. In addition, the NBA's sponsorship of the Women's National Basketball League is an attempt to tap into the market for women's professional sports. Scholars will no doubt want to analyze the success or failure of these marketing experiments to probe just what direction sports will take in the next century. After all, if international expansion and attempts to win over more female fans do not work, where will owners turn for more revenue? If those marketing tactics do work, how will that impact the business of sport? Of course, each league's attempt to garner more money will be accompanied by legal battles that will have to be fought over such unresolved issues as franchise movement and pay-per-view television. All of this should provide scholars with plenty of material for study as professional sports continues to evolve over the next few years.

Scholars in search of the most current research in sports business or sports law can consult several quality journals dedicated to examining the current issues in each field. Those interested in the business of sport might consider *American Economic Review, American Journal of Economics and Sociology, Athletic Business, British Journal of Management, Business Journal, Business Law Review, Canadian Journal of Economics, International Economic Review, Journal of Economic Studies, Journal of Social and Political Economic Studies, Journal of Sports Management, Media Sports Business, Quarterly Journal of Business and Economics, Sports Business, Sports inc.,* or *Sports Marketing Quarterly.* For recent articles on the field of sports law or on legal issues that are impacting the world of sports, one might try *Detroit College of Law Entertainment and Sports Law Forum,*

*Harvard Law Review, Journal of Legal Aspects of Sport, Journal of Legal Studies, Marquette Sports Law Journal, Seton Hall Journal of Sport Law, The Sports Lawyer, University of Miami Entertainment and Sports Law Review, University of Michigan Law Review,* or *Villanova Sports and Entertainment Law Journal.*

## REFERENCES

### Books

Abrams, Roger. *Legal Bases: Baseball and the Law.* Philadelphia, PA: Temple University Press, 1999.

Ammon, Rob, Jr., Peter J. Farmer, and Aaron Mulrooney. *Sport Facility Planning and Management.* Morgantown, WV: Fitness Information Technologies, 1996.

Andelman, Bob. *Stadium for Rent: Tampa Bay's Quest for Major League Baseball.* Jefferson, NC: McFarland, 1993.

Appenzeller, Herb. *Sports and Law: Contemporary Issues.* Charlottesville, VA: Michie Company, 1985.

Baim, Dean. *The Sports Stadium as a Municipal Investment.* Westport, CT: Greenwood Press, 1994.

Benson, Michael. *Ballparks of North America: A Comprehensive Historical Reference to Baseball Grounds, Yards, and Stadiums.* Jefferson, NC: McFarland, 1989.

Bergin, Ron. *Sponsorship, Principles and Practice: A Practical Guide to Entertainment, Sport, Music and Event Marketing.* Nashville, TN: Amusement Business, 1989.

Berry, Robert, and Glenn M. Wong. *Law and Business of the Sports Industries: Common Issues in Amateur and Professional Sport.* Dover, MA: Auburn House Publishing Company, 1986.

Berry, Robert, William Gould, and Paul Staudohar. *Labor Relations in Professional Sports.* Dover, MA: Auburn House Publishing, 1986.

Brooks, Christine. *Sports Marketing Strategies: Competitive Business Strategies for Sports.* Englewood Cliffs, NJ: PrenticeHall, 1994.

Burk, Robert. *Never Just a Game: Players, Owners and American Baseball to 1920.* Chapel Hill, NC: University of North Carolina Press, 1994.

Carpenter, Linda. *Legal Concepts in Sport: A Primer.* Reston, VA: American Association for Lifestyles and Fitness, 1995.

Carter, David. *Keeping Score: An Inside Look at Sports Marketing.* Grants Pass, OR: Oasis Press, 1996.

————. *You Can't Play the Game if You Don't Know the Rules: Career Opportunities in Sport Management.* Manasses Park, VA: Impact Publications, 1994.

Champion, Walter T. *Fundamentals of Sports Law.* Deerfield, IL: Clark Boardman Callaghan, 1990.

————. *Sports Law in a Nutshell.* St. Paul, MN: West Publishing Company, 1993.

Clement, Annie. *Law in Sport and Physical Activity.* Indianapolis, IN: Benchmark Press, 1988.

Condon, George. *The Man in the Arena.* Cleveland, OH: A. C. Sutphin Foundation, 1995.

Cuneen, Jacqueline, and M. Joy Sidwell. *Sport Management Field Experiences.* Morgantown, WV: Fitness Information Technologies, 1994.

Danielson, Michael N. *Home Team: Professional Sports and the American Metropolis.* Princeton, NJ: Princeton University Press, 1997.

DeSensi, Joy T., and Danny Rosenberg. *Ethics in Sport Management.* Morgantown, WV: Fitness Information Technologies, 1996.

Dougherty, Neil J. *Sport, Physical Activity and the Law*. Champaign, IL: Human Kinetics Books, 1994.

Drowatzky, John. *Legal Issues in Sport and Physical Education Management*. Champaign, IL: Stipes Publishing, 1993.

Euchner, Charles C. *Playing the Field: Why Sports Teams Move and Cities Fight to Keep Them*. Baltimore, MD: Johns Hopkins Press, 1994.

Fizel, John, Elizabeth Gustafson, and Lawrence Hadley, eds. *Baseball Economics: Current Research*. Westport, CT: Praeger, 1996.

Friedman, Alan, ed. *Team Marketing Reports' 500 Great Sport Promotion Ideas: Successful New Ideas to Increase Revenue*. Chicago: Team Marketing Reports, 1994.

Garvey, Edward. *The Agent Game: Selling Players Short*. Washington, D.C.: Federation of Professional Athletes: AFL/CIO, 1984.

Gorman, Jerry. *The Name of the Game: The Business of Sports*. New York: John Wiley & Sons, 1994.

Graham, Peter J. *Sport Business: Operational and Theoretical Aspects*. Dubuque, IA: Brown & Benchmark, 1993.

Graham, Stedman, Joe Jeff Goldblatt, and Lisa Delphy. *The Ultimate Guide to Sport Event Management and Marketing*. Chicago: Irwin Professional Publishers, 1995.

Greenberg, Martin J. *Sports Law Practice*. Charlottesville, VA: Michie Company, 1993.

Gruver, Edward. *The American Football League: A Year-by-Year History, 1960–1969*. Jefferson, NC: McFarland, 1997.

Harris, David. *The Rise and Decline of the NFL*. New York: Bantam Books, 1987.

Hay, Robert D. *Sports Marketing: Texts and Cases*. Santa Barbara, CA: Kinko's Publishing Group, 1985.

Helitzer, Melvin. *The Dream Job: $port Publicity, Promotions and Marketing*. Athens, OH: University Sports Press, 1996.

Hladczuk, John. *Sports Law and Legislation: An Annotated Bibliography*. New York: Greenwood Press, 1991.

Howard, Dennis, and John L Compton. *Financing Sport*. Morgantown, WV: Fitness Information Technologies, 1995.

Huizenga, Robert. *You're OK. It's Just a Bruise*. New York: St. Martin's, 1994.

Johnson, Arthur T. *Minor League Baseball and Local Economic Development*. Urbana, IL: University of Illinois Press, 1993.

Katz, Donald R. *Just Do It: The Nike Spirit in the Corporate World*. New York: Random House, 1994.

Kerrane, Kevin. *Dollar Sign on the Muscle*. New York: Simon & Schuster, 1989.

King, Peter. *Football: A History of the Professional Game*. Birmingham, AL: Oxmoor House, 1993.

Klatell, David. *Sports for Sale: Television, Money and the Fans*. New York: Oxford University Press, 1988.

Klinkowitz, Jerry. *Owning a Piece of the Minors*. Carbondale, IL: Southern Illinois University Press, 1999.

Koehler, Robert W. *Law: Sport Activity and Risk Management*. Champaign, IL: Stipes Publishing, 1987.

Lee, Teresa A. *Legal Research Guide to Television Broadcasting and Program Syndication*. Buffalo, NY: W. S. Hein, 1995.

Lewis, Guy, ed. *Successful Sport Management*. Charlottesville, VA: Michie Company, 1985.

Lowe, Stephen R. *The Kid on the Sandlot: Congress and Professional Sports, 1910–1992*. Bowling Green, OH: Bowling Green University Press, 1995.

Lowenfish, Lee. *The Imperfect Diamond: A History of Baseball's Labor Wars*. New York: Da Capo Press, 1991.

Maloy, Bernard P. *Law in Sport: Liability Cases in Management and Administration*. Indianapolis, IN: Benchmark Press, 1988.

Mangan, James, and Paul D. Staudohar. *The Business of Professional Sports*. Urbana, IL: University of Illinois Press, 1991.

Marburger, Daniel. *STEE-RIKE FOUR! What's Wrong with the Business of Baseball?* Westport, CT: Praeger, 1997.

McKinnon, Matthew C., and Robert McCormick. *Sports Law*. Detroit, MI: Lupus, 1992.

Miller, Edward. *The Baseball Business: Pursuing Pennants and Profits in Baltimore*. Chapel Hill, NC: University of North Carolina Press, 1990.

Miller, Lori. *Sport Business Management*. Gaithersburg, MD: Aspen Publishers, 1997.

Morgan, Jon. *Glory for Sale: Fans, Dollars and the New NFL*. New York: Bancroft, 1997.

O'Brien, D. B., and J. O. Overby. *Legal Aspects of Entrepeneurship*. Morgantown, WV: Fitness Information Technologies, 1997.

Parkhouse, Bonnie L., ed. *The Management of Sport: Its Foundations and Applications*. St. Louis, MO: Mosby, 1996.

Patten, Phil. *Razzle Dazzle: The Curious Marriage of Television and Professional Football*. Garden City, NY: Dial Press, 1984.

Pearson, Daniel. *Baseball in 1989: Players vs. Owners*. Bowling Green, OH: Bowling Green University Popular Press, 1993.

Pietrusza, David. *Major Leagues: The Formation, Sometimes Absorption and Mostly Inevitable Demise of 18 Professional Baseball Organizations*. Jefferson, NC: McFarland, 1998.

Pitts, Brenda. *Case Studies in Sports Marketing*. Morgantown, WV: Fitness Information Technologies, 1998.

Pitts, Brenda, and David K. Stotlar. *Fundamentals of Sports Marketing*. Morgantown, WV: Fitness Information Technologies, 1996.

Quirk, Charles E., ed. *Sports and the Law: Major Legal Cases*. New York: Garland Publishing, 1996.

Quirk, James, and Rodney D. Fort. *Hard Ball: The Abuse of Power in Team Sports*. Princeton, NJ: Princeton University Press, 1998.

———. *Pay Dirt: The Business of Team Sports*. Princeton, NJ: Princeton University Press, 1992.

Raterman, Dale. *How to Get a Job in Sports*. Indianapolis, IN: Master's Press, 1995.

Rekes, Linda. *Citizenship Through Sports and Law*. Minneapolis, MN: West Publication Company, 1995.

Richmond, Peter. *Ballpark: Camden Yards and the Building of an American Dream*. New York: Simon & Schuster, 1993.

Rosentraub, Mark S. *Major League Losers: The Real Cost of Sport and Who's Paying for It*. New York: Basic Books, 1997.

Sands, Jack. *Coming Apart at the Seams: How Baseball Owners, Players and Television Executives Have Led Our National Pastime to the Brink of Disaster*. New York: Macmillan, 1993.

Schaaf, Phil. *Sports Marketing: It's Not Just a Game Anymore*. Amherst, NY: Prometheus Books, 1995.

Schlossberg, Howard. *Sports Marketing*. Cambridge, MA: USA Blackwell Business, 1996.

Schubert, George W., Rodney Smith, and Jesse Trentadue. *Sports Law*. St. Paul, MN: West Publication Company, 1990.

Scully, Gerald. *The Business of Major League Baseball*. Chicago: University of Chicago Press, 1989.

————. *The Market Structure of Sports*. Chicago: University of Chicago Press, 1995.

Sheehan, Richard. *Keeping Score: The Economics of Big-Time Sports*. South Bend, IN: Diamond Communications, 1996.

Shropshire, Kenneth L. *Agents of Opportunity: Sports Agents and Corruption in Collegiate Sports*. Philadelphia, PA: University of Pennsylvania Press, 1990.

————. *Careers in Sports Law*. Chicago: American Bar Association, 1990.

Simon, Ron. *The Game Behind the Scenes: Negotiating in the Big Leagues*. Stillwater, MN: Voyager Press, 1993.

Sleight, Steve. *Sponsorship: What It Is and How to Use It*. New York: McGraw-Hill, 1989.

Sommers, Paul, ed. *Diamonds Are Forever: The Business of Baseball*. Washington, D.C.: The Brookings's Institution, 1992.

*Sport: Dollars and Sense*. Milwaukee, WI: National Sport Law Institute of Marquette Law School, 1993.

*Sport Sponsor Factbook*. Chicago: Team Marketing Report, 1993.

*Sport Summit Sports Business Directory*. Bethesda, MD: E. J. Krause & Associates, 1995.

Staudohar, Paul D. *Playing for Dollars: Labor Relations and the Sports Business*. Ithaca, NY: ILA Press, 1996.

————. *The Sports Industry and Collective Bargaining*. Ithaca, NY: IRL Press, Cornell University, 1989.

Stein, Gil. *Power Plays: An Inside Look at the Big Business of the National Hockey League*. New York: Birch Lane, 1997.

Stotlar, David K. *Successful Sport Marketing*. Madison, WI: WCB Brown & Benchmark, 1993.

Sullivan, Neil. *The Diamond Revolution: The Prospects for Baseball after the Collapse of Its Ruling Class*. New York: St. Martin's, 1992.

Thoma, James. *Sport Governance in the Global Community*. Morgantown, WV: Fitness Information Technologies, 1996.

Uberstine, Gary. *Covering All the Bases: A Comprehensive Research Guide to Sports Law*. Buffalo, NY: W. S. Hein, 1988.

U.S. Congress. *Professional Sports Community Protection Act of 1985*. Washington, D.C.: USGPO, 1985.

Van der Smissen, Betty. *Legal Liability and Risk Management for Public and Private Entities*. Cincinnati, OH: Anderson Publishing, 1990.

Vanderzwaag, Harold J. *Policy Development in Sport Management*. Westport, CT: Praeger, 1998.

Walker, Sheila M. *National Sports Festival Planning Manual: A Guide to Contradictory Multi-Sport Events*. Colorado Springs, CO: U.S. Olympic Committee, 1985.

Wascovich, Terence R. *The Sports Marketing Guide*. Cleveland, OH: Ohio Points Ahead Press, 1993.

Weiss, Ann. *Money Games: The Business of Sport*. Boston: Houghton-Mifflin, 1993.

Whitford, David. *Playing Hardball: The High Stakes Battle for Baseball's New Franchises*. New York: Doubleday, 1993.

Wilson, Neil. *The Sports Business*. London: Piatkus, 1988.

Wong, Glenn M. *Essentials of Amateur Sports Law*. Westport, CT: Praeger, 1994.

————. *The Sport Lawyer's Guide to Legal Periodicals: An Annotated Bibliography*. Buffalo, NY: W. S. Hein, 1994.

Yasser, Raymond L. *Sports Law: Cases and Materials*. Cincinnati, OH: Anderson Publishing, 1990.

Zeigler, Earle F. *Management Competency Development in Sport and Physical Education*. Champaign, IL: University of Illinois Press, 1995.

Zimbalist, Andrew. *Baseball and Billions*. New York: Basic Books, 1992.

————. *Unpaid Professionals: Commercialism and Conflict in Big-Time College Sport.* Princeton, NJ: Princeton University Press, 1999.

Zimbalist, Andrew, and Roger G. Noll, eds. *Sports, Jobs, and Taxes: The Economic Impact of Sports Teams and Stadiums.* Washington, D.C.: The Brookings's Institution, 1997.

## Journals

*American Economic Review* (Princeton, NJ)

*American Journal of Economics and Sociology* (New York, NY)

*Athletic Business* (New York, NY)

*British Journal of Management* (New York, NY)

*Business Journal* (Boston, MA)

*Business Law Review* (Norwell, MA)

*Canadian Journal of Economics* (Burbury, British Columbia, Canada)

*Detroit College of Law Entertainment and Sports Law Forum* (Detroit, MI)

*Harvard Law Review* (Cambridge, MA)

*International Economic Review* (Philadelphia, PA)

*Journal of Economic Studies* (Birmingham, AL)

*Journal of Legal Aspects of Sport* (New York, NY)

*Journal of Legal Studies* (Chicago, IL)

*Journal of Social and Political Economic Studies* (Washington, D.C.)

*Journal of Sports Management* (Champaign, IL)

*Marquette Sports Law Journal* (Marquette, MI)

*Media Sports Business* (New York, NY)

*Quarterly Journal of Business and Economics* (Lincoln, NE)

*Seton Hall Journal of Sport Law* (New York, NY)

*Sports Business* (Woodbridge, Ontario, Canada)

*Sports inc.* (New York, NY)

*The Sports Lawyer* (Miami, FL)

*Sports Marketing Quarterly* (Chicago, IL)

*University of Miami Entertainment and Sports Law Review* (Miami, FL)

*University of Michigan Law Review* (Ann Arbor, MI)

*Villanova Sports and Entertainment Law Journal* (Villanova, PA)

# 3

# Sport and Education

For many of us, it is tempting to view sport as mere diversion, as an activity that is essentially nonserious, playful, and escapist. For others, it is impossible to remove sport from the realm of larger, weightier concerns. Sport is seen as an arena for proving oneself or for establishing superiority over another individual, town, state, or country. Perhaps nowhere is this spirit more evident than at the Olympics, where fans from across the globe wave flags in hopes that their athletes will bring home coveted medals from the valued athletic space that is the Olympic arena, medals that somehow signify a nation's greatness. In the case of professional leagues, sport functions both as a vehicle by which investors can make money and through which local fans can gain a fragile, somewhat indescribable, but no less real, ascendancy over those who live in other cities by vanquishing their teams on the gridiron or the diamond. Anyone living in Boston in the mid-1980s, for instance, knows that the great Celtic-Laker battles of that time were as much about imagined cultural superiority as about whose basketball team was better. A Celtic victory somehow affirmed all that was right with clam chowder, Faneuil Hall, and *Cheers*. Still, others insist that sport has a higher purpose, one that is purely educational and self-affirming in nature, one that exists outside the economic and political forces that provoke competition, one that is dedicated to helping people live longer, healthier lives. In my own discipline of English studies, some scholars insist that sport is a vital academic subject, one that is sometimes essential for understanding the culture in which a novel, film, or poem is produced. To an extent, then, sport is interesting because it has so many faces and has the ability to address a number of vital human needs and emotions. Not surprisingly, sport is used to fulfill several, often conflicting, functions within our current institutional framework of education, its several forms existing as a rather unwieldy, at times volatile, three-part blend. The most prominent part is the big business strand of college sports, consisting mostly of Division I football and men's basketball programs, whose popularity nets some colleges and universities millions of dollars annually. Scholars examining college sports have focused on the processes by which Division I schools make or lose money and what other benefits these schools get from their commercial venture. Most of the scholarship, however, is aimed at the negative consequences of what is often referred to as "big-time" college athletics. These include gambling, steroid use, alcohol and drug abuse, crime, academic fraud, cheating, racism, sexism, and the privileging of athletes over the rest of the student body. In contrast to this is a body of academic work that explores how schools from kindergarten to university are using sport to educate their students on how they can use physical activity to enhance their lives. These works chronicle the recent history of physical education and concentrate on how schools are dealing with a variety of contemporary problems facing physical educators. These include funding programs, choosing between intramural and varsity programs, counseling, providing programs for disabled students, creating special programming for kids, solving ethical concerns and legal problems, and developing an effective overall philosophy by which to operate a physical education program that is helpful to all students while not breaking the school's budget. Finally, there has been in the last two decades an effort by many professors to use sport within their academic disciplines. Sport has, in fact, become an acceptable academic subject that many disciplines have been quick to adopt. Courses in the sociology of sport, sport psychology, sport history, and the literature of sport are just a few of the sport-related classes that dot the academic map. Accordingly, a number of fine classroom texts, pedagogical manuals, and research databases have been created to help those interested in incorporating sport into their classroom pedagogy or research projects. This chapter will discuss what scholars have had to say about key issues in each of the three areas in which sport and education intersect, focusing mostly on the current conflict between educators who want to see sport used as a tool to enhance the physical and academic well-being of students and those that benefit from big-time college sports.

## INTERCOLLEGIATE SPORTS: PROBLEMS AND POSSIBILITIES

Anyone surveying the cultural landscape of colleges and universities cannot help but notice the centrality of intercollegiate sport to campus life. From the intimate arenas of Division III schools to the mega stadiums of big-time football powerhouses, winning the big game is important to students, alumni, and fans. Though many have long lauded sport for its alleged ability to develop character and leadership traits in young men and women, there is clearly something deeper that makes sporting contests such a vital part of college life. After all, when one's team is down by six points and has a fourth and goal from the one-yard line with time running out, one is not usually concerned with how well the halfback's gridiron experience has enhanced his academic or social development. The only consideration is whether or not he will be able to plow into the end zone and bring greater glory to the old alma mater and a certain, undefined personal satisfaction to us. Most scholars agree that victories appeal to our most basic sense of pride, that we simply feel a bit better about ourselves when our college bests another school in the athletic arena. It is interesting and somewhat disturbing that many Americans choose to attach notions of our superiority to collegiate athletic achievement instead of academic or other humanitarian pursuits. Wilford S. Bailey and Taylor D. Littleton's *Athletes and the Academy: An Anatomy of Abuses and a Prescription for Reform* asserts that we do this because sports give us annual, highly visible celebrations of rituals that nostalgically connect us with important moments in our past, allowing us to cast fond remembrance on the triumphs of youth. "Sports through their popular and ceremonial appeal to alumni could serve—and do still—as a core of identity and remembrance, their stadiums and coliseums bearing names and symbolic decorations of past triumphs that consecrate both field and court in ways impossible of application to laboratories or classrooms" (Bailey 1991, 6). If sports does, in fact, allow us to celebrate our lives and our traditions, John Bale argues in *The Brawn Drain: Foreign Student Athletes in American Universities* that this is only so because sports provide Americans with an arena of festive entertainment that is by itself intoxicating. For Bale, the electricity of the band belting out the school fight song, the emotional rendition of the alma mater at half time, and the tailgate parties with old friends outside the sacred stadium all contribute to our fascination with and love for college sports (Bale 1991, 27).

Still, the question remains as to why Americans choose to engage in this regenerative process within the context of sports instead of a science fair, poetry reading, or service project. The best explanation for our college sport fixation is offered by Donald Chu in *The Character of American Higher Education and Intercollegiate Sport*. According to Chu, the answer lies in the power of tradition. We celebrate ourselves through college sport because higher education has spent a century or more training us to do so. Chu's book does an excellent job of detailing how big-time college sports developed within the framework of American higher education around the end of the nineteenth century. He is careful to emphasize that the rise of college sports hinged on two factors: societal values and money. American universities operated as by-products of a society that valued rugged individualism, that craved virile heroes, and that valued athletic space as a training ground for male leaders that would advance American interests at home and abroad. As Chu writes, "Dreams of rugged individual success and idealized images of dynamic action had to be reconciled with the realities of life dominated by corporate organizations. The public, hungry for heroes that embodied traditional dreams, cultivated sport figures such as The Four Horsemen of Notre Dame" (Chu 1989, 56). Because sports, especially football, were valued by the public, college presidents gradually embraced athletics as a way to market their schools. Chu writes, "The American colleges and universities of the late nineteenth and early twentieth centuries were limited in both their current resources and their ability to acquire further resources. Survival required addition of programs and modification of traditional mission to suit potential students and the public imagination" (Chu 1989, 33). Success on the gridiron meant increased alumni support, more applications from perspective students, and, for some schools, hefty profits from the games. Of course, "college leadership could hardly fail to notice the national exposure afforded heretofore minor schools such as Notre Dame and Swarthmore," who cashed in on early football success (Chu 1989, 57). Thus, from its infancy, big-time college sports has been closely tied with money, prestige, and alumni pride.

While tradition and school pride still provide fuel for the big-time college sports machine, money continues to be the chief catalyst for intercollegiate sport. Colleges and universities may theoretically engage in sport to ensure the physical development of students, to inflate school spirit, or to carry out the humanistic belief that colleges have a duty to nurture students in a holistic fashion that is in keeping with the ancient Greek philosophy of making complete individuals by perfecting the mind and the body. Of course, the egos of key alumni can never be ruled out as a factor, especially considering the cultural power accorded sport in the United States. Still, the main reason that big-time sport exists today is that most schools want a piece of what has become a very lucrative industry. Gary Funk's *Major Violations: The Unbalanced Priorities in Athletics and Academics* is one of several books that provides staggering statistics on just how profitable college sports have become for those who play and succeed at the highest levels. For instance, Funk discusses the ramifications of the National Collegiate Athletic Association's (NCAA) 1989 deal with CBS, in which the network agreed to pay $1 billion to broadcast the NCAA basketball championship from 1991–1997. The deal got the attention of colleges by calling for even greater payouts than the deal that expired in 1990 after paying each Final Four participant a cool $1,432,500. With such pots of gold looming at the end of the road to the Final Four, schools have spent millions to upgrade facilities and hire big-name coaches who might lead them to the promised land (Funk 1991, 66–69). Football's vault, though accessible to fewer schools because of mammoth operating costs, is even more lucrative than that of basketball. According to Dana Brooks's *Racism in College Athletics: The African-American Athlete's Experience*, schools that went to bowl games in 1990 divided $57 million (Brooks 1993, 271). The figure has grown each year with major bowl participants netting between $5 and $8 million in 1997. The top football schools are money-making machines. The University of Florida not only sells out its 85,000-seat stadium, but it also leases luxury boxes for as much as $30,000 per game (Brooks 1993, 272). Both the University of Tennessee and the University of Michigan have over 105,000 seats that are filled for every game. In *Win at Any Cost: The Sellout of College Athletics*, Francis Dealy writes that Michigan's football program earned $12.8 million for the school in 1989, accounting for 64 percent of the athletic department's revenue (Dealy 1990, 156). Michigan is perhaps rivaled only by Notre Dame, which, as the only major school with its own network television contract, is paid in excess of $7 million per year by NBC to allow the network to broadcast its home football games. Dealy estimates that "Boston College earned an extra $10 million from [Heisman Trophy winner] Doug Flutie, and Georgetown University benefitted by $30 million when Patrick Ewing played for the Hoyas" (Dealy 1990, 156). At many schools, money sports are so popular that alumni and fans have to make donations to the school just to secure the right to pay for tickets. Dennis Howard's *Financing Sport* provides a detailed account of how college athletic programs rake in money. Included is a discussion of Ohio State's "point system," in which football fans can gain points toward the purchase of bowl tickets or upgraded basketball tickets by donating large sums for the right to buy football tickets. Donators can fall into one of several levels of membership in the "Buckeye Club" depending on how much they want to contribute. The only difference is that the more one spends the closer one gets to the fifty-yard line in football and center court in basketball. At many schools, donations of $10,000 to secure top seats are not uncommon (Howard 1995, 390). As Funk sums up, "Modern collegiate sport is, essentially, a monetary endeavor" (Funk 1991, 65).

## THE POWER OF TELEVISION

Most scholars have focused their attention on the consequences of this monetary endeavor. Perhaps the most disturbing result has been the schools' loss of control over athletics to the television networks and corporate sponsors whose money drives the industry. One of the main problems is that while there is a great deal of television money to be had, only the most successful teams can actually make enough to break even or make a profit. Thus, most teams are bound to accrue significant deficits because only a few teams can make it to the big games. In his highly readable *Out of Bounds: How the American Sports Establishment Is Being Driven by Greed and Hypocrisy and What Needs to Be Done About It*, Congressman Tom MacMillan summarizes the problem: "As TV dollars pour in, the colleges expand their programs, becoming more dependent on TV money. The networks, not the schools, are calling the shots" (MacMillan 1992, 131). The effects of this dependence can be devastating. In *The Old College Try: Balancing Academics and Athletics in Higher Education,* James Thelin discusses the 1984 Supreme Court ruling that gave television networks the right to negotiate football contracts with individual teams and conferences rather than with the NCAA. Before the decision, the NCAA had the power to limit the number of games aired on television and the right to dictate which games would be shown. Thus, the NCAA was able to negotiate profitable deals for its member schools by showing only the best games during prime viewing slots. There were no "weak" games flooding the market and taking the luster off the sport. In fact, the NCAA was so adept that its 1984 television agreement called for networks to pay colleges $74 million for the season. When the Supreme Court ruling came down, however, the agreement was nullified and television networks bargained freely with teams and conferences (Thelin 1989, 55). The result was that the networks stepped into college football's driver's seat. Not only did they spend only $30.8 million in 1984 for more games than they would have received under the old $74 million agreement, but they also put athletic directors in the position of having to chase them for more revenue. Even powerful Notre Dame had to play eight games on television on the exact days and times requested by the networks in order to equal the amount of revenue it garnered from three telecasts under the old contract. As Murray Sperber writes in *College Sports Inc.: The Athletic Department vs. The*

*University*, athletic departments launched into a "futile scramble to make up the lost revenue and—the worst error—maintain spending at pre-1984 levels. The result was greater deficits for a larger number of programs and an accelerating loss spiral that continues to this day" (Sperber 1991, 54).

Colleges are now forced to play games when and where the networks say. This is why one sees basketball games tipping off at 9:30 p.m. (EST). It is also why many football teams play at least twelve regular season games. Brigham Young even played fifteen games in 1996, resulting in more lost class time for students but more television money for the school. Of course, the athletic departments also have to live with some of the dictates of the advertisers that help sustain the television networks and of the corporate sponsors that now subsidize college sports as part of their marketing strategy. Anheuser-Busch, for instance, is one of the top sponsors of the NCAA basketball tournament. Without the beer manufacturer, it is unlikely that CBS could pay $1 billion to the colleges. However, as Dealy points out, this puts colleges in the position of essentially advocating student drinking. Dealy laments that "despite the U.S. Surgeon General's declaration that underage drinking is the nation's number one health problem, the NCAA conspires with Anheuser-Busch and CBS to stimulate minors to use an illegal drug, beer" (Dealy 1990, 143). Sperber's book puts forth several similar examples, including that of the University of Denver, which, in order to cover the rising costs of running a large athletic program, accepted money from both Coors and Anheuser-Busch. "That alcohol consumption, especially of beer, has reached epidemic proportions on campuses across America did not bother the University of Denver" (Sperber 1991, 63). Sperber's book forces readers to deal with what may be the biggest problem for colleges in the twenty-first century: how to run a profitable, honest program that is healthy for student athletes when the athletic departments are increasingly controlled by television networks and corporations that pay more of the bill each year. As Sperber writes, "This practice undermines one of the fundamental tenets of American colleges and universities—their independence" (Sperber 1991, 64).

The endless chase for revenue has left athletic departments in an expensive chase after a mirage. Most schools spend millions trying to reach the Final Four or the Orange Bowl only to lose much of their investment. According to Thelin's *Games Colleges Play: Scandal and Reform in Intercollegiate Athletics*, "A glance at a university budget shows that annual operation of a large varsity sports program costs about the same as running a professional school in engineering, law or even medicine. It is standard practice for a head football coach to be paid at least as much as an academic dean" (Thelin 1997, 1). The problem is that in order to get to the big money games, schools have to have great players. In order to procure such athletes, schools have to invest millions in state-of-the-art facilities and pay top dollar for coaches who can recruit game-breaking players. Most big-time college coaches earn six- or seven-figure salaries, and football and men's basketball coaches at most schools are paid much more than tenured faculty. Sperber claims that in 1988 the average pay for nine assistant football coaches at the University of Iowa was $50,000, while the average pay for assistant professors with Ph.D.s was $32,800. He goes on to recount some rather disturbing facts, including the story of Indiana University's athletic department where all ranking officials, including the weight room attendant and basketball trainer, were paid more than most associate professors in 1989 (Sperber 1991, 96). The result of this lavish spending has been annual losses for most schools. According to MacMillan, "The NCAA estimates that 70 percent of the organization's 298 Division I programs currently operate at deficits" (MacMillan 1992, 122). Sperber, who dedicates an entire chapter to debunking myths about college athletics, asserts that the idea that college sports are profitable is a myth thrust before the public by colleges to justify their big business approach to college athletics. Sperber writes that "of the 802 members of the NCAA, the 493 members of the NAIA, and the 1,050 nonaffiliated junior colleges, only 10 to 20 athletic programs make a consistent albeit small profit. The rest—over 2,300 institutions—lose anywhere from a few dollars to millions annually" (Sperber 1991, 2). For those looking for exact financial statistics for individual schools, conferences, or divisions, the NCAA publishes a guide entitled *Revenue and Expenses of Intercollegiate Athletic Programs* that analyzes the gains and losses of member schools over five-year periods.

One of the biggest concerns for educators is that monetary loss is hardly the only problem plaguing athletic departments. Several scholars have charged college administrations with sanctioning an athletic system that fosters abusive behavior antithetical to any educational agenda a university might have. For instance, in their desperation to cash in on the television windfall, some schools have cheated by violating recruiting regulations or by engaging in academic fraud. Once again, Sperber does a fine job of explaining just how schools and their "boosters" try to circumvent the NCAA recruiting regulations. Usually, colleges will woo students with expensive meals, lavish hotel rooms, monetary payments to family members, cars, stereos, or other incentives. "On many campuses, these also include attractive members of the opposite sex who 'date' the recruit for a weekend" (Sperber 1991, 248). Brian Bosworth's *The Boz: Confessions of a Modern Anti-Hero*, Stu Whitney's *Behind the Green Curtain: The Sacrifice of Ethics in Michigan State's Rise to Football Prominence*, Charles Thompson's *Down & Dirty: The Life and Times of Oklahoma Football*, and Douglas Looney and Don Yeager's *Under the Tarnished Dome: How Notre Dame Betrayed Its Ideals for Football Glory* are just a few of several books, many written by former players, that provide a litany of egregious violations committed by programs over the last two decades. Of course, many of these schools incur NCAA penalties resulting in loss of scholarships, television and bowl revenue, and recruiting visits. In the last two decades, Southern Methodist, Miami, Clemson, Mississippi, Oklahoma, Auburn, and Washington are just a handful of top notch programs who were found guilty and punished for numerous violations. Sperber's book chronicles the stories of several schools who have earned NCAA censures for rather incredible and embarrassing recruiting escapades.

## PROBLEMS FOR STUDENT ATHLETES

Scholars are careful to stress that not only does this sort of preferential treatment for athletes put schools in jeopardy, it also has negative consequences for the student, who is encouraged to believe that this fantasy world of pleasure will continue and that he will not have to deal with classes, grades, and the realities of college life. Again, the previously listed books by former college athletes provide colorful reading for anyone who doubts that most recruited athletes do experience a type of culture shock when confronted with the daily grind of college life. As Sperber concludes, "Of all methods devised for preparing seventeen-year-olds for life as student-athletes, the recruiting process, and its highlight weekend visit, is probably the worst" (Sperber 1992, 249). Before leaving the subject of recruiting, it is necessary to mention a fine book by Ted Weissberg entitled *Breaking the Rules: The NCAA and Recruitment in American High Schools*. In it, Weissberg produces hard evidence that confirms much of Sperber's findings and validates many of the experiences related by former college stars such as Bosworth and Thompson. In addition, the author discusses some other abuses, including the practice known as "overbooking." This refers to the fact that schools routinely offer more scholarships than they actually have to give because they think that not all of the recruits will accept them. However, when too many accept, the school can wait a long time before telling some of the students that their offer has been rescinded. Often, this leaves student athletes without a place to go to school. As Weissberg writes, "The practice is within NCAA regulations. But it works against student-athletes, especially those with marginal talent. Overbooked student-athletes often wind up without any scholarships and their plans to attend college can be ruined at the last second" (Weissberg 1995, 99).

A second major area of cheating is academic fraud. Clarence Underwood has written a tremendous book called *The Student-Athlete: Eligibility and Academic Integrity* which explains just how schools cheat in this area to ensure the eligibility of their student athletes. Underwood compiled evidence on several different cases of academic fraud and grouped the cases into three different categories. The first is transcript forgery, which involves a school altering a player's high school or college transcript so that he can gain admission to a program. The second category is referred to as "academic abuse" in which students already at the college receive credit for classes they never actually took. Usually the player gets a "A" or a "B" in a class in which he was enrolled but never attended. The idea is that the good grade will average in with his other poor grades to keep him eligible. Finally, financial aid abuse is another area in which schools can illegally give students scholarship money disguised as loans. Often, these "loans" are nothing more than unreported scholarships donated by wealthy boosters (Underwood 1984, xi). Underwood introduces several case studies that give the reader an understanding of exactly how these violations take place and a disturbing idea of just how often they occur.

Scholars and former athletes continue to remind us that, in addition to cheating, commercialized college sports never seems to be able to free itself from connections with ethical backsliding. Bosworth, Thompson, and Looney all speak of drug parties, sexual orgies, illegal payments, numerous acts of violence against both male and female students, and gambling. In 1996, Boston College's football team reprimanded several players for gambling on the team's games. According to Dealy, "Close to two dozen football players at the University of Colorado were arrested between 1987 and 1989 on charges ranging from rape to assault" (Dealy 1990, 127). The University of Nebraska's 1996 National Championship was sullied because of the participation of running back Lawrence Phillips and nose tackle Christian Peter. Peter had been found guilty of sexual assault and a few other lesser charges, while Phillips had been found guilty of beating up his girlfriend. Despite a media barrage that featured an emotional interview with Peter's victim and a bloody picture of Phillips' battered victim, both men played in Nebraska's Fiesta Bowl win over Florida and made key plays to propel the Cornhuskers to victory. As Funk writes, the crimes of Phillips, Peter, and other college athletes are products of a system that seems to be dedicated not to molding teenagers into strong adults, but instead to manipulating kids to win games and make money with little concern for their ethical development. "Why should a nation whose habits fuel illegal billion-dollar industries in drugs, gambling, and prostitution expect abstinence from 19-year-olds? What our society has reaped is a blighted athletic crop of some administrators, coaches, athletes, and boosters to whom ethics mean little" (Funk 1991, 99).

In addition, the current system of big-time college athletics discriminates against a large cross-section of students. Brooks's *Racism in College Athletics: The African-American Athlete's Experience* is one of the best books to tackle the problem of racism in the world of commercialized college sports. Brooks provides analysis and statistics that prove that while African-American males do most of the work in the big-money sports of football and basketball, they get little from their schools except publicity that may help to launch a few select players into the professional ranks. Brooks leaves little doubt that the majority of players on top teams that contend for the big money in college sports are African Americans and that "as the payoff for successful seasons has soared, the reliance on African-American athletes has ascended" (Brooks 1993, 60). Yet, it is also clear that African-American players that do not make the pros are in great danger of leaving college with little more than their memories. Most never earn a degree. For instance, between 1980 and 1985, less than one-third of all African-American male athletes received a diploma. In 1985, only 26.6 percent of all African-American athletes graduated from their respective colleges compared with 52.3 percent of white student athletes who successfully matriculated (Brooks 1993, 93). In addition, blacks were disproportionately victimized by Proposition 48, a 1988 NCAA resolution that imposed minimum academic standards on student athletes who wanted to remain eligible for sports. In the first two years after the rule went into effect, African-American athletes composed 84 percent of its casualties. Perhaps part of the problem is that few of these students had the benefit of competing for an African-American coach who could serve as a positive role model for their charges. According to Brooks, despite heavy reliance on African-

American athletes, only a handful of football and basketball programs have black coaches or administrators. For example, as late as 1987, only 2 Division I athletic directors, 3 Division I football coaches, and 25 of 273 Division I basketball coaches were black. As Brooks writes, "African-American athletes recruited to big-time college programs are also part of a corporate/entertainment world. They are hired to perform on the athletic fields and in the arenas to generate monies, media interest and public relations for the university" (Brooks 1993, 283). Unfortunately, most of these athletes never receive a degree, and their intellectual development is largely sacrificed at the alter of financial gain.

Big-time college athletic departments have also neglected women's athletics under the assumption that women's sports, unlike football, men's basketball, or hockey, can not make profits and are therefore untenable for programs obsessed with the bottom line. Greta Cohen's *Women in Sport: Issues and Controversies* is a diverse book that discusses several ways in which the current collegiate sports system discriminates against women. Perhaps the most shocking chapter is "Gender Equity Strategies for the Future," written by Donna Lopiano, the executive director of the Women's Sports Foundation. Lopiano introduces several eye-opening statistics before hashing out possible remedies. For instance, as of 1989 women athletes received less than 33 percent of all college scholarship money, and less than 18 percent of athletic budgets went to women. That same year, female athletes made up only 35 percent of all college athletes despite the fact that women comprised over half the total student population. In 1991, women athletes garnered only 29 pages of newspaper coverage for every 527 of men's coverage (Cohen 1995, 104). The news was even worse for women coaches and administrators. In 1991, only 14 of 121 conference commissioners were women. While nearly 90 percent of women's athletic programs were headed by women in 1972, only 16 percent were headed by women in 1992. Of 106 big-time football schools, only one had a female athletic director in 1992 (Cohen 1995, 105). Lopiano asserts that the main reason for this inequity is that big-time athletic schools have become corporate entities controlled by business interests that care little for academic achievement or social equality: "Athletic directors and football and basketball coaches have had unquestioned power for a long time. They have abused that power by wasting money, giving themselves huge salaries compared with those of other teachers and professors, and bringing scandal and charges of unethical conduct down upon their institutions, which has, in turn, damaged public confidence in higher education" (Cohen 1995, 114). Not only has it damaged the public's confidence in America's colleges and universities, it has also hindered women athletes from reaping the potential benefits of athletic competition.

As badly as minority and women student athletes have been shortchanged, perhaps no group has been neglected as much as the nonparticipant student body, a group that might make up 80–95 percent of the students at most schools. Scholars that have written about current abuses in college athletics have devoted little time to the fact that much of any school's athletic budget is covered by tuition and special athletic fees from students who have little or no chance or desire to play on a team. Often, these fees can run into hundreds of dollars per year and do not necessarily include tickets to big-time football or basketball games. Sperber is one of only a few scholars that mentions the problem. He does a thorough job of dismantling the myth that athletic department profits help students by bolstering other university departments in which any given student might be working. He convincingly points out that some schools must divert funds from the greater university budget to make sure that the cost of athletics are covered. Amazingly, Sperber estimates that at some programs nearly 80 percent of the athletic budget is covered by monies provided by students that have no access to varsity teams, most of which are exclusively composed of recruited and/or scholarship athletes (Sperber 1991, 143). MacMillan also laments the unfair burden carried by nonparticipant students to support college sports. He discusses the University of Maryland's $4.75 million deficit in 1991, writing that it "would have been more staggering if not for the millions of dollars of fees levied on its students" (MacMillan 1992, 123). Both MacMillan and Sperber issue a much-needed call for fairness to the rank and file of the student body. Either all of the positions on all of the teams should be opened up to all of the paying customers at a school, or that school should not charge any student fees for activities in which nearly all students are barred from participating.

## A DUBIOUS HISTORY AND POTENTIAL SOLUTIONS

Perhaps the common denominator for all of the problems in college athletics is that schools are essentially trying to have the best of two worlds that mix like oil and water. They want to maintain amateurism while reaping the benefits of a system that closely resembles that of a professional league. Kenneth Shropshire's *Agents of Opportunity: Sports Agents and Corruption in College Sports* does a fine job of showing how this impossible balancing act puts student athletes in vulnerable positions. The author persuasively argues that the demands placed on college athletes by big-time schools are basically those that are placed on most professional athletes. Football players, for instance, are required to practice year round, deal with an often critical media corps, and spend more hours on football in season than one might work in a forty-hour work week. Of course, that player still must go to class like other students, and he still has the monetary needs of other classmates. Shropshire points out that "most students require more money than they can get through their scholarships" (Shropshire 1990, 32). Because it is impossible timewise and because it is often against NCAA rules, these student athletes can not get jobs to make money. Thus, they often turn to gambling or illegal booster contributions. Recently, student athletes have fallen prey to agents who float players "loans" that are illegal under NCAA rules. Once a player is found to have accepted money from an agent he forfeits his remaining eligibility and is forced to try his hand in the professional ranks. This action has two consequences. The first is that players who do not make the pros have no way to return to college because their scholarship would have been revoked. The second is that the schools can be heavily penalized for allowing their athletes to break NCAA rules. This was the case for the University of Massachusetts in 1995 when the school had to forfeit several wins and its Final Four appearance because its star player, Marcus Camby, had accepted money from an agent. Camby's decision to accept money cost his school millions of dollars in revenue. Shropshire's book contains several examples of schools and athletes that have been hurt by illegal deals with agents (Shropshire 1990, 1–32). The author's argument is convincing, in part, because he is largely nonjudgmental. He simply points out how college athletics' insistence on trying to balance a professional system with amateur rules has placed both colleges and athletes in dangerous positions.

It is important to note that, while it can be argued that college sports has become more corrupt in recent years, several scholars have written entertaining books showing that college athletics has always been somewhat of a commercial venture or at least an activity whose purpose was far from being educational. Ronald Smith's *Sports and Freedom: The Rise of Big-Time College Athletics* provides readers with a thorough and riveting account of how college athletic programs evolved from small, student-run organizations to the unwieldy, corporate structures of the late twentieth century. Smith makes it clear that college sports have rarely existed to fulfill an educational mission. For instance, Smith chronicles the development of a fierce rivalry between Harvard and Yale in rowing, America's first intercollegiate sport. Competitions in the 1850s and 1860s drew large crowds, intense media coverage, and serious gambling activity. In addition, the races featured sizeable monetary payments to the winners. Smith's account of the races does not sound that different from a contemporary newspaper account of a Florida-Georgia football game, commonly referred to as the world's largest outdoor cocktail party.

The Harvard-Yale saga continued to dominate rowing concerns through the 1860's. Crowds, possibly as large as 25,000, came to see the meets. The students attending the Lake Quinsigamond meets would often become disorderly with demonic yelling, obscene songs, and drunken sprees which, according to one reporter, was a 'grand bacchanalian carnival.' On one occasion it resulted in chinaware thrown through hotel windows, carpets ripped up, furniture destroyed, and doors battered down. Police arrested more than a score of young people, who were both jailed and fined. The Yale faculty was concerned about the 'gross immoralities' attending the races and voted to cooperate with the Harvard faculty to suppress the annual event, but with no success. (Smith 1988, 36)

Smith goes on to recount stories of how "special" students, ringers, were brought in to win big meets and later, with the advent of football, important gridiron contests. According to Smith, schools knew that "importing athletes under the name of 'special students' was a sham." But "leaders soon saw the possibilities of using the 'special' category to harbor athletes, just as universities learned nearly a century later to use federal subsidies to stockpile students who were economically deprived but athletically gifted" (Smith 1988, 183).

Contrary to popular myth, things did not improve much in the first half of the twentieth century. Smith's *Big-Time Football at Harvard, 1905* is a fascinating read that uses old letters and journals to reconstruct what football was like in Cambridge at the turn of the century. Smith is diligent in showing how the game was certainly a commercial enterprise for the university, one that was replete with the same type of academic fraud that one might see today. For instance, Harvard's game with Yale that year drew 40,000 paying customers to Harvard Stadium. The Crimson lost 6–0, but the set-back was not the result of not having the best players on the field. Smith relates several stories of how Harvard coaches and officials arranged jobs for students, smoothed over legal difficulties, kept questionable students above water academically, and buried news stories that would embarrass the school and force the administration to remove the lads in question from the team (Smith 1994, 13–16). Bailey's *Athletes and the Academy: An Anatomy of Abuses and a Prescription for Reform* discusses the corruption that resulted in the reform movement of 1929. According to Bailey, the "Carnegie Report" to American colleges and universities chided higher education for allowing rampant materialism through "an opulent athletic power structure," the increased commercialization of athletics through "the domain of advertizing and public relations," "the professional nature of a student athlete's duty," "the exaggerated place of athletics in higher education," and "the sordid system of subsidized recruitment" (Bailey 1991, 9). Likewise, Thelin points out in *Games Colleges Play: Scandal and Reform in College Athletics* that the 1951 reform movement launched by the American Council on Education's Presidential Committee was inspired by a long string of gambling scandals that plagued college sports in the late 1940s and early 1950s (Thelin 1997, 103–106). As journalist Rick Telander points out in his thoughtful commentary on college football, *The Hundred Yard Lie,* "big-time college football has always been corrupt" (Telander 1996, 192). There really is no golden era of pure, clean college sports, some innocent time which we must try and recreate. If anything, writers like Smith, Bailey, Thelin, and Telander reveal that the first step in any reform process may be the recognition that college sports as big business has rarely been financially successful for most schools and has never been in line with any university's educational goals.

Thus, the questions remain. What can be done with our current system of college athletics? Can it be altered and reformed without being fully dismantled, or do we need to scrap it entirely and build anew? Scholars have not been shy to advance several proposals designed to make college sports a more just, clean, and educational arena in the twenty-first century. Some academics feel that most of the problems with college athletics stem not from any inherent flaws in the system, but instead lie with the NCAA. In *Undue Process: The NCAA's Injustice for All,* Don Yaeger chronicles several problems with the way the NCAA does business. According to Yaeger, the NCAA will never stop cheating because it spends only 2 percent of its budget on enforcement, its investigations are mismanaged and unnecessarily costly and time consuming, its penalties are often too harsh for minor violations, its departments are understaffed, its rules are vague and so needlessly complex that colleges have a hard time obeying them, and its investigators are often untrained and do not keep accurate records of their findings (Yaeger 1991, 127–133). Yaeger introduces ten steps intended to make the NCAA a better manager of college athletics. These include things as simple as mandatory tape-recorded interviews during all investigations and increased staff sizes, to rather nebulous demands to make drastic changes in the infractions committee and to overhaul the appeals process. Yaeger's suggestions to invest in proper training to ensure professionalism and to allow the NCAA to subpoena witnesses to find the truth in its investigations seem sound.

Arthur Fleisher's *The NCAA: A Study in Cartel Behavior* also focuses on the NCAA as being the chief problem in college sports. However, unlike Yaeger, Fleisher suggests that the problem is with the NCAA's structure as a cartel that acts to protect the business interests of its clients. Fleisher is hardly judgmental. He does not comment on whether he thinks that this commercial function is appropriate for the NCAA. He simply asserts that it exists and that it causes problems because it forces the NCAA to do impossible things. The first is to run all sports, including the vast majority that do not produce profits, in the same way as it runs the big business ventures of football and basketball. The second is that it calls for the NCAA to administer the same rules and policies to big-time sports programs and small Division III schools that clearly run amateur programs. Fleisher insists that the NCAA must change to account for these inconsistencies, in effect suggesting that the NCAA must cease to function as a cartel and adopt a fully amateur approach that is in line with its formal regulations, or change the regulations and admit that college sports is a business venture that must be subject to governance by a cartel (Fleisher 1992, 6–16). Implicit in Fleisher's argument is the idea that the NCAA could break into two sections with two different sets of rules and expectations. One would be oriented toward the amateur philosophies of most colleges and the other would serve the universities that want to engage in big-time college sports.

Other scholars agree with Fleisher and Yaeger that the basic system need not be destroyed, but have different ideas as to which parts of the system are most in need of repair. Together, their works act as a fairly comprehensive list of reforms that are necessary if colleges are to keep the current system. Underwood, for instance, introduces seventeen measures that schools can adopt to prevent academic fraud. Among the most promising is that students who qualify for Pell Grants and other forms of aid should be allowed to keep that aid in addition to their athletic scholarship. This would help the athlete meet incidental expenses and reduce the student's reliance on booster money or other illegal forms of aid. In addition, Underwood argues that "the NCAA should develop a program in conjunction with the public school system to promote the importance of an education" (Underwood 1984, 146). The idea behind such a program would be to teach future student athletes good academic study habits before they reach college. Chu compliments Underwood by insisting that academic development ought to be bolstered by a renewed emphasis on ethical education for both students and administrators. "The college that does not root out the obvious vileness within it presents an image that decays all higher education. The moral institution must face the timeless challenge of trying to do what is right" (Chu 1989, 201). Important to note is that Chu argues that a key part of doing the right thing is making sure that all students have access to athletic opportunity on campus. "So long as college and big-time sport leadership endorse and act upon the assumption that sport is an educational experience for the primary benefit of athletes, then the history of college sport clearly shows that problems will persist" (Chu 1989, 199). Weissberg extends Chu's idea, insisting that the key to reform is the narrowing of distance between student athletes and the rest of the student body. Such reform seems sound. After all, if there were no athletic scholarships and no recruiting, and the college teams were composed of regular students that survived a tryout to which every qualified student could take part, it is conceivable that athletic budgets would be greatly reduced at the same time that student opportunity to access athletic money would be maximized. The problem is that, while many faculty members may like this idea, many fans, alumni, and students actually do not like it. Thus, most scholars who offer reforms are left wondering whether any modifications will take place until America loses its fascination with the big game.

Most scholars agree that, even if the current system can not be reworked in a completely fair manner, some changes can be made within the system. Brooks, for example, offers several plausible suggestions that might improve the college sporting experience of African-American athletes. Some promising ideas include early intervention programs in which colleges or the NCAA target high school students that loom as future athletes and provide them with academic guidance and training so that they arrive on campus prepared for college classes. Also intriguing is the humane notion that young athletes ought to have money made available to them so that they can go home a few times a year to maintain connections with family and gain support from loved ones. This can be especially important to eighteen-year-old African Americans who are away from home for the first time at predominantly white schools. Brooks also favors making freshmen players ineligible so that they can concentrate on academics, hiring more African-American administrators and coaches as role models, and creating special opportunities for student athletes to get involved with campus activities outside of sports so that they integrate into the college community as students and not just as athletes. Of course, Brooks falls in line with most other scholars when he insists that "all other goals, including making money, are secondary to meeting the educational needs of student-athletes" (Brooks 1993, 278–282). Not surprisingly, many advocates for women's sports also believe that, considering that most women's sports will not make profits in the near future, a reduced emphasis on making money will be crucial in the effort to build more and better sports for women. Lopiano also posits that schools must hire more female administrators and coaches, that schools must be forced to release all financial expenditures on an annual basis so as to be sure that equal amounts are being spent on men's and women's sports, and that, through lawsuits and NCAA governance, all schools bring their programs into compliance with the congressional Title IX legislation of 1972, which ensures both genders equal athletic funding at all schools that receive government support (Cohen 1995, 109–114). Certainly, it seems reasonable that at least some of these reforms will be enacted as external pressure mounts on colleges to rework their athletic programs. As Lopiano writes, "The unfavorable media coverage, which questions higher education by association, has brought college presidents out of their ivory towers and into the dangerous streets of alumni-supported athletics. Athletic programs have given presidents the ammunition for reform and a general public supportive of such efforts" (Cohen 1995, 114).

Some scholars have turned their efforts away from specific flaws in the current system of college sports and have instead focused on what, if anything, needs to be done to alter the fundamental structure of the entire system. Sperber contends that there are merely two alternatives. Schools can either fully adopt a professional setup whereby athletic departments become fully independent of university budgets and balance their own books on the strength of their product, or they can give up the chase for the almighty dollar and be content with a truly amateur system in which both expenses and rewards for winning would be severely reduced. As Sperber writes, "If schools insist that their athletic programs be either self-sufficient separate businesses or genuine student activities, the current financial chicanery and fraud—as well as the drain on university resources—would end" (Sperber 1991, 349). In *The Political Economy of College Sports,* Nand Hart-Nibbrig rejects both of these options as being impractical. The author argues that the professional model does not account for the fact that most sports do not make money. He convincingly contends it would be impractical for most schools to fund all sports via football and basketball revenues when many schools do not even break even on those sports. Likewise, he argues that the amateur model will not work because no one wants what would essentially amount to an intramural program. Hart-Nibbrig is honest in his assessment of America's love for big-time sports and concludes that it is simply impractical for schools to abandon what amounts to their most effective way to reach the public. "To the extent that universities must appeal to the public for funds, then we can expect the performance of sports teams—the most publicly visible component of the university—to improve substantially. Unless the amateur option can deal with this larger issue, it can hardly resolve the systematic pressures associated with college sports" (Hart-Nibbrig 1986, 113). Hart-Nibbrig introduces a third model, which he calls "corporate athleticism," as being the only viable alternative to the professional or amateur models. In essence, the corporate athletic model is the system now in place. Though the author concedes that steps must be taken to moderate "illegal or corrupt practices," he asserts that, considering the political realities of higher education, there is really nothing that can be done except to work within the current system where television and corporate funding fuel programs that can potentially satisfy both the public need for grand entertainment and the academic community's desire for broad participation. "But since powerful incentives to political reform are largely absent, the most likely prospect is that the present sports system will slowly evolve. Rules will be modified in a piecemeal fashion, and modest efforts will be made periodically to preserve cherished symbols of amateurism" (Hart-Nibbrig 1986, 114). As mentioned, Hart-Nibbrig does see the necessity for some reform and asserts that changes will gradually bring the system into an acceptable light with most constituencies. As he concludes, even faculty will be able to live with a slightly altered system. "Although the commercialization of sport has evolved new forms, on the historical evidence this commercialization process is not fundamentally incompatible with academic values" (Hart-Nibbrig 1986, 114).

Thelin expresses the opinion of many scholars in *The Old College Try* when he argues that, considering the diverse sizes and goals of colleges and universities in the United States, all schools should be able to choose what type of program they want to run. For instance, schools may choose a "commercial model," which would feature athletes who would not necessarily be students working to make money for the school. Another alternative would be the "symbolic model" in which athletic departments, because of their symbolic importance to the school and community, could continue to operate at deficits that be made up by siphoning money from other departments. The "subsidy model" is similar except that the debt is paid annually out of state funds. The "extracurricular model" would function much like the amateur model already described, complete with nonrecruited, nonscholarship players that compete for little money or notoriety. Finally, the "academic model" would not rule out scholarships or recruiting, but it would do away with big money, big crowds, pressure to win, long trips to play opponents, and anything else that might interrupt an athletes academic progress. Here, sport itself would even be used as a tool to educate the student in terms of leadership and management skills (Thelin 1989, 97–101). A key codicil to Thelin's argument is that no matter what athletic model a school chooses for itself, the control of college sports needs to transfer from the NCAA and athletic departments to college presidents and faculty. Thelin persuasively contends that college presidents cannot be expected to reform athletics because any reforms that result in even a few losing seasons would likely mean the president's quick termination at the hands of trustees who like to win the big game. Similarly, athletic directors are too dependent on winning to be expected to institute changes that might result in subpar on-field results. Thus, Thelin proposes that faculty take an active role in designing and implementing policy that would clean up current abuses while allowing colleges to decide exactly what type of system they want to have (Thelin 1989, 63–83).

## COLLEGIATE PHYSICAL EDUCATION

While the direction that reform will likely take remains a hot subject for scholarly debate, one thing seems clear. Those who advocate any form of big-time college sports are probably going to be at odds with physical educators who view sport as a way to enhance the overall education and life experience of students, faculty, and staff. For those interested in the history of physical education in the United States, there are a handful of well-written, informative books that discuss how key figures, philosophies, movements, legislation, and other important factors have reshaped the discipline in each period of American history. While the complex nature and sheer volume of the material is difficult to summarize, scholars Betty Spears and Richard Swanson have postulated that most of America's physical education experiences can be grouped into one of six "themes," each of which helps the reader understand a significant part of the discipline's development. Betty Spears and Richard Swanson's *History of Sport and Physical Activity in the United States* remains the classic of the history of physical education and stands with Mabel Lee's *A History of Physical Education and Sports in the United States,*

Angela Lumpkin's *Physical Education: A Contemporary Introduction*, John Rickards Betts' classic *America's Sporting Heritage 1850–1950*, and Benjamin Rader's *American Sports: From the Age of Folk Games to the Age of Spectators* as one of the most complete and influential books on the subject.

The first theme introduced by Spears and Swanson is that of cultural diversity. The authors assert that American physical education has always been and continues to be influenced by the sporting practices and philosophies of the country's various ethnic groups. For instance, Rader provides a definitive analysis of the gymnastic (turnverein) movement that, in part, shaped the American sporting scene in the mid-nineteenth century. The movement was ignited by German immigrants who opened gymnasiums in the 1850s and 1860s in order to preserve ethnic customs through sport in the face of an American society that demanded assimilation. However, it was not long before the "Turners" did assimilate, allowing gymnastics to spread all over the country (Rader 1983, 92). According to Lee, "The following cities established physical education in their schools using the German system: Cincinnati, 1855; Cleveland, 1870; Milwaukee, 1876; Omaha, Kansas City, and La Crosse, 1885; Chicago, 1886; Davenport, 1887; St. Louis, 1888; Los Angeles, Oakland, Moline, Detroit and Erie, 1890; Indianapolis, San Francisco, Spokane, and Dayton, 1892; and St. Paul, 1894" (Lee 1983, 84). In areas of the country with little Germanic influence, gymnastic programs from other ethnic groups took hold. In Boston, the Swedish system of gymnastics was introduced into all public schools by 1890. Lee writes that "within a year of its introduction into the Boston public schools alone, over 60,000 students were taking Swedish gymnastics" (Lee 1983, 85). Lee, Spears and Swanson, and Rader all provide commentary on how the native sporting practices of new Americans have altered physical education in this country over the last century and a half. For information on how recent immigrants from Asia, Mexico, Central America, Cuba, and the former Soviet Union are currently impacting American physical education, it is necessary to look to the academic journals that contain the discipline's new scholarship. *Health Education Quarterly*; the *Journal of Sport History*; the *Journal of Physical Education, Recreation and Dance*; and the *Journal of the Philosophy of Sport* would all be good starting places for scholars interested in these and other contemporary issues.

The second theme of note is how the values that have governed daily living in the United States have influenced physical education at any given point in the country's history. For example, Lee makes the point that physical education was slow to develop in Puritan New England because religious leaders were skeptical of any activity whose intent was to develop what was regarded as a sinful body. Though some physical instruction did take place, it was often limited to strictly monitored military drills that could be rationalized as being necessary for the common defense (Lee 1983, 16–17). Between 1820 and 1850, however, physical education was encouraged at colleges such as Harvard and Yale, whose principle function was to train ministers and secular leaders, because school administrators saw physical activity as a way for students to develop sharp minds and buoyant spirits (Spears and Swanson 1995, 88–91). Perhaps the best example of how societal values reshaped American physical education is provided by Rader's account of the "Muscular Christian" movement of the late nineteenth century. The movement had many faces but was, in general, characterized by a feeling that America's youth were physically soft and spiritually weak. The reasons for this feeling were many. Some former Civil War officers felt that their sons were becoming weak because they did not have any battles in which to sharpen their physical and spiritual resolve. Men such as Theodore Roosevelt and Supreme Court Justice Oliver Wendall Holmes, Jr., lamented the condition of America's young men and looked to sport as a way to inculcate this lost youth with true manly virtues. "To the advocates of the new sporting ideology, modern life had become too soft and effeminate. Frontiers and battlefields no longer existed to test manly courage and perseverance. Apart from sports, men no longer had arenas for proving their manliness" (Rader 1983, 149). Still, most of the concern stemmed from the fact that the country's post-Civil War industrial surge had created a rather untenable situation for city governments. As industry developed, millions of Americans flocked to New York, Chicago, Philadelphia, and other centers of commerce, creating overcrowded, unsanitary conditions. Often parents had to work long hours outside the home, leaving children who did not work to fend for themselves in cities full of danger and vice. When cities ill-equipped to handle the negative consequences of the industrial revolution found themselves with sickly youths who were often forced to live and work in crime-ridden urban areas with insufficient physical, educational, and religious programs, concerned citizens and officials established the Young Men's Christian Association (YMCA) and the Young Women's Christian Association (YWCA) to minister to both the physical and spiritual needs of inner city boys and girls. In 1906, the Playground Association of America was founded to create areas in cities where both children and adults could exercise. By the end of the century, the first scholastic athletic leagues began play. Early twentieth-century developments included the founding of the Boy Scouts of America (1910) and the Girl Scouts of the U.S.A. (1912), both of which included sports as part of their overall philosophy for developing America's youth into strong leaders (Rader 1983, 146–169). By the 1920s the concern for children's health was so strong among Americans that nearly every state had both scholastic sports programs and physical education programs in place in public schools, a dual model that continues to this day.

The third theme around which American physical education has progressed is that of social organization. Spears and Swanson contend that the desire for certain social groups to cement their bonds, celebrate their values, and further their agendas has influenced American sport. In the colonial period, for example, physical education was rarely organized. It usually consisted of fathers schooling their sons on how to engage in the sporting practices of their class. The sons of the gentry were taught "horse racing, fox hunting and other gentlemanly sports," while "common men hunted, fished, and had their shooting matches" (Spears and Swanson 1995, 332). In *A Sporting Time: New York City and the Rise of Modern Athletics, 1820–1870*, Melvin Adelman argues that, despite the fact that Americans have historically viewed baseball as having pastoral origins, the game actually developed in major cities such as New York in the mid-nineteenth century as the result of upper- and middle-class amateur clubs that sought to prove the worth of their professions. Adelmen writes: "New York butchers were typical of this group, known as lusty chaps who glorified in their stamina and physical prowess. With the growing popularity of baseball, artisans also could win prestige within the larger community of players and fans, thereby further enhancing their standing in their own communities" (Adelman 1986, 141–142). As with sporting movements within most groups, baseball would soon exert its influence on physical education across the country. After the Civil War, the sport was played with gusto within all segments of the population. Baseball was played at colleges, and professional baseball thrived as early as the 1860s and 1870s, giving millions of school children the inspiration to play and establishing baseball as our national pastime by the early twentieth century.

The fourth theme involves the effects of technology on sporting activity. Lee, Spears and Swanson, Adelman, Rader, and Betts comment on how technological developments have changed the face of American physical education over the last century and a half. Examples include improved techniques of mass production, which made for the industrialization that would bring so many Americans to cities after the Civil War. So many people in one place allowed for the development of the amateur baseball leagues, the scholastic leagues, and the previously mentioned reforms in physical education for children. In addition, communications technology such as the telegraph, and subsequently the telephone, and advances in transportation such as a modernized system of train travel and cement roads allowed for increased sporting participation and interest in the last half of the nineteenth century. In the last section of his book, Rader provides an intriguing analysis of how technology has reshaped physical education in the United States in the last twenty years. Rader traces the impact of technology on individual sports, such as golf and tennis; team sports, such as football; college sports; and Olympic sports. He concludes that technology has swept Americans into an age of spectatorship. Television, for instance, has combined with advances in print journalism to bring the drama of sports to every living room in America. As such, it has turned us into a nation of spectators, men and women who watch sports as much as we engage in them. Rader provides several statistics to show that America's spectatorial passion has resulted in the glorification of such sports as basketball, football, baseball, and, recently, hockey and soccer, all of which feature highly paid athletes who function as heroes and role models to American children (Rader 1983, 346–355). Not surprisingly, this has altered physical education, resulting in curriculums that now tend to focus on these popular spectator sports. Rader explains the relationship between technology, spectator sports, and the physical education of children.

The triumph of spectator-centeredness had significant implications for the history of American sports. First, it focused public attention on professional sports. Professional sports served as models for nearly all levels of sport. The professional model reached down to the level of preadolescent youth sports. Little League Baseball had outfield fences, dugouts, grandstands, and even a "draft" system, and Pop Warner football teams had nine-year-old cheerleaders. To succeed at the highest levels, especially in individual sports, youngsters had to begin to specialize at a tender age. Tennis players, for instance, often began to engage in systematic training by the age of five or six. Carefully designed programs to select the most promising future athletes in early childhood became a reality. Modern technology assisted in this endeavor as well as in improving the performances of athletes. (Rader 1983, 358–359)

Thus, while technology has greatly increased the ability of physical educators to use sport to enhance the lives of Americans, it has also resulted in some serious problems that teachers must fight to overcome.

The fifth theme of American physical education is its changing emphasis from serving only a small segment of the American populace to literally serving the entire nation. As mentioned, early periods of physical education tended to involve elite gentlemen training their sons to observe upper-class standards of conduct or exclusive colleges teaching young men and a few young women of privilege how to use physical exercise as a way to enhance their intellectual and spiritual development. In the twentieth century, physical education has changed to focus on the individual development of all people. For instance, Spears and Swanson provide a good discussion of what the 1972 Title IX legislation has meant to the development of both girls' scholastic sports and women's college sports, and also to physical education curriculums that have changed to meet girls' needs (Spears and Swanson 1995, 324–329). Rader devotes an entire chapter to analyzing the effects of civil rights legislation on the participation of minority athletes in scholastic sports and physical education programs. Lumpkin discusses one of the newest trends in physical education pedagogy, the individualized education program (IEP), which, in some school systems, has revolutionized the field. With an IEP, a teacher can work with disadvantaged students to develop a physical fitness regimen that is specifically designed with that student in mind. The student may even get to construct the IEP, depending on the program. Regardless, the IEP allows each student to develop at his or her own rate under the guidance and encouragement of trained professionals and has greatly increased the opportunities of handicapped children to realize the benefits of sports (Lumpkin 1994, 255–258). In no small way, educational techniques such as IEPs have lead to public celebrations such as the Special Olympics, where handicapped athletes receive medals not only for winning, but for participating. Certainly, one of the nice features of this theme is its emphasis on individual achievement in noncompetitive environments, something that stands in contrast to the modern emphasis on team sports where winning is the highest virtue.

The final theme introduced by Spears and Swanson is that of the "American Dream," in which Americans undertake sporting activity because it is fun and, as such, is viewed as being part of the good life. The authors assert that much of American physical education in the past has sprung from Americans' desire to play. Likewise, this emphasis has resulted in a contemporary recreational movement that involves Americans teaching themselves or learning from professionals hundreds of different sporting activities. As Spears and Swanson write, "The period between 1945 and 1993 was generally affluent and brought the 'good life' within reach of many Americans. With money to spend on non-essentials and more opportunity to pursue leisure time interests, people turned to sport and the active life in greater and greater numbers" (Spears and Swanson 1995, 333). Volleyball, golf, tennis, ice hockey, skiing, swimming, aerobics, softball, and power walking are just a few activities that have exploded in recent years as Americans of all ages and creeds have found their athletic niche. As Spears and Swanson point out, this recreational boom can be seen as the coming to fruition of a "sports for all" philosophy that has dominated American physical education in the last half of the twentieth century. Under this philosophy, educators and government officials have shaped policies such as the Civil Rights Amendment that have increased opportunities for all Americans. Most scholars agree that Americans will probably continue to enjoy recreational sporting activities and that physical educators will likely continue to search for new ways to implement the sports for all curriculum well into the twenty-first century (Spears and Swanson 1995, 333). Some informative sources on recreation sporting opportunity include Susan J. Grosse and Donna Thompson's *Leisure Opportunities for Individuals with Disabilities: Legal Issues*, Lynn Winston's *Recreation and Sports,* and Bernie Schock's *Parents, Kids and Sports*, all of which provide information on how to find and get started in any number of recreational opportunities.

## THE PHILOSOPHY OF PHYSICAL EDUCATION

Scholars in the field of physical education will no doubt continue to research how these six themes operate in America. However, the greatest concern of contemporary physical educators, in general, is how to philosophically approach their discipline. This has been a subject of much scholarly debate. Considering that the story of American physical education is essentially the continuing saga of an eclectic mix of divergent movements, it is not surprising that the philosophy of most of these teachers is a blend of at least five traditional philosophies that have influenced the development of the field. Lumpkin's *Physical Education: A Contemporary Introduction* does a tremendous job of explaining how teachers at all levels work elements of each philosophy into their classroom pedagogy. Idealism, for instance, springs from the ancient Greek concept that for an individual to attain virtue and to glimpse truth, the individual must have a well-developed mind and body that complement each other, allowing the individual to develop as a complete person. Usually, instruction is teacher-centered, often involving a lecture in which a model of exercise is displayed for the student. All such lectures and examples are designed to inculcate moral and spiritual values into the student through discussion of physical activity. Because idealism tends to go heavy on theory and light on actual physical activity, many educators temper its effects by employing elements of pragmatism, a philosophy that asserts that the main goal of physical education should be to prepare the student to be a healthy member of society that can interact with others in a positive, meaningful way. Pragmatism is currently riding a crest of popularity because it fits snugly with prevailing postmodern ideas that emphasize individual experiences and "truths" over time-tested lessons that allegedly enlighten each student. Thus, pragmatism calls for each teacher to encourage physical activity that helps students gain practical skills that they need at that moment to help them be better citizens. For example, a manager might encourage employees of IBM to play on the company softball team so as to bolster feelings of comraderie and to foster a needed sense of cooperation among workers. On the other hand, a teacher might encourage a shy student going off to college to run track under the theory that competing in an individual sport would boost confidence. Also diverging from idealism is realism, which revolves around the idea that education should alert students to the truths contained in the natural world. All physical activities, therefore, should be composed of drills and projects that force the student to come to grips with the scientific realities of the world. For instance, a physical fitness instructor will sometimes have clients engage in a highly structured, closely monitored exercise program in order to attain a weight and muscle mass that, scientifically, has been determined to be ideal for a person of the client's size and age. A fourth philosophy, naturalism, is most noteworthy for insisting that the point of physical education is to allow an individual to gain self-confidence, self-esteem and simple pleasure from playful interaction with the natural world. For the Naturalist, physical education is experimental and self-directed. A teacher operating under this philosophy might take students on a hike and, with little or no instruction, encourage them to enjoy themselves on the way to their destination. The goal of the hike would be that each student would develop physically through the strenuous nature of the hike, socially by interacting with peers along the way, and creatively by figuring out the best way to negotiate different parts of the trail. Finally, existentialism has, in the twentieth century, developed as a popular philosophy that asserts that the role of physical education is to encourage students to resist societal truths that are embodied in social rituals and traditions in favor of carving out personal truths based on their own experiences. Existentialism calls for instructors to put important questions before students, but to resist answering them. At most, a teacher might help students come up with several possible answers before leaving them to discuss which one, if any, they will adopt as their own. In terms of practical applications, a teacher might make up a game that has no basis in Western tradition in order to force students to grapple with complex moral issues such as what constitutes fairness or what it means to be a team player. The theory is that because students would be unfamiliar with any traditions or social values embedded in the new game, they would be forced to wrestle with the issues presented on their own without reference to societal precedent. While acknowledging that these five theories inform most of the contemporary American physical education curriculum, Lumpkin also gives brief descriptions of other philosophies that have influenced the development of the field. Among these is asceticism, an almost Puritanical belief that the body is inherently disruptive to the soul and must be brought under control by physical activities designed to quell its evil tendencies. A similar philosophy is scholasticism, which asserts that physical education should discipline the body so that it does not interfere with the mind's intellectual pursuits. On the other hand, humanism asserts the importance of developing the body for its own sake, as something beautiful and worthy of admiration. Finally, progressivism stresses an individual's creative development through self-initiated physical activities (Lumpkin 1994, 34–45).

Of course, educators must not only debate how to create the most effective programs possible by blending the best elements from each philosophical model, but must also consider which ethical philosophies they will encourage students to use to solve the hundreds of ethical questions that surround practitioners. Without a doubt, the profession of physical education has gotten more complex in the last half of the twentieth century. As with society in general, there has been a general move from clearly defined rights and wrongs that guided educators to a highly subjective brand of morality that often leaves teachers, students, and players faced with difficult decisions. In addition, the evolution in sport from a playful activity guided by a loose series of "rules" to a serious, highly structured affair in which considerable pressure is applied to athletes to win awards and money has given rise to several new ethical questions. Though she does not attempt to hash out possible answers, Lumpkin catalogs several of the most pressing ethical dilemmas facing today's physical educators, including the following: Should athletes have to follow a coach's orders even if they are dehumanizing? Should material rewards be given to teams composed of young children? Should a coach be allowed to verbally abuse an official or a player? Should all students be required to pay an athletic fee? Should an athlete use performance-enhancing drugs? Should a coach teach athletes how to circumvent rules under the pretense that it is just part of the game? Should teachers encourage students to see physical fitness and skill as tools by which to exert control over others and reap material rewards at the expense of defeated opponents? Should sports competitions be open to players of both sexes? Should teachers instruct students on how to play through injuries? Should students be instructed on how to take advantage of the weaknesses of others? Should children be cut from sports teams? Should teachers instruct students in the art of psychological manipulation? Can an educator teach the importance of playing for fun and for the physical and social enjoyment afforded by sports when students are constantly bombarded with messages that emphasize winning as the chief good in sport (Lumpkin 1994, 47)?

Joy De Sensi's *Ethics in Sport Management* is one of several books that provides highly readable discussions about several ethical theories used by physical educators to resolve some of these dilemmas. In the book, De Sensi profiles three teleological theories, all of which rely on the notion that ethical decisions should be made on the basis of what is good for an individual or group. Perhaps the most dominant theory in contemporary practice is egotism, the theory that ethical choices should be made on the basis of what is psychologically and materially beneficial to the student. Thus, when it comes down to betting against one's own team, one's main considerations should be whether or not one can make money without feeling any guilt. While this theory is ingrained in American culture because of the popular assumption that everyone has to look out for oneself in a dog-eat-dog world, egotism has several obvious flaws, not the least of which is that it hinges on a willingness to consistently undermine the welfare of others in favor of one's own selfish gains. Unlike egotism, utilitarianism posits that ethical choices are those that do the largest amount of good for the largest number of people. This approach can often be quite effective. In the previous example of the gambling student, a utilitarian approach would have necessitated the player choosing not to gamble, thus removing the danger that he or she would lose money and, more importantly, that his or her team would lose the game and suffer possible sanction if the incident ever came to light. However, utilitarianism also has its drawbacks. De Sensi offers the example of a football coach who makes millions for his school by putting an injured star player back in the game to make a game-saving play. The player aggravates the injury, lapses into a coma, and dies. Suspiciously, utilitarianism says that, despite the death of a single player, the coach made the right decision because the win secured money and happiness for almost everyone. A third ethical option is referred to as situation ethics. This theory asserts that there is no such thing as ethical standards or absolute rules. Instead, educators must adopt new ethical judgments for each singular dilemma they encounter. The appeal of this theory is that it takes into account the fact that different situations can contain unusual circumstances that call for unique responses. One obvious problem is that these responses must spring from some theory that the instructor already knows. It is, as De Sensi points out, impossible to approach each new situation with a blank slate. Another problem is that a teacher runs the risk of abandoning tried and true virtues learned from past cases in favor of a dangerous moral relativism (De Sensi 1996, 55–65). As De Sensi admits, "Many people already know that torture, slavery, rape, incest, and a host of other abhorrent activities are morally wrong, no matter what. Yet the relativistic strain in situation ethics leaves open the wrongfulness of such acts" (De Sensi 1996, 65).

De Sensi also offers a compelling discussion of three deontological theories, those that focus on making ethical decisions on the basis of some deeply held, traditional belief irrespective of consequences. Once again, each of these theories harbors both positive and negative aspects. One of the dominant Western deontological theories is the biblical golden rule, the essence of which is that an ethical decision is one in which one does to others what one would do to oneself. The humanistic appeal of this approach is that it is other-centered and, as such, tends to build bridges between disparate members of a community. For instance, if during a hockey game a player chooses not to exercise his option to deliberately hurt the other team's star player by delivering a legal but deadly hit when the star is in a vulnerable position, it might serve as a lesson in sportsmanship to impassioned, young fans of both teams. The problem is that in a world where egotism is often the dominant philosophy, those who practice the golden rule often get burned. This is the great trap that the golden rule presents. It is, perhaps, the best hope for resolving ethical dilemmas. But unless both sides are equally thoughtful, the process will likely degenerate into a manipulative situation that will make everyone involved suspicious of such altruistic ethical practices in the future.

Another ethical deontological theory is represented by Kantian ethics, where, through the power of their own reason, individuals create maxims from which they make ethical decisions. One of the chief tests of these maxims is that they must have universal appeal that creates a sense of duty in those who believe in them. For instance, one maxim might be that one should not cheat. The appeal of Kantian ethics is that it places each of its adherents under the obligation of doing what is in theory universally agreed upon, in this case that each person would be duty bound not to cheat. Again, as with the golden rule, the main problem is that this theory has no regard for consequences. It is common knowledge, for instance, that most hockey players cheat. The common practices of holding, spearing, and grabbing sticks are not celebrated and are often masked under the phrase "he's taking his fair advantage," but all hockey players know that not to execute these moves often means losing the game. In this situation, cheating is justified because there is tacit agreement among most players that it is permissible to take one's fair advantage in the name of winning. Yet another problem with Kantian ethics is that human reason is both fallible and highly individualistic. There is no guarantee that any maxims will be morally sound, and it is extremely unlikely that all people will agree on the same maxim.

Ross's prima facie duties is a third deontological theory that attempts to solve the problems of Kantian ethics by accounting for exceptions to any given maxim. For instance, an educator adhering to Ross's scheme might alter the cheating maxim to state that one should not cheat unless one can advance a cause that is so noble that it justifies cheating. Ross's system seems more practical that Kant's, but the problem remains that there can be no agreement of just what a noble cause might be. No matter how many exceptions Ross tries to account for, he can not possibly account for them all, and the exceptions he does define are often subject to multiple interpretations (De Sensi 1996, 66–80). Thus, one can see that deontological ethical theories, like teleologic theories, have elements that appeal to teachers and students of physical education ethics, but none offers a foolproof way of resolving critical ethical issues. This lack of certainty is the fire that continually fuels the debate of how to best teach students to practice and teach ethics within the field of physical education.

A final area of ethical theory that De Sensi explores is justice. Here the premise is that one should make ethical decisions on the basis of what is just. The trick is to supply a definition for justice. Those who hold the egalitarian view believe that just decisions are those that treat everyone equally but that also allow for special help for those that are disadvantaged. This is a compelling, but tricky definition for educators. Conflicts inevitably arise. For instance, if a coach has a limited amount of financial aid to give his or her players to attend a camp, does he or she spread it out equally or give it to those who need it most, leaving the middle- to upper-class kids to pay their own way. Egalitarianism suggests that either way is permissible, but that does not leave the coach with an easy choice. No matter what he or she decides, people will be disgruntled, and egalitarianism provides no way of knowing if one way is more ethical than the other. This illustrates the single biggest downfall of ethical theories. Most of them only work in conjunction with other theories. In this example, if the wealthier parents heeded the dictates of utilitarian ethics and decided that their full payment for their kids would be best for everyone, all would be well. Likewise, if all of the parents thought of each other according to the golden rule and agreed that each player deserved an equal amount of aid, problems could be averted. Often, however, egotism disturbs this delicate process, giving ethical decisions based on any theory less chance of success. It seems as though an uphill battle looms no matter what theoretical approach a teacher might use. For instance, another definition of justice is offered by libertarians, who claim that a just ethical decision is one that does not restrict the freedom of those whose actions are not directly hurting anyone else. Under this definition, it would be all right to take steroids to improve athletic performance, despite the fact that performance-enhancing drugs are disastrous to a person's health. Utilitarianism suggests that a just decision is one that leads to societal improvement. De Sensi points out, however, that this type of thinking often leads to favoring economic concerns over social or health concerns (De Sensi 1996, 90). For instance, a decision on the part of an athletic director to allow her basketball team to play a nationally ranked opponent halfway across the country on a Monday night might work for the greater financial good of the school but could do considerable harm to the academic efforts of the players on the team. A final definition is posed by Marxists, who argue that a just decision is one that frees people from any economic circumstance that might be hindering their development as an individual. Thus, a Marxist might argue that it would be ethical for the basketball players mentioned previously to refuse to travel such a distance to play a game because it would only enhance their servitude to the school while hindering their intellectual development. However, as is often the case with Marxism and many other ethical theories, what sounds good in theory rarely works in practice. If the players refused to play, they would likely lose their scholarships and have to leave school, a situation that would hardly facilitate their intellectual progress (De Sensi 1996, 80-94). Thus, it seems as though the ethical debate will rage on for physical educators as each teacher figures out how to balance a delicate blend of several preferred theories with the unpredictability of human nature.

## CONTEMPORARY ISSUES IN PHYSICAL EDUCATION

Several scholars have addressed a number of important issues that physical education teachers will have to deal with as the profession enters the next millennium. In *Sports Management at Schools and Colleges*, Harold Vanderzwaag points out that one of the greatest challenges will be ensuring that all students have equal access to athletic opportunity. He explains that "the real difficulty seems to be in the tendency to overlook the fact that the sport program extends beyond the athlete to mass participation. The students at large must feel that they have an adequate opportunity to be involved with an organization that epitomizes the action of sport. They cannot be shoved off into a corner in an intramural program that receives scant attention or in a gym class that has an atmosphere of 'glorified recesses'" (Vanderzwaag 1984, 217). As more students pay larger mandatory athletic fees, administrators will have to either justify giving most of those resources to a select group of athletes or, more likely, to search for ways to make physical fitness or intramurals the main focus for the program so that all students can get their money's worth. Closely related to this debate is the fact that, in an age of intense competition where prep stars strive mainly for college scholarships and college players play with one eye on the pros, both faculty and administration will have to make sure student athletes are more students than athletes. As Vanderzwaag comments, "What is most needed is an elimination of the hypocrisy that has surrounded school and college sport for too many years. We cannot continue with the procedure of presenting the lofty conception of the student athlete and then, at the same time, continue to offer programs in which the athlete is a student in only a nominal sense" (Vanderzwaag 1984, 219). In *Physical Education and Kinesiology in North America: Professional and Scholarly Foundations*, Earle Zeigler argues that the only way to do this is to change our focus from competitive sport to playful, noncompetitive athletic activity. According to Zeigler, once schools promote sports participation that results in nonmaterial rewards such as personal growth, all students will reap the benefits of physical activity in a way that is consistent with any academic curriculum (Zeigler 1994, 379). Tougher academic standards; the possibility of less scholarships and recruiting, both of which severely restrict overall student participation; and policy changes that move sports programs away from varsity competition and toward a less competitive, more inclusive program that would accommodate all students will be critical items on school agendas in coming years.

As educators continue to act on the sports for all philosophy, creating more athletic options for disabled persons will continue to be an important issue. Already, several quality books exist that address the sporting needs of the disabled. *Leisure Opportunities for Individuals with Disabilities: Legal Issues*, edited by Susan J. Grosse and Donna Thompson, is a must read for anyone interested in the most important laws that guarantee handicapped persons athletic opportunity. Among other issues, the editors clearly explain The Rehabilitation Act of 1973 and The Americans with Disabilities Act of 1992, how civil rights legislation aided the cause of disabled persons, the responsibility of schools to provide athletic access for the handicapped, and the guidelines that private athletic facilities such as campgrounds must follow in order to ensure potential use by people with special needs. Lynn Winston's *Recreation and Sports*, David Stewart's *Deaf Sport: The Impact of Sports Within the Deaf Community*, and Red Durgin's *A Guide to Recreation, Leisure and Travel for the Handicapped* provide accounts of how important sport is for those with disabilities and list sporting activities in which handicapped persons take part nationwide. Perhaps the most exhaustive book on the subject is Michael Paciorek's *Sports and Recreation for the Disabled*, which contains a complete list of annual sporting activities specifically designed for people with disabilities. Paciorek also lists phone numbers and addresses for hundreds of organizations dedicated to promoting sport for the disabled, and he includes instruction on how to implement specific programs for the deaf, the blind, the mentally impaired, amputees, and those with spinal cord injuries. The book is a must for teachers. In all, Paciorek shows how instructors can implement no less than fifty-three sports designed for handicapped students into their physical education curriculum.

The topic of how to use new technology in physical education will be important as the possibility for computer-based instruction gradually becomes economically feasible for some schools. While little has been written so far, Bonnie Mohnson's *Using Technology in Physical Education* is representative of the kind of works to which teachers will have access in the next century. Mohnson explains several ways that coaches and teachers can use advanced technology to enhance their students' sporting experiences. Laser disk technology is already being used to allow athletes to compare their performance to ideal models that are programmed into a computer. Mohnson writes that, in addition to Olympic athletes using this method to improve their efficiency, "our students can also analyze their own movement using this method and compare it to a model performance in order to determine what areas they need to improve in" (Mohnson 1995, 19). Instructors can also use computer-assisted instruction (CAI) to allow students to get a feel for how an athletic act, such as pole vault, should look before they actually try it. Mohnson chronicles the story of an inner city teacher that used CAI to instruct students in what they would encounter in the great outdoors before the class embarked on a long camping trip (Mohnson 1995, 103). Finally, Mohnson discusses how teachers will be able to take advantage of such things as distance learning and virtual reality to make for better physical education classes in the future. Her conclusion that "we must all begin our journeys and keep up with these advances in order to find positive applications for their use in physical education" seems an appropriate call toward what will no doubt be a huge area for both coaches and teachers (Mohnson 1995, 131).

Anyone interested in major issues at the secondary school level will want to read Irvin Keller's *Administration of High School Athletics*, which offers several suggestions as to how schools might answer their most difficult questions. According to Keller, the biggest challenge for all schools will be how to pay for increasingly expensive sports programs, while at the same time providing quality physical education programs that serve the entire student body. The author offers several tips on how schools might raise more money to combat rising costs but hints that schools confronted with ever-increasing costs of operation may be forced to make the choice to either cut varsity sports or parts of the physical education program (Keller 1984, 385–388). Like Keller, many scholars believes that unless they opt for noncompetitive physical education programs, schools will be caught in an endless battle to raise more and more money to pay for scholastic sports. Vanderzwaag thinks that this will result in school athletic departments acting as nothing more than public relations agents in charge of raising money and drumming up support for varsity teams whose bills will constantly threaten to put the school in debt (Vanderzwaag 1984, 243). William Stier has written a book entitled *Fundraising for Sport and Recreation*, which anticipates this dilemma. Stier offers complete instruction on how schools can engage in fundraisers designed to garner anywhere from $3,000 to $10,000. The author includes activities as simple as pancake breakfasts to events such as dance marathons and carnivals that require a significant amount of time and planning. The book is informative and entertaining and is a must read for administrators and teachers trying to keep physical education programs afloat into the next century.

John Olson's *Administration of High School and Collegiate Athletic Programs* argues that there are seven major challenges facing secondary school educators. In addition to finances, Olson asserts that schools will have to guard against legal challenges to school policies, especially those involving eligibility standards, Title IX violations, injuries to players, and the use of nonfaculty coaches. Furthermore, schools will have to fight to maintain control of athletic policy as boosters, taxpayers, and parents who have to contribute more money to varsity sports seek to dictate how their money will be spent. Another key decision that educators will have to make is what type of program they can feasibly run. Many schools will likely have to decide between running a large varsity sport program or a more comprehensive physical education program designed for the entire student body. Those schools that continue to run large scholastic sports programs will have to combat both the increased pressure felt by many students to win and achieve college scholarships and the level of escalating violence in sports where the difference between winning and losing is often perceived as the loss or gain of an award or possibly even of a college scholarship. Finally, Olson makes the point that those in physical education will be faced with many ethical questions regarding both their role as a teacher and student behavior. For instance, educators will have to determine if drug testing for athletes is a viable option for guarding against the use of deadly performance-enhancing drugs, or what the minimum academic guidelines for eligibility will be. Earle Zeigler's *Ethics and Morality in Sport and Physical Education* contains several case studies that force readers to confront difficult issues that educators face. These include whether a coach should teach players to obey or manipulate rules, whether coaches should authorize the use of painkillers, whether schools should give financial aid or special admission on the basis of athletic merit, whether competitive sport is good for student development, and whether or not schools should use high academic standards to determine student eligibility (Zeigler 1984, 74–89). Keller also analyzes six crucial issues for junior high school educators. The first and most important is that educators in this age group must allow all students to get as much athletic experience as possible. This should include plenty of physical activity but should also involve an ample amount of classroom instruction that indoctrinates the student to the theories and philosophies of the discipline. If possible, Keller urges that coaches institute "no-cut" policies and de-emphasize the importance of winning, especially in gym classes where fair play, team work, and other noncompetitive values should take center stage. Keller also insists that the number of practices and games be limited so as to allow students to put most of their time into academic work. Finally, the author insists that all schools hire coaches that are full members of the faculty even if they are not the "best" coach for the job. This is intended to prevent both possible neglect on the part of the coach and lawsuits from parents. The theory is that full-time faculty members will likely have students' academic interests at heart and are more easily held accountable by schools and parents (Keller 1984, 350–361).

Those wanting to find information about current issues surrounding physical education and sports in elementary schools can choose from a number of fine sources. Lawrence D. Bruya has edited *Where Our Children Play: Elementary School Playground Equipment* and *Play Spaces for Children: A New Beginning*, both of which contain several informative essays on new trends in physical education for children. The books are replete with helpful hints for teachers of school children. Those interested in using sport as part of elementary school pedagogy can consult David Ritchie's *Sport and Recreation* and Don Wulffson's *How Sports Came to Be*, which use sport to explain parts of American history. Likewise, Neil Duncan's *Sport Technology*, Robert Gardner's *Experimenting with Science in Sports*, and George Coulter's *Science in Sports* all use sports to generate student interest in science. Time-Life for Children has released a book entitled *Play Ball: Sports Math* that uses sports situations to teach students basic mathematical skills. Evaleen Hu's *A Level Playing Field: Sport and Race* and Nathan Aeseng's *The Locker Room Mirror: How Sports Reflects Society* can be used to teach important lessons on racism, sexism, and fair play, as well as to teach students about contemporary American society. Lowell Dickmeyer's *Winning and Losing*, Nate Zinsser's *Dear Dr. Psych*, and Robert Ross Olney's *Imaging: Think Your Way to Success in Sports and in the Classroom* are psychological works that attempt to answer questions often asked by elementary-aged students. The importance of winning and losing, trying one's best, how one can learn sound morals through sporting activity, and how one can use sport to complement classroom work are discussed. Finally, Lillian Morrison's *The Break Dance Kid: Poems of Sport, Motion and Locomotion*, Arnold Adoff's *Sport Pages*, and R. R. Knudson and May Swenson's *American Sports Poems* offer entertaining and inspirational poetry for students. All three texts contain poems that are playful, powerful, and clever and thus would be perfect for teachers trying to engender an interest in writing among students. As sport grows more popular with children, educators will write more books such as these that will continue to aid teachers in their quest to use sport as a teaching tool.

## SPORTS AND THE ACADEMIC CURRICULUM

Over the last two decades, sport has become an important area of study for scholars in many academic disciplines. Several works now exist in most fields that would be suitable for classroom use. For instance, scholars hoping to use sport to teach history might consider Donald Spivey's *Sport in America: New Historical Perspectives*, Benjamin Rader's *American Sports: From the Age of Folk Games to the Age of Spectators*, Paul Zingg's *The Sporting Image: Readings in American Sport History*, or George Sage's *Sport and American Society: Selected Readings*, all of which either discuss the history of sport or use sport as a vehicle through which to examine American history. English professors could structure an effective sports literature course around David Vanderwerken's *Sport Inside Out: Readings in Literature and Philosophy* or George Plimpton's *The Norton Book of Sports*. Cultural studies scholars have the luxury of choosing from several excellent texts.

Some titles include Richard Mandell's *Sport: A Cultural History*, Greta Cohen's *Women in Sport: Issues and Controversies*, Michael Messner and Donald Sabo's *Sport, Men, and the Gender Order: Critical Feminist Perspectives*, Jeremy MacClancy's *Sport, Identity and Ethnicity*, George Eisen and David K. Wiggins's *Ethnicity and Sport in North American History and Culture*, and David Rowe's *Popular Cultures: Rock Music, Sport and the Politics of Pleasure*. All of these works are well written and use sport to tackle current issues in gender, ethnic, and popular studies. Psychology students might read Richard Cox's *Sport Psychology: Concepts and Applications*, Jeffrey Goldstein's *Sports, Games and Play: Social and Psychological Perspectives*, or Arnold LeUnes's *Sport Psychology: An Introduction*. Budding sociologists could rely on Andrew Yankannis's *Sport Sociology: Contemporary Themes*, John W. Loy's *Sport, Culture and Society: A Reader on the Sociology of Sport*, or Conrad Vogler and Stephen Schwartz's *The Sociology of Sport: An Introduction*. In the business field, Paul Staudohar's *Playing for Dollars: Labor Relations and the Sports Business*, Bonnie Parkhouse's *The Management of Sport: Its Foundations and Applications* and Brenda Pitts's *Fundamentals of Sports Marketing* stand out because of their clarity and completeness. Finally, in the disciplines of religion and philosophy, William Morgan's *Philosophic Inquiry into Sports*, Charles Prebish's *Religion and Sport: The Meeting of Sacred and Profane*, Shirl Hoffman's *Sport and Religion*, and Drew Hyland's *Philosophy of Sport* are all fine texts from which a professor could conduct a course.

There are three books that discuss how to incorporate sports-related courses into the curriculum of several different disciplines. These books provide theoretical discussions aimed at justifying the use of sport in the humanities and tips as to how to most effectively implement a course focusing on sport. William J. Baker's *Sports and the Humanities*: *A Symposium* lays the groundwork for establishing sport as a legitimate academic subject. It contains several essays, including Frank B. Ryan's "Sports and the Humanities: Friends or Foes" and Robert J. Higgs's "Sports and the Humanities: State of the Union," which comment on why sports-related courses are not only appropriate for study at university level, but are actually vital for teachers and students who truly wish to understand both American and international cultures. Perhaps the most intriguing essay is Betty Spears's "Sport Studies in the Schools: Some Specific Proposals," in which the author records the views of some prominent scholars who defend the integration of sport into the established curriculums of their various fields. The essay covers philosophy, sociology, psychology, and history. Spears, who is a historian, sums up the potential of sport for those in her field. "The history of sport provides unique opportunities for students to study the cultures of the groups which make up the cultures of the United States and Canada. The history of American sport covers North Americans, Europeans, Africans, Asians and peoples from other countries that immigrated to America" (Baker 1983, 107). Like those she interviews, Spears gives several specific examples of how one might use sport in the classroom. She writes, "The sports of any era can be investigated as part of the culture being studied. The Roaring Twenties produced a bevy of sport stars reflecting the country's prosperity and changing social values" (Baker 1983, 108).

Another fine work is *Sport in the Classroom: Teaching Sport-Related Courses in the Humanities*, edited by David Vanderwerken. Published in 1990, the work is a compilation of essays from professors who have taught sport-related courses in history, philosophy, sociology, religion, anthropology, and interdisciplinary studies. Vanderwerken, an English professor at Texas Christian University, includes at least two entries from each field and provides an excellent essay on how to use sport to teach a course on American sport literature. The best thing about the book is its comprehensive nature. For instance, in addition to the professor's discussion of the theory behind the course, its intended goals, methods used, techniques that worked or failed, and suggestions for those who would like to teach a similar course, each of the essays contain a full, detailed syllabus and a recommended reading list. It seems as though each essay brings out a particularly valuable teaching technique. For example, Donald Mrozek's "'It Ain't Nothin' Until I Call It': What Belongs in a Course on Sports History?" discusses how a professor can use audiovisuals to illustrate most of the concepts a class might undertake in a course on twentieth-century American history. Don Morrow's "Reflections on Teaching Canadian Sport History" discusses the difference between teaching undergraduate and graduate courses on sport history. Morrow provides two different syllabi so that readers can get a feel for exactly how they might construct similar courses. Jay Coakley's "Teaching the Sociology of Sport: It's More than a Reflection of Society" discusses how the teaching of sport sociology has changed over the last three decades before presenting a syllabus that represents how a professor can take advantage of what previous scholars have done to present a course that tackles most of the key contemporary issues in the field. No matter what one's discipline, each of the essays should be read carefully by anyone considering a proposal of a course in sport studies. Perhaps the most important essay is Neil Isaacs's "Teaching at the Cutting Edge: Sport-Related Courses and Curricular Legitimacy." The author shows how professors of courses on sport can defend their courses as appropriate for the academic curriculum. Isaacs, a professor of literature from the University of Maryland, provides no less than five syllabi for various courses on sport literature, showing how adaptable and diverse sport is as an academic tool.

Finally, *Dimensions of Sport Studies,* edited by Donald Chu, is an excellent book for any scholar who wants a brief overview of the philosophy, sociology, psychology, or history of sport. The book does two things particularly well. First, it provides an excellent analysis of the critical work available in all four disciplines until 1982. In doing so, it acquaints scholars with much of the foundational work in each field. Second, each chapter contains a "Substantive Concerns" section, in which the author discusses a broad range of goals that scholars in each discipline seek to pursue, as well as the current methods being used by scholars to answer key questions in the field. The chapter entitled "The Rise of Sport" is one of few pieces of academic writing that clearly and concisely discusses the significance of sport in several cultures, including those that exist in North America, China, and Europe, and that provides an analysis of how and why sports developed in those cultures. The book also contains chapters on women in sport and race in sport that could also be used by cultural studies scholars looking for material to use in projected courses.

Finally, there are several journals and databases that contain current research on college sports, physical education, and sport as an academic practice. The *Physical Education Index* is a good starting point for any student looking for information on sport and education. It catalogues articles from over 140 journals that focus on some aspect of sport's many intersections with education. Some of the best journals include *American Journal of Health Promotion; Athletics Administration; International Journal of Education Reform; Issues in Education; Journal of Health Education; Journal of Physical Education, Recreation and Dance; Journal of School Health; Journal of Sport and Exercise Psychology; Journal of Sport and Social Issues; Journal of Sport History; Journal of Teaching in Physical Education; Journal of the Philosophy of Sport; Physical Education Digest; Physical Educator;* and *Quest.* Researchers might also want to consult the *Education Index* and *Current Journals in Education* (CIJE) both of which contain articles from hundreds of journals. In addition, The *Educational Resources Information Center* (ERIC) is an invaluable compilation of recent studies on sport and education. One of the best ways to follow current debates in college athletics or the discipline of physical education is to access weekly editions of *The Chronicle of Higher Education*, whose contributors usually have their finger on the pulse of college and university campuses across America. The Sports Information Resource Center produces SPORTSDiscus, a database that indexes thousands of works on sport from all disciplines, including dissertations. Another great Internet source is the *North American Sports Library Network* (NASLIN). Those interested in NASLIN should contact Gretchen Ghent at the University of Calgary Library at gghent@acs.ucalgary.ca.

## REFERENCES

### Books

Aaseng, Nathan. *The Locker Room Mirror: How Sports Reflects Society.* New York: Walker & Co., 1993.

Adelman, Melvin. *A Sporting Time: New York City and the Rise of Modern Athletics, 1820–1870.* Urbana, IL: University of Illinois Press, 1986.

Adoff, Arnold. *Sport Pages.* New York: Lippincott, 1986.

Bailey, Wilfred S., and Taylor D. Littleton. *Athletes and the Academy: An Anatomy of Abuses and a Prescription for Reform.* New York: American Council of Education, 1991.

Baker, William J., ed. *Sports and the Humanities: A Symposium.* Orono, ME: University of Maine Press, 1983.

Bale, John. *The Brawn Drain: Foreign Student Athletes in American Universities.* Urbana, IL: University of Illinois Press, 1991.

Betts, Rickards John. *America's Sporting Heritage, 1850–1950.* Reading, MA: Addison-Wesley, 1974.

Bosworth, Brian. *The Boz: Confessions of a Modern Anti-Hero*. New York: Charter Books, 1989.

Brooks, Dana H. *Racism in College Athletics: The African-American Athlete's Experience*. Morgantown, WV: Fitness Information Technologies, 1993.

Bruya, Lawrence. *Play Spaces for Children: A New Beginning*. Reston, VA: American Alliance for Health, Physical Education, Recreation and Dance, 1988.

———. *Where Our Children Play: Elementary School Playground Equipment*. Reston, VA: American Alliance for Health, Physical Education, Recreation and Dance, 1988.

Burke, Michael. *Outrageous Good Fortune*. Boston: Little, Brown, 1984.

Chu, Donald. *The Character of American Higher Education and Intercollegiate Sport*. Albany, NY: State University of New York, 1989.

———. *Dimensions of Sport Studies*. New York: John Wiley & Sons, 1982.

———, ed. *Sport and Higher Education*. Champaign, IL: Human Kinetics Books, 1985.

Cicciarella, Charles. *Sport Competition Structures*. Charlotte, NC: Premium Software, 1994.

Cohen, Greta, ed. *Women in Sport: Issues and Controversies*. Newbury Park, CA: Sage Publications, 1995.

Copeland, Barry. *Funding Sources in Physical Education, Exercise and Sport*. Morgantown, WV: Fitness Information Technologies, 1995.

Coulter, George. *Science in Sports*. Vero Beach, FL: Rourke Publishing, 1995.

Cox, Richard. *Sport Psychology: Concepts and Applications*. Madison, WI: Brown & Benchmark Publishing, 1994.

Dealy, Frances. *Win at Any Cost: The Sellout of College Athletics*. New York: Carol Publishing Group, 1990.

De Sensi, Joy. *Ethics in Sport Management*. Morgantown, WV: Fitness Information Technologies, 1996.

Dickmeyer, Lowell. *Winning and Losing*. New York: F. Watts, 1984.

Dougherty, Neil, ed. *Physical Education and Sport for the Secondary School Student*. Reston, VA: American Alliance for Health, Physical Education, Recreation and Dance, 1983.

Duncan, Neil. *Sport Technology*. New York: Bookwright Press, 1992.

Durgin, Red, ed. *A Guide to Recreation, Leisure and Travel for the Handicapped*. Toledo, OH: Resource Directories, 1985.

Eisen, George, and David K. Wiggins. *Ethnicity and Sport in North American History and Culture*. Westport, CT: Greenwood Press, 1994.

Fleisher, Arthur. *The NCAA: A Study in Cartel Behavior*. Chicago: University of Chicago Press, 1992.

Freeman, William Harden. *Physical Education and Sport in a Changing Society*. Boston: Allyn & Beacon, 1997.

Funk, Gary. *Major Violations: The Unbalanced Priorities in Athletics and Academics*. Champaign, IL: Leisure Press, 1991.

Gardner, Robert. *Experimenting with Science in Sports*. New York: F. Watts, 1993.

Gerdy, John R. *The Successful College Athletic Program: The New Standard*. Phoenix, AZ: Oryx Press, 1997.

Goldstein, Jeffrey, ed. *Sports, Games and Play: Social and Psychological Viewpoints*. Hillsdale, NJ: L. Erlbaum Associates, 1989.

Graham, Jan. *Sports*. Austin, TX: Raintree, Steck and Vaughn, 1995.

Graham, Peter J. *Sport Business: Operational and Theoretical Aspects*. Dubuque, IA: Brown & Benchmark, 1993.

Griffin, Robert. *Sports in the Lives of Children and Adolescents*. Westport, CT: Praeger, 1998.

Grosse, Susan J., and Donna Thompson, eds. *Leisure Opportunities for Individuals with Disabilities: Legal Issues.* Reston, VA: American Alliance for Health, Physical Education, Recreation and Dance, 1993.

Hamblin, Robert. *Win or Win: A Season with Ron Shumate.* Cape Girardeau, MO: Southeastern Missouri State University Press, 1992.

Hart-Nibbrig, Nand. *The Political Economy of College Sports.* Lexington, MA: Lexington Books, 1986.

Hoffman, Shirl, ed. *Sport and Religion.* Champaign, IL: Human Kinetics Books, 1992.

Howard, Dennis. *Financing Sport.* Morgantown, WV: Fitness Information Technologies, 1995.

Hu, Evaleen. *A Level Playing Field: Sport and Race.* St. Paul, MN: Lerner Publishing Co., 1995.

Hyland, Drew. *Philosophy of Sport.* New York: Paragon House, 1990.

Johnson, John. *Promotion for Sports Directors.* Chicago: Human Kinetics Books, 1996.

Keller, Irvin. *Administration of High School Athletics.* Englewood Cliffs, NJ: PrenticeHall, 1984.

Knudson, R. R., and May Swenson. *American Sports Poems.* New York: Orchard Books, 1988.

Lapchick, Richard, and John Brooks Slaughter. *The Rules of the Game: Ethics in College Sport.* Phoenix: Oryx Press, 1994.

Lawrence, Paul. *Unsportsmanlike Conduct: The NCAA and the Business of College Football.* New York: Praeger, 1987.

Lee, Mabel. *A History of Physical Education and Sports in the United States.* New York: John Wiley & Sons, 1983.

LeUnes, Arnold. *Sport Psychology: An Introduction.* Chicago: Nelson-Hall, 1996.

Looney, Douglas, and Don Yaeger. *Under the Tarnished Dome: How Notre Dame Betrayed Its Ideals for Football Glory.* New York: Simon & Schuster, 1993.

Loy, John W., ed. *Sport, Culture and Society: A Reader on the Sociology of Sport.* Philadelphia: Lea and Febiger, 1981.

Lumpkin, Angela. *Physical Education: A Contemporary Introduction.* St. Louis, MO: Mosby, 1994.

MacClancy, Jeremy. *Sport, Identity and Ethnicity.* Herndon, VA: Berg Publishing, 1996.

MacMillan, Tom. *Out of Bounds: How the American Sports Establishment Is Being Driven by Greed and Hypocrisy and What Needs to Be Done about It.* New York: Simon & Schuster, 1992.

Mandell, Richard. *Sport: A Cultural History.* New York: Columbia University Press, 1984.

Mason, James. *Modern Sports Administration.* Englewood Cliffs, NJ: PrenticeHall, 1988.

Messner, Michael, and Donald Sabo. *Sport, Men, and the Gender Order: Critical Feminist Perspectives.* Champaign, IL: Human Kinetics Books, 1990.

Mohnson, Bonnie. *Using Technology in Physical Education.* Champaign, IL: Human Kinetics Books, 1995.

Morgan, William, ed. *Philosophic Inquiry into Sports.* Champaign, IL: Human Kinetics Books, 1995.

Morrison, Lillian, ed. *The Break Dance Kid: Poems of Sport, Motion and Locomotion.* New York: Lothrop, Lee and Shepherd, 1985.

Nuwer, Hank. *Recruiting in Sports.* New York: Watts, 1989.

Olney, Robert Ross. *Imaging: Think Your Way to Success in Sports and in the Classroom.* New York: Atheneum, 1985.

Olson, John, ed. *Administration of High School and Collegiate Athletic Programs.* Philadelphia, PA: Saunders College, 1987.

Paciorek, Michael. *Sports and Recreation for the Disabled*. Carmel, IN: Cooper Publishing Group, 1994.

Parkhouse, Bonnie, ed. *The Management of Sport: Its Foundations and Applications*. St. Louis, MO: Mosby, 1996.

Pitts, Brenda. *Fundamentals of Sport Marketing*. Morgantown, WV: Fitness Information Technologies, 1996.

*Play Ball: Sports Math*. Alexandria, VA: Time-Life for Children, 1993.

Plimpton, George, ed. *The Norton Book of Sports*. New York: W. W. Norton, 1992.

Prebish, Charles. *Religion and Sport: The Meeting of Sacred and Profane*. Westport, CT: Greenwood Press, 1993.

Rader, Benjamin. *American Sports: From the Age of Folk Games to the Age of Spectators*. Englewood Cliffs, NJ: PrenticeHall, 1983.

————. *In Its Own Image: How Television Has Transformed Sports*. New York: Free Press, 1984.

Raiborn, Mitchell. *Revenues and Expenses of Intercollegiate Athletic Programs: Analysis of Financial Trends and Relationships, 1985–1989*. Overland Park, KS: NCAA, 1990.

Ritchie, David. *Sport and Recreation*. New York: Chelsea House, 1996.

Rooney, John. *The Recruiting Game: Toward a New System of Intercollegiate Sports*. Lincoln, NE: University of Nebraska Press, 1987.

Rowe, David. *Popular Cultures: Rock Music, Sport, and the Politics of Pleasure*. Thousand Oaks, CA: Sage Publications, 1995.

Sack, Allen, and Ellen Staurowsky. *College Athletes for Hire: The Evolution and Legacy of the NCAA's Amateur Myth*. New York: Praeger, 1998.

Sage, George. *Sport and American Society: Selected Readings*. Reading, MA: Addison-Wesley, 1980.

Salter, David, ed. *Blueprint for Success: An In-Depth Analysis of NCAA Division III Athletics, and Why It Should Be the Model for Intercollegiate Reform*. Dumont, NJ: F. Merrick Publishing, 1993.

Schock, Bernie. *Parents, Kids and Sports*. Chicago: Moody Press, 1987.

Schropshire, Kenneth. *Agents of Opportunity: Sports Agents and Corruption in College Sports*. Philadelphia, PA: University of Pennsylvania Press, 1990.

Schultz, Ron. *Looking Inside Sports Aerodynamics*. Santa Fe, NM: John Muir Publications, 1992.

Smith, Ronald A., ed. *Big-Time Football at Harvard, 1905*. Urbana, IL: University of Illinois Press, 1994.

————. *Sports and Freedom: The Rise of Big-Time College Athletics*. New York: Oxford University Press, 1988.

Spears, Betty, and Richard Swanson. *History of Sport and Physical Activity in the United States*. Dubuque, IA: W. C. Brown & Co., 1995.

Sperber, Murray. *College Sports Inc.: The Athletic Department vs. The University*. New York: Holt, 1991.

————. *Onward to Victory: The Crisis that Shapes College Sports*. New York: Holt, 1998.

Spivey, Donald, ed. *Sport in America: New Historical Perspectives*. Westport, CT: Greenwood Press, 1985.

Staudohar, Paul. *Playing for Dollars: Labor Relations and the Sports Business*. Ithaca, NY: ILA Press, 1996.

Steel, Edward. *Counseling College Student-Athletes: Issues & Interventions*. Morgantown, WV: Fitness Information Technologies, 1996.

Stewart, David. *Deaf Sport: The Impact of Sports within the Deaf Community*. Washington, D.C.: Gallaudet University Press, 1991.

Stier, William. *Sport Fund-Raising for Sport and Recreation*. Madison, WI: Brown and Benchmark, 1994.

Telander, Rick. *The Hundred Yard Lie*. Urbana, IL: University of Illinois Press, 1996.

Thelin, James. *Games Colleges Play: Scandal and Reform in Intercollegiate Athletics*. Baltimore, MD: Johns Hopkins University Press, 1997.

———. *The Old College Try: Balancing Academics and Athletics in Higher Education*. Washington, D.C.: George Washington University Press, 1989.

Thompson, Charles. *Down & Dirty: The Life and Crimes of Oklahoma Football*. New York: Carrol & Graf, 1990.

Underwood, Clarence. *The Student-Athlete: Eligibility and Academic Integrity*. East Lansing, MI: Michigan State University Press, 1984.

Vanderwerken, David. *Sport Inside Out: Readings in Literature and Philosophy*. Ft. Worth, TX: TCU Press, 1985.

———, ed. *Sport in the Classroom: Teaching Sport-Related Courses in the Humanities*. Rutherford, NJ: Fairleigh Dickinson University Press, 1990.

Vanderzwaag, Harold. *Sports Management at Schools and Colleges*. New York: John Wiley & Sons, 1984.

Vogler, Conrad, and Stephen Schwartz. *The Sociology of Sport: An Introduction*. Englewood Cliffs, NJ: PrenticeHall, 1993.

Walsh, Jim. *Everything You Need to Know about Collegiate Sports Recruiting: A Guide for Players and Parents*. Thousand Oaks, CA: Andrews & McMeel, 1997.

Walter, Byers. *Unsportsmanlike Conduct: Exploiting College Athletics*. Ann Arbor, MI: University of Michigan Press, 1995.

Weissberg, Ted. *Breaking the Rules: The NCAA and Recruitment in American High Schools*. New York: Watts, 1995.

Whitford, David. *A Payroll to Meet: A Story of Greed, Corruption and Football at SMU*. New York: Macmillan, 1989.

Whitney, Stu. *Behind the Green Curtain: The Sacrifice of Ethics and Academics in Michigan State's Rise to Football Prominence*. Grand Rapids, MI: Master's Press, 1990.

Winston, Lynn. *Recreation and Sports*. Bloomington, IL: Accent Press, 1985.

Wolff, Alexander. *Raw Recruits*. New York: Pocket Books, 1990.

Wulffson, Don. *How Sports Came to Be*. New York: Lothrop, Lee & Shepherd, 1980.

Yaeger, Don. *Undue Process: The NCAA's Injustice for All*. Champaign, IL: Sagamore Publishing, 1991.

Yankannis, Andrew. *Sport Sociology: Contemporary Themes*. Dubuque, IA: Kendall/Hunt Publishing Co., 1987.

Zeigler, Earle. *An Introduction to Sport and Physical Education Philosophy*. Dubuque, IA: WCB Brown, 1989.

———. *Ethics and Morality in Sport and Physical Education*. Champaign, IL: Stipes Publishing Company, 1984.

———. *Physical Education and Kinesiology in North America: Professional and Scholarly Foundations*. Champaign, IL: Stipes, 1994.

———. *Professional Ethics for Sports Management*. Chicago, IL: Stipes, 1997.

Zimbalist, Andrew. *Unpaid Professionals: Commercialism and Conflict in Big-Time College Sports*. Princeton, NJ: Princeton University Press, 1999.

Zingg, Paul. *The Sporting Image: Readings in American Sport History*. Lanham, MD: University Press of America, 1988.

Zinsser, Nate. *Dear Dr. Psych*. Boston: Little, Brown, 1991.

## Journals

*American Journal of Health Promotion* (St. Louis, MO)
*American Journal of Public Health* (Washington, D.C.)
*Athletics Administration* (Lexington, KY)
*Chronicles of Higher Education* (Washington, D.C.)
*Current Journals in Education* (CD-ROM)
*Education Index* (CD-ROM)
*Educational Resources* (CD-ROM)
*International Journal of Education Reform* (Lancaster, PA)
*Issues in Education* (Riverside, CA)
*Journal of Health Education* (Reston, VA)
*Journal of Physical Education, Recreation and Dance* (Reston, VA)
*Journal of School Health* (Kent, OH)
*Journal of Sport and Exercise Psychology* (Champaign, IL)
*Journal of Sport and Social Issues* (Thousand Oaks, CA)
*Journal of Sport History* (University Park, PA)
*Journal of Teaching in Physical Education* (Champaign, IL)
*Journal of the International Council for Health, Physical Education, Recreation, Sport and Dance* (Reston, VA)
*Journal of the Philosophy of Sport* (Champaign, IL)
*North American Sport Library Network* (Calgary, Alberta, Canada)
*Physical Education Digest* (Sudbury, Ontario, Canada)
*Physical Education Index* (CD-ROM)
*Physical Educator* (Indianapolis, IA)
*Quest* (Champaign, IL)

# 4

# Sport: Ethnicity and Race

Over the last two decades, several factors have combined to push race and ethnicity onto the academic stage. Perhaps the most significant factor was the civil rights legislation of the 1960s, which forced America's white power structure to include members of minority groups into mainstream societal institutions. Changes have been slow but steady in the area of higher education. More minority students and faculty, an increasingly influential African-American middle class, and rapidly growing Asian-American and Hispanic-American populations have combined with a new emphasis on diversity and multiculturalism within the academy to establish Cultural Studies, African-American Studies, Chicano Studies, Asian-American Studies, and other ethnic study concentrations within such established disciplines as sociology, history, and English. At the same time that postmodern relativity and multiculturalism have taken root on college campuses, sports, which has over the course of the twentieth century assumed a place of considerable importance in the lives of Americans, have become a highly visible arena in which minority athletes have excelled. If sport has evolved into a secular or civil religion in the United States, baseball, basketball, and football, which are dominated by African-American and Hispanic-American players, have become the chief denominations. The media and several interested scholars have not missed the fact that the major deities in this sporting faith usually represent minority groups. Despite some challenges by Larry Bird, the scepter of power in the National Basketball Association (NBA) has been passed from Julius Erving to Magic Johnson to Michael Jordan. Though the marquis position of quarterback has remained largely white, the National Football League's (NFL) popularity was built on the achievements of African-American stars such as Walter Payton, Jerry Rice, Emmett Smith, Art Monk, Joe Greene, Franco Harris, and countless others. No Major League Baseball team could compete without stars from Mexico, the Dominican Republic, Cuba, and Puerto Rico. For every Greg Maddox and Mark Maguire there is a Pedro

Martinez or Sammy Sosa. All of this has caused scholars to sit up and take notice of the relationship between sport, race, and ethnicity in the United States. Most of the writing centers around the sporting history and contemporary experiences of African Americans, but there is a growing body of literature that covers the importance of sport in the lives of Native Americans, Hispanics, Jewish Americans, and other ethnic groups. In the last decade, scholars have laid the foundation for further academic inquiry by concentrating on how sport has functioned historically for various minority groups, how the media is affecting public perceptions of minority athletes, and how sport functions as an important source of ethnic pride both in the United States and internationally. This chapter will highlight some of those works so as to provide a starting point for those interested in launching research projects in one of the hottest areas in Sport and Leisure Studies.

## SPORT AND ETHNIC IDENTITY

Every year people risk their lives by running with the bulls through the streets of Pamplona, Spain. Quite a few get injured and occasionally one dies. Soccer hotbeds in Europe and South America are known for their passionate dedication to the game and their single-minded allegiance to local teams. When emotions run high for national games or matches between towns that represent different ethnic groups, riots that result in injury and death are not uncommon. It is, in fact, one of the most notable things about soccer for the average American. Every country contains within its borders several different ethnic groups that use sport as a means of establishing identity. According to Jeremy MacClancy, author of *Sport, Identity and Ethnicity*, "sports help to define moral and political community. They are vehicles of identity, providing people with a sense of difference and a way of classifying themselves and others." He continues to say that "sports are ways of fabricating in a potentially complex manner a space for oneself in their social world" (MacClancy 1996, 3–4). MacClancy's book contains nine essays that show how this process of ethnic identity formation via sporting ritual works throughout the world. Two of the best are Martin Stokes's "Strong as a Turk: Power, Performance and Representation in Turkish Wrestling" and Peter Parkes's "Indigenous Polo and Politics of Regional Identity in Northern Pakistan." The former illustrates the hierarchy that exists between men in various ethnic enclaves in Turkey based on their performances between the ropes, while Parkes's piece demonstrates how ethnic groups that hold power in Pakistan use sport, in this case polo, to establish their superiority over any competing groups. Other essays in the volume focus on how nations function as ethnic entities that attempt to parlay athletic triumphs into nationalistic campaigns. Two such essays are MacClancy's "Nationalism at Play: The Basques of Vizcaya and Athletic Bilbao" and "Our Blood Is Green: Cricket, Identity and Social Empowerment among British Pakistanis," both of which show how ethnicity refers to a broader range of conditions than we give it credit for.

By contrast, George Eisen and David Wiggins's *Ethnicity and Sport in North American History and Culture* focuses on how important sport has been to the assimilation efforts of first- and second-generation ethnic groups in the United States. In "Forty-Eighters and the Rise of the Turnverein Movement in America," Robert Knight Barney shows how mid-nineteenth-century German immigrants formed gymnastic clubs known as turnvereins for two main reasons. The first was to promote fitness and to create familiar social structures for newly arrived German immigrants. The second was to give these new Americans a socio-political organization in which they could unite to formulate and promote their positions on any number of issues. Most of the turnvereins, for instance, worked in concert to elect Republican presidents, to abolish slavery, to retain voting rights while halting the Nativist movement that fueled resentment against immigrants, and to preserve and spread German culture in the United States. As Barney writes, "The turnverein offered Forty-Eighters an organizational center for espousing the social and political causes in which they believed so strongly. A consistent theme of purpose pervaded the declarations of Forty-Eighter Turners who commented on the purposes of the turnverein" (Eisen and Wiggins 1994, 21).

Another excellent essay is "The Shamrock and the Eagle: Irish Americans and Sport in the Nineteenth Century," in which Ralph Wilcox demonstrates that sport had two important functions for first-generation Irish immigrants in late nineteenth-century America. First, sport gave the Irish a way to hold onto the traditions of their homeland. To this end, organizations such as the Gaelic Athletic Association, the Gaelic Athletic Union, the Irish-American Athletic Association, and the Irish Counties Athletic Union were formed in eastern cities around the turn of the century. They were dedicated to keeping alive traditional Irish games, such as Gaelic football, as a way of maintaining some sense of traditional Irish identity in their new land. As Wilcox writes, "Their clannish attachments to the Land of Erin remained strong as national groups such as the Clan Na Gael promoted sport to ensure that their fellow countrymen's roots were never forgotten" (Eisen and Wiggins 1994, 71). On the other hand, through these same organizations, Catholic churches, and businesses that relied heavily on Irish labor, Irish immigrants began playing baseball and other traditionally American sports. By the first decade of the twentieth century, the Irish were playing baseball in record numbers, not only as a way of having fun and celebrating their heritage, but as a way of assimilating into the American mainstream, as a way of showing that they were just "as American as the next person engrossed in the national pastime" (Eisen and Wiggins 1994, 71). This dual use of sport has been the norm for many ethnic groups since the late eighteenth century and continues to resonate in Hispanic- and Asian-American sporting activities. Other essays in *Ethnicity and Sport in North American History and Culture* make this quite clear. In all, the book features essays on early Native Americans, early twentieth-century Jewish communities, Italian Americans, the use of sport by Japanese Americans in World War II internment camps, African Americans in rural and urban settings, Hispanic Americans, and ethnic women in urban settings.

Some fine works exist that shed light on the historical meanings that sport has held for Jewish Americans. In *Jews and Gender: Responses to Otto Weininger*, Nancy Harrowitz explains how athletic participation has long been an uphill battle for Jews because deeply entrenched myths pictured them as weak, clumsy, undeveloped intellectuals who had no place in sports: "The Jewish male predicament grew out of a long and ambivalent involvement with the masculine norms of nineteenth-century Europe. These standards of behavior and feeling brought the 'racial' dichotomy of German and Jew into every sphere of life, confirming the deficient character of Jewish experience" (Harrowitz 1995, 144). Harrowitz goes on to show how science, philosophy, literature, social customs, and political wrangling have all contributed to a lack of sporting opportunity and a sense of inferiority for Jewish athletes.

On the other hand, *Ellis Island to Ebbets Field: Sport and the American Jewish Experience* is a book in which author Peter Levine shows how American Jews have used sport to counter negative stereotypes. He has two chapters on the development of basketball in Jewish inner-city neighborhoods from the 1920s through the 1950s. He includes descriptions of what the sport meant to local teams such as the Talmud Torah Athletic Club in Minneapolis as well as several interviews with Jewish professional players from the 1940s and 1950s. Of the latter he concludes that "with basketball they learned about American values, tried out new identities, thought new thoughts, challenged their roots, and made choices—all within Jewish bounded space. Their story demonstrates the possibilities for living in the United States as Americans in ways that do not deny a real Jewish presence and a fierce pride in being Jewish (Levine 1993, 51). This idea of sport as a bridge between American and Jewish cultures became even more intense for many Jews who played baseball, for the national pastime was America's game, the only visible sport to which the entire nation paid attention. Jews who, in fact, excelled on the diamond were seen as more comletely American; Jewish excellence on the baseball field, meant that Jewishness and Americanness went hand in hand. Levine includes an informative section on the development of sandlot and amateur baseball in Jewish communities, but his best chapter is on the powerful impact that Jewish professional baseball players had on American Jews. Levine profiles Hank Greenberg, Carl Levin, Al Rosen, Andy Cohen, and other Jewish stars, showing how important it was to Jewish adults and children to have folk heroes that were baseball players who were worshiped by both Jews and Gentiles. Levine also includes an excellent chapter on how important boxing was to Jews as a means of showing the world that they were not weak, but were instead tough and strong in the most masculine sense. In a way, Jewish domination of the sport in the 1920s and 1930s was more important than Jewish participation in baseball from the 1930s onward. "Despite its reputation as a disreputable sport, no other activity provided such a clear way to refute stereotypes of the weak, cowardly Jew that anti-Semites employed to deny Jewish immigrants and their children full access to opportunities" (Levine 1993, 162). Those who like Levine's work will also want to try Steven Riess's *Sports and the American Jew,* a collection of essays that continues to debunk stereotypes that Jews and sports do not mix. All of the essays in the book clearly demonstrate that sports has long been a significant institution in Jewish-American life. The book is particularly noteworthy because several of the essays show how Jews, denied entry into prestigious Protestant clubs, established their own network of sports clubs; became promoters, administrators and owners; and went into manufacturing of sporting goods so as to solidify their connection with American sport.

Those searching for more information on the role of baseball in Jewish culture should read Eric Solomon's "Jews and Baseball: A Cultural Love Story," which is located in Eisen and Wiggins's *Ethnicity and Sport in North American History and Culture*. Solomon is an expert on literature and films that involve the Jewish relationship with the game in the first half of this century. In the process of profiling and explaining the significance of these texts, he offers several reasons why baseball was so important to Jews. One of the biggest reasons was, of course, that the all-American game offered Jews "a superb avenue for acculturation—where a minority group emulates the dominant culture's values and customs—and assimilation—where a minority group is absorbed into the dominant culture" (Eisen and Wiggins 1994, 77). Solomon's more intriguing second reason is that baseball's emphasis on history, usually in the form of statistical comparisons, analysis, and argumentation, appealed to Jews, whose education often centered on analyzing events from the past, while also emphasizing close reading of and arguments over the Torah. A third reason explored by Solomon is the fact that professional baseball became a city game and Jews were essentially an urban people. As Jews spread throughout cities such as New York, the professional teams became a way of distinguishing themselves from other Jews in different parts of the city. "If one grew up in Flatbush, one followed the Dodgers, in 'the shadow of Coogan's Bluff,' the Giants, in the Bronx (perhaps) the Yankees; other multiple-team cities like Boston or Chicago brought forth similar urban allegiances" (Eisen and Wiggins 1994, 77). Most of all, baseball gave Jews a common ground in the United States, a center that was distinctly American in which they could celebrate their status as uniquely American Jews. "For the Jewish arrival, baseball was the shtetl—a center of perception and community with strong cultural traditions, psychological sanctions, and emotional commitments—and a shul, a center of belief and ritual. Thus, to know and love baseball was to know and love America" (Eisen and Wiggins 1994, 78).

Another quality book is Allen Bodner's *When Boxing Was a Jewish Sport*. Bodner, whose father was a boxer in New York in the 1920s, gives us a clear, vivid picture of Jewish life in twentieth-century New York City. He explains the economic conditions that pulled many first- and second-generation Jews to the squared circle in the 1920s and 1930s, but also examines the psychological needs of Jews during this time that led to their pre-eminence in the ring. He profiles many Jewish boxers and, because the leading Jewish newspaper, the *Daily Forward*, did not cover boxing because it was held in such low regard by Jewish religious and community leaders, his depictions have a second function of rescuing some colorful boxers from anonymity. In addition to Bodner's book, several articles on sports and Jewish culture can be accessed via the database SPORTSDiscus, one of the best collections of articles on sports that a researcher would ever hope to find. A handful of the hundreds of recent articles includes Solomon's "Counter Ethnicity in the Jewish-Black Baseball Novel: The Cases of Jerome Charyn and Jay Neugeboren," which accounts for the popularity of baseball fiction with Jews; George Eisen's "Children and Play in the Holocaust: Games among Shadows," which presents a historical analysis of play during the Holocaust; and Saul Ross's "Jewish Ethics and Sport: Toward a Jewish Philosophy of Physical Education and Sport," which explores how Judaic philosophy has been used to foster singular sporting practices.

## AFRICAN AMERICANS AND SPORT

Perhaps because of their long, brutal history in the United States and their many singular contributions to the athletic history of the country, African Americans have been the subject of many fine scholarly and popular books. The best general history of African-American sporting experience is Wiggins's *Glory Bound: Black Athletes in a White America*. Wiggins is undoubtedly an expert on the subject, and the book is essentially a compilation of eleven essays that he has written over the last two decades. The book is broken up into three parts. The first part covers the games and activities of slaves and the rise of African-American athletes as dominant jockeys and boxers in the late nineteenth century. The second part focuses on the civil rights movement and its effect on sports. Chapters include the 1936 Olympics, the integration of professional baseball, the 1968 Olympic boycott, the career of Muhammad Ali, and protests against racial bias on university campuses. Finally, part three offers insight into the debate about black superiority in certain sports such as football, basketball, and track and also includes a chapter on the psychology of the contemporary black athlete. The final chapter is a tribute to one of the first and quite possibly most important historians of black sport, Edwards Bancroft Henderson, without whose efforts at chronicling black sports in the early decades of this century the stories of many important events and players would have been lost. All of the chapters in this book are meticulously researched and well written, but two in particular stand out. The first is "The Play of Slave Children in the Plantation Communities of the Old South, 1820–1860," in which Wiggins shows how sport was often the most important part of slave life because it was one area where they had some autonomy, where they could let loose and express themselves in a way that brought inexpressible joy in the face of a monotonous, grueling existence. Not only did sporting activity bring relief, but it also afforded slaves a chance to build their own traditions apart from the humiliating white customs that largely defined their lives. "These were ideal times for children to become familiar with organization, the customs, and the leaders of their community. Through their mutual experiences they learned how their community made decisions, organized clandestine meetings, provided for common recreational activities, and organized itself to be as free as possible from the structures of their overseer or master" (Wiggins 1997, 12). Sports, then, have been a way of establishing positive, affirmative identities for African Americans from the very beginning of their American experience. In a way, this double-edged sporting experience still pervades black athleticism. This is the subject of "The Notion of Double-Consciousness and the Involvement of Black Athletes in American Sport." Just as the slaves struggled to use sport to fashion their own identities within the overall context of white control, black athletes throughout the twentieth century have struggled with the same question: How does a minority athlete subject to discrimination use sport as a means of self-fulfillment and still please a white power structure that finances and manages the greater sporting structures of the society? Wiggins examines how different African Americans have tried to do this and shows that the most successful stars have been the ones to successfully balance the multiple roles required of them. "Outstanding black athletes were able to compete with other Americans for status and social equality because they realized early on that success in this country was ultimately linked with the process of adaptation and differentiation and the need to assume multiple roles" (Wiggins 1997, 220).

Other helpful histories include Rob Ruck's *Sandlot Seasons: Sport in Black Pittsburgh*, in which the author examines the importance of noninstitutionalized, "sandlot" sport both in terms of how it improved the quality of life for black Americans in the pre-civil rights era, and how it functioned as an important stepping stone toward organizing Negro leagues in baseball and other sports. Thus, the book works both as a specific history, one that is complete with profiles of key figures and events of the evolution in black athletics in Pittsburgh, and as a microcosm of what was happening in black communities throughout the nation in the first half of the twentieth century. By contrast, Arthur Ashe's voluminous *A Hard Road to Glory: A History of the African-American Athlete* is a very general, three-part history of black athletes from 1600 to the present. Ashe is thorough, and his work is an excellent reference source for any scholar trying to locate general information about specific athletes or on black participation in any given sport during any era of the United States. Finally, Harry Edwards's *The Struggle That Must Be*, is a provocative work that shows how a thoughtful, personal account of life experience can be a powerful historical tool. Though personal anecdotes have long been the bane of traditional historians, Edwards's words are resonant in that they speak for a generation (at least) of African-American athletes.

One of the best books on the rise of black baseball is Neil Lanctot's *Fair Dealing and Clean Playing: The Hilldale Club and the Development of Black Professional Baseball, 1910–1932*. Lanctot describes the process by which several factors combined to push the Philadelphia Hilldale Baseball Club to the top of the black baseball world. These factors included the massive migration of African Americans from the South to more liberal northern cities at the beginning of the twentieth century. This migration became more pronounced during World War I when munitions demands made thousands of factory jobs for migrating blacks. Lanctot writes that "over a 20-year period, the steady migration of southern blacks into northern cities had resulted in the establishment of substantial African-American communities increasingly capable of supporting their own professional baseball teams" (Lanctot 1994, 43). Not only did black people with money want to see men of their race take part in the national game, but many whites were interested in black teams. White teams liked to play clubs like Hilldale because they offered quality competition and would play for a small percentage of the gate. In addition, black teams were often in high demand because the game was becoming so popular that there were hundreds of white teams looking for opponents. In addition, it seems that white America was quite interested in interracial competition, and "barnstorming," extended tours by black ball clubs whereby these clubs would challenge white teams throughout any given region of the country, became all the rage in the 1920s and 1930s. As Lanctot argues, "Interracial games continued to be extremely popular, especially among white fans" (Lanctot 1994, 58). Lanctot concludes his book by recounting the demise of Hilldale due to the more powerful Negro league teams, which, ironically, would eventually be undone by the integration of Major League Baseball.

Several other quality works exist that illuminate the world of the Negro leagues and black baseball in general in the pre-integration era. Robert Peterson's *Only the Ball Was White: A History of Legendary Black Players on All-Black Professional Teams* is a highly readable, landmark book that still stands as one of the best recitations of how the Negro leagues did business, and what they meant both to black communities and to America in general. James Overmyer's *Queen of the Negro Leagues: Effa Manley and the Newark Eagles* recounts the story of a feisty white women who lived as a light-skinned black women for most of her days, and who effectively ran the Newark team in the 1930s and 1940s. It will surprise some readers to find out how much power Manley had in Negro baseball and in the integration process. Another group that ensured the success of both the Negro Leagues and the integration of white baseball was the black press. Jim Reisler's *Black Writers/Black Baseball: An Anthology of Articles from Black Sportswriters Who Covered the Negro Leagues* is a wonderful collection of writings from black sportswriters such as Wendell Smith of the *Pittsburgh Courier* and Sam Lacy of the *Baltimore Afro-American*, men who not only helped to popularize black baseball, but who were one of the prime catalytic agents in the integration process. The clever, passionate, insightful columns of these writers should not be missed by anyone who values good writing; they are an invaluable and entertaining source of knowledge about Negro league baseball. Finally, there are three books that provide concise histories of three Negro league teams. Paul Debono's *The Indianapolis ABC's: History of a Premier Team in the Negro Leagues* is a short history of black baseball in Indianapolis, which has an informative chapter on the development of the Negro National League. Ruck's *Sandlot Seasons: Sport in Black Pittsburgh* contains the story of the Pittsburgh Crawfords, and Jules Tygiel's*The Jackie Robinson Reader* has a chapter on Robinson's stint with the Kansas City Monarchs. Brent Kelley's *Voices from the Negro Leagues: Conversations with 52 Baseball Standouts of the Period 1924–1960* is also a quality oral history that focuses mostly on the Negro National League.

Tygiel is also the ranking authority on the integration of Major League Baseball. Both *The Jackie Robinson Reader* and *Baseball's Great Experiment: Jackie Robinson and His Legacy* provide detailed, almost step-by-step accounts of how

Robinson landed his position with the Brooklyn Dodgers in 1947. Tygiel does a particularly good job of showing the reader just how many people were actually a part of that long process. While reading both books, one comes to appreciate the dignity and savvy baseball sense of Branch Rickey and the patience and wisdom of Rachael Robinson. Mostly, one is left with a new understanding of just how pivotal the writers of the black press were both in getting the process off the ground and in ensuring its success. Tygiel echoes Wiggins's articles, "Wendell Smith, the *Pittsburgh Courier Journal,* and the "Campaign to Include Blacks in Organized Baseball," which is located in Wiggins's *Glory Bound: Black Athletes in a White America.* Both writers show how these writers fostered the integration campaign, secured allies within the white press to help fuel the fires, arranged tryouts for black players with major league clubs, and roomed with Robinson for his first two years with Brooklyn so as to shield him from the countless racial attacks he suffered. *Baseball's Great Experiment* focuses more on the backdoor politics and business decisions that led to integration, while *The Jackie Robinson Reader* concentrates on Robinson's life and what he meant to that generation of black Americans. The other book about Robinson that scholars should consult is Joseph Dorinson and Joram Warmund's *Jackie Robinson: Race, Sport, and the American Dream,* in which several scholars, sportswriters, and friends capture just what kind of person Robinson was and how he developed into a legend in the 1950s.

Three other books about the integration of baseball are Larry Moffi's *Crossing the Line: Black Major Leaguers, 1947–1959* and *This Side of Cooperstown: An Oral History of Major League Baseball in the 1950s,* also edited by Moffi, and David Zang's *Fleet Walker's Divided Heart: The Life of Baseball's First Black Major Leaguer.* Moffi's *Crossing the Line* provides fairly detailed biographies on all the black players that put in major league service as part of the first wave of integration and includes quotes from those players about what their experiences were like. *This Side of Cooperstown* is more of a general baseball history meant to show the reader what the game was like in the 1950s. However, there is an excellent chapter on Vic Power, who played with the Philadelphia and Kansas City Athletics, the Cleveland Indians, the Minnesota Twins, the California Angels, and the Philadelphia Phillies as a utility player from 1954–1965. Power tells in his own words what it was like to be one of the first black ball players and to endure endless racial insults with very little recourse. Zang's book is a wonderfully written critical appraisal of Fleet Walker, which focuses on the hardships faced by the first wave of black major league ball players.

The formation and maintenance of black masculinity is a key issue that runs through most of the materials on black sports history, integration, or Negro baseball. The oral histories, in particular, provide fascinating insight into how black players had to practice a kind of schizophrenic masculinity that had distinctly public and private sides. In private, they could make their own rules and standards for being manly, but in a public sphere dominated by whites they had to display coolness under pressure, toughness and leadership on the field, and submissiveness off the field. One of the best essays to reflect the pain and confusion this masculine dilemma caused black athletes for most of this century is "Pain and Glory: Some

Thoughts on My Father," located in Don Belton's *Speak My Name: Black Men on Masculinity and the American Dream*. The essay is Quincy Troupe's reflection on his father, Quincy Troupe, Sr., a great baseball player in the old Negro leagues before integration. Troupe's essay is a moving depiction of what his father meant to him then and what he means to him as an adult now that he can look back over time and survey how his dad lived out his complicated masculinity. Troupe's piece is testimony to how Troupe, Sr., and hundreds of other black players served as important role models to black boys in the early part of this century. They were courageous athletes who gave the boys confidence that they could walk humbly but with great dignity and flair in a white world.

Two contemporary books that examine the relationship between sport and black masculinity are Geoffrey Canada's *Reaching Up for Manhood: Transforming the Lives of Boys in America* and Richard Majors's *Cool Pose: The Dilemmas of Black Manhood in America*. Canada, the president and CEO of the Rheedlen Centers for Children Families, shows how athletics, while providing some means of self-fulfillment and hope for black boys, actually helps to perpetuate some rather harmful conditions, including gender stress; misperceptions of the male role; and old, destructive male myths about building identities based on conquest and otherness. He offers several solutions for this situation, the foremost of which is strong father-son relationships where boys receive guidance from loving dads who should understand the proper place of sport in the lives of their sons. While Canada's focus is on the state of black youth in general, Majors focuses specifically on how young black males use sport as both an avenue to a better life and as an arena in which they foster their own identity that exists as a shield against the racism that they encounter every day in the United States. Majors shows exactly how this works, and his book features many interviews with black, male athletes whose stories corroborate his theories. Like Canada, Majors concludes that using athletics as a psychological defense against poverty, fatherlessness, lack of education, and white oppression is harming black youth by robbing them of the joys of athletics, steering them away from educational pursuits that could actually help them financially and emotionally, and allowing them to put off dealing with real problems such as racism and poverty in productive ways.

## RACISM AND SPORTS

What one notices in the writings of Canada, Majors, and other historians and sociologists writing on the subject of African-American participation in sports is that their books and articles usually filter down to one dominant idea: how racism has impacted black players. According to scholar John Hoberman, racism in the world of athletics has been perpetuated by fears of black superiority that are grounded in a longstanding but dubious tradition of racial biology. In *Darwin's Athletes: How Sport Has Damaged Black America and Preserved the Myth of Race*, Hoberman dedicates several chapters to explaining how the medical establishment has consistently manufactured and propagated the idea that blacks are a more physically gifted race than whites. He argues that "the persistence of 'southern' fixation on racial biology in modern Western culture is one of the least discussed aspects of our own engagement with the issue of race, and its focus on the alleged peculiarities of the black body has long provided the emotional and conceptual foundation for speculations about racial athletic aptitude" (Hoberman 1997, 148). White physicians have over the years insisted, among other things, that slavery toughened blacks in a way that would ensure performances that whites, not having gone through the same "developmental" experience, would never deliver. The myth of the power of black skin as being more resistant to sun and rain than white skin is another factor that has contributed to the myth of racial superiority, as is the notion that blacks have greater lung capacity and thus greater "vital capacity " for all physical activity than whites. Hoberman goes to great lengths to explain all of the medical "wisdom" that helped originally foster the idea that blacks were, more than anything else, physical human beings, while whites were more cerebral in nature. For the other side of the myth of racial biology is that blacks have so much physical ability only at the expense of cerebral capacity. Hoberman shows not only how the medical and academic communities have worked to preserve this troubling dichotomy, but how the media continually sustains it by portraying white athletes as "smart players," who display "bulldog leadership," "a tireless work ethic," and "great character," while describing black players in purely physical terms (Hoberman 1997, 49–50). The unfortunate problem with all of this is that many blacks and whites have accepted the idea that blacks are physically superior but mentally deficient people. The consequences have been that black achievement in the narrow realm of sports has received tremendous media attention, while little notice has been paid to more significant advancements made in intellectual arenas where success could lead so many more black people to better lives than sports ever could. Thus, Hoberman sees this biological myth as paralyzing black youth, trapping them within a very limiting myth of physical prowess. "Here too there is no point in speaking hypothetically, since African Americans' attachment to sport has been diverting interest away from the life of the mind for most of this century. The rejection of academic achievement as a source of clan pride is already rampant among black boys, whose preferred role models are rappers and athletes" (Hoberman 1997, 4).

While Hoberman focuses on the power of negative stereotypes on current black youths, several other authors have focused their attention on what higher education is doing to help black athletes compete on an equal playing field. One of the foremost scholars in this area is Richard Lapchick, head of the Institute for the Study of Sport at Northeastern University, whose books have both exposed racial discrimination on college campuses and called for specific reforms. Three of his books are particularly useful for understanding the progress that as been made by black athletes on college campuses in the last two decades. The first is *Broken Promises: Racism in American Sports*, which catalogues some of the most significant problems and reforms of the early 1980s. The second is *Five Minutes to Midnight: Race and Sport in the 1990s*, which discusses the progress that has been made in the late 1980s and early 1990s. The last is *Sport in Society: Equal Opportunity or Business as Usual?* in which Lapchick analyzes how schools are doing in terms of graduating minority athletes, hiring minority coaches and administrators, and achieving racial diversity and sensitivity on campus. Another scholar who has written on racism in college sports is Dana Brooks, whose *Racism in College Sports: The African-American Athlete's Experience* provides an in-depth analysis of the problems that black student athletes continue to face in college programs. He offers excellent chapters on the effects of academic reforms such as propositions 42 and 48 on black players, and his chapter on how much money black players make at some universities versus how many of those players graduate is eye opening. Finally, Kenneth Shropshire's *In Black and White: Race and Sport in America* functions as an exposé of racism in professional sports. Shropshire shows how minorities suffer discrimination, usually in very subtle ways, in terms of getting coaching jobs, front office positions, and endorsement deals. He is relentless in exposing media bias but is most concerned with showing the reader why there are so few blacks in on or off the field managerial positions in professional sports.

## NATIVE AMERICANS AND HISPANIC AMERICANS

Those interested in the historical significance of sports in Native-American culture should start with Joseph B. Oxendine's *American Indian Sports Heritage: Cultural Significance of American-Indian Sports History*. Oxendine divides his book into two sections, one on Indian sporting activities from the pre-Columbian era through the end of the nineteenth century and one dealing specifically with twentieth-century developments. In the first section, one of the best chapters is "Indian Concepts of Sport," in which the author explains how Indian sport developed within various tribal cultures as a means of fulfilling important functions of everyday life. According to Oxendine, most "games of skill and dexterity were rarely played by adults for mere amusement or fun. Rather, they were played for some purpose that was a matter of importance to the community." Indeed, "athletic contests started out as rites" (Oxendine 1995, 5). Most of the contests were part of religious rituals that were of the utmost importance to the tribes. Sports were a central component, for instance, in mortuary practices, attempts to heal the tribe or an individual of sickness, ceremonies designed to foster favorable climatic conditions, and celebrations of fertility rites. Oxendine describes how different tribes worked sport into these various rituals, going into impressive depth considering the paucity of primary resources on the subject. He concludes that "Indian sport was intimately related to ritual and ceremony. In addition to the pure joy involved in participation, sport was used as a means by which the Indians communicated with a higher spirit, seeking blessings on their individual or communal welfare" (Oxendine 1995, 33).

Oxendine's second section explains how Indian sport moved away from ritual and ceremony and toward competition for bragging rights within and between tribes in the late nineteenth and first half of the twentieth centuries. One of the most interesting chapters in this part of the book is "Sports Programs at the Carlisle and Haskell Schools," in which the author discusses the rise of Indian schools as part of a greater movement on the part of white Americans to move Indians off reservations and into mainstream society. Athletics were seen as being vital to this process, and sports, especially those such as baseball and football that were closely identified with the American experience, were staples of the Indian school curriculum. One of the most important functions of sport at these schools was not to bring Indians closer to white society, but to provide a space in which Indian solidarity was achieved by bringing Indians from antagonistic tribes together on one team united by the common goal of defeating their white opponents. As Oxendine explains, "The athletic teams at Indian schools provided a morale boost and rallying focus for the total Indian population. In addition, a cohesion among Indian tribes was affected by these viable successes" (Oxendine 1995, 202). Oxendine contends that this success and solidarity is part of why the federal government worked to close schools like Haskell and Carlisle. His chapter is quite entertaining and keeps the spirit of the two schools alive. Oxendine follows this discussion with a chapter that centers on Jim Thorpe as a symbol of the lasting significance of the Indian schools, a man who, armed with training he received at Carlisle, was able to give Native Americans a sense of pride because of his athletic success on the national scene. The final chapter of the book provides the reader with short biographical sketches of other great Indian athletes who made their mark on the American athletic stage from 1900–1930.

Another excellent source for those interested in Native-American sports history is Peter Nabokov's *Indian Running: Native American History and Tradition*, in which the author describes the importance of running to Indians from the late seventeenth century to the present. The book is both informative and entertaining, featuring the use of countless anecdotes and primary writings that give the work a vibrancy and color often absent in traditional academic works. Various chapters deal with uses of running by the Aztec, Hopi, Pueblo, and Inca Indians, kick-stick running, running as ritual, running in white competitions, and running as a religious exercise. One of the best chapters is "Window Rock to Ganado, 9 August," which explains how Navajo girls have used running as part of a puberty ceremony called Kinaalda. "During the four-day rite, when extended family and friends honor her first menstruation, the girl might run up to three times a day, just as dawn lightens the sky. Each run should be longer than the last, for how far she ultimately gets determines how long she will live" (Nabokov 1987, 139). The chapter, like others in the book, contains many of the songs and chants that went along with such running ceremonies. Articles that complement Nabokov's history include George Eisen's "Early European Attitudes Toward Native American Sports and Pastimes," located in Eisen and Wiggins's *Ethnicity and Sport in North American History and Culture*; T. Alcoze's "Sports as Training for Life: A Native Perspective," in Saul Ross and Leon Charette's *Persons, Minds and Bodies: A Transcultural Dialogue Amongst Physical Education, Philosophy and the Social Sciences*; and "Pre-Columbian Native American Sport," located in Allen Guttmann's *A Whole New Ball Game: An Interpretation of American Sports*.

Although little research has been done on Native Americans and sport, even less information is available on Americans of Hispanic descent. There are, however, some quality books and articles that shed some light on the subject. Peter Bjarkman's *Baseball with a Latin Beat: A History of the Latin American Game* is a fascinating work that provides a detailed discussion of the historical importance of baseball in Caribbean lands. In a similar manner, Ruck's *The Tropics of Baseball: Baseball in the Dominican Republic* shows what the game has meant to Dominicans throughout the twentieth century. The last chapter, "The City of Shortstops," is particularly helpful in understanding the importance of baseball heroes to the Dominican people. In *Baseball on the Border: A Tale of Two Laredos*, Alan Klein discusses the political and social ramifications of baseball on the Texas-Mexico border. The work is noteworthy because of Klein's ability to show how sport continues to be a highly political act, in this case one that has deep consequences for the identity and sense of well-being of large groups of Spanish-speaking peoples in both the United States and Mexico. Samuel Regalado's *Viva Baseball! Latin American Major Leaguers and Their Special Hunger* chronicles the struggles of Latin American professional baseball players in the United States from the late 1800s to the present. One of the leading scholars in the field is Joseph Arbena, whose *Annotated Bibliography of Latin American Sport: Pre-Conquest to the Present* and *Sport and Society in Latin America: Diffusion, Dependency and the Rise of Mass Culture* are both tremendous sources of information of the subject. Helpful articles include H. L. Pinzon's "Multicultural Issues in Health and Education Programs for Hispanic-Latino Populations in the United States," K. Sanders-Phillips's "The Ecology of Urban Violence: Its Relationship to Health Promotion Behaviors in Low-Income Black and Latino Communities," Regalado's "Baseball in the Barrios: The Scene in East Los Angeles Since World War II," and G. Pye's "The Ideology of Cuban Sport," all of which explain various aspects of the complex relationship between sport and Spanish-speaking people both in the United States and in surrounding countries. Hopefully, the continued rise of Cultural Studies, Latin American Studies, Chicano Studies, and like programs will mean the production of more works on the historical and current importance of sport to those whose ethnic origins place them under the wide umbrella of Hispanic Studies.

Those looking for information on media representations of minority athletes should consult Aaron Baker and Todd Boyd's *Out of Bounds: Sport, Media and the Politics of Identity,* which contains a section entitled "Sports, Race and Representation." It includes three excellent essays, including Kent Ono's "America's Apple Pie: Baseball, Japan-Bashing, and the Sexual Threat of Economic Miscegenation," John Sloop's "Mike Tyson and the Perils of Discursive Constraints: Boxing, Race, and the Assumption of Guilt," and Boyd's "The Day the Niggaz Took Over: Basketball, Commodity Culture, and the Black Masculinity."

Naturally, one should consult the online database SPORTSDiscus or any of several fine journals for latest information on the intersection of sport, race, and ethnicity. Journals that regularly carry articles in this area include *African-American Review, Black Scholar, Canadian Journal of Latin American and Caribbean Studies, Hispanic American Historical Review, Jewish Heritage, Jewish*

History, Journal of African-American Men, Journal of Afro-Latin American Studies and Literature, Journal of American Culture, Journal of American History, Journal of Black Studies, Journal of Ethnic History, Journal of Latin American Affairs, Journal of Latin American Jewish Studies, Journal of Latin American Studies, Journal of Sport and Social Issues, Modern Judaism, Race and Nation, Race and Society, and Sociology of Sport Journal.

## REFERENCES

### Books

Adelson, Bruce. Brushing Back Jim Crow: The Integration of Minor League Baseball in the American South. Charlottesville, VA: University of Virginia, 1999.

Arbena, Joseph. An Annotated Bibliography of Latin American Sport: Pre-Conquest to the Present. New York: Greenwood Press, 1989.

————. Latin American Sport: An Annotated Bibliography. Westport, CT: Greenwood Press, 1999.

————. Sport and Society in Latin America: Diffusion, Dependency and the Rise of Mass Culture. New York: Greenwood Press, 1988.

Ashe, Arthur. A Hard Road to Glory: A History of the African-American Athlete. New York: Amistad, 1993.

Baker, Aaron, and Todd Boyd. Out of Bounds: Sports, Media and the Politics of Identity. Bloomington, IN: University of Indiana Press, 1997.

Belton, Don, ed. Speak My Name: Black Men on Masculinity and the American Dream. Boston: Beacon Press, 1995.

Bjarkman, Peter C. Baseball with a Latin Beat: A History of the Latin American Game. Jefferson, NC: McFarland, 1994.

Bodner, Allen. When Boxing Was a Jewish Sport. Westport, CT: Praeger, 1997.

Brooks, Dana. Racism in College Athletics: The African-American Athlete's Experience. Morgantown, WV: Fitness Information Technologies, 1993.

Canada, Geoffrey. Reaching Up for Manhood: Transforming the Lives of Boys in America. Boston: Beacon Press, 1998.

Debono, Paul. The Indianapolis ABC's: History of a Premier Team in the Negro Leagues. Jefferson, NC: McFarland, 1994.

Dorinson, Joseph, and Joram Warmund, eds. Jackie Robinson: Race, Sports, and the American Dream. New York: M. E. Sharpe, 1998.

Echevarria, Roberto Gonzalez. The Pride of Havana: A History of Cuban Baseball. New York: Oxford University Press, 1999.

Edwards, Harry. The Struggle that Must Be. New York: Macmillan, 1980.

Eisen, George. Children and Play in the Holocaust: Games among the Shadows. Amhearst, MA: University of Massachusetts Press, 1990.

Eisen, George, and David Wiggins. Ethnicity and Sport in North American History and Culture. Westport, CT: Greenwood Press, 1994.

Entine, Jon. Taboo: Why Black Athletes Dominate Sports and Why We're Afraid to Talk about It. London: Public Affairs Press, 1998.

George, Nelson. Elevating the Game: Black Men and Basketball. New York: Harper Collins, 1992.

Guttmann, Allen. A Whole New Ball Game: An Interpretation of American Sports. Chapel Hill, NC: University of North Carolina Press, 1988.

Harrowitz, Nancy. *Jews and Gender: Responses to Otto Weininger*. Philadelphia, PA: Temple University Press, 1995.

Hoberman, John. *Darwin's Athletes: How Sport Has Damaged Black America and Preserved the Myth of Race*. Boston: Houghton-Mifflin, 1997.

Ibrahim, H. "Comparative Leisure and Recreation." *Journal of Physical Education, Recreation and Dance* 60 (1989): 33–64.

James, C. L. R. *Beyond a Boundary*. Durham, NC: Duke University Press, 1992.

Kelley, Brent. *Voices from the Negro Leagues: Conversations with 52 Baseball Standouts of the Period 1924–1960*. Jefferson, NC: McFarland, 1997.

Klein, Alan. *Baseball on the Border: A Tale of Two Laredos*. Princeton, NJ: Princeton University Press, 1997.

Lanctot, Neil. *Fair Dealing and Clean Playing: The Hilldale Club and the Development of Black Professional Baseball, 1910–1932*. Jefferson, NC: McFarland, 1994.

Lapchick, Richard. *Broken Promises: Racism in American Sports*. New York: St. Martin's, 1984.

———. *Five Minutes to Midnight: Race and Sport in the 1990s*. Lanham, MD: Madison Books, 1991.

———. *Sport in Society: Equal Opportunity or Business as Usual?* Thousand Oaks, CA: Sage Publications, 1996.

Levine, Peter. *Ellis Island to Ebbets Field: Sport and The American Jewish Experience*. New York: Oxford University Press, 1993.

MacClancy, Jeremy, ed. *Sport, Identity and Ethnicity*. Herndon, VA: Berg, 1996.

Majors, Richard. *Cool Pose: The Dilemmas of Black Manhood in America*. New York: Simon & Schuster, 1993.

Moffi, Larry, ed. *Crossing the Line: Black Major Leaguers, 1947–1959*. Jefferson, NC: McFarland, 1994.

———, ed. *This Side of Cooperstown: An Oral History of Major League Baseball in the 1950s*. Iowa City, IA: University of Iowa Press, 1996.

Nabokov, Peter. *Indian Running: Native American History and Tradition*. Santa Fe, NM: Ancient City Press, 1987.

Overmyer, James. *Queen of the Negro Leagues: Effa Manley and the Newark Eagles*. Lanham, MD: Scarecrow Press, 1998.

Oxendine, Joseph B. *American Indian Sports Heritage: Cultural Significance of American-Indian Sports History*. Lincoln, NE: University of Nebraska Press, 1995.

Peterson, Robert. *Only the Ball Was White: A History of Legendary Black Players on All-Black Professional Teams*. New York: Oxford University Press, 1992.

Pinzon, H. L., and Perez, M. A. "Multicultual Issues in Health Education Programs for Hispanic-Latino Populations in the United States." *Journal of Health Education* 28 (1997): 314–316.

Pye, G. "The Ideology of Cuban Sport." *Journal of Sports History* 13 (1986): 119–127.

Regalado, Samuel. "Baseball in the Barrios: The Scene in East Los Angeles since World War II." *Baseball History* 1 (1986): 47–59.

———. *Viva Baseball! Latin American Major Leaguers and Their Special Hunger*. Urbana, IL: University of Illinois Press, 1998.

Reisler, Jim. *Black Writers/Black Baseball: An Anthology of Articles from Black Sportwriters Who Covered the Negro Leagues*. Jefferson, NC: McFarland, 1994.

Riess, Steven. *Sports and the American Jew*. Syracuse, NY: Syracuse University Press, 1997.

Ross, Saul, and Leon Charette, eds. *Persons, Minds, and Bodies: A Transcultural Dialogue amongst Physical Education, Philosophy and the Social Sciences*. North York, ON: University Press of Canada, 1988.

Ruck, Robert. *Sandlot Seasons: Sport in Black Pittsburgh.* Urbana, IL: University of Illinois Press, 1993.

———. *The Tropics of Baseball: Baseball in the Dominican Republic.* New York: Carroll & Graf, 1993.

Sailes, Gary. *African Americans in Sport: Contemporary Sport.* New Brunswick, NJ: Transaction Publishers, 1998.

Sanders-Phillips, K. "The Ecology of Urban Violence: Its Relationship to Health Promotion Behaviors in Low-Income Black and Latino Communities." *American Journal of Health Promotion* 10 (1996): 308–317.

Shropshire, Kenneth. *In Black and White: Race and Sport in America.* New York: New York University Press, 1996.

Solomon, Eric. "Counter Ethnicity and the Jewish-Black Baseball Novel: The Cases of Jerome Charyn and Jay Neugeboren." *Modern Fiction Studies* 33 (1987): 49–63.

Tygiel, Jules. *Baseball's Great Experiment: Jackie Robinson and His Legacy.* New York: Oxford University Press, 1997.

———. *The Jackie Robinson Reader.* New York: Dutton, 1997.

Wiggins, David K. *Glory Bound: Black Athletes in a White America.* Syracuse, NY: Syracuse University Press, 1997.

Zang, David. *Fleet Walker's Divided Heart: The Life of Baseball's First Black Major Leaguer.* Lincoln, NE: University of Nebraska Press, 1997.

## Journals

*African-American Review* (Terre Haute, IN)

*Black Scholar* (Oakland, CA)

*Canadian Journal of Latin American and Caribbean Studies* (London, Ontario, Canada)

*Hispanic American Historical Review* (Miami, FL)

*Jewish Heritage* (Los Angeles, CA)

*Jewish History* (Waltham, MA)

*Journal of African-American Men* (New Brunswick, NJ)

*Journal of Afro-Latin American Studies and Literature* (Los Angeles, CA)

*Journal of American Culture* (Bowling Green, OH)

*Journal of American History* (Bloomington, IN)

*Journal of Black Studies* (Thousand Oaks, CA)

*Journal of Ethnic History* (Atlanta, GA)

*Journal of Latin American Affairs* (Washington, D.C.)

*Journal of Latin American Jewish Studies* (Ann Arbor, MI)

*Journal of Latin American Studies* (New York, NY)

*Journal of Sport and Social Issues* (Thousand Oaks, CA)

*Modern Judaism* (Binghamton, NY)

*Race and Nation* (Las Vegas, NV)

*Race and Society* (Stamford, CT)

*Sociology of Sport Journal* (Champaign, IL)

# 5

# Sport and Gender

There are no doubt some scholars who would not include a separate chapter on gender in a work such as this one. After all, gender issues play into every discipline. Any discussion of the economics, history, philosophy, psychology, or legal aspects of sport would have to include particular interests and concerns of both men and women. Still, America's abiding interest in gender issues runs deep. Relationships between men and women are the most likely fodder for television sit-coms, talk shows, and dramas. News programs rarely take a night off from the front lines of the gender war, routinely feeding viewers a steady diet of domestic abuse, sex discrimination, funding to combat prostate cancer, or other gender-related stories that are part of our seemingly never-ending fascination with the subject. The growth of Women's Studies and Cultural Studies programs at most colleges and universities reflects that even the stodgy gatekeepers of the academy's curriculum are grudgingly beginning to recognize the legitimacy of the study of gender. Certainly for the last two decades, gender has been one of the most sensitive areas in the sports world. Title IX and the insurgence of women's athletics has for a number of reasons kept gender issues on the front pages of sports sections across the nation. How will Title IX affect men's athletic opportunities? How will its implementation affect the profit margins of university programs? If women can try out for men's teams, why can men not try out for women's squads? Is it legal to have single gender professional sports leagues such as the Women's National Basketball Association? What constitutes equal opportunity when it comes to sports? How is the success of women's sports changing the way we think about gender? These are only a few of the questions whose answers are being played out on our athletic fields and in our newspapers, courtrooms, and classrooms every day. Discussions of these questions can now be undergirded by a number of scholarly books that examine gender and sport from a variety of different angles. For instance, redefinitions of what makes a literary "classic" in the field of English

Studies have led to the recognition of creative works that eloquently and insightfully speak to the unique importance of sport in the lives of men and women. Women's Studies scholars, sociologists, historians, and other academics have begun to define women's sports history, to critically comment on how contemporary gender issues in athletics might affect sports for men and women in the future, to articulate feminist approaches to sport, to examine the relationship between masculinity and sport in different periods, and to analyze how sport is viewed by gays and lesbians. This chapter will profile some of the major works written on these and other subjects in the last two decades, focusing on how the study of gender has enhanced our understanding of the function and importance of sport in Western society.

## THE HISTORY OF WOMEN'S SPORT

Though there are several quality books that examine the historical development of sport in various cultures, it is only in the last few years that a handful of scholars have begun to provide us with glimpses of the sundry roles sport has played in women's lives over the years. Allen Guttmann's *Women's Sports: A History* provides the reader with two excellent discussions. The second, which makes up the last two chapters of the book, examines current controversies within women's sports. Most of the work, however, is dedicated to showing how women of the past used sport to entertain themselves, to win the respect of men, to promote female solidarity, to maintain a healthy lifestyle, and to train themselves for greater economic or political functions. As one peruses Guttmann's well-researched, highly readable work, one cannot help but understand that, even though women have been denied athletic access for most of recorded history, sport has always been central to women's existence. For instance, the chapter entitled "From Egyptians to Etruscans" shows that hunting was an important activity for some women in various ancient societies and that sports were seen as a way of keeping fit and having fun. "Archeological finds from ancient Egypt suggest that men and women of every social stratum, from mighty dynastic rulers to the humblest peasants, mingled freely in their daily lives without the strict segregation by gender which kept respectable Greek women sequestered in their homes" (Guttmann 1991, 9). This mingling included sport. Guttmann has chapters on the role of female athletes in Sparta, Medieval and Renaissance Europe, Victorian England, and Europe during the modern period. His chapter on "Women's Sports and Totalitarian Regimes" is particularly interesting, confronting the reader with the ironic reality that many totalitarian regimes, while restricting women's sporting privileges at the grass-roots level, actually have been instrumental in establishing women's athletic programs. Though these programs were designed solely to bring greater glory to the state, the performance of female athletes from such countries as East Germany, the Soviet Union, and China showed the world just how good women's sports can be.

Those interested in the role of sport in the lives of colonial American women should consult Scott Crawford's article "Pioneering Women: Recreational and

Sporting Opportunities in a Remote Colonial Setting" or Nancy Struna's "Good Wives and Gardiners, Spinners and Fearless Riders: Middle and Upper-Rank Women in the Early American Sporting Culture." Both are located in *From "Fair Sex" to Feminism: Sport and the Socialization of Women in the Industrial and Post-Industrial Eras*, edited by J. A. Mangan and Roberta Park. Since Crawford writes about poor women on the frontier and Struna about society women, the articles nicely complement each other and give the reader a fairly broad view of women's sporting experience during the period. While the loose, fluid rules of frontier life allowed women to engage freely in competitive sport with each other and with men, the more rigid rules that governed polite society forced women to develop their own sporting pastimes and rules within the accepted domestic sphere. Struna writes that this was important because it marked the "initial defining of a woman's sporting sphere, a process which was and would continue to be simultaneously radical and conservative. The women's sporting sphere was radical in so far as it was innovative: new networks and activities engaged in by women in a new domain, private leisure. But the sport of women by women also retained traditional elements . . . it did not destroy the centuries-old position of women as spectators in the public domain of male competition" (Mangan and Park 1987, 249–250).

Like most of the works on women's sports history, the authors in Mangan and Park's anthology are mostly dedicated to analyzing the period between 1880 and 1930. Several of the essays discuss the role of newly founded physical education programs on women's athletic development around the turn of the century. Kathleen McCrone's "Play Up! Play Up! And Play the Game! Sport at the Late Victorian Girls' Public School" provides insight into the types of sports in which British girls competed, the Victorian ideal of favoring participation, moral development, and health concerns over competition, and the importance of sport to the girls' sense of identity and well-being. Sheila Fletcher's "The Making and Breaking of a Female Tradition: Women's Physical Education in England, 1880–1980" extends McCrone's analysis by detailing the transformation of British physical education from a moralizing tool to a competitive training ground for modern life. Roberta Park's "Sport, Gender and Society in a Translantic Victorian Perspective" looks at the important role that athletic programs at women's colleges in America played in expanding the opportunities for female athletes. She concludes that "higher education and athletic sport were both instrumental in the transformation of American concepts regarding the feminine ideal in the late 1800s" (Mangan and Park 1987, 76). Quality programs at Oberlin, Vassar, and Wellesley became models for other schools, and their influence over the young ladies of the wealthy class soon led, along with other factors, to the development of the "new woman," the strong, independent, well-educated and athletic Gibson girl of the 1890s. Donald Mrozek's "The Amazon and the American 'Lady': Sexual Fears of Women as Athletes" charts the development of these new women and shows that much of the resistance to women's athletics in the early twentieth century can be traced to male fears of the Gibson girl and her sisters, most of whom were seen as "Amazons," masculine women that threatened to usurp coveted male roles. "It was bad enough if a man could not manage to 'behave like

a man'; but his dilemma worsened if women refused to behave 'like women' "
(Man and Park 1987, 285).

The rest of the essays in Mangan and Park's book deal with the view that the
medical profession of the late nineteenth century had of women and how that view
impacted women's sport. Of particular interest is an essay by Carroll and Charles
Rosenberg entitled "The Female Animal: Medical and Biological Views of Women
and Their Role in Nineteenth-Century America." The authors contend that men,
increasingly uncomfortable with women's expanding role in the work force and in
society in general, reacted by trying to use medical science to stem the rising
"threat" of female athleticism. While consenting that some physical activity was
morally and physically beneficial, most doctors concluded that "woman was the
product and prisoner of her reproductive system," and that she should engage only
in light physical activity designed to prepare her for the rigors of childbirth
(Mangan and Park 1987, 15). As the Rosenbergs conclude, "It was inevitable that
many men would seek in domestic peace and constancy a sense of continuity and
security so difficult to find elsewhere in society. They would expect—at the very
least—their wives, their daughters, their family relationships generally to remain
unaltered. When their female dependants seemed ill-disposed to do so, such men
responded with a harshness sanctioned increasingly by the new gods of science"
(Mangan and Park 1987, 30). The article's bibliography, like that of Paul
Atkinson's "The Feminist Critique: Physical Education and the Medicalization of
Women's Education," is quite extensive and provides several leads for anyone
interested in the impact of the medical world on women's athletics.

Several other works shed light on the role of sport in the lives of turn-of-the-
century women in both Britain and America. Reet Howell's *Her Story in Sport: A
Historical Anthology of Women in Sports* contains over twenty quality articles that
focus on American and Canadian women's sporting experience. Three articles are
particularly informative. The first is Mary Lou Squires's "Sport and the Cult of
True Womanhood: A Paradox at the Turn of the Century," in which the author
argues that women's sport reflected the conflict and tension between what men
demanded of women and what some women wanted to do to change what it meant
to be a woman. Sport remained for the most part an activity that was relatively
noncompetitive. Bicycling and recreational tennis or golf were popular in part
because they were viewed by men as being in keeping with traditional female roles.
They were seen as activities that were morally and physically beneficial for young
women destined to be domestic caretakers of a great nation. On the other hand,
colleges were also stressing the value of competitive sport as a means of enjoyment
and preparation for being stronger and more independent than the previous
generation of women. As Squires writes, "College women of the 1890–1910 era
served as a socio-cultural bridge between the past and the future. The restraints of
the past were reflected in the dress and playing rules of the new sports activities:
whereas, the freedom of the future was reflected in competitive sports participation" (Howell 1982, 105).

In "The Effect of Changing Attitudes Toward Sexual Morality upon the
Promotion of Physical Education for Women in Nineteenth Century America,"

Patricia Vertinsky shows that the use of sport as a moral tool was also a double-edged sword for women. Physicians, educators, and others that valued traditional female roles sought to use rigid physical education and activities programs to teach girls how to have respect for their bodies and to use exercise as a means of promoting a self-disciplined lifestyle free of the dissipating influences of premarital sexual activity. On the other hand, early feminists, particularly those from Elizabeth Cady Stanton to Margaret Sanger who fought for birth control, abortion rights, and overall control by women of their bodies, promoted competitive athletics as a way of teaching women to assert control over their own lives (Howell 1982, 170–171). For an overall summation of the factors that caused athletic women to play a dual role in which they inched toward independence while still placating the demands of the past, one should consult Howell's "Generalization on Women and Sport," though the author perhaps too optimistically concludes that "by the end of the nineteenth century the American sportswoman had arrived" (Howell 1982, 138).

Kathleen E. McCrone's *Playing the Game: Sport and the Emancipation of English Women: 1870–1914* provides an interesting and accurate depiction of the effect of the Victorian women's movement on sports for women in Britain around 1900. Focusing her discussion on how early English feminists combated traditional conceptions of femininity, concerns over sexual immorality, religious dogma, the politics of the medical field, and educational discrimination, McCrone lets the reader feel how difficult it was for women to make even modest gains in athletic participation, and her passionate, descriptive writing drives home the significance of the women who advanced the cause of women's athletics at that time. She concludes that "the emergence of the Victorian sportswoman was part of the same broad movement of social transformation that saw middle-class women contradict received definitions of their sex's true nature and challenge a system that restricted opportunities for development by becoming university students, medical doctors, and municipal voters. In its own way sport was just as significant to the ultimate goals of feminism" (McCrone 1988, 289).

Two other excellent books are Kathy Peiss's *Cheap Amusements: Working Women and Leisure in Turn-of-the-Century New York* and Ruth Sparhawk's *American Women in Sport, 1887-1987: A 100-Year Chronology*. Peiss provides an eye-opening account of why working women played, how they played, and what their leisure activities, including sports, meant to them. Her work provides a nice contrast with that of other scholars who mostly deal with middle- and upper-class sporting initiatives. Sparhawk gives us a concise version of women's sporting experience in America. Her book contains four sections, each reflecting what the author sees as four distinct periods in the development of women's athletics. These include the "Pre-organization Era" from 1887 to 1916, in which women struggled to fight athletic discrimination without much institutional help; the "Organizational Era" from 1917 to 1956, in which women formed several organizations that helped them gain athletic opportunity; the "Competitive Period from 1957 to 1971, in which women made significant, but limited strides in competitive athletics; and the "Title IX Era," in which women have made significant progress toward equality with men. Sparhawk's book is particularly good for those researchers interested in getting a broad understanding of the key events that defined each period.

There are three books that would be useful for anyone seeking a greater understanding of the development of women's sport since World War II. The most comprehensive is Mary Jo Festle's *Playing Nice: Politics and Apologies in Women's Sports*. Festle gives the reader an in-depth look at key developments that have influenced women's athletics in every decade since the Great War. Her explanations for the reasons behind roadblocks to women's sports in the 1950s, the reasons for the slight changes of the 1960s, and the political and social reasons behind the adoption of Title IX in the 1970s are particularly convincing. She demonstrates her keen understanding both about how Title IX has affected sports in America for women and about how poor enforcement procedures and the conservative politics of the Reagan 1980s delayed the impact of the ruling. For those wondering why it took so long for Title IX to have major effects on the sports scene, Festle's work is the book to consult. Guttman's *Women's Sports: A History* is a good companion piece to Festle's book, which ends with the end of Reagan's presidency. Guttman concentrates his discussion on what he sees as the three key issues facing women in the 1990s. These include how women might redefine sporting goals based on new-found resources and public approbation, how women will balance the desire to be a good athlete and still be feminine, and how women will combat the supposed patriarchal tendency to devalue female athletes by objectifying them as sexual, erotic performers. Finally, Howell's *Her Story in Sport: A Historical Anthology of Women in Sports* contains an entire section called "On the Road to Equality," which analyzes the events that led to the cataclysmic events of the 1970s and which thoroughly explains Title IX. Any researcher interested in reading the actual language of the amendment, while also getting a critique of each part of it, will want to access this chapter.

There are several other notable works that illuminate the heretofore darkened recesses of women's sports history. Mary Boutilier's *The Sporting Woman* is a good primer for those interested in a general synopsis of the history of the female athlete in America. Janet Woolum's *Outstanding Women Athletes: Who They Are and How They Influenced Sports in America* is a good resource because, though its discussion is quite general, the book provides short biographies on many female athletes with whom most people would be unfamiliar. Many of these athletes were crucial to the development of women's sports in the nineteenth and twentieth centuries. Susan Johnson's *When Women Played Hardball* and Lois Browne's *Girls of Summer: The Real Story of the All-American Girls Professional Baseball League* are excellent accounts of women's professional baseball at mid-century that provide us with an entertaining and informative view of what it was like to be a professional female athlete in the 1940s and 1950s. Finally, Kim Marie Vaz's *Black Women in America* contains some fascinating articles that aid our understanding of the history of the black female athlete in America. Of particular interest is an article entitled "Performing Their Visions: African-American Women in Sport," which uses articles from black newspapers to chronicle the experience of black women athletes between the world wars. The article is also significant because it challenges and contradicts Arthur Ashe's assumption that until recently "most black women spent very little time engaged in competitive, organized sport" (Vaz 1995, 294).

## SPORT AND MEN'S LIVES

Works on women's sports history are not the only gender-based studies of sport to appear in the last few years. Some scholars have turned their attention to what sport has meant to men over the last century and a half. Academics have been particularly interested in why men have embraced sport so tenaciously as something central to their identity. As with the women's histories, works on men tend to focus on the decades of the late nineteenth and early twentieth centuries as a crucial time in which sport's historical link with masculinity became intensified through institutionalization. Michael Kimmel argues in *Manhood in America: A Cultural History* that sport became so important to men at the turn of the century because it functioned as a way of coping with a burgeoning industrialized economy. For the average, "common" man who existed as a number on an assembly line, sport was an arena in which the individual, physical act still mattered, a place where a man could prove his own worth apart from the confining, dehumanizing structure of work. By contrast, the sons of the elite, who would be the captains of industry and leaders of the political machine that would sustain big business, saw sport as a preparatory training ground for their future roles. Sports would teach these boys about aggressiveness, winning, and endurance. They would learn how to overcome adversity, deal with pain, and conquer enemies. Kimmel points out that it was this upper-class drive to ready its sons for competition in the modern world that led to the development of the boys' dime novels of Horatio Alger and Gilbert Patton, which functioned as instructional manuals on how to be a manly man. "In boys' fiction heroes like Frank Merriwell embodied the strenuous ideal found in sports, excelling at every sport, always winning the big game for Yale even when the chips were down without any compromise of his manly or moral virtues" (Kimmel 1991, 142).

Kimmel agrees with scholar Todd Crosset that men's fear of feminization, which was rampant at the end of the century, also contributed to men's use of sport as a vehicle by which to differentiate themselves from women and current conceptions of femininity. Crosset's "Masculinity, Sexuality, and the Development of Early Modern Sport" appears in Michael Messner and Don Sabo's *Sport, Men, and the Gender Order: Critical Feminist Perspectives* and is a valuable piece for understanding the basic social, political, economic, and technological reasons for male fears of women at the time. Crosset also shows how men used sport as a means of establishing their superiority over women and over any men who could not succeed in the valued masculine space of the athletic field. Crosset argues that "sport served as one of the social institutions of the late nineteenth century that played a critical role in socializing men to define themselves as biologically superior to women. Sport as we know it originated during this period" (Messner and Sabo 1990, 51). Football, which rose to popularity on college campuses in the early 1900s, is perhaps the best example of how men used sport as a power structure that featured male heroes and female admirers. Michael Oriard's *Reading Football: How the Popular Press Created an American Spectacle* is the book to read for anyone who wants to understand how men's gender concerns fueled the popularity of football in America.

Messner and Sabo's collection also includes several essays by authors who argue that the development of sport was closely linked to moral concerns. For instance, Crosset's essay includes a section on how the nineteenth-century medical community's belief that masturbation led to lazy, maladjusted boys caused educators to insist that boys engage in sports as a way of relieving stress and learning self-discipline. It was hoped that this would stop the harmful sexual practice and aid in the production of morally fit young men. As Crosset writes, "Many believed that sport was an activity that regenerated the body and made for more efficient use of sperm" (Messner and Sabo 1990, 52). Kimmel's "Baseball and the Reconstitution of American Masculinity" is another essay that confirms Crosset's assertion. Kimmel argues that baseball rose in stature during the period in part because it was seen as the perfect remedy for the moral morass in which young boys were allegedly ensnared. According to Kimmel, baseball was a sport that was seen as being physically demanding, intellectually challenging, and morally uplifting. This combination was especially important because it satisfied the demands of several important groups. Educators liked the cerebral aspect of the game, while masculinists loved the physical rigor displayed on the diamond. The moral aspect most appealed to those who supported the Muscular Christianity movement. Most groups applauded the idea that all three elements together could foster quite a manly environment. "American Courage, Confidence, Combativeness; American Dash, Discipline, Determination; American Energy, Eagerness, Enthusiasm; American Pluck, Persistence, Performance; American Spirit, Sagacity, Success; American Vim, Vigor, Virility. Such values were not only American but Christian, replacing the desiccated values of a dissolute life with the healthy vitality of American manhood" (Messner and Sabo 1990, 61).

Other quality books that establish the reasons behind male sport participation around 1900 include Timothy Chandler and John Nauright's *Making Men: Rugby and Masculine Identity*, Wanda Wakefield's *Playing to Win: Sport and the American Military, 1989–1945*, and J. A. Mangan and James Walvin's *Manliness and Morality: Middle-Class Masculinity in Britain and America, 1800–1940*. Sport's popularity with men at the time, as it is today, was closely tied to notions of superiority. Men used sport as a way to convince themselves not only that they were superior to women or to other men, but that groups to which they belonged were superior to other groups. Chandler and Nauright's book is one of the best for clarifying how men of different European cultures used sport, in this case rugby, to assert national, ethnic, religious or class identity, and superiority. By contrast, Wakefield proves that, at least in America, sport gained popularity because the military saw it as one of the best ways to train troops that were tough, sharp, disciplined, and battle ready. Wakefield has a wonderful, entertaining chapter on

Theodore Roosevelt's introduction of sport into military training in the late 1800s as the Americans prepared for the Spanish-American War. She continues to trace the development of sport as military training exercise through the end of World War II. Finally, Mangan and Walvin's collection of essays gives the most comprehensive treatment of the period in the sense that each essay tackles a different underlying cause of male sports involvement. Topics include technological, medical, familial, religious, educational, military, sociological, and psychological explanations for the rise of sport in men's lives at the turn of the century. Any gender scholar would find Peter Stearns's "Men, Boys and Anger in American Society, 1860–1940" particularly interesting because the author clearly demonstrates how male rage, so much feared and despised in the contemporary period, was once a cornerstone on which boys' identities were built.

Some scholars have directed their research toward an examination of what men get from sports today. In *Men's Lives,* Kimmel and Messner conclude that boys are attracted to sport because it allows them to attain a sense of self-worth and public approbation while still maintaining distance from society. Boys have only to excel on the field in order to cement affirming connection with society. They do not have to risk sharing secrets, getting angry, or going through any of the painful ups and downs of normal relationship building. "The rule-bound, hierarchical world of sport offers boys an attractive means of establishing an emotionally distant (and thus safe) connection with others" (Messner 1992, 174). The theme of distance is also the subject of Ava Rose and James Friedman's "Television Sport as Mas(s)culine Cult of Distraction," one of several tremendous essays that appears in Aaron Baker and Todd Boyd's *Out of Bounds: Sports, Media, and the Politics of Identity.* The authors suggest that many boys and men watch and play sports for one main reason: to escape a complex reality where it is increasingly more difficult to understand what it means to be a man by retreating into a sports world where traditional male roles, characteristics, and qualities are maintained. In the sports world, men are virile, heroic, and in control. They dominate while women cheer. A man may work for a woman, and he may be bossed around at home. But when he turns on the football game, he can still see men being praised, even idolized for their exploits: "The masculine universe constructed by television sports seems to work to reinforce this patriarchal power structure" (Baker and Boyd 1997, 12).

*Out of Bounds* also contains a section devoted exclusively to analyzing how minority men use sport. The best of the essays is Todd Boyd's "The Day the Niggaz Took Over: Basketball, Commodity Culture, and Black Masculinity." Boyd argues that young black men look at sport as having two distinct functions. First, it provides an arena of opportunity that is highly valued by whites, highly visible, and highly accessible for black athletes. While Boyd would consent that the odds are stacked against any aspiring professional athlete, he makes the point that the sports world offers a ray of hope to young black men who do not see a future in any of the traditional avenues to success. While this is clearly a problem, it is an important reason why black athletes play. Perhaps a bigger reason is the fact that sport gives black men the forum to act out against racism. After all, they are on stage and have a captive audience in front of which to attack it. Boyd offers Charles Barkley as an example of a contemporary player who continually uses his status to make powerful social and political statements. Such statements can be verbal or physical, such as wearing distinctive clothing (the black arm band) or engaging in a certain style of play. According to Boyd, the main point is that "African American males, through sports, can create a space of resistance and free expression that announces a relative notion of empowerment, while at the same time acknowledging the racial and class hierarchies that still dominate sports and society as a whole" (Baker and Boyd 1997, 133). Other helpful sources on the subject of why minority youth play sport include Don Sabo and Russ Runfola's *Jock: Sport and Male Identity*, Robert Ruck's *Sandlot Seasons: Sport in Black Pittsburgh,* Peter Levine's *Ellis Island to Ebbet's Field: Sport and the American Jewish Experience,* Peter Nabokov's *Indian Running: Native American History and Tradition,* and Alan Klein's *Baseball on the Border: A Tale of Two Laredos.*

Klein's *Little Big Men: Bodybuilding Subculture and Gender Construction* is another comprehensive book that explains why some boys and men are so attached to sport. Klein asserts that many male athletes compete in sports such as bodybuilding because the emphasis on a muscular, hypermasculine appearance helps them compensate for general feelings of inferiority on a number of fronts. For men who feel insecure in their masculinity either because they feel feminine, are in prison, have lost a job or suffer from a lack of education, muscles and physical prowess are often used to make up for feelings of inadequacy. "Hypermasculinity is an exaggeration of male traits, be they psychological or physical. Psychologists see hypermasculinity as rooted in confusion and/or insecurity. The more insecure the man, the greater his tendency to exaggerate, to proclaim his maleness" (Klein 1993, 221). According to Klein, the most crucial aspect of athletics for men, especially when it comes to ultra physical sports like bodybuilding, is that it allows men to prove that they are not feminine, that they are tough, rugged, and everything a man should be. "Whether one looks at hypermasculinity through a psychological or sociological lens, there is embedded in it a view of radical opposition to all things feminine" (Klein 1993, 221). Of course, Klein falls in line with sociologists like Messner, Sabo, and Kimmel when he asserts that one of the biggest reasons for sports participation among heterosexual males is that it proves to the world that they are not gay. According to Klein, "The athlete's identity is, in our society, never in question." Klein is quick to point out that because of this athletics also affords boys a chance to display homosocial behavior that would be otherwise impermissible. "Rather than behave in all aspects as male conventions dictate, it is the athlete who, because he is the highest embodiment of masculinity in our society, is allowed to behave in certain ways that other men are not. Only athletes and women are allowed to touch and hug each other in our culture. Athletes are only allowed to do this because their masculinity is beyond doubt" (Klein 1993, 219). Anyone interested in how insecurity, homophobia, and sexism help to explain boys' sporting experiences should take the time to read Klein's study.

## SPORT AND HEALTHY CONCEPTIONS OF GENDER

Most scholars agree that the result of male use of sport to fashion identity has been mixed at best. While most agree that sport can be a vital activity for promoting physical health, fostering mental and emotional well-being, building self-esteem, and teaching life skills such as leadership, cooperation and self-confidence, every scholar seems to see the current relationship between men and sport as being at least somewhat dysfunctional. In Harry Brod's *The Making of Masculinities: The New Men's Studies*, for example, Messner points out that sport has become such a dominant factor in determining what it means to be male that boys who are not athletically inclined are often stigmatized. Not only do these boys suffer through adolescence, but the boys who excel at sports and come to build their identity around athletic success are often forced into a process of continual conquest and winning in order to retain their feelings of self-worth. Naturally, this is impossible. As Messner writes, "It means that the young man must continually prove, achieve, and then reprove, and reachieve his status. As a result, many young athletes learn to seek and need the appreciation of the crowd to feel that they are worthy human beings" (Brod 1987, 199). In *Jock: Sport and Male Identity*, Sabo and Runfola dedicate several chapters to explaining how this type of selfish, narcissistic, unstable identity based on defeating 'others' harms a man's ability to develop relationships with other men, who he sees as competitors; with women, who he sees as a mere component to his masculine self; or with himself, who must always be falling short of the impossible demands of his rigid masculine code. Of course, Klein's *Little Big Men: Bodybuilding Subculture and Gender Construction* is instrumental in showing how this type of masculine sporting experience fosters homophobia, sexism, and insecurity in men.

The natural question is how sport can be transformed into a healthier activity for both men and women. Some scholars, mostly feminist theorists, have offered suggestions about how we can retheorize sport in order to develop a more affirming athletic system. In *Feminism and Sporting Bodies: Essays on Theory and Practice*, Ann Hall describes the functions of a good theory and then discusses how feminist theorists have attempted to fulfill these roles within their works on sport. According to Hall, a usable theory needs to explain the historical relationship between gender and sport, to discuss how people have resisted inequalities inherent within this relationship, to analyze how dominant groups have manipulated the relationship to reinforce inequalities as a way of keeping power, and to devise ideas for change that will be mutually beneficial for both genders. Hall argues that feminist theorists have taken the lead in trying to develop a "new history" whose goal is "to reconstruct the lives of real women who have had to negotiate a place for themselves within the repressive social relations of their time" (Hall 1996, 37). She analyzes the works of several feminist historians who, in undertaking this process, have also chronicled patterns of women's resistance and patriarchal counterresistance. In a final chapter, Hall offers several suggestions about how to change sport for the better, all of which stem from her belief that all reforms must be initiated with the idea of achieving equity as opposed to equality. For Hall this seems to mean that there must be an emphasis not just on getting more girls and women involved in sport, a process that results in mere numerical equality, but on engendering permanent institutional change so that the way we conduct and construct sport is systemically altered. She includes a case study profiling feminist praxis in Canada to define what she views as the appropriate method of putting a good theory into practice. Her book is also an excellent bibliographic source for feminist writings on sport.

Another highly readable, informative book is Mary Boutilier's *The Sporting Woman*. Boutilier offers chapters in women's sports history, psychological dimensions of women's sporting experience, the impact of the family unit on the female athlete, and the social context of women's play. Still, her book is most valuable because of its clear explanations of the four main feminist theoretical approaches to sport. Boutilier describes the goals of liberal feminism, radical feminism, Marxist feminism, and socialist feminism and provides a thoughtful discussion on the positives and negatives of each school of thought. Liberal feminism is praised as being the most influential face of the movement, one that the author credits with working within established male bureaucracies to foster much of the athletic opportunity that young women have today. "They believe that the correction of past abuses and oversights is possible from within the present structure. For a liberal feminist there is no reason to suspect the aims, motives, or commitment of those who control the media, the business community, and the sporting establishment. They are simply responsive to market demands" (Boutilier 1983, 245). With the explosion of women's sports participation and popularity over the last decade, it seems that liberal feminists were right. However, Boutilier still criticizes liberal feminism for being too closely tied with the current patriarchal system of sports and for seeing women as a homogeneous group instead of a diverse body whose interests often conflict. Marxist feminist thought hinges on the idea that until women control the majority of economic resources within a society, they will never gain sporting equality because the teams, the arenas, and all of the businesses that support the immense sporting monolith in most countries will always be operated by men who can not be trusted to serve women. Radical feminists insist that women must have full control over female sporting experience if it is to be truly valuable for girls and women. All male, hierarchical structures that support the current athletic system must be torn down and rebuilt in terms consistent with feminist ideals. Boutilier gives credence to some of the Marxist and radical feminist critiques of sport but is quick to expose the overly theoretical, often impractical nature of each. Boutilier then spends several pages explaining the merits of the socialist feminist model, which she sees as attempting to take the best elements of each of the other theories and blend them into a cogent theory that can work within established systems so as to reinvent the entire athletic enterprise in a way that will help men and women of all races, classes, religions, and ethnic groups.

In *Sporting Females: Critical Issues in the History and Sociology of Women's Sport*, Jennifer Hargreaves provides a similar discussion on the merits and shortcomings of the four types of feminist approaches. Like Boutilier, she favors a holistic approach that utilizes the best ideas of liberal, Marxist, and radical feminism. Such an approach would be dedicated to "a co-operative venture with men for qualitatively new models in which differences between the sexes would be unimportant" (Hargreaves 1994, 40). Hargreaves's work contains two unique chapters that are must reads for gender studies researchers. The first, "Nature and Culture: Introducing Victorian and Edwardian Sports for Women," diagnoses the prime historical dilemma for women athletes as being society's general belief in the "false" dichotomy of nature and culture. According to the author, men have always been identified with factors of human-produced culture, including work, war, politics, and sport, for which they were well suited because of their biological make-up. Women, on the other hand, have been identified with nature, especially the natural functions of childbirth, motherhood, and domestic nurturing. Hargreaves makes a powerful case that this binary classification "is the essence of biological reductionism. Biological ideas were used specifically to construct social ideas about gender and to defend inequalities between men and women in sports" (Hargreaves 1994, 43). In another chapter, "Femininity or Masculinity," she shows how the stereotypes that have emanated from the nature-culture classification have evolved into current notions of masculinity and femininity that remain problematic for women in sport. The last chapter, "Gender Relations and Power," analyzes how these stereotypes are continually reinforced by media coverage. Like Boutilier's book, this work is an excellent source for understanding women's sporting experience from 1850–2000 and is a tremendous bibliographic resource.

Although usually working from a profeminist perspective, some theorists have begun to develop theories of masculinity, focusing on how men use athletics to develop identity and how this affects the world of sport. As Don Sabo and Michael Messner comment in *Sex, Violence and Power in Sports: Rethinking Masculinity*, a profeminist approach to men and sport "is critical in that it sees men and masculinity as a problem. It recognizes that there is something rotten in the ways that manhood has been defined" (Sabo and Messner 1994, 194). Sabo and Messner wrote this book on the heels of *Sport, Men and the Gender Order: Critical Feminist Perspectives*, and both works promote the idea that gender has no ultimate source. It is, instead, a complex societal construction based on interlocking systems of social codes, political patronage, and economic control that allows men to develop identities whose core is the oppression of women and gay men. Sport is simply a tool used by men to keep this hegemonic masculinity intact. Though the work of Messner and Sabo is important, it is decidedly one dimensional. It leaves out the experiences of hundreds of thousands of men who enjoy sport without any thoughts of domination or conquest. Likewise, the thoroughly postmodern theoretical presuppositions of the authors do not reflect the views of any male athlete or scholar who might believe in transcendent values regarding gender and the process of identity formation. A book that better covers the wide range of values and theoretical positions of the diverse men's movement is Kenneth Clatterbaugh's *Contemporary Perspectives on Masculinity: Men, Women and Politics in Modern Society*. Clatterbaugh does not focus specifically on sport, but he does give accurate, relatively objective accounts of the different facts of the men's movement from which the reader can see how various men view gender issues. Profeminist men, Christian men, gay men, black men, mythopoetic men, and masculinists are all represented, and it does not take too much imagination on the part of the reader to see that men within all of these groups would have very different views about how sport should be altered to better serve the development of strong boys. Still, for those looking for suggestions from profeminist men's studies scholars on what to actually do to improve sports, one might consult the works of Messner and Sabo, or the earlier works of Sabo and Runfola, all of which propose alternatives to current sporting practice. Hopefully, as men's studies emerges as an important discipline, more works, both theoretical and anecdotal, will be written that focus on the complex role of sport in men's lives as we enter a new century in which men are as likely as women to encounter gender discrimination.

## SPORT AND CONTEMPORARY GENDER ISSUES

Sports theorists writing on gender have cast their attention on several contemporary issues that currently effect the way men and women play. One of the most important is the effect that Title IX continues to have on high school and college sports. Howell's *Her Story in Sport: A Historical Anthology of Women in Sport* contains a section entitled "On the Road to Equality," which features the full text of the Title IX amendment and a complete discussion of what each part of the law was intended to do. Another helpful book is Frank Aquila's *Title IX: Implications for Education of Women*. Though a bit outdated, the book is still quite useful because Aquila explains the Title IX regulations, answers frequently asked questions about the ruling, and provides an entire chapter of hypothetical situations to which the law would apply. Those looking for models of implementation of Title IX might try Teresa Isaac's *Sex Equity in Sports Leadership: Implementing the Game Plan in Your Community*. Isaacs is nothing if not thorough, and her book takes the reader through a detailed process on how to use local schools, parents, businesses and media to establish and maintain sports equity programs. The author alerts the reader about how to deal with many of the usual challenges to Title IX and the pitfalls that often accompany an implementation program. Finally, Ken Dyer's *Sportwomen Toward 2000: A Celebration* is an affirming work that gives an international perspective on Title IX while providing descriptions of several programs in European countries and Australia that are their equivalents to Title IX. Dyer's focus is on what countries around the world are doing to help girls and women enjoy sports.

In *Challenging the Men: The Social Biology of Female Sporting Achievement*, Dyer confronts another key gender issue in the world of athletics, the effects on performance of physiological differences between men and women. His conclusion is that while there are significant differences in terms of height, muscle mass, arm and leg length, weight, and overall strength that generally favor men, these variations can be minimized by training procedures that include good coaching, top-notch facilities, and proper psychological motivation. Dyer includes evidence to back up his claim that as women get better training and more encouragement from media, family, peers, schools, churches, and governments, they are gradually narrowing the performance gap with men. As he says of biological factors, "The evidence which leads us to question their importance and their inevitability comes from a number of directions. First, there are marked and continuing improvements in women's performance in a wide range of sports. Second, there are demonstrable effects of entirely social factors on performance. Third, the physical and psychological differences between the sexes that have been considered normal in western societies have changed in recent years and look like they will change even more in the future" (Dyer 1982, 91). Dyer's work is confirmed in the more recent work of Christine Wells. In *Women, Sports and Performance,* Wells admits that there are physiological differences between the sexes but insists that "currently, performance ratios between the sexes are less than 10% and are continuing to decline. This implies that sex role expectations and environmental factors, such as opportunities for participation at an early age and the availability of expert coaching, play a major role in sex differences in sport performance" (Wells 1991, 49). Both Wells and Dyer successfully debunk several myths that have hampered women over the last two centuries. They conclude, for example, that menstruation is not a handicap to training or performance, women's sex organs are no more vulnerable than men's organs, hard training will not hurt a woman's body, pregnancy is not deleterious to athletic performance, and women neither peak athletically before men, nor do they get injured more than men. Other interesting works that expand on these arguments include Adrienne Blue's *Grace under Pressure: The Emergence of Women in Sport* and Greta Cohen's *Women in Sport: Issues and Controversies,* both of which warn women not to let competition with male performance distract them from other important athletic goals such as personal fulfillment and pure enjoyment.

Another huge issue is the effect that the media has on the way we perceive athletes, particularly female competitors. The best book on this subject is Pamela Creedon's *Women, Media and Sport: Challenging Gender Values.* Creedon includes several essays that analyze the way television, radio, magazines, and newspapers have covered female athletes over the last fifty years. For the most part, women have been neglected by the media. What images do exist however, speak to the fact that women have undergone, as Creedon would say, a kind of "symbolic annihilation" at the hands of the media, which has portrayed women as vulnerable, fragile, passive, weak, timid creatures that are, above all, sexual beings: "Specific findings from this research literature suggest that visual production techniques, language, terminology and commentary applied to women's sport are selectively imposed by the media to provide a highly stereotypical feminized view—one that tends to sexualize, commodify, trivialize and devalue women's sporting accomplishments" (Creedon 1994, 36). Overall, Creedon includes thirteen quality essays in the book that deal with such topics as representation of minority women athletes in the media, how women can influence the media as journalists and as spectators, and what women's sports must do to gain more favorable media coverage. Creedon remains quite positive about this proposition, citing the fact that women's sports draw bigger audiences every year. This is proven by Gina Daddario in *Women's Sport and Spectacle: Gendered Television Coverage of the Olympic Games.* Daddario smoothly shows how, over the last three to four Olympiads, women have gradually come to be the driving force behind media coverage. Primarily this is true for two reasons. The first is that women make up the lion's share of the audience, and the television networks in particular must be sensitive to their viewing preferences. The second is that the addition of more women's sports has meant more women winning medals in exciting competitions. While Daddario stops short of saying that this type of female influence on the media will permeate other sports coverage, her argument makes it clear that images of women in the media are changing for the better.

Interestingly, little attention has been given to men's issues such as how Title IX will affect opportunities for men and boys in athletics, how media images of men affect aspiring male athletes, or how evolving notions of what it means to be masculine are changing the way men and boys are forced to compete. Two quality books that take men's issues seriously, however, are Kevin Quirk's *Not Now Honey, I'm Watching the Game: What to Do When Sports Come Between You and Your Mate* and David Savran's *Taking It Like a Man: White Masculinity, Masochism, and Contemporary American Culture.* A glance at the title causes one to assume that Quirk's book will be light-hearted and jovial. Quirk actually provides us with a serious look at what male obsession with sports can mean to a marriage. He also examines the effects of sports addiction of fathers on sons. Quirk includes several anecdotes and offers a number of techniques that men and women have used to overcome this dilemma in their marriage. It is particularly important for fathers who have children because it shows them how to put sport into the proper perspective for their sons and daughters. Savran's book is a fascinating, well-researched work that asserts that boys and men, particularly white males, are being marginalized today in an effort to accommodate the demands of women. In a compelling analysis that covers the domestic arena, the workplace, government, education, the media, and sport, among others, Savran shows how men and boys are shortchanged by a society which incorrectly, but willingly, sees them as privileged victimizers and oppressors. Savran's work is daring and hopefully will be a signal to other men's studies scholars not to be shy about producing male positive scholarship that actively asserts that boys and men are suffering discrimination on a number of fronts. Certainly, scholars should have no qualms about speaking out against such treatment.

Gay and Lesbian issues have only recently been addressed by scholars of sport. There are, however, some quality works on the subject. One is Helen Lenskyj's *Out of Bounds: Women, Sport and Sexuality* in which the author warns women in no uncertain terms that an important part of breaking down harmful stereotypes of what it means to be feminine is combating discrimination against lesbians within the women's sporting community. She contends that "homophobia has created rifts between women in sport, as in the women's movement at large" (Lenskyj 1986, 107) and offers several examples of how that has hurt women's athletics in the past. Mainly, she concentrates on explaining the difficulty that women have had in the past because their muscular frames, aggressive attitudes, and athletic postures have been associated with lesbianism, which has and continues to be an albatross for most women. Lenskyj spends most of her book advancing the controversial argument that this does indeed happen and will not stop until lesbianism is accepted as normal. On the men's side, Brian Pronger contends that gay men use sport as a means of protesting hegemonic masculinity. In *The Arena of Masculinity: Sports, Homosexuality, and the Meaning of Sex,* Pronger gives several examples of how sporting success, once considered to be the ultimate indicator that a man could not be gay, is now one of the prime ways that gay men seek to legitimize their various styles of masculinity. His book is unique and, at times, shocking, but it is the best on the market for the scholar who wants to understand gay mens' historical and present relationship with athletics. Anyone searching for candid stories of what it is like to be a gay athlete will want to read Dan Woog's *Jocks: True Stories of America's Gay Male Athletes*, a book that features candid portrayals of actual high school, college, and professional gay players.

While many books that deal with gender and sport focus on one or two main topics, there are two works that are defined primarily by their comprehensive nature, which makes them the perfect works through which to examine contemporary issues in gender and sport. They are Greta Cohen's *Women in Sport: Issues and Controversies* and Susan Birrell and Cheryl Cote's *Women, Sport and Culture.* Cohen's book contains essays on a number of interesting topics, including how gender-specific toys influence athletic preference, athletic opportunities for women with disabilities, and special challenges faced by women of color. Birrell and Cote's work is by far the most complete treatment of gender and sport that currently exists. It contains chapters on the history of gender and sport, theoretical approaches to the subject, exploitation of athletes based on gender, gender issues faced by coaches and administrators, the impact of Title IX, homophobia, gender stereotypes and their effect on sport, the effect of the media on gender issues in athletics, and special problems faced by men and women in sport throughout history. Anyone looking for a textbook on the subject should start their search with this work, all of whose essays are meticulously researched and clearly written. Finally, Michael Dierdorff's *Atalanta: An Anthology of Creative Work Celebrating Women's Athletic Achievements*, Donald Hall's *Fathers Playing Catch with Sons*, and Ronald Rapoport's *A Kind of Grace: A Treasury of Sportswriting by Women* provide a less academic way to understand what sport means to men and women. Each of these works contains poems, stories, and essays written by men and women about the importance of athletics in their lives, and thus all provide a human touch to a subject that is increasingly coming under academic scrutiny.

Finally, with gender being such a hot topic in today's academic world, there is no shortage of journals that carry the most recent research on the relationship between gender and sport. Some of the journals that regularly include such articles include *American Woman, Gender and Society, Journal of African-American Men, Journal of American Culture, Journal of American History, Journal of Men's Studies, Journal of Popular Culture, Journal of Sport and Social Issues, Journal of Women's Health, Journal of Women's History, Off Our Backs: A Woman's*

*News Journal, Sociology of Sport Journal, Woman Studies, Women's Sport and Fitness,* and *Women's Studies Quarterly.*

## REFERENCES

### Books

Aquila, Frank. *Title IX: Implications for Education of Women.* Bloomington, IN: Phi Delta Kappa Education Report, 1981.

Baker, Aaron, and Todd Boyd, eds. *Out of Bounds: Sports, Media, and the Politics of Identity.* Bloomington, IN: Indiana University Press, 1997.

Bandy, Susan, and Anne Darden. *Crossing the Boundaries: An International Anthology of Women's Experiences in Sport.* Champaign, IL: Human Kinetics Books, 1999.

Benedict, Jeff. *Public Heroes, Private Felons: Athletes and Crimes Against Women.* Boston: Northeastern University Press, 1997.

Berlage, Gai Ingham. *Women in Baseball: The Forgotten Story.* New York: Praeger, 1994.

Birrell, Susan, and Cheryl Cote, eds. *Women, Sport and Culture.* Champaign, IL: Human Kinetics Books, 1994.

Blue, Adrienne. *Grace under Pressure: The Emergence of Women in Sport.* Toronto, ON: Sedgewick and Jackson, 1987.

Boutilier, Mary. *The Sporting Woman.* Champaign, IL: Human Kinetics Books, 1983.

Brod, Harry, ed. *The Making of Masculinities: The New Men's Studies.* Boston: Allyn and Unwin, 1987.

Browne, Lois. *Girls of Summer: The Real Story of the All-American Girls Professional Baseball League.* Toronto, ON: Harper Collins, 1993.

Burstyn, Varda. *The Rites of Men: Manhood, Politics, and the Culture of Sport.* Toronto, ON: University of Toronto Press, 1999.

Cayleff, Susan. *Babe: The Life and Legend of Babe Didrickson Zaharias.* Urbana, IL: University of Illinois Press, 1995.

Chandler, Timothy, and John Nauright. *Making Men: Rugby and Masculine Identity.* London: F. Cass, 1996.

Clatterbaugh, Kenneth. *Contemporary Perspectives on Masculinity: Men, Women and Politics in Modern Society.* Boulder, CO: Westview Press, 1997.

Cohen, Greta, ed. *Women in Sport: Issues and Controversies.* Newbury Park, CA: Sage Publications, 1995.

Creedon, Pamela J., ed. *Women, Media and Sport: Challenging Gender Values.* Newbury Park, CA: Sage, 1994.

Costa, Margaret D. *Women and Sport: Interdisciplinary Perspectives.* Champaign, IL: Human Kinetics Books, 1994.

Daddario, Gina. *Women's Sport and Spectacle: Gendered Television Coverage of the Olympic Games.* Westport, CT: Praeger, 1998.

Denfield, Rene. *Kill the Body, the Head Will Fall: A Closer Look at Women.* New York: Warner Books, 1997.

Dierdorff, Michael. *Atalanta: An Anthology of Creative Work Celebrating Women's Athletic Achievements.* Los Angeles: Papier-Mache Press, 1984.

Drollinger, Karen. *Grace and Glory: Profiles of Faith and Courage in the Lives of Top Women Athletes.* Dallas, TX: Word Publications, 1990.

Dyer, Kenneth F. *Challenging the Men: The Social Biology of Female Sporting Achievement.* St. Lucia: University of Queensland Press, 1982.

————. *Sportswomen Towards 2000: A Celebration.* Richmond, Australia: Hyde Park Press, 1989.

Etue, Elizabeth. *On the Edge: Women Making Hockey History.* Toronto, ON: Second Story Press, 1996.

Festle, Mary Jo. *Playing Nice: Politics and Apologies in Women's Sports.* New York: Columbia University Press, 1996.

Garber, Mary. *Interviews with Mary Garber.* Washington, D.C.: The Foundation, 1991.

Green, Tina Sloan. *Black Women in Sport.* Reston, VA: American Alliance for Health, Physical Education, Recreation and Dance, 1981.

Guttmann, Allen. *Women's Sports: A History.* New York: Columbia University Press, 1991.

Hall, Ann. *Feminism and Sporting Bodies: Essays on Theory and Practice.* Champaign, IL: Human Kinetics Books, 1996.

Hargreaves, Jennifer. *Sporting Females: Critical Issues in the History and Sociology of Women's Sport.* New York: Routledge, 1994.

Hilkey, Judy. *Character Is Capital: Success Manuals and Manliness in Gilded Age America.* Chapel Hill, NC: University of North Carolina, 1997.

Howell, Reet, ed. *Her Story in Sport: A Historical Anthology of Women in Sports.* West Point, NY: Leisure Press, 1982.

Isaac, Teresa Ann. *Sex Equity in Sports Leadership: Implementing the Game Plan in Your Community.* Lexington, KY: Eastern Kentucky State University Press, 1989.

Johnson, Susan. *When Women Played Hardball.* Seattle, WA: Seal Press, 1994.

Kimmel, Michael. *Manhood in America: A Cultural History.* New York: Free Press, 1991.

Kimmel, Michael, and Michael Messner. *Men's Lives.* Boston: Allyn and Bacon, 1992.

Klein, Alan. *Baseball on the Border: A Tale of Two Laredos.* Princeton, NJ: Princeton University Press, 1997.

————. *Little Big Men: Bodybuilding Subculture and Gender Construction.* Albany, NY: State University of New York Press, 1993.

Lenskyj, Helen. *Out of Bounds: Women, Sport and Sexuality.* Toronto, ON: Women's Press, 1986.

Levine, Peter. *Ellis Island to Ebbets Field: Sport and the American Jewish Experience.* New York: Oxford University Press, 1993.

Macy, Sue. *Winning Ways: A Photographic History of Women in Sports.* New York: Henry Holt, 1996.

Madden, W. C. *The Women of the All-Girls Professional Baseball League: A Biographical Dictionary.* Jefferson, NC: McFarland, 1997.

Mangan, J. A., and Roberta Park. *From "Fair Sex" to Feminism: Sport and the Socialization of Women in the Industrial and Post-Industrial Eras.* London: F. Cass, 1987.

Mangan, J. A., and James Walvin. *Manliness and Morality: Middle-Class Masculinity in Britain and America, 1800–1940.* New York: St. Martin's, 1987.

Marlene, Adrian. *Sports Women.* New York: Karger, 1987.

Martz, Sandra, ed. *More Golden Apples: A Further Celebration of Women and Sport.* Manhattan Beach, CA: Papier-Mache Press, 1986.

McCrone, Kathleen. *Playing the Game: Sport and the Physical Emancipation of English Women, 1870–1914.* Lexington, KY: University of Kentucky Press, 1988.

Messner, Michael. *Power at Play: Sports and the Problem of Masculinity.* Boston: Beacon Press, 1992.

————. *Sex, Violence and Power in Sports: Rethinking Masculinity.* Freedom, CA: Crossing Press, 1994.

Messner, Michael, and Donald Sabo, eds. *Sport, Men and the Gender Order: Critical Feminist Perspectives.* Champaign, IL: Human Kinetics Books, 1990.

Nabokov, Peter. *Indian Running: Native American History and Tradition.* Santa Fe, NM: Ancient City Press, 1987.

Nelson, Mariah Burton. *Are We Winning, Yet? How Women Are Changing Sports and Sports Are Changing Women.* New York: Random House, 1991.

———. *The Stronger Women Get, The More Men Love Football: Sexism and the American Culture of Sport.* New York: Harcourt, Brace, 1994.

Oriard, Michael. *Reading Football: How the Popular Press Created an American Spectacle.* Chapel Hill, NC: University of North Carolina Press, 1993.

Peiss, Kathy. *Cheap Amusements: Working Women and Leisure in Turn-of-the-Century New York.* Philadelphia, PA: Temple University Press, 1986.

Postow, Betsy C. *Women, Philosophy and Sport: A Collection of New Essays.* Metuchen, NJ: Scarecrow Press, 1983.

Powe-Allread, Alexandra, and Michelle Powe, eds. *The Quiet Storm: A Celebration of Women in Sport.* Indianapolis, IN: Master's Press, 1997.

Pronger, Brian. *The Arena of Masculinity: Sports, Homosexuality, and the Meaning of Sex.* New York: St. Martin's, 1991.

Quirk, Kevin. *Not Now Honey, I'm Watching the Game: What to Do When Sports Come Between You and Your Mate.* New York: Fireside Books, 1997.

Rapoport, Ronald. *A Kind of Grace: A Treasury of Sportswriting by Women.* Berkeley, CA: Zenobia Press, 1994.

Remley, Mary. *Women in Sport: An Annotated Bibliography and Resource Guide, 1900–1990.* Boston: G. K. Hall, 1991.

Reynolds, Bill. *Glory Days: On Sports, Men, and Dreams that Don't Die: A Memoir.* New York: St. Martin's, 1998.

Robinson, Laura. *Crossing the Line: Violence and Sexual Assault in Canada's National Sport.* Toronto, ON: McClelland & Stewart, 1998.

Ruck, Robert. *Sandlot Seasons: Sport in Black Pittsburgh.* Urbana, IL: University of Illinois Press, 1993.

Ryan, Joan. *Little Girls in Pretty Boxes: The Making and Breaking of Elite Gymnasts and Figure Skaters.* New York: Doubleday, 1995.

Sabo, Donald, and David Frederick Gordon, eds. *Men's Health and Illness: Gender, Power and the Body.* Thousand Oaks, CA: Sage Publications, 1995.

Sabo, Donald, and Michael Messner. *Sex, Violence and Power in Sports: Rethinking Masculinity.* Freedom, CA: Crossing Press, 1994.

Sabo, Donald, and Russ Runfola, eds. *Jock: Sport and Male Identity.* Englewood Cliffs, NJ: PrenticeHall, 1980.

Salter, David. *Crashing the Old Boys' Network: The Tragedies and Triumphs of Girls and Women in Sports.* Westport, CT: Praeger Publishers, 1996.

Sandoz, Joli, and Joby Winans, eds. *Whatever It Takes: Women on Women's Sport.* New York: Farrar, Strauss & Giroux, 1999.

Sault, Nicole. *Many Mirrors: Body Image and Social Relations.* New Brunswick, NJ: Rutgers University Press, 1994.

Savran, David. *Taking It Like a Man: White Masculinity, Masochism, and Contemporary American Culture.* Princeton, NJ: Princeton University Press, 1998.

Shangold, Mona M. *Women and Exercise: Physiology and Sports Medicine.* Philadelphia, PA: F. A. Davis, 1994.

Sherrow, Victoria. *Encyclopedia of Women's Sport.* Santa Barbara, CA: ABC-Clio, 1996.

Sparhawk, Ruth. *American Women in Sport, 1887–1987: A 100-Year Chronology.* Metuchen, NJ: Scarecrow Press, 1989.

Spierenburg, Pieter, ed. *Men and Violence: Gender, Honor, and Rituals in Modern Europe and America.* Columbus, OH: Ohio State University Press, 1998.

Stanley, Gregory Kent. *The Rise and Fall of the Sportswoman: Women's Health, Fitness and Athletics, 1860–1940.* New York: P. Lang, 1995.

Thorngren, Connie M. *Games Yet to Be Played: Equity in Sport Leadership.* Newton, MA: Women's Educational Equity Act Publishing Center, 1994.

Tricard, Louise. *American Women's Track and Field: A History, 1895 Through 1980.* Jefferson, NC: McFarland, 1996.

Vaz, Kim Marie, ed. *Black Women in America.* Newbury Park, CA: Sage Publications, 1995.

Wakefield, Wanda Ellen. *Playing to Win: Sports and the American Military, 1898–1945.* Albany, NY: State University of New York Press, 1997.

Wells, Christine L. *Women, Sports and Performance: A Physiological Perspective.* Champaign, IL: Human Kinetics Books, 1991.

Woog, Daniel. *Jocks: True Stories of American Gay Athletes.* Los Angeles: Alyson Books, 1998.

Woolum, Janet. *Outstanding Women Athletes: Who They Are and How They Influenced Sports in America.* Phoenix, AZ: Oryx Press, 1992.

## Journals

*American Woman* (New York, NY)
*Gender and Society* (Santa Barbara, CA)
*Journal of African-American Men* (New Brunswick, NJ)
*Journal of American Culture* (Bowling Green, OH)
*Journal of American History* (Bloomington, IN)
*Journal of Men's Studies* (Harriman, TN)
*Journal of Popular Culture* (Bowling Green, OH)
*Journal of Sport and Social Issues* (Thousand Oaks, CA)
*Journal of Women's Health* (Larchmont, NY)
*Journal of Women's History* (Bloomington, IN)
*Off Our Backs: A Women's News Journal* (Washington, D.C.)
*Sociology of Sport Journal* (Champaign, IL)
*Woman Studies* (North York, Ontario)
*Women's Sport and Fitness* (Boulder, CO)
*Women's Studies Quarterly* (New York, NY)

# 6

# Sport and Literature

Great authors who have written about sport include Roger Angel, Pat Conroy, Robert Coover, Frank DeFord, Don DeLillo, David James Duncan, Frederick Exley, Richard Ford, Peter Gent, Eric Greenberg, Donald Hall, William Kennedy, W. P. Kinsella, Maxine Kumin, Peter Lefcourt, Jason Miller, Joyce Carol Oates, Wilfred Sheed, and John Updike. The list could be much longer. These are only a few of the many authors whose works represent the maturation of the sports narrative. The process has been a long one, over a century in the making. It started in the late nineteenth century with sports books for adolescent boys; writers such as Owen Johnson, Gilbert Patten, and John R. Tunis became household names in the early decades of the twentieth century, especially Patten, whose chronicles of Yale's all-American boy, Frank Merriwell, became staple reading for two generations of young readers. These men wrote alongside Jack London, Ernest Hemingway, and other more canonical writers whose works on sports have been long revered by the academy. Naturally, the relationship between art and sports has hardly been limited to novels, drama, or poetry. Artists as diverse as Andy Warhol and Leroy Nieman have used sport as the basis for artistic endeavor, with Nieman relying on the genre of sport art almost exclusively at one point during his brilliant career. Recently, architectural firms have brought a new aesthetic to sports, transforming the usual stadiums into nostalgic cathedrals such as The Ballpark in Arlington, Texas, or Oriole Park at Camden Yards in Baltimore, Maryland.

In many ways sport is art, so the link between athletics and the traditional arts should not be surprising. The number of novels, other fiction and nonfiction works, and volumes of poetry written in the last twenty years is impressive. This chapter will profile some of these works that, in the eyes of some scholars, have lent legitimacy to the idea that sports literature is a genre worthy of critical study. The recognition of this legitimacy has resulted in several fascinating critical inquiries from scholars such as Michael Oriard, Christian Messenger, and Wiley Umphlett, whose books have blazed a new intellectual path through the jungles of academe. The works of these and other critics will also be discussed. In addition, various bibliographic works and periodicals that routinely contain works of sports fiction, nonfiction, or critical articles will be mentioned.

## CRITICAL WORKS ON THE LITERATURE OF SPORTS

The number of critical works on sports literature is small, but the books that do exist are quite good. Perhaps the first major work along these lines was Christian Messenger's *Sport and the Spirit of Play in American Fiction: Hawthorne to Faulkner*. Written in 1981, the book is still a classic in the field and is indispensable reading for anyone who wants to understand how sport and cultural conceptions of play have impacted American writers from the early 1880s through World War II. The book should be read in preparation for Messenger's *Sport and the Spirit of Play in Contemporary Fiction*, which features a thorough examination of how writers such as Coover, Exley, Ken Kesey, John Knowles, Jenifer Levin, John Irving, Norman Mailer, and a host of others have used sport to comment on politics, social issues, and everyday life in America. Messenger's method is fascinating because he combines the best of the traditional approach of a historical critic, who uses the historical context of each text to examine that text, with the cutting edge technique of a cultural critic, who looks at the texts to shed light on how people used sport or games at the time the book was written and how this usage allows us to better understand life at the time. It is this double-edged quality that truly makes the work stand out.

Like Messenger, Michael Oriard's work usually involves a dichotomous historical and cultural approach. Written in 1982, *Dreaming of Heroes: American Sports Fiction, 1868–1980* is perhaps the best book for anyone hoping to understand the factors behind the rise of sports literature and its subsequent periods of evolution. Oriard warns the reader that his "focus is primarily thematic rather than historical" but admits that "the organization of my chapters is roughly chronological nonetheless" (Oriard 1982, 22). Indeed, Oriard steers his reader through the history of the American sports novel, addressing the juvenile novel that initially dominated the genre; the works of adult novelists such as Jack London, Ring Lardner, and Zane Grey who kept Americans entertained before World War II; the serious and often morose fiction of the 1950s and 1960s; and the permissive, experimental and sometimes raunchy works of the late 1960s to the 1980s. In doing so, Oriard lives up to his thematic intentions, covering what he sees as basic American concerns. Nostalgia, idealism, innocence, youth, aging, urbanization and the loss of the pastoral ideal, sexual mores and gender roles, morality and mortality, fears of war, crises of meaning, and our never-ending quest for significance are all covered in this engaging, highly entertaining book that is a must for students of American culture.

In 1991, Oriard released his comprehensive *Sporting with the Gods: The Rhetoric of Play and Game in American Culture*. Part of the *Cambridge Studies in American Culture* series, the book explores how we can use American concepts of play to better understand American culture at any given point in the history of the country. The heart of the book rests on the notion that "the popular rhetoric of 'play' and 'games', in other words, is profoundly ideological, yet it is not at all straightforward. The function of rhetoric is to persuade. Sometimes the sporting rhetoric overtly resists the prevailing political power of the day; sometimes it endorses, promotes and enhances it; sometimes it seems to resist but tacitly augments the power arrangements through its evasions" (Oriard 1991, xvi). Oriard examines the function of athletic banter and customs in several American epochs, including the nineteenth-century western frontier; the antebellum South; gambling venues, such as the nineteenth-century horse-racing track; the boardrooms and political meetings of the early twentieth century; and the countercultural movements of the 1960s. It is fascinating study for both cultural historians and linguists.

Several other scholars have used distinct literary methods to comment on the literature of sport. For instance, in *Ground Rules: Baseball and Myth*, Deeanne Westbrook uses archetypal theories of myth to explain the power of baseball literature. Relying on the theoretical works of Friedrich Nietzsche, Paul de Man, Paul Ricoeur, Jacques Lacan, and Eric Gould, Westbrook advances the following notion: "Whether fragmentary or coherent, dangerous or life enhancing, primitive or modern, evolutionary or constant, myth, the narrative that discloses a sacred world, abides and exerts its influence, for good or ill, in our world" (Westbrook 1996, 8). Baseball and baseball literature can be understood by analyzing the myths that it reinforces and subverts. Westbrook's work is compelling and has great breadth. She discusses August Wilson's "Fences" and its reliance on the art of bricolage, the concept that an artist pieces together a work of art by relying on the bits and pieces of past myths and theories. By diagnosing these seemingly stray pieces and how the author uses them to piece together a work of art, we can not only understand our past, but our present as well. She applies other concepts of myth criticism to Mark Harris's *Bang the Drum Slowly*, W. P. Kinsella's *The Iowa Baseball Confederacy*, Eric Greenberg's *The Celebrant*, Bernard Malamud's *The Natural*, and other novels in a convincing and thoughtful analysis.

By contrast, James Moore and Natalie Vermilyea's *Earnest Thayer's "Casey at the Bat": Background and Characters of Baseball's Most Famous Poem* is a vastly entertaining and informative biographical study of the classic sports poem, penned by Thayer in 1888. The authors discuss Thayer's family background, his political and economic positions when he wrote the poem, his career as a Harvard student and journalist, the reception of the poem, and its use by other authors throughout history. There can be little doubt that Thayer's subject was the California League team from Stockton, and Moore and Vermilyea reveal the circumstances in which Thayer wrote the poem (the fear of a pennant slipping away) and provide insight into personalities such as Cooney, Flynn, Barrows, and Jimmy Blake that populate the poem. Controversy still rages over the man on whom Casey was based. Was it the legendary Mike "King" Kelly, a Boston slugger who had been playing winter ball in San Francisco when Thayer was in California? Was it Sam Winslow, Thayer's childhood friend and captain of the 1885 Harvard nine? Or was it a variety of other figures that crossed Thayer's path, who later in life made their unique cases that they were, in fact, the goat of the poem? It is worth the read to find out the answers to these questions. Anyone who wants to see how biographical criticism can be effectively practiced and how a piece of literature can be used as a political tool by individuals and institutions should take a look at this book.

In *Laurel & Thorn: The Athlete in American Literature*, Robert J. Higgs uses sports literature to trace America's preoccupation with masculine ideals. His analysis is deeply rooted in the traditions of the Ancients, relying on comparisons between literary portrayals of athletes over the course of the twentieth century and the legendary figures of Apollo, Dionysus, and Adonis. Higgs concludes that "this study has shown that in the view of American authors, most publicly applauded representations of beauty, prowess, or versatility are suspect if not fraudulent. In twentieth century literature there is the unmistakable conviction that strength and beauty, the athletic ideal, must forever be sought but can never be defined or achieved" (Higgs 1981, 181). This view is born out in the stereotypical portrayals of Apollonian heroes. Such caricatures include "the dumb athlete, the leisure-class gentleman, the southern knight, the WASP ideal, the muscular Christian, the booster alumnus, the Hollywood model, and the brave new man" (Higgs 1981, 181). Of course, there is also derision of the Dionysian hero, whose wild, mindless sensuality is often his downfall. The faults of the Adonis are also exposed, but as with the Apollonian and Dionysian models, no alternative masculine code is offered, only the insistence that sports literature reveals the ever-present dilemma of manhood: one must participate in all of the rituals, traditions, and models that are sure to undermine one's happiness and health.

Another fascinating work from a literary standpoint is Timothy Morris's *Making the Team: The Cultural Work of Baseball Fiction*. Morris's boldest statement is that the search for authorial intent, while laudable, is hardly necessary when interpreting a literary work. Instead, he deliberately misreads what he believes to be the intent of several pieces of juvenile fiction in order to prove that the true function of those *texts* was to prepare the juvenile reader for an adult world of crime, disappointment, and perversion. Normally, we do not think of a Frank Merriwell adventure this way, and it is certain that Patten did not intend to convey these ideas. Yet, as Morris writes, "I misread in this way because I believe that juvenile texts—indeed, any texts, do cultural work that their authors do not intend. Kids' books are usually not fair game for such practices, but I intend to treat them no differently from any serious text" (Morris 1997, 10). In so doing, Morris constructs not only a great book about sport literature, but also produces a fabulous piece of literary criticism, one that is unusual in that it is sufficiently academic and clearly written at the same time. He not only shows us how sports literature has developed logically as a genre with no radical break as it moved from primarily juvenile literature to adult novels, but concludes by making a broader statement in the manner of Foucault or Barthes: "We cannot separate books into literary and non-literary; we simply read them. We read them, I argue, in pretty much the same way, and they are all culturally significant" (Morris 1997, 11). There is no "good" literature; there is only literature or text. By considering juvenile literature in a rigorous manner usually left for the adult works, Morris gives us a good explanation of how sport literature has functioned culturally over the decades and why it has evolved to its present state.

As one might suspect from the fact that baseball was our national game without challenge for nearly a century, baseball literature has more often than not been the main subject for critics writing about sports literature. One fine example is Cordelia Candelaria's *Seeking the Perfect Game: Baseball in American Literature.* The author skillfully describes the rituals and traditions that led to the genesis of baseball fiction in the nineteenth century and goes on to discuss nine different motifs that have defined baseball books over the last century, including the sport's aboriginal roots, folk development, the restorative functions of sport, the game's celebration of the human spirit and quest for the ideal, the use of sport by gentlemen, the false myths regarding baseball's origins, baseball's relationship to American business, the political functions of baseball, and baseball as a text in itself. Ultimately, Candelaria issues the following conclusion about baseball fiction: "Its development has been from subliterary treatments sentimentalizing the game, such as the work of Gilbert Patten; to greater realism, as in Ring Lardner, and greater literary sophistication as in Bernard Malamud; to multidimensional metafictions encapsulating baseball as fiction within fiction, for example the work of Coover and Roth" (Candelaria 1989, 146). Candelaria discusses each of these movements in the context of the nine motifs.

Two other unique critical books are Neil David Berman's *Playful Fictions and Fictional Players: Game, Sport, and Survival in Contemporary American Fiction* and Gregory S. Sojka's *Earnest Hemingway: The Angler as Artist.* Berman shatters the notion that a safe, separate world of play exists within sport and analyzes how five contemporary sports novels prove that this notion of play as a safe zone has been harmful to American society. He discusses, for instance, the repercussions of failed attempts at play on the life of one individual in Leonard Gardner's *Fat City,* the potential disaster that looms for society in Don DeLillo's *End Zone,* and the disintegration of modern values and the utility of language in Lawrence Shainberg's *One on One.* Unlike Berman, Sojka focuses on one author, analyzing several of Hemingway's fishing stories such as "Big Two-Hearted River," *The Old Man and the Sea,* and *Islands in the Stream.* He shows how each of the Hemingway angling heroes, Nick Adams, Santiago, and Thomas Hudson, attains self-mastery by fulfilling the requirements of what Sojka calls Hemingway's "aesthetic of contest." This code calls for a man to simply be the master of himself, the only thing a man can truly aspire to in a meaningless universe. The best way to attain this state of grace is by conquering nature in one of several contests, including hunting, bullfighting, mountain climbing, or, in the case of the characters examined by Sojka, fishing. Both Berman and Sojka's books are a bit hard to read because of the print quality, but both add keen insight to the field of sport literature.

The best critical anthology on the market is Wiley Lee Umphlett's *The Achievement of American Sports Literature: A Critical Appraisal,* a volume whose pages are filled with the writing of some of the best scholars of American literature on the scene today. The first section of the book is entitled "The Creative

Literature—Fiction, Drama (Film), and Poetry" and features analytical essays on sport fiction of the twentieth century. Each of the essays is thoughtful and well written, covering a different aspect of the genre. For instance, Umphlett's "Formulaic Sources of the American Sports Fiction Tradition: The Code of Quality Performance in Juvenile Sports Fiction" profiles some of the games, stories, traditions, and rituals that resulted in the first generation of sports novels for kids, while Leverett Smith's "John R. Tunis's American Epic: or, Bridging the Gap Between Juvenile and Adult Sports Fiction" explains how Tunis's fiction irrevocably shaped his loyal childhood readers' future adult conceptions of life and fiction. Robert Cochran's "The Bench Warmer with a Thousand Faces: Sports Fiction and the Democratic Ideal" discusses how sports literature acts politically as a champion of the unsung hero, the average citizen without whose unheralded effort no true team or societal achievement could ever take place. The rest of the articles are noteworthy not only for their overall quality, but for their emphasis on great literature that has not received much attention. Christian Messenger's "Expansion Draft: Baseball Fiction of the 1980s" covers the work of writers such as John Hough, Jr., Robert Mayer, James McManus, Gary Morganstein, David Ritz, and Wilfred Sheed, whose deep and entertaining baseball fictions have delighted connoisseurs of sport fiction and which should soon receive the critical attention from the academy they richly deserve. Like Messenger, Ronald Giles focuses on the contemporary scene, examining several films from the 1970s and 1980s, including *Raging Bull, Personal Best, Hoosiers,* and *Fat City.* Don Johnson's "'Who the Hell Are You, Kid?': The New Baseball Poem as a Vehicle for Identity" and Brooke Horvath and Sharon Carson's "Women's Sports Poetry: Some Observations and Representative Texts" both examine how new poetic voices are using sport to explore the elusive nature of subjectivity in the latter stages of this century. Poets whose works are discussed include Richard Jackson, Maxine Kumin, William Matthews, Arthur Smith, May Swenson, and Judith Wright.

The second section of the book is entitled "The Supplemental Literature—Criticism, Philosophy, Autobiography, History, and Special Studies" and includes articles that deal with larger issues within the field of sports literature. For example, Lyle Olsen's "The Inception and Reception of a Journal: The Story of Sport Literature's Search for a Voice and an Identity" tells the story of *Aethlon,* formerly *Arete,* which continues to be the only journal for sports literature. As Olsen's piece points out, the journal has faced many obstacles but continues to be the forum for new fiction and criticism relating to sports literature. In addition to writing *Laurel & Thorn: The Athlete in American Literature*, Higgs is a frequent contributor to *Aethlon.* His "The Agonic and the Edenic: Sport Literature and the Theory of Play" works hand-in-hand with Daniel Herman's "Sport, Art, and Aesthetics: A Decade of Controversy (1978–88)," as both try to articulate a theory of sport that might be applied to foster understanding of its literature. Mary McElroy's "Athletes Displaying Their Lives: The Emergence of the Contemporary Sports Autobiography" examines the cultural effects of the confessional sports autobiography that exists today. She argues that it has at least two huge effects.

One is to provide minority and female athletes with a forum in which they can speak their mind on crucial issues; the second is to subvert the myth that athletes are great people who should be idolized. Finally, Oriard's "Sports History/Sports Literature: Some Future Directions and Challenges" deals with the future of sports as an area of critical inquiry within the humanities. Oriard calls for an expansion in scope on the part of scholars of sport literature, who should be including examinations of mass literature of all forms, including journalism and mass marketing materials, into their methods of analysis. He also advocates projects that deal with the history of sports language and sports iconography that would incorporate methods used by social historians. In short, Oriard advocates combining the methods used by traditional literary scholars with procedures used by other disciplines in the humanities. Oriard's ideas will no doubt prove prophetic as the humanities become more and more interdisciplinary in the next century.

A final critical book worth mentioning is Richard Fotheringham's *Sport in Australian Drama*, in which the author discusses the role that sport has played on the Australian stage from 1788 to 1990. His topics range from the origins of the hippodrama in the late eighteenth century to the use of sport in feminist and multicultural dramas of the 1980s. In between, he discusses the celebration of sport in nineteenth-century theater, the use of sport by the drama industry to promote its productions, the golden age of sports drama (1880–1910), the sporting play and the development of Australian nationalism, sport in Australian film, and sport in the modern drama. In addition to giving the reader a close look at Australian theater and life, the book is both meticulously researched and clearly written.

One of the best features of all of the critical books profiled so far is the bibliography. Each book contains a full-length list of citations and resources that is invaluable to the researcher. Fiction and nonfiction books and articles are included, and while there is some overlap between the works, each author includes sources that are unique. There are at least three books that are only intended as bibliographies that might be helpful to those looking for even more complete resource lists. The first is Suzanne Wise's *Sports Fiction for Adults: An Annotated Bibliography of Novels, Plays, Short Stories and Poetry with Sporting Settings*. The author organizes the book by sport and, as advertised, provides short annotations for each reference that explain the general subject of the work in question. The book is quite a find for the sport researcher because Wise exhaustively tackles the works on a plethora of subjects. For instance, airplane racing, bridge, camping, cockfighting, decathlon, dog shows, gliding, handball, hurdling, mountaineering, polo, rodeos, roller skating, shot-putting, skin diving, surfing, walking, and wildfowling are included along with baseball, basketball, football, ice hockey, soccer, and other higher profile sports. Another quality bibliography is Grant Burns's *The Sports Pages: A Critical Bibliography of Twentieth-Century American Novels and Stories Featuring Baseball, Basketball, Football and Other Athletic Pursuits*. Burns is more "canonical" than Wise. He features lists of materials written about the big three, and supplements these lists with shorter sections of several other "minor" sports. Besides the sheer volume of material that Burns covers, the best thing about his work is the length and substance of his annotations. Each entry is accompanied by a full explanation of what happens in the story in question. Occasionally, Burns offers his opinions about the quality of a given work and the cultural tasks it performs. Finally, Mike Shannon's *Diamond Classics: Essays on 100 of the Best Baseball Books Ever Published* functions as a type of bibliographic work in that it provides in-depth commentary on what Shannon judges to be the best works ever written on the sport of baseball. He includes critical works, creative nonfiction, novels, dramas, short stories, and poems. The book starts with a profile of David Voigt's scholarly trilogy, *American Baseball* and ends with a synopsis of Ring Lardner's *You Know Me, Al*, perhaps the most "classic" piece of baseball literature ever penned. In between, he covers most of the influential works written over the course of the last century. His commentary on these works is highly informative because it combines a short summary of each work with a discussion of the work's importance at the time in which it was written, as well as its significance to scholars today.

## CREATIVE NONFICTION

Perhaps the most contemplative, passionate writing about sport over the last twenty years has come in the form of creative nonfiction. These essays and epistles have no single source; the only criteria for engaging in this type of writing is that one be in love with sport. Former players, sportswriters, coaches, and poets with a love for their chosen games have produced deep, heart-felt works that have changed the way many of us think about our athletic passions. One of the best books is Donald Hall's *Fathers Playing Catch with Sons: Essays on Sport.* Hall writes about several sports, but the majority of the work is dedicated to his lifelong devotion to baseball. He offers essays that speak to the timelessness of the game, observing that perhaps no other force has built lasting connections between men of his generation. The most important of these relationships is between the father and the son. As Hall writes: "And I him, and my father and my son, and my mother's father when the married men played the single men in Wilmot, New Hampshire, and my father's father's father who hit a ball with a stick while he was camped outside Vicksburg in June of 1863, and maybe my son's son's son for baseball is continuous, like nothing else among American things, an endless game of repeated summers, joining the long generations of all the fathers and all the sons" (Hall 1986, 46). Hall's writing is witty, insightful, and profoundly human. It is a work for many fathers and sons and for all baseball devotees who have always believed that "baseball sets off the meaning of life precisely because it is pure of meaning," that its rhythms are open to all who seek order, connection, and transcendence (Hall 1986, 51).

One of Hall's chapters is dedicated to baseball writers whose works shaped his life and art. One such scribe is Roger Angell, the long-time writer for *The New Yorker* whose eloquent musings on the grand old game have captivated readers for the last two decades. *The Summer Game, Five Seasons,* and *Late Innings* have all enjoyed success, but his best entry might be *Season Ticket: A Baseball Companion.* Its pages contain Angell's thoughts on the events that defined the 1984–1988 major league seasons and include every type of writing imaginable. He is analytical and dedicates entire chapters to describing the subtleties of holding runners on base or the intricate psychological maneuvers of a pitcher and a batter as they square off with men on base. He is nostalgic about great men who are leaving the game, such as former Baltimore manager Earl Weaver, or about great venues, such as Fenway Park in Boston, that he knows cannot last forever. He is funny when describing the habits and foibles of baseball fans, who even with the best of intentions can let their passions carry them into silly tirades and frantic fits of worry. He reminds us why we are fans; why we find pennant races so thrilling; why we love to get caught up in a team, an athlete, or a season when there is really no pressing reason we should do so. Of course, he does all of this while still covering the awful aspects of the game that have soured many fans. As Angell writes: "Most of us fans fall in love with baseball when we are children, and those who come aboard as adults often do so in a rush of affection and attachment to a local team that has begun to win. These infatuations are ferociously battered and eroded by various forces" (Angell 1988, 418). Angell's book helps us deal with our anger toward these "forces," including exorbitant salaries, spoiled players, heartbreaking defeats, and lost seasons. He reminds us of why we fell in love with the game in the first place, and why we still persevere, patching up the relationship after each disappointment. He ends his last chapter in the Hall of Fame, the house for all the great heroes and memories of the past: "We know they are there, tucked away up-country and in the back of our minds; old men, and younger ones on the way, who prove and sustain the elegance of our baseball dreams" (Angell 1988, 419).

There are so many good books dedicated to baseball that it is impossible to cover them all in this chapter, but two other writers that must be mentioned are Roger Kahn and Thomas Boswell. Both have authored several books that shed light on why baseball continues to grip our nation. Two of Boswell's best are *Why Time Begins on Opening Day* and *How Life Imitates the World Series*, but his less heralded *The Heart of the Order* also deserves some plaudits. In it, Boswell covers several aspects of the game but focuses especially on how its greatest players allow us to understand the game better. For instance, Don Mattingly, the great Yankee first baseman, is the shortstop on Boswell's team because he best exhibits the characteristics of the quintessential shortstop: quiet determination, the perseverence to work through injuries, consistency, and that indefinable quality we call heart. These are not only the qualities of a great middle infielder, they are the things that draw us to baseball. According to Boswell, we find beauty, symmetry, aesthetic pleasure of all kinds, and intellectual fulfillment in baseball more so than any other sport. His glowing descriptions of athletes, managers, and ball parks attest to his commitment to this belief, but it is the humorous "99 Reasons Why Baseball Is Better Than Football" that stays in the reader's memory. The list is too lengthy to include here, but it is sure to spark laughter and controversy in most fans. Boswell's diversity is mirrored in Roger Khan's *Memories of Summer: When Baseball Was an Art and Writing about It a Game.* Khan blends humor, subtle analysis, and warm nostalgia to his discussion of recollections of his childhood summers in Brooklyn, his allegiance to the Dodgers, his sadness and anger at their departure for Los Angeles, and his realization of just how important baseball and the Dodgers were to his life as a young man and to the life of his community.

At least three other pieces of creative nonfiction should be mentioned. These are S. S. Hanna's *Beyond Winning: Memoirs of a Women's Soccer Coach*, Joyce Carol Oates's *On Boxing*, and Oriard's *The End of Autumn: Reflections of My Life in Football*. *Beyond Winning* is the story of Dr. S. S. Hanna, an English professor by trade, and his successful attempt to start a women's soccer program from scratch at tiny Geneva College in Pennsylvania. Though Hanna's prose lacks the aesthetic beauty and rich vibrancy of writers such as Hall and Angell, his story is one that we need to hear. It is the tale of a professor and students whose dedication to amateur athletics was so intense that they played on despite the lack of proper facilities and equipment, little funding, and almost no initial institutional support. It is, in short, a book that gives one a glimpse of college coaches, professors, and athletes acting the way they would if college sports were truly about education, personal growth, and amateur ideals. Oates's work is a short, highly philosophical meditation on boxing and its place in American society over the last half century. Reverberating with feminist overtones, *On Boxing* forces the reader to take a second look at how boxing has performed cultural work as a hypermasculine activity that reinforces the awful patriarchal machismo we keep hearing so much about. The book is much more than this, however. Oates looks deep into the heart of boxing and offers some fascinating insights on why the violence, extreme physicality, pain, and intensity of the sport captivates its audiences. Finally, Oriard's reminiscence of his twenty years as a football player is worth the read because any person for whom sports was an integral part of growing up can identify with his stories. In describing his past, he takes you back to your childhood and moves you through adolescence and early adulthood, allowing you to better understand yourself and your relationship with sports.

## FICTIONAL ANTHOLOGIES

Very close to creative nonfiction are fictional anthologies by one author. Many such works contain both fiction and nonfiction essays, and often the material is rich with cultural and philosophical insight. At least three such works stand out above the rest. One is Mike Shannon's *The Day Satchel Paige and the Pittsburgh Crawfords Came to Hartford, N.C.*, a collection of seven stories and sixty-five short poems that speak to every aspect of a fan's experience. Shannon deals with obsession, the pain of disappointment, the peculiar nature of the thrill of experiencing emotional highs through the feats and victories of others, the special relationships that develop between fans whose only connection is a team that really has no interest in their lives except for their capacity as economic entities, and the pure joy of playing and watching sport. The best part about the book, however, is that all its lessons and deeper concerns are couched in funny stories and clever poems. For instance, the story that gives the book its title is especially hilarious. It recalls memories of barnstorming days when white and black teams alike whipped across the country taking on all challengers who dared face their exciting and unpredictable brand of baseball. In the story, the Pittsburgh Crawfords of the Negro League venture to small-town North Carolina to play the local team. Everyone turns out to see the great Satchel Paige. Unfortunately for the racist throng, Paige and the boys have pulled a fast one on them. Instead of Paige on the mound, The Crawfords send Alvin, the team batboy and mascot. They pass him off as Paige, and the white audience is enthralled when the Crawfords spank the Hartford Aces 16–3. Everyone has a good laugh on the ride to Richmond, where Paige awaits them for a game that very night. The reader laughs with the Crawfords, knowing that a bit of revenge has been exacted. The townspeople have paid full price to watch a mascot and have praised him to high heaven. It is funny, but it is also meaningful. The racism that has infected our country is exposed, and the love of baseball shared by the members of the Crawfords is celebrated. Shannon's book is more than anything else a celebration of the spirit of baseball, the soul of the game that reinvigorates us every spring.

A second anthology is Thomas McGuane's *An Outside Chance: Classic and New Essays on Sport*. McGuane's essays are meditations of a man alone on a river, thinking about the beauty of his surroundings, the sacredness of his angling activity, and the wonderful, yet temporal nature of his life and all that is in it. His prose is eloquent and his insights comforting. His topics range from the specific fishing techniques and dilemmas he discusses in "Close to the Bone," to touching, respectful tributes to nature in "Molly," a fond reminiscence about his old hunting dog, to man's relationship with nature in "Angling Versus Acts of God." At times McGuane is comedic and rebellious, as in "Wading the Hazards," which celebrates the exploits of an adolescent, outlaw caddie, who takes out his frustrations on the patrons of a snobby country club. He closes the book with an essay called "Midstream," in which he laments the new American preoccupation with making sports into materialistic enterprises that must serve some economic end. The business golf date is not McGuane's cup of tea. If you long to be lost in thought while fishing in the middle of a stream and to experience sporting pleasures just for the sensual fulfillment they bring, you will not be able to put McGuane's book down.

The final fictional anthology by a single author is Peter La Salle's *Hockey Sur Glace*. It is one of my favorite books because it is one of the few works that contains good hockey writing. La Salle traces his love of the sport to the ponds of northern Rhode Island, and he dedicates his first story, "Hockey Angles," to a nostalgic reflection on his youth. From tales of hockey dreams, he moves on to stories of high school conquests and college adventures, all the while reminding the reader of the unique nature of ice hockey. Like the sport, La Salle's narrative gets in your blood. It makes you want to play again, to experience the rush of moving at top speeds, at precarious angles, armed with blades on your feet and a piece of lumber in your hands. Lost in the pages of La Salle's tribute to the sport, former players are reminded that there is nothing like hockey outdoors on a frozen pond.

For those who want to get a good "feel" for sports literature by sampling the writings of several different authors, there are a handful of good general anthologies from which to choose. Each of these anthologies would be useful to any teacher who wants to put together a class on sports literature. One of the most recent editions is *The Norton Book of Sports*, edited by George Plimpton. The book is organized in four sections, one for each season of the year. Still, the designations are purely arbitrary, and each section is stocked with essays, poems, and short stories that use sport to comment not only on the importance of sport to Americans, but also on the nature of American culture at different points in the nation's history. Plimpton includes canonical authors such as Mark Twain, whose "The Celebrated Jumping Frog of Calaveras County" is the first entry in the book, but also includes some fine pieces by fabulous authors who are rarely read today. These include a hilarious play by Don Marquis, one of the foremost humorists of the 1920s. The play is entitled "Why Professor Waddems Never Broke A Hundred." It is the story of Professor Waddems, an avid golfer, who is so angered when his concentration is broken by Dr. Green, a famous surgeon, that he kills Green for the good of society. The judge clears Waddems of all charges, complimenting him for his sound judgment and suggesting to the jury that there is still time left for nine holes if they expedite the case. The dark humor is wonderful and Marquis's story is charmingly disturbing. What is he suggesting? Are we so absorbed by our sporting passions that our values have become warped, or, like Dr. Green, have we become too serious, allowing our professional ambitions to dull our sense of play? This double-edged quality whereby the stories please the reader emotionally and sensually while still provoking intellectual thought on important issues is what makes the works in *The Norton Book of Sports* so clever.

Two other excellent collections are *The Twentieth Century Treasury of Sports*, edited by Al and Brian Silverman, and *Sport Inside and Out: Readings in Literature and Philosophy*, edited by David Vanderwerken and Spencer Wirtz. Both overlap Plimpton's volume to some degree, but most of the material in each anthology is distinct. For instance, Vanderwerken and Wirtz focus heavily on philosophical writings. They include "The Natural Religion" by Michael Novak, the noted theologian from Stanford University whose works pioneered efforts to understand how spiritual aspects of sport operate on a regional basis. Also included is writing from social scientists such as Hans Lenk, whose essays such as "Action Theory and the Social Scientific Analysis of Sports Action" paved the way for further interdisciplinary inquiry into sport. Another nice feature of the book is that it is broken into substantive sections, each of which addresses an important aspect of life. The importance of religion, myth, philosophy, aesthetics, social customs, language, fantasy, humor, death, time, the participant, the spectator, and the community are all addressed, and the reader is struck by the quality of sports literature and its cultural power. By contrast, *The Twentieth Century Sports Treasury* is important because the Silvermans stocked the volume with long pieces of literature that give the reader a chance to experience great authors in heartier doses than a poem or mini-short story can provide. For instance, the editors include excerpts from some of the best sports novels of all time, such as Don DeLillo's *End Zone*, Eliot Asinof's *Man on Spikes,* and Mark Harris's *The Southpaw*. In addition, the volume contains stories by William Faulkner, F. Scott Fitzgerald, and Jack London that one rarely sees in other anthologies. Of course, the classics are there as well, and works such as Irwin Shaw's "The Eighty Yard Run," perhaps the best sports short story of all time, sit near Ring Lardner's classic satire, "The Champion." One does not usually think of curling up with a good anthology on a warm summer's day by a lake, but either *Sport Inside and Out* or *The Treasury* would neatly fit into such idyllic scenes.

Three other quality general anthologies are *Men in Sports: Great Stories of All Time from the Greek Olympic Games to the World Series*, edited by Grant Aymar, *Show Me a Hero: Great Contemporary Stories about Sport*, edited by Jeanne Schinto, and *A Literature of Sports*, edited by Thomas Dodge. The latter, compiled around 1980, is the oldest of the bunch. Though Dodge could not include some of the great literature written in the 1980s and 1990s, his work is a quality volume that has some unique features. One strength is its organization. The book is sectioned into areas that deal with significant human experience. Examples include the quest for thrill, rites of passage, aging, love, our need for competition, our enjoyment of the irreverent, and our relationship with authority. The volume is heavy on poetry and contains some of the best sports poems ever written. By contrast, Schinto's edition was published in 1995 and focuses on contemporary writing. Consequently, she includes the works of some of America's best current authors, such as Toni Cade Bambara, Ethan Canin, Ellen Gilchrist, Mark Helprin, Don Lee, Monica Wood, and Jay Woodruff. Finally, Aymar's work spans the centuries, lining up some of the best sports stories ever written from the classical age to the present. His volume is distinct because it is organized by sport and contains writings from a diverse set of authors that include Bob Cousy, Sir Arthur Conan Doyle, Ken Dryden, Zane Grey, Homer, Rudyard Kipling, Theodore Roosevelt, and Jules Verne. Again, all of the pieces are worthy of reading.

For those who prefer to read about specific sports, there is no shortage of quality anthologies whose writings focus on one game. Naturally, baseball anthologies are the easiest to find, but volumes on golf are nearly as plentiful. Two of the more interesting baseball books are *Taking the Field: The Best of Baseball Fiction*, edited by George Bowering, and *Writing Baseball*, edited by Jerry Klinkowitz. Bowering's work lives up to its billing. Naturally, it does not contain all of the great baseball stories, and it leaves out poetry, but the stories that fill this volume are superb. Examples include Damon Runyon's "Baseball Hattie," Jack Kerouac's "Ronnie on the Mound," Andre Dubus's "The Pitcher," and Sergio Ramirez's "The Centerfielder." Other feature authors include Ring Lardner, Nelson Algren, Richard Wilbur, David Carkeet, and W. P. Kinsella. Klinkowitz's book is organized in six sections: nostalgic tales about past sporting experiences, tales from the minors, stories from scouts, player memoirs, writings by professors, and essays from fans. The nostalgia section contains essays from renowned writers such as Paul Auster and Gerald Rosen, a former New York Giants batboy who now teaches at Sanoma State College in California. The fan's section is also noteworthy because it contains excerpts from Neil Sullivan's angry, elegiac lament *The Dodgers Move West* and William Least Heat Moon's captivating nonfiction novel *Blue Highways*, as well as an amusing slice of Americana by Garrison Keillor entitled "Three New Twins Join Club in Spring Training."

Some of the better golf readers are John Updike's *Golf Dreams: Writings on Golf,* John Feinstein's *A Good Walk Spoiled,* James Finegan's *Blasted Heaths and Blessed Greens,* William Hallberg's *Perfect Lies: A Century of Great Golf Stories,* and M. Scott Peck's *Golf and the Spirit.* Only Hallberg's edition contains fiction, featuring entries by F. Scott Fitzgerald, Owen Johnson, Jack London, Walker Percy, John Updike, and P. G. Wodehouse. Finegan's book is a philosophical treatise on the best greens and fairways of Scotland, while Feinstein's work is one of the best for understanding the rigors and pressures of the PGA Tour. Updike and Peck both discuss how golf can be good for body and soul. Peck is a medical doctor, and his work is fascinating because he makes a scientific argument while still managing to sound like a golf fan.

Basketball is in some ways the most "American" of all sports, yet it has produced only a handful of quality works of fiction. Two of the better anthologies are *The Schoolyard Game: An Anthology of Basketball Writings,* edited by Dick Wimmer, and *Full Court: A Literary Anthology of Basketball,* edited by Dennis Trudell. *Full Court* is the more comprehensive of the two and contains essays by such stellar writers as Bobbie Ann Mason, Herbert Wilner, Pete Fromm, John Updike, and John Edgar Wideman. The stories are not grouped under any subheadings, but topics range from the thrill of first dribbling a basketball to one's horrible sense of loss at having to walk away from the game. From fast breaks to slam dunks, from junior high school games to national championships, the book has something for every hoops fan, as does *The Schoolyard Game,* a more compact work that nevertheless contains some great writing that Trudell's book does not feature. For instance, excerpts from Pat Conroy's *The Great Santini,* Philip Roth's classic American novel *Goodbye Columbus,* and other fine novels appear in the book, alongside stories by contemporary scribes Tom Boswell and Ron Shelton. There is also a fine essay from the late Pete Axthelm, one of the best basketball writers who has ever lived.

Other single sport anthologies include Martin Greenberg's *In the Ring: A Treasury of Boxing Stories,* Robert Byrne's *Byrne's Book of Great Pool Stories,* John Wiebusch and Brian Silverman's *A Game of Passion: The NFL Literary Companion,* Dick Francis and John Welcome's *The Dick Francis Treasury of Great Racing Stories,* Garth Battista's *The Runner's Literary Companion,* and Peter Fromm's *King of the Mountain: Sporting Stories.* Greenberg's work is probably the best boxing anthology available and includes stories by all the legendary chroniclers of the squared circle: Ernest Hemingway, Jack London, Ring Lardner, Paul Gallico, and Budd Schulberg. Likewise, *A Game of Passion* represents the best football writing to date. Irwin Shaw, Don DeLillo, James Dickey, Ray Bradbury, Frederick Exley, August Wilson, Gay Talese, and Gary Cartwright are featured authors. Byrne's book proves that billiards have not eluded the view of major literary figures. Some of the better stories in the anthology are Alexander Pushkin's "The Captain's Daughter," Leo Tolstoy's "Recollections of a Billiard Scorer,"and A. A. Milne's "A Billiard Lesson." *The Dick Francis Treasury* includes Arthur Conan Doyle's classic "Silver Blaze," Sherwood Anderson's "I'm a Fool," and John Galsworthy's "Had a Horse," among others.

Fromm's collection is a tribute to human sporting experience in the great outdoors. *The Runner's Literary Companion* is one of the best anthologies on sport. It stands out even among the other quality collections mentioned here. Works by Toni Cade Bambara, Evelyn Waugh, James Beuchler, Joyce Carol Oates, Max Apple, Walt Whitman, W. H. Auden, Margy Piercy, Richard Wilbur, Grace Butcher, and A. E. Housman, whose "To an Athlete Dying Young" stands with Alan Sillitoe's "The Loneliness of the Long-Distance Runner" as two of the greatest sports poems ever written, are included.

One of the most promising fictional developments of the 1990s has been the rise of women writing about sports. Not only are there several good novels and poems by women, but there are a number of fine anthologies that house fiction written by women, much of which is dedicated to analyzing and describing women's sporting experience in the United States. One of the earliest volumes to appear on the scene was *Diamonds Are a Girl's Best Friend*, edited by Elinor Nauen. The book is packed with beautifully crafted stories by some of America's best contemporary writers. For example, historian Doris Kearns Goodwin's "From Father, With Love" recounts her early infatuation with the game based on her relationship with her father; poet Marianne Moore's classic essay "Baseball and Writing" remind us of the powerful relationship that exists between sport and art; and novelist Anna Quindlan's "A Baseball Wimp" reminds us how the infectious spirit of a good pennant race can arrest the attention of even the most laissez faire city dweller. There are several essays by women who loved to play baseball before they ever thought of being spectators, and there is pleasure, pain, and ambivalence in the essays. Also included are excerpts from Annie Dillard's *An American Childhood* and Shirley Jackson's *Raising Demons*, as well as some unique analyses of baseball by poet May Swenson, feminist activist Mariah Burton Nelson, and novelist Ellen Cooney.

Another tremendous book is *A Whole Other Ball Game: Women's Literature on Women's Sport*, edited by Joli Sandoz. This book is the first anthology dedicated exclusively to women's sports. It features poems by Adrienne Rich and Tess Gallagher and personal essays from Toni Cade Bambara, Margy Piercy, and Judith Wright. All of the entries deal with the importance of competition to women. For instance, Ellen Gilchrist's "Revenge" describes the pain and anguish of being denied the right to compete in the south in the 1940s. In "The Lady Pitcher" Cynthia Macdonald depicts the tension she felt at softball's College World Series as an athlete expected to compete aggressively at the highest levels and a young lady expected to maintain a certain grace and dignity. Carolyn Kremers's "When I am 98" is about how sport helps young girls become women. Mariah Burton Nelson's "Competition" shows how athletic contests draw women together, acting as feminist enterprises that promote sisterhood. Other works deal with losing or winning the big game, playing in a game for the first time, the pain of leaving the competitive arena, the importance of sport to cementing lifelong relationships, the role sport plays in making women feel comfortable with their bodies and in shaping conceptions of self, and a host of other topics.

Three other collections of note are *Uncommon Waters: Women Write about Fishing*, edited by Holly Morris, *Women on Hunting*, edited by Pam Houston, and Nauen's *Ladies, Start Your Engines: Women Writers on Cars and the Road*. The former is one of the few volumes dedicated to capturing the experiences of a growing number of women anglers. It includes essays by Lillian Hemingway, Margaret Atwood, and Audre Lord, among others. Houston's work is a combination of fictional hunting tales written by women, such as those penned by Joyce Carol Oates, Margaret Atwood, and Annie Dillard, and nonfiction stories from women writing about their actual hunting adventures. As one might suspect, Nauen's edition is marginally about auto racing, but it is more a celebration of women's relationships with their cars. There are essays about racing, fixing cars, important moments that took place in cars, and cars that hold great memories. It is truly a fun book to read, dotted with essays from the likes of Eudora Welty, Flannery O'Connor, and Edith Wharton. Who would not like to read "Cars I Have Known," a revealing essay about the various autos that Carolyn Cassidy rode in over the years with husband Neil, perhaps the quintessential car thief of all time?

## SPORTS POETRY

Many of the works profiled so far in this chapter feature sports poetry. Still, there are several books devoted exclusively to poems about sport. One of the best is *Hummers, Knucklers, and Slow Curves: Contemporary Baseball Poems*, edited by Don Johnson. All of the poems are about baseball, and as Johnson admits, "the poems are as varied, evocative and mysterious as the game they attempt to describe" (Johnson 1991, xix). Little League games, long bus rides in the minors, lazy nights in the right field bleachers, pennant races, baseball language, baseball as a spiritual activity, diamond memories, and home run trots are just a few of the topics covered by some of America's best poets. These include Gregory Corso, Donald Hall, Rolph Humphries, Lillian Morrison, and Robert Penn Warren. Another volume of baseball poems is *Baseball, I Gave You the Best Years of My Life*, edited by Richard Grossinger and Lisa Conrad. Though it does contain a few short stories, the book is mostly poetry about the grand old game.

Other volumes of sports poetry include *American Sports Poems*, edited by R. R. Knudson and May Swenson; *This Sporting Life*, edited by Emilie Buchwald and Ruth Roston; Robert Mitchell's *The Heart Has Its Reasons: Reflections on Sports and Life*; and John Lee's *The Hockey Player Sonnets*. Lee won the 1987 People's Poetry Award as well as the Charterhouse Award of London, England. His hockey poems stem from his long relationship with the sport as a fan and his comparatively short stint as a player. Lee took up the game as an adult in mid-life and his poems reflect a refreshing and complex appreciation for the game and for the important role sport plays in life beyond youth. Mitchell's work is equally compelling because, as the title might indicate, he writes intensely about his emotional relationship with sport. His graceful poetic style is easy to read, and he uses it to draw the reader into his passion about games past and present. Mitchell makes you *feel* sport and its power. *American Sports Poems* is a complete anthology of poems written by a diverse group of writers whose only similarity is their love of athletic pursuits. Some of the best poets of the century are featured, including Robert Frost, Louise Gluck, Randall Jarrell, Archibald MacLeish, Ogden Nash, Theodore Roethke, Carl Sandberg, Delmore Schwartz, Anne Sexton, Karl Shapiro, and E. B. White. Finally, *This Sporting Life* is notable because it houses the work of contemporary poets such as Alixa Doom, Donald Allen Evans, Susan Firer, Gary Gildner, Tom Hansen, Judith Emlyn Johnson, Roseann Lloyd, William Meissner, Barbara Petoskey, Austin Straus, and Al Zolynas. The poems are grouped by sport.

## THE SPORTS NOVEL

While poetry has gained in popularity over the last decade, the state of any genre is still defined by the quality of its novels. Judging from the number of good novels either primarily or secondarily about sport written over the last two decades, the field of sports literature must be very healthy indeed. The number is so great that it would be impossible to even list them here, much less talk about them even for a short length of time. Thus, I will try to comment on a few novels that seem to be representative of the different directions that the sports novel has taken over the last twenty years. For instance, the autobiographical novel or confessional memoir has become one of the more popular types of sports literature in recent years. One of the best examples of this is Gary Gildner's *The Warsaw Sparks*. Gildner, a professor of English and a gifted writer, went to Poland in the late 1980s to teach poetry. He ended up gratifying another of his passions: baseball. He formed an amateur team and, acting as player-coach, taught his teammates the game complete with all of its uniquely American myths and rituals. The book is the story of the Polish people and their struggles. It is a gritty story of the harshness of life in socialist Poland, and the hopes and dreams the young Polish players find in the game of baseball, dreams that are inflamed by their barnstorming tour of North America. Sometimes we have to look to the "other" to get a clearer picture of ourselves; that is what this book allows the American reader to do. If you want to know why Americans love baseball and what it means to be American, read this book.

Another type of story is the redemption novel. Usually, this type of narrative forces us to see both the goodness and the seaminess in sport. Eric Goodman's *In Days of Awe* is a good example of such a work. It is the tale of a superstar pitcher Joe Singer, "Jewish Joe Singer" as Goodman refers to him, who has it all. He is a great pitcher at the top of his game, and he enjoys his beautiful wife and his heroic status in the community. It is not until he is implicated in a gambling scheme, suspended from the game, and dumped by his wife that he learns how special baseball is. He can never go back to the game, and we feel the depth of his anguish. Yet, we also see how his departure from the game of his youth allows him to grow. He gains distance from the shallow world of professional sport and is able to see how it was warping his view of life. Finally, he comes to terms with God and himself and finds love and purpose in a realistic way that makes the reader think he has matured into a stable adult. Still, the beauty of the game lingers in the back of our minds and Goodman is careful not to condemn the game. Rather, he forces us to distinguish the game we love from the institution we frequently hate. Another novel in this vein is William Kennedy's Pulitzer prize winning *Ironweed*, perhaps one of the finest novels written in the 1980s, which chronicles the sad journey of Francis Phelan, a washed-up ball player who desperately tries to come to terms with several old ghosts.

Closely related to the redemption tale is the reform novel, the story that is intended by the author as a political act for the purpose of igniting change. Though these works can sometimes be a bit heavy-handed and "preachy," there are some fine efforts that make for good reads. One such book is Dan Doyle's *"Are You Watching, Adolph Rupp?"* the story of a corrupt college basketball program, an honest but beleaguered coach, and the effects of the modern system of college sports on young athletes. The book is filled with shady gamblers, angry, hyper-masculine fathers that try to live through their sons, abusive parents, power hungry alumni, and many fine people who try to fight the system and to recapture the essence of sport and all that is good about intercollegiate athletics. Doyle is the director of the Institute for International Sport at the University of Rhode Island and a committed educator. This is his first novel and if his characters are sometimes a bit exaggerated, his sentiments are genuine. Certainly, his diagnosis of the problem in college sports is accurate, and his solutions, inherent within the narrative, are not overly dogmatic or dripping with pathos.

Some of the best sports novels are actually philosophical inquiries. Such is the case with the novels of David James Duncan, author of *The River Why* and *The Brothers K*. The former is in the tradition of Izaak Walton's *The Compleat Angler*. It contains enough fishing instruction and reminiscence to satisfy any fisherman but is principally the story of Gus Orviston's quest for meaning. He eventually finds it, in a way, but the journey is the important thing. That is where he and the reader learn about nature, God, human relations, and the possibility of truth. *The Brothers K* is a bit different. It is a work about baseball, religion, and family. More specifically, it is about the spiritual role that baseball plays as a family is torn apart. Duncan asks some tough questions about how family members from generations with such different fundamental beliefs can maintain their love, and how sacrifice and love can exist between people with such diverse world views.

There are, of course, many types of other novels. The mystical tale of sporting transcendence is always good for a change of pace. Works such as Michael Murphy's *Golf in the Kingdom*, newly released in 1994, is a good example. We get to watch the hero transformed on a magical golf course. Also, there is the novel of experience, usually written by former athletes. One decidedly fun romp is *Ruffians*, a raunchy, fast-paced tale of greed and corruption in the National Football League, written by former Atlanta Falcon defensive tackle Tim Green. For pure entertainment, there is the comic novel, of which David Carkeet's *The Greatest Slump of All Time* is a good example. Gay and lesbian sports novels are few in number, but one of the better ones is Peter Lefcourt's *The Dreyfus Affair*, the comical and rather jolting story of a second baseman who falls in love with his shortstop during a tight pennant race. There are many fine mystery writers who use sport as a backdrop for their stories of murder and mayhem. Troy Soos's novels are as much expeditions through classic ballparks as they are mysteries; but they are good stories of murder and justice, and if you have never been to Boston you might try *Murder at Fenway Park.* For various lists of sports novels, one can check the bibliographies of most of the anthologies and critical texts mentioned in this chapter, but I have tried to list some of the best sports novels in the bibliography that follows this chapter. If you cannot find something to your liking on one list, try another. There is something on the market for everyone.

## PERIODICALS RELATED TO SPORTS LITERATURE

Any scholar in need of quality academic articles on sport and literature should start with *Aethlon: The Journal of Sport Literature,* the ultimate source of scholarship on the subject. There are, of course, several reputable journals that regularly include articles from both established scholars and new voices in the field. Journals that frequently feature articles on sports and literature include *American Literary History; American Quarterly; Australian Magazine; China Sports; International Sports Journal; Journal of American Culture; Journal of American Folklore; Journal of Canadian Studies; Journal of Latin American Culture; Journal of Men's Studies; Journal of Popular Culture; Journal of Ritual Studies; Journal of the Philosophy of Sport; Modern Fiction Studies; Nine: A Journal of Baseball History and Social Policy Perspectives; Sport, Education and Society; Sporting Heritage; Sports Illustrated; Sports in Japan;* and *South Atlantic Review.* A complete list of related periodicals is located in Appendix 2 at the end of this volume. One might also consult the database SPORTSDiscus or the website for *Sportsjones* magazine at www.sportsjones.com.

Perhaps the explosion of criticism, fiction, and nonfiction works about sport are a surprise to some people. It should not be. After all, in a society that patronizes even the most marginal, silly sporting events (the X games), that idolizes even the most bizarre athletes (Dennis Rodman),and that elects its governors from the ranks of former professional wrestlers (Jesse Ventura), how could the sporting obsession not pour into the pages of our national literature? It is very likely that the literary and critical efforts of our best writers and scholars will continue to be directed toward the fields, stadiums, and streams that attract us so much. Sport is just too much a part of most Americans' personal lives and far too important on the national and international scenes not to grab the attention of novelists, poets, and academicians. Perhaps a better question is why it took so long for sport to be viewed as a worthy subject for a great writer or a serious scholar?

## REFERENCES

### Books

Alguire, Judith. *Iced.* Norwich, VT: New Victorian Publications, 1996.
Angell, Roger. *Late Innings.* New York: Simon & Schuster, 1982.
———. *Five Seasons.* New York: Popular Library, 1978.

————. *Season Ticket: A Baseball Companion*. New York: Ballantine Books, 1988.

Ardizzone, Tony. *Heart of the Order*. New York: Holt, 1986.

Asinof, Eliot. *Man on Spikes*. 1955. Reprint. Carbondale, IL: Southern Illinois University Press, 1998.

Aymar, Grant. *Men in Sports: Great Sports Stories of All Time from the Greek Olympic Games to the World Series*. New York: Crown Publishers, 1994.

Bandy, Susan J. *Coroebus, Triumphs: The Alliance of Sport and the Arts*. San Diego, CA: San Diego Sate University, 1988.

Battista, Garth, ed. *The Runner's Literary Companion*. New York: Breakaway Books, 1994.

Beckham, Barry. *Double Dunk*. Los Angeles: Holloway House, 1989.

Berman, Neil David. *Playful Fictions and Fictional Players: Games, Sport and Survival in Contemporary Fiction*. Port Washington, NY: Kennikat Press, 1981.

Bickham, Jack. *Dropshot*. New York: Forge, 1990.

Bjorkman, Peter. *Baseball and the Game of Life*. New York: Vintage, 1991.

Bledsoe, Lucy Jane. *In Sweat: Stories and a Novella*. Seattle, WA: Seal Press, 1995.

Bookbinder, Bernie. *Out at the Old Ball Game*. Bridgehampton, NY: Bridge Works Publications, 1995.

Boswell, Thomas. *The Heart of the Order*. New York: Doubleday, 1989.

————. *How Life Imitates the World Series*. Garden City, NY: Doubleday, 1982.

————. *Strokes of Genius*. Garden City, NY: Doubleday, 1982.

————. *Why Time Begins on Opening Day*. New York: Penguin, 1984.

Bouton, Jim, and Eliot Asinof. *Strikezone*. New York: Viking, 1994.

Bower, George. *The Jordans*. New York: Arbor House, 1984.

Bowering, George. *Taking the Field: The Best of Baseball Fiction*. Red Deer, Alberta, Canada: Red Deer College Press, 1990.

Brooks, K. S., ed. *Thru the Smokey End Boards: Canadian Poetry about Sports and Games*. Vancouver, BC: Polestar Press, 1996.

Brown, Rita Mae. *Sudden Death*. New York: Bantam, 1983.

Bryson, William. *The Babe Didn't Point: And Other Baseball Stories about Iowans and Sports*. Ames, IA: Iowa State University Press, 1989.

————. *A Walk in the Woods*. New York: Broadway Books, 1997.

Buchwald, Emilie, and Ruth Rolston, eds. *This Sporting Life*. Minneapolis, MN: Milkweed Editions, 1997.

Burns, Grant. *The Sports Pages: A Critical Bibliography of Twentieth-Century American Novels and Stories Featuring Baseball, Basketball, Football and Other Athletic Pursuits*. Metuchen, NJ: Scarecrow Press, 1987.

Butler, Jack. *Jujitsu for Christ*. New York: Penguin, 1988.

Byrne, Robert. *Byrne's Book of Great Pool Stories*. Orlando, FL: Harcourt Brace & Co., 1995.

Candelaria, Cordelia. *Seeking the Perfect Game: Baseball in American Literature*. Westport, CT: Greenwood Press, 1989.

Carkeet, David. *The Greatest Slump of All Time*. New York: Harper and Row, 1984.

Carney, Gene. *Romancing the Horsehide: Baseball Poems on Players and the Game*. Jefferson, NC: McFarland, 1993.

Chafets, Zeev. *Hang Time*. New York: Warner Books, 1996.

Charyn, Jerome. *El Bronx*. New York: Mystery Press, 1997.

Coben, Harlan. *Deal Breaker*. New York: Dell, 1995.

————. *Fade Away*. New York: Dell, 1996.

————. *One False Move*. New York: Delacorte, 1998.

Cody, Liza. *Backhand*. New York: Bantam, 1993.

Conroy, Pat. *The Lords of Discipline*. Boston: Houghton-Mifflin, 1980.

————. *The Prince of Tides*. Boston: Houghton-Mifflin, 1986.

Cooney, Ellen. *All the Way Home*. New York: Putnam, 1984.

Coover, Robert. *Whatever Happened to Gloomy Gus of the Chicago Bears*. New York: Simon & Schuster, 1987.

Crews, Harry. *The Knockout Artist*. New York: Harper and Row, 1988.

Crider, William. *Winning Can Be Murder: A Sheriff Dan Rhodes Mystery*. New York: St. Martin's, 1996.

Davis, Terry. *Vision Quest*. New York: Viking, 1979.

Deford, Frank. *Everybody's All-American*. New York: Viking, 1981.

DeLillo, Don. *End Zone*. Boston: Houghton-Mifflin, 1972.

Dershowitz, Alan. *The Advocate's Devil*. New York: Warner, 1994.

Dodge, Thomas. *A Literature of Sports*. Lexington, MA: D. C. Heath, 1980.

Doyle, Dan. *Are You Watching, Adolph Rupp?* Kingston, RI: Stadia Publishers, 1989.

Duff, Gerald. *Indian Giver*. Bloomington, IN: Indiana University Press, 1983.

Duncan, David James. *The Brothers K*. New York: Doubleday, 1992.

————. *The River Why*. New York: Bantam, 1983.

Early, Gerald, ed. *Body Language: Writers on Sport*. St. Paul, MN: Graywolf Books, 1999.

Evensen, Bruce. *When Dempsey Fought Tunney: Heroes, Hokum and Storytelling in the Jazz Age*. Knoxville, TN: University of Tennessee Press, 1996.

Everett, Percival. *Suder*. New York: Viking, 1984.

Fehler, Gene. *Center Field Grasses: Poems from Baseball*. Jefferson, NC: McFarland, 1991.

Feinstein, John. *A Civil War: Army vs. Navy*. Upland, PA: DIANE Books, 1997.

————. *A Good Walk Spoiled*. Old Tappan, NJ: Macmillan, 1998.

————. *Hard Courts: Real Life on the Professional Tennis Tour*. New York: Random House, 1992.

————. *A Season on the Brink*. Old Tappan, NJ: Macmillan, 1986.

————. *Winter Games*. Boston: Little, Brown & Co., 1995.

Finegan, James. *Blasted Heaths and Blessed Greens*. New York: Simon & Schuster, 1996.

Fisher, Anne Kinsman. *The Legend of Tommy Morris: A Mystical Tale of Timeless Love*. San Rafael, CA: Amber-Allen Publications, 1996.

Ford, Richard. *The Sportswriter*. New York: Vintage, 1986.

Fotheringham, Richard. *Sport in Australian Drama*. New York: Cambridge University Press, 1992.

Fowler, Karen Joy. *The Sweetheart Season*. New York: Holt, 1996.

Francis, Dick, and John Welcomer, eds. *The Dick Francis Treasury of Great Racing Stories*. New York: W. W. Norton, 1989.

Fromm, Peter. *King of the Mountain: Sporting Stories*. Mechanicsburg, PA: Stackpole Books, 1994.

Gardner, Leonard. *Fat City*. New York: Popular Library, 1969.

Geist, Bill. *Little League Confidential: One Coach's Completely Unauthorized Tale of Survival*. Toronto, ON: Maxwell Macmillan, 1992.

Gent, Peter. *The Conquering Heroes*. New York: D. I. Fire, 1994.

————. *The Franchise*. New York: Random House, 1983

————. *North Dallas After Forty*. New York: Villard, 1989.

Gethers, Peter. *Getting Blue*. New York: Delacorte, 1987.

Gildner, Gary. *The Warsaw Sparks*. Iowa City, IA: University of Iowa Press, 1990.

Goodman, Eric. *In Days of Awe*. New York: Alfred A. Knopf, 1991.

Gordon, Alison. *Night Game: A Kate Henry Mystery*. Toronto, ON: M&S Publications, 1997.

Granger, William. *The New York Yanquis*. New York: Arcade Publications, 1995.

Green, Tim. *The Dark Side of the Game: My Life in the NFL*. New York: Warner Books, 1997.

————. *Outlaws*. New York: Harper-Collins, 1997.

————. *Ruffians: A Novel*. Atlanta, GA: Turner Publishing, Inc., 1993.

————. *Titans*. New York: St. Martin's, 1995.

Greenberg, Eric. *The Celebrant*. New York: Everett House, 1982.

Greenburg, Martin H., ed. *In the Ring: A Treasury of Boxing Stories*. New York: Bonanza Books, 1986.

Gregorich, Barbara. *She's on First*. New York: Contemporary Books, 1987.

Grossinger, Richard, and Lisa Conrad, eds. *Baseball, I Gave You the Best Years of My Life*. Berkeley, CA: North Atlantic Books, 1992.

Gustafson, Lars. *The Tennis Players*. New York: New Directions, 1983.

Guy, David. *Football Dreams*. New York: New American Library, 1982.

Hall, Donald. *Fathers Playing Catch with Sons: Essays on Sport*. New York: Dell, 1986.

Hallberg, William. *Perfect Lies: A Century of Great Golf Stories*. Garden City, NY: Doubleday, 1989.

————. *The Rub of the Green*. Garden City, NY: Doubleday, 1988.

Hanna, S. S. *Beyond Winning: Memoirs of a Women's Soccer Coach*. Boulder, CO: University of Colorado Press, 1996.

Hannah, Barry. *The Tennis Handsome*. New York: Knopf, 1983.

Harris, E. Lynn. *And This Too Shall Pass*. New York: Doubleday, 1996.

————. *Just as I Am*. New York: Doubleday, 1994.

Harris, Mark. *Bang the Drum Slowly*. New York: Knopf, 1956.

————. *The Southpaw*. New York: Permabook, 1954.

Harrison, Robert. *Green Fields and White Lines: Baseball Poems*. Jefferson, NC: McFarland, 1995.

Hassler, John. *The Love Hunter*. New York: Morrow, 1981.

Hays, Donald. *The Dixie Association*. New York: Simon & Schuster, 1984.

Hester, Martin L. *Another Jackie Robinson*. Greensboro, NC: Tudor Publications, 1996.

Higgs, Robert J. *Laurel & Thorn: The Athlete in American Literature*. Lexington, KY: University of Kentucky Press, 1981.

Hitchcock, George. *The Racquet; or, Viajes for American Lejana*. Brownsville, OR: Story Line Press, 1993.

Hoffman, Marian. *Norman Rockwell's American Sportsman*. New York: Crescent Books, 1990.

Holtzer, Susan. *Bleeding Maize and Blue*. New York: Doubleday, 1997.

Hornby, Nick. *Fever Pitch: A Fan's Life*. New York: Penguin, 1982.

Hough, John. *The Conduct of the Game*. New York: Harcourt Brace Jovanovich, 1986.

Houston, Pamela, ed. *Women on Hunting*. Hopewell, NJ: The Ecco Press, 1995.

Hoyt, Richard. *Red Card: A Novel of World Cup, 1994*. New York: Forge, 1994.

Humber, William, and John St. James. *All I Thought about Was Baseball: Writings on a Canadian Pastime*. Toronto, ON: University of Toronto Press, 1996.

Irving, John. *The Hotel New Hampshire*. New York: E. P. Dutton, 1981.

Jenkins, Dan. *Life Its Ownself*. New York: Simon & Schuster, 1984.

Johnson, Donald, ed. *Hummers, Knucklers, and Slow Curves: Contemporary Baseball Poems*. Champaign, IL: University of Illinois Press, 1991.

Jordan, Pat. *The Cheat*. New York: Villard, 1984.

Kahn, Roger. *Memories of Summer: When Baseball Was an Art and Writing About It a Game*. New York: Hyperion, 1997.

————. *The Seventh Game*. New York: New American Library, 1982.

Kennedy, William. *Ironweed*. New York: Viking, 1983.

Kerrane, Kevin, and Richard Grossinger. *Into the Temple of Baseball*. Berkeley, CA: Celestial Arts Press, 1990.

Kinsella, W. P. *Box Socials*. Toronto, ON: Harper-Collins, 1992

———. *Diamonds Forever: Reflections from the Field, the Dugout, and the Bleachers*. Toronto, ON: Harper-Collins, 1997.

———. *The Dixon Cornbelt League, and Other Baseball Stories*. New York: Harper-Collins, 1995.

———. *The Further Adventures of Slugger McBatt*. Boston: Houghton-Mifflin, 1982.

———. *Iowa Baseball Confederacy*. Boston: Houghton-Mifflin, 1986.

———. *Shoeless Joe*. New York: Ballantine Books, 1983.

———. *The Thrill of the Grass*. New York: Penguin, 1984.

Klinkowitz, Jerry. *Basepaths*. Baltimore, MD: Johns Hopkins University Press, 1995.

———. *Short Season and Other Stories*. Baltimore, MD: Johns Hopkins University, 1988.

———. *Writing Baseball*. Chicago: University of Illinois Press, 1991.

Kluger, Steve. *Changing Pitches*. New York: St. Martin's, 1984.

Knudson, R. R., and May Swenson, eds. *American Sports Poems*. New York: Orchard Books, 1988.

Kram, Mark. *Miles to Go*. New York, Morrow, 1982.

Lamott, Anne. *Crooked Little Heart*. New York: Pantheon Books, 1997.

Landvik, Lorna. *Your Oasis on Flame Lake*. New York: Fawcett Columbine, 1997.

Lardner, Ring. *You Know Me, Al*. New York: C. Scribner's Sons, 1925.

LaSalle, Peter. *Hockey Sur Glace*. New York: Breakaway Books, 1996.

LeClair, Thomas. *Passing Off*. Sag Harbor, NY: Permanent Press, 1996.

Lee, John B. *The Hockey Player Sonnets*. Waterloo, ON, Canada: Penumbra Press, 1991.

Lefcourt, Peter. *The Dreyfus Affair*. New York: Harper-Collins, 1992.

Lelchuk, Alan. *Playing the Game*. Dallas, TX: Baskerville Publications, 1995.

Levin, Jenifer. *Sea of Light*. New York: Dutton, 1993.

———. *Water Dancer*. New York: Poseidon, 1982.

Links, Bo. *Follow the Wind*. New York: Simon & Schuster, 1995.

Lorenz, Thomas. *Guys Like Us*. New York: Viking, 1980.

Lupica, Mike. *Jump*. New York: Villard, 1995

Malamud, Bernard. *The Natural*. New York: Farrar, Straus and Giroux, 1952.

Mayer, Robert. *The Grace of Shortstops*. New York: Doubleday, 1984.

McCloskey, John. *Mr. America's Last Season Blues*. Baton Rouge, LA: Louisiana State University Press, 1983.

McCown, Clint. *The Member-Guest: A Novel in Stories*. New York: Doubleday, 1995.

McGuane, Thomas. *An Outside Chance: Classic and New Essays on Sport*. Boston: Houghton-Mifflin, 1990.

McManus, James. *Chin Music*. New York: Crown, 1985.

McNab, Tom. *The Fast Man*. New York: Simon & Schuster, 1988.

Messenger, Christian K. *Sport and the Spirit of Play in American Fiction: Hawthorne to Faulkner*. New York: Columbia University Press, 1981.

———. *Sport and the Spirit of Play in Contemporary Fiction*. New York: Columbia University Press, 1990.

Mitchell, Robert. *The Heart Has Its Reasons: Reflections on Sports and Life*. South Bend, IN: Diamond Publications, 1995.

Monninger, Joseph. *Second Season*. New York: Atheneum, 1987.

Moore, James, and Natalie Vermilyer. *Earnest Thayer's "Casey at the Bat": Background and Characters of Baseball's Most Famous Poem*. Jefferson, NC: McFarland, 1994.

Morganstein, Gary. *The Man Who Wanted to Play Centerfield for the New York Yankees*. New York: Atheneum, 1983.

Morris, Holly, ed. *Uncommon Waters: Women Write about Fishing*. Seattle, WA: Seal Fiction, 1991.

Morris, Timothy. *Making the Team: The Cultural Work of Baseball Fiction*. Urbana, IL: University of Illinois Press, 1997.

Morris, Willie. *Always Stand in Against the Curve and Other Sports Stories*. Oxford, MS: Yoknapatawpha Press, 1983.

Murphy, Michael. *Golf in the Kingdom*. London: Viking, 1972, 1994.

Murray, Frank. *Every Young Man's Dream*. Chicago: Silver Books, 1984.

Nauen, Elinor, ed. *Diamonds Are a Girl's Best Friend*. Boston: Faber & Faber, 1993.

———. *Ladies, Start Your Engines: Women Writers on Cars and on the Road*. Boston: Faber & Faber, 1996.

Navratilova, Martina. *Killer Instinct: A Jordan Myles Mystery*. New York: Villard, 1997.

Nelson, Kent. *Toward the Sun*. New York: Breakaway Books, 1998.

Newcombe, Jack. *In Search of Billy Cole*. New York: Arbor House, 1984.

Norman, Geoffrey. *Blue Chipper: A Morgan Hunt Novel*. New York: Morrow, 1992.

Nunn, Ken. *Tapping the Source*. New York: Delacorte, 1984.

Oates, Joyce Carol. *On Boxing*. Garden City, NY: Doubleday, 1987.

———. *You Must Remember This*. New York: Dutton, 1987.

Olsen, Toby. *Seaview*. New York: New Directions, 1983.

Olshan, Joseph. *Nightswimmer*. New York: Simon & Schuster, 1994.

Oriard, Michael. *Dreaming of Heroes: American Sports Fiction, 1868–1980*. Chicago: Nelson-Hall, 1982.

———. *The End of Autumn: Reflections of My Life in Football*. New York: Garden City Press, 1982.

———. *Sporting with the Gods: The Rhetoric of Play and Game in American Culture*. Cambridge: Cambridge University Press, 1991.

Orodenker, Richard. *The Phillies Sports Reader*. Philadelphia, PA: Temple University Press, 1996.

———. *Twentieth Century American Sportswriters*. Detroit, MI: Gale Research, 1996.

———. *The Writer's Game: Baseball and Writing in America*. New York: Twayne, 1996.

Parker, John L. *And Then the Vulture Eats You*. Tallahassee, FL: Cedarwinds Publications, 1994.

———, ed. *Once a Runner*. Tallahassee, FL: Cedarwinds Publications, 1990.

Peck, M. Scott. *Golf and the Spirit*. New York: Random House, 1999.

Pipkin, Turk. *Fast Greens*. New York: Dial Press, 1996.

Plimpton, George. *The Curious Case of Sidd Finch*. New York: Macmillan, 1987.

———, ed. *The Norton Book of Sports*. New York: W. W. Norton, 1992.

Pomeranz, Gary. *Out at Home*. Boston: Houghton-Mifflin, 1985.

Quarrington, Paul. *Home Game*. New York: Doubleday, 1983.

Reid, Elwood. *If I Don't Six*. New York: Doubleday, 1998.

Reilly, Rick. *Missing Links*. New York: Doubleday, 1996.

Revoyr, Nina. *The Necessary Hunger*. New York: Simon & Schuster, 1997.

Ritz, David. *The Man Who Wanted to Bring the Brooklyn Dodgers Back to Brooklyn*. New York: Simon & Schuster, 1981.

Rosen, Charles. *The House of Moses All-Stars*. New York: Seven Stories Press, 1996.

Rosen, R. D. *Strike Three, You're Dead*. New York: Signet, 1985.

Rutman, Leo. *Five Good Boys*. New York: Viking, 1982.

Sandoz, Joli, ed. *A Whole Other Ballgame: Women's Literature on Women's Sport*. New York: Farrar, Strauss & Giroux, 1997.

Sandoz, Joli, and Joby Winans, eds. *Whatever It Takes: Women on Women's Sport*. New York: Farrar, Strauss & Giroux, 1999.

Schiffer, Michael. *Ballpark.* New York: Simon & Schuster, 1982.

Schinto, Jeanne, ed. *Show Me a Hero: Great Contemporary Stories about Sport.* New York: Persea Books, 1995.

Shainberg, Lawrence. *One on One.* New York: Pocket Books, 1972.

Shannon, Michael. *The Day Satchel Paige and the Pittsburgh Crawfords Came to Hartford, N.C.* Jefferson, NC: McFarland, 1992.

———. *Diamond Classics: Essays on 100 of the Best Baseball Books Ever Published.* Jefferson, NC: McFarland, 1989.

———. *Tales from the Dugout: The Greatest True Baseball Stories Ever Told.* Chicago: Contemporary Books, 1997.

Sheed, Wilfred. *The Boys of Winter.* New York: Knopf, 1987.

Shields, David. *Heroes.* New York: Simon & Schuster, 1984.

Shriver, Lionel. *Double Fault.* New York: Doubleday, 1997.

Silverman, Al, and Brian Silverman. *The Twentieth Century Treasury of Sports.* New York: Viking, 1992.

Small, David. *Almost Famous.* New York: Norton, 1982.

Snyder, Don J. *Veteran's Park.* New York: Franklin Watts, 1987.

Sojka, Gregory. *Earnest Hemingway: The Angler as Artist.* New York: Peter Lang Publishing, 1985.

Soos, Troy. *Hunting a Detroit Tiger.* New York: Kensington Books, 1997.

———. *Murder at Ebbets Field.* New York: Kensington Books, 1995.

———. *Murder at Fenway Park.* New York: Kensington Books, 1994.

———. *Murder at Wrigley Field.* New York: Kensington Books, 1996.

Stark, Sharon. *A Wrestling Season.* New York: Morrow, 1987.

Stein, Harry. *Hoopla.* New York: Knopf, 1983.

Stout, Glenn, ed. *The Best American Sports Writing 1999 (an annual).* Boston: Houghton-Mifflin, 1980–2000.

Sullivan, Mark. *The Fall Line.* New York: Kensington Books, 1994.

Terry, Douglas. *The Last Texas Hero.* Garden City, NY: Doubleday, 1982.

Toomey, Pat. *On Any Given Sunday.* New York: Fine, 1984.

Trudell, Dennis, ed. *Full Court: A Literary Anthology of Basketball.* New York: Breakaway Books, 1996.

Tuckman, Bruce. *Long Road to Boston.* Tallahassee, FL: Tradewinds Publications, 1995.

Umphlett, Wiley Lee. *The Achievement of American Sports Literature: A Critical Appraisal.* Cranbury, NJ: Associated University Presses, 1991.

Updike, John. *Golf Dreams: Writings on Golf.* New York: Knopf, 1996.

———. *Rabbit Angstrom: A Tetrology.* New York: Knopf, 1995.

Vanderwerken, David, and Spencer Wirtz. *Sport Inside and Out: Readings in Literature and Philosophy.* Fort Worth, TX: Texas Christian University Press, 1985.

Vogan, Sara. *In Shelley's Leg.* St. Paul, MN: Graywolf Press, 1985.

West, Paul. *Out of My Depths.* Garden City, NY: Doubleday, 1983.

Westbrook, Deeanne. *Ground Rules: Baseball and Myth.* Champaign, IL: University of Illinois Press, 1996.

Wiebusch, John, and Brian Silverman, eds. *A Game of Passion: The NFL Literary Companion.* Atlanta, GA: Turner Publications, 1994.

Willard, Nancy. *Things Invisible to See.* New York: Knopf, 1984.

Wilner, Herbert. *A Quarterback Speaks to His God.* Berkeley, CA: Cayuse Press, 1987.

Wimmer, Dick. *The Schoolyard Game: An Anthology of Basketball Writings.* New York: Simon & Schuster, 1992.

Winegardner, Mark. *Prophets of the Sandlots: Journey with a Minor League Scout.* New York: Atlantic Monthly Press, 1990.

————. *Veracruz Blues*. New York: Viking, 1996.
Wise, Suzanne. *Sports Fiction for Adults: An Annotated Bibliography of Novels, Plays, Short Stories and Poetry with Sporting Settings*. New York: Garland Publishing, 1986.
Woodward, Caroline. *Disturbing the Peace*. Vancouver, BC: Polestar Books, 1990.
Young, Al. *Ask Me Now*. New York: McGraw-Hill, 1980.

## Journals

*Aethlon: The Journal of Sport Literature* (Johnson City, TN)
*American Literary History* (Oxford, England)
*American Quarterly* (Baltimore, MD)
*Australian Magazine* (Sydney, Australia)
*China Sports* (Beijing, China)
*International Sports Journal* (West Haven, CT)
*Journal of American Culture* (Bowling Green, OH)
*Journal of American Folklore* (Bowling Green, OH)
*Journal of Canadian Studies* (Ottawa, Ontario, Canada)
*Journal of Latin American Culture* (Oxford, England)
*Journal of Men's Studies* (Johnson City, TN)
*Journal of Popular Culture* (Bowling Green, OH)
*Journal of Ritual Studies* (Pittsburgh, PA)
*Journal of the Philosophy of Sport* (Champaign, IL)
*Modern Fiction Studies* (West Lafayette, IN)
*Nine: A Journal of Baseball History and Social Policy Perspectives* (Edmonton, Alberta, Canada)
*South Atlantic Review* (Atlanta, GA)
*Sport, Education and Society* (Abington, England)
*Sporting Heritage* (Bickley, England)
*Sports Illustrated* (New York, NY)
*Sports in Japan* (Tokyo, Japan)

# 7

# Sport: Philosophy and Religion

Sport's intersection with philosophy and religion prompts some of the most provocative and important questions for sports scholars. Athletes, coaches, and academics have always questioned why we participate in sports, why we value sport, and what sport means to countries, towns, schools, and individuals. Still, the formal study of the philosophy of sport is a relatively recent development. Johan Huizinga's *Homo Ludens: A Study of the Play Element in Culture* (1960), Roger Callois's *Man, Play and Games* (1961), and Howard Slusher's *Man, Sport and Existence: A Critical Analysis* (1967) laid the original groundwork in the field and opened the doors for current sport philosophers. Those interested in discussions of these and other early works in the philosophy of sport should consult Jack Higgs's *Sports: A Reference Guide*, which expertly profiles the works that defined the field until 1980. This chapter will profile the major concerns of scholars of sport philosophy over the last two decades, concentrating on metaphysical questions such as why and how we play and what play means to us, ethical questions that examine how sport affects character development and a participant's ability to deal with ethical dilemmas presented within the sporting context, and aesthetic questions dealing with sport's relationship to art and the ramifications of this relationship for players and spectators. Another area of interest for academics has been the impact of political ideology on sport philosophy, especially the differences in athletic philosophies of authoritarian and democratic governments. Also important is the branch of philosophy known as ontology, which concerns itself with how humanity's spiritual dimensions are played out in the context of sport. Indeed, an important part of any discussion of the philosophy of sport must be the close ties shared between religion and sport, a topic that has always been important for athletes. It is rare, indeed, that we do not see some athlete engage in a religious ritual before or during a big game. Pregame prayer, superstitious routines, and postgame tributes to God are par for the course in contemporary athletics. This chapter will discuss recent scholarly research on the relationship between sport and religion, focusing on two main questions: Is sport a religion? How does religion operate within athletic constructs? In addition, this chapter will analyze recommended texts for classroom use and profile what some scholars say about what makes sport philosophically and spiritually valuable.

## THE MEANING OF SPORT

Following the lead of Huizinga, Callois, and Slusher, many scholars have speculated on why we play and what our play means. Perhaps the best book with which to begin one's inquiry into these questions is Robert Osterhoudt's *The Philosophy of Sport: An Overview*. Osterhoudt thoroughly explains five main philosophic systems and their implications for sports and includes sections that profile the strengths and weaknesses of each system's relation to sport. The first is the naturalistic philosophy of sport, which contends that we play in order to physically and spiritually reconnect ourselves to nature. We play mostly for the bodily sensations that are achieved while engaging in a cross-country race in which we chart a course through a natural setting. For those who counter with the idea that nearly everything can be considered natural and that we play for mental fulfillment as much as physical stimulation, there is idealism, a philosophy championed by such notables as Plato, Lao-tze, Buddha, and Pythagoras. Idealism posits that we play to connect ourselves to ideas or knowledge that exists on a higher plane. The body is thus subordinated to the mind and is only used to provide our brains with a healthy body in which to operate. In "sporting activities that emphasize the idea-centered character of reality, sublime and arduous activities which serve largely social aims, are preferred over others" (Osterhoudt 1991, 177). Of course, the problem with idealism is that it does not account for the physical enjoyment we get from playing sports. Both idealism and naturalism are examples of dualistic philosophies of sport, systems that see the human mind and body as separate and largely adversarial, so that one must be subordinate to the interests of the other. Other philosophies, such as pragmatism, are holistic in nature, holding that we engage in sports because they do things we like for our entire person. In particular, pragmatism asserts that we participate in sport because it leads to practical benefits, such as good health, a sense of well-being, new ideas, and human connection. No matter what, our participation is utilitarian. We play for positive results in our life. This is perhaps the philosophy that is most evident in contemporary America, where parents encourage their children to play sports to make friends and build character, high school kids play to earn scholarships, and college athletes labor with an eye toward the professional ranks. Closely related to pragmatism is realism, a philosophy that springs from the notion that there is nothing present in the universe except the physical, material realm. Our engagement in sport represents our attempt to make sense of the world and the fragmented nature of its reality. For instance, a realist might hold that people participate in mountain climbing to come to grips with their place in the world or to figure out their relationship with nature. A final holistic philosophy is existentialism, whose proponents hold that we play because the sporting experience allows us to consistently construct and reconstruct our identities through vital, subjective experiences. The idea here is that the human conception of self is simply our impression of all of our experiences. Sporting experiences are physical, mental, and spiritual and allow the participant to forge a series of truths about him or herself. Osterhoudt points out that each of these three holistic philosophies has the same problem. They do not account for the spiritual side of human life, the fact that many people are religious and consider their play to have some spiritual element that is greater than the self-realization extolled by the existentialist (Osterhoudt 1991, 174–187).

Osterhoudt's book is one of two works that does a masterful job of discussing the views of dominant philosophers and the implications of their views for sports from Ancient Greece to the twentieth century. Chapter four of his book is entitled "The Main Philosophic Periods/Figures and Their Implications for Sport." Zoroaster, Confucius, Epicures, Anselm, Aquinas, Kant, Rousseau, Hegel, Marx, Kierkegaard, Bentham, Mill, Jaspers, Sartre, Santayana, and Wittgenstein are only a handful of the philosophers whose thoughts he profiles, making sure to stress their application to sports. The book is thus a well-written guide to the world's most influential philosophies and to their relationship to athletics. Another such book is Robert Mechikoff and Steven Estes's *A History and Philosophy of Sport and Physical Education: From Ancient Greece to the Present.* The authors' strategy is much the same as Osterhoudt's, but the organization is different. Instead of chronicling the thoughts of philosophers in different ages from all over the world, Mechikoff and Estes focus on the contributions from scientists, philosophers, and educators in every age to show how the three types of knowledge together contributed to the way people of that age viewed sport. For instance, they discuss how the scientific theories of Isaac Newton and Francis Bacon combined with the philosophical dictates of Rene Descartes and the educational ideas of John Locke and Francois Rabelais to define the parameters for sporting practices in sixteenth-century Europe (Mechikoff and Estes 1993, 94–107). The authors do this for Ancient Greece and Rome, Medieval Europe, the Enlightenment, Northern Europe in the nineteenth century, colonial America, nineteenth-century America, and twentieth-century Europe and America. They also offer three chapters that analyze how world philosophies have impacted the Olympic games throughout their history, paying close attention to how the Olympics has changed over the course of the twentieth century because of new philosophic developments in science, education, and politics.

Mechikoff and Estes also offer a clear discussion that could help any student of sport philosophy distinguish between what is meant by existential views of sport as opposed to phenomenological conceptions of athletics. According to the authors, "Existence precedes essence, which accounts for the term *existentialism.* This means that each individual creates himself or herself through choices and experiences and that a person is the sum total of all his or her choices or experiences" (Mechikoff and Estes 1993, 381). Thus, sport from this viewpoint is simply the attempt by an individual to fashion an identity based on something that he or she likes in the sporting experience. For instance, a young man who wants to cultivate a macho identity might want to play football, ice hockey, or even try his hand at boxing because to be a boxer or a football player might signify an identity that is tough, manly, and virile in the mind of the boy. By contrast, phenomenology is much like realism. "From a metaphysical standpoint, the body is viewed monistically as a means of fundamental access to the world, the instrument of communication to the world. The body is not an instrument of the mind or an enemy of reason, but an individual's avenue to the world of experience in knowledge" (Mechikoff and Estes 1993, 383). Thus a phenomenological view of sport, like an existential one, denies any spiritual component to athletic activity. There is no higher truth to be reached. The only celebration is of the self, existentially of the self's sense of identity, and phenomenologically of the self's physical and mental knowledge gained through its sporting interaction with the material world. Mechikoff and Estes not only discuss these two philosophical views in a way that is understandable, but also offer some intriguing discussion questions meant to give students a chance to play with the main concepts presented by each philosophy.

Another book of interest is Carolyn Thomas's *Sport in a Philosophic Context*, which cleverly organizes its discussion of sport philosophy into three sections: classical theories of play, recent theories of play, and modern theories of play. Thomas provides thorough explanations for the theories in each category, including some practical applications and potential drawbacks. Classical theories include two theories of surplus energy, one that posits that play results from our need to use our excess energy, and the other that asserts that we use the excess energy for play because it triggers a pleasurable response in us. Instinct theories contend that we play because of an unlearned, innate capacity to respond playfully to different situations, while the concept of recapitulation involves the idea that this innate tendency to play actually results from our desire to reproduce the playful behaviors adopted by humans during the various stages of our evolution. Thomas points out that these two explanations are unsatisfactory because, although play does seem natural, it is clearly a learned behavior that springs from specific societal circumstances. Preparation theory accounts for this by contending that we play in order to prepare us for things we will face later in life. This is perhaps the classical theory that comes closest to contemporary America, where we incessantly tout sport as something that will prepare our children for the bigger game of life. Another theory that has contemporary resonance is that of relaxation, the not-so-novel idea that energy spent in play not only relaxes us, but actually invigorates us as well (Thomas 1983, 60–61).

Thomas also analyzes what she calls recent theories of play, by which she seems to mean theories that were prominent in the later nineteenth and early twentieth centuries. One of the more intriguing of these is Catharsis, the idea that we engage in sport because it provides us with an emotional release. The concept is usually associated with the idea that sport allows people to work out frustrations and relieve both psychological and physiological stress. The theory has not fully been borne out by psychological studies, but its prevalence in American society is evident. Clearly, some athletes do play to work through problems, but just as many exhibit sporting behaviors that resemble the theory of generalization, which asserts that we play in order to revisit experiences that have been pleasant for us at work. The theory is somewhat plausible, especially when extended to include the behaviors that children learn in school, their version of work. After all, if compromise is satisfying to a person in the workplace, there is a chance that he or she might continue to enjoy the good feelings of compromise in sports. Such a person might be a good captain, at least in terms of making sure that all the players on a team feel like they are being treated fairly. Closely related to generalization is developmental theory, which states that play actually represents human attempts to impose subjective value on reality. In other words, we play because play, by nature, is fluid. It can be anything we want it to be and thus can function as a place where we can reinforce values that are pleasing or reassuring to us (Thomas 1983, 66–67). Again, this is quite common in modern athletics. For instance, athletes might wear a red ribbon on their uniform to make a political statement or pray in the end zone after a touchdown in an attempt to infuse their sporting experience with religious meaning that reaffirms their faith.

Thomas also advances two modern theories of play, both of which are prevalent within the American sports establishment. The first is arousal theory, which says that we play because we naturally seek physical and emotional highs. Put simply, sports make us feel intensely. They let us know that we are alive through moments of optimal arousal that might include winning a big game or putting every last ounce of energy into finishing a triathalon. Arousal theory works hand in hand with competence theory, which says that we play in order to achieve some goal that makes us feel good about ourselves (Thomas 1983, 70). This may include making friends as a kid, making business contacts as an adult, feeling healthy or winning a scholarship. The idea, which seems consistent with much of postmodern American ideology, is that we do things because they make us feel good, either through physical and emotional stimulation or because they in some way give us a skill that will help us in some other area of our lives. Again, Thomas provides a lengthy discussion of how these theories developed, exactly how they operate in today's world, and how each falls short of fully explaining human play. She makes the point that, although she categorizes the theories by period, almost all of these theories should be seen as partial explanations for our sporting habits, a range of behaviors that are so broad and diverse that no one theory could fully account for them.

R. Scott Ketchmar is another leader in the field of sport philosophy. His works include *Practical Philosophy of Sport*, in which he relates three contemporary explanations for why we engage in athletics. The first is commonly referred to as runaway individualism. The idea here is that our society values individualism in a few ways. First, we judge our citizens on their ability to be self-reliant. Second, a major part of what Americans believe to be a healthy identity is self-expression. Sport, then, is one vehicle by which we come to be self-reliant and individually expressive, thus satisfying our country's definition of a successful or complete person. A football player, for instance, must take full responsibility for doing his part to help the team win, but he can also express himself by dancing in the end zone. A second theory is called excessive survivalism. It asserts that sports teach us lessons and equip us with tools that help us survive contemporary life where we are judged either as winners or losers: "Victories seem to be important even if they have to be gained by bending the rules and playing weak opponents. Symbolically and psychologically, if not actually, to survive in our culture is to be a winner. Sport and athletics offer some of the best stages society has for rehearsing, reenforcing, and acting out this survival commitment" (Ketchmar 1994, 98). Yet a third explanation for play is oppressive rationalism, which simply contends that we play because it has a purpose for us as individuals or for society. Sports, for instance, might be a way to a better economic position for those good enough to be professionals or might be a way to advance a political or social cause, such as the San Francisco Giants implementation of an AIDS Awareness Day in 1995. It is interesting that each of these theories begins with a negative word, "runaway," "oppressive," and "excessive," that indicates that we have gone too far in each of these directions. Ketchmar clearly thinks so and dedicates several pages to explaining how playing for these reasons can be quite detrimental. For instance, the author believes that excessive survivalism reinforces an unhealthy way of looking at people as either winners or losers. Since there are usually only a few winners and several "losers," most people are always bound to be on the short end of the stick. Ketchmar does a nice job of explaining the dangers associated with each of these theories, contending that their common pitfall is that they corrupt the fun nature of sports, which when played properly can bring out the best each participant has to offer, allowing him or her to feel intense enjoyment (Ketchmar 1994, 95–105).

Those interested in a discussion on psychoanalysis or Zen might consult Drew Hyland's *Philosophy of Sport*. Hyland defines the relationship between psychoanalysis and sport as being the process by which we can see how a person's unique psychological make-up determines his sporting behavior. Hyland's discussion is good and underscores the fact that the problem with psychoanalysis is that it involves so many complex factors, such as the effects of the person's religion, family, education, and physical appearance on his or her outlook on life, that it is hard to use. All of these factors must be accounted for before a plausible psychoanalytic explanation of sporting practice can be rendered. What is more appealing is the use of sociological categories to narrow down the parameters of psychoanalysis. For instance, Hyland shows how one can examine the psychological reasons why Asian Americans participate in certain sports but not in others. Hyland also provides a nice discussion of Zen, which holds that we play sports because they allows us to fully realize ourselves by attaining "peak experiences." Just what those are and how we come by them is difficult to determine, but two books, Eugen Herrigel's *Zen in the Art of Archery* and Robert Pirsig's famous *Zen and the Art of Motorcycle Maintenance: An Inquiry into Values*, might help the reader get a sense of what a peak experience is. Most of Hyland's book advances his theory of why we play, an intriguing blend of ideas that he calls "responsive openness." The idea behind responsive openness is that sport gives us the opportunity to wrestle with some of the concepts and issues that define our existence. For instance, one of the concepts that we must address is finitude, the idea that life will end and that it has many limits for us while we are alive. Sport forces us to deal with limits of movement (no use of hands in soccer) and time (shot clock), and forces us to confront our own mortality when we deal with our inability to play a sport any longer. This is most visible with professional athletes who usually leave their sports in their mid-thirties (Hyland 1990, 129). Other elements of responsive openness include possibility, which forces us to confront the unforeseen but which also encourages us to imagine potentially positive solutions; freedom, which refers to our recognizance of our free will and the responsibility for positive action that goes with it; risk-taking, trust, value, and fun, which makes us grapple with that which we find pleasurable in life and why. All of these elements of responsive openness are designed to improve our understanding of ourselves, making it easier for us to navigate our way through an increasingly complex society.

Two other books worth consulting because of their unique approach to answering the question of why we play are Allen Guttmann's *The Erotic in Sports* and Betsy Postow's *Women, Philosophy, and Sport: A Collection of New Essays.* Guttmann advances the idea that we play sport in part because it allows us to engage our body and the bodies of others in a meaningful, erotic manner. Thus, at the heart of sport is a deep physiologic satisfaction. Guttmann offers compelling historical evidence that humans have always loved sport for this reason, including examples from antiquity, the Middle Ages, the Renaissance, and throughout the modern period. His analysis of Fox Television's *American Gladiators* is indicative of the kind of writing in the book:

Extremely muscular men and women, who have obviously spent innumerable hours "pumping iron," compete in a series of unique physical contests. Dressed in a variety of skimpy science-fiction outfits that accentuate different parts of their anatomy (e.g., women's thighs, men's pectoral muscles), the contestants wrestle, batter one another with padded poles, swing from rings, climb a cushioned pyramid from which other contestants try to hurl them to the floor, scale a wall under the same adverse condition, race up inclined treadmills that roll them backwards if they weaken, endeavor to knock or pull each other from elevated platforms, and compete in a number of other newly invented sports, most of which allow for the ample demonstration of physical prowess and the generous display of secondary sex characteristics. The women, who seem invariably to be blond if they are not African Americans, compete in exactly the same sports as the men. When not competing, the male and female contestants smile, gyrate seductively, flex and swagger. It is difficult to imagine a more egregious assertion of the erotic element in sports. (Guttmann 1996, 72)

The essays in Postow's book are not as colorful but are just as informative because they deal specifically with women's philosophies of sport. Included are women's conceptions of justice that can be fulfilled in sport, the use of sport by women to resolve typically female conflicts such as how to reconcile the feminine behaviors traditionally expected of women with modern demands of an increasingly competitive capitalist marketplace, and new philosophies of how to promote sports in society that include "feminine values" so as to make sport a healthy, beneficial experience for both boys and girls. Those interested in what a feminine value is and how they might transform our philosophies of sport should focus on J. Theodore Klein's essay, "Philosophy of Education, Physical Education, and the Sexes."

## ETHICAL CONCERNS IN SPORT

Another important area of philosophy is the study of ethics. One of the better introductions to how ethical considerations operate within the world of sports is Warren P. Fraleigh's *Right Actions in Sport: Ethics for Contestants*. He points out that the athletic arena is an excellent training ground for tackling tough ethical questions because it provides us with a background in which the moral nature of action is always in question. As Fraleigh writes, "Persons associated with sports contests for a significant length of time are aware of many instances in which questions arise about morally right actions" (Fraleigh 1984, 1). Much of Fraleigh's work is dedicated to explaining the process by which we make ethical decisions in sports. Though his analysis is painstakingly complete and laden with countless examples, he basically concludes that each person needs to cultivate a worldview that includes an established set of criteria against which they compare the rightness and wrongness of actions. The person then applies those standards to the ethical dilemmas they face in athletics. For instance, a Christian might ask what the Bible says about cheating or if it offers any guidelines that might address whether it is acceptable to foul an opponent intentionally. Fraleigh does not discuss many of the hundreds of frameworks of reference a person might have for determining whether an action is right or wrong, but he does answer the question about how we can cope with the fact that this method of making ethical decisions will result in any number of divergent opinions. For Fraleigh, the main contribution of sports to a society's ethical improvement is that any ethical question posed within a sporting event should be answered with regard to what is best for the team rather than what is best for oneself: "In the sports world we can see that everyone is better off if everyone follows moral rules rather than rules of self-interest. The latter would invite chaos, distrust, fear, and rampant disregard of one participant for other participants. Now, when we adopt the position that we ought to be moral in its more general sense because it is consistent with a world that is better for everyone, we establish a general recipe for guidance in specific sports situations" (Fraleigh 1984, 12). Therefore, it does not matter what one's system of reference is as long as community concerns are elevated above individual interests. This method can then be transferred to society so that ethical decisions that affect a nation or any given community are made on the basis of what is best for everyone (Fraleigh 1984, 10–12).

Fraleigh's analysis seems somewhat idealistic, but he is up front with his readers in telling them that his goal is not to examine how current ethical issues are played out in sports, but to analyze how sports can function in a way that leads to ethical improvement for society. By contrast, in *Ethical Decisions in Sport: Interscholastic, Intercollegiate, Olympic and Professional* Edward Shea analyzes several potential frameworks from which an athlete might make ethical decisions that can lead to his or her individual character development. Shea discusses the ramifications on ethics of capitalism, democracy, authoritarian governments, self-centered values, concepts of duty, moral relativism, power, dominance, masculine and feminine stereotypes, and several other factors that influence an athlete's core framework of values. Unlike Fraleigh, Shea thinks the ethical questions presented by sport are beneficial not because they lead to an ethical process that promotes community well-being, but because they provide the opportunity for each individual to grow intellectually and morally as they wrestle with each question to either reenforce or alter their current moral views (Shea 1996, 59–66). A question such as "Should I cheat if it will help me win?" for instance, forces an athlete to sharpen his or her cerebral skills by looking at every side of the situation to determine all of the positive and negative ramifications of the act. The athlete would have to consider the effects of the act on his or her reputation, career, friends, and family. No matter what decision the athlete makes, he or she will have changed from the process of having to make it. Of course, the change can be negative as well as positive, and Shea makes it clear that students should not look upon the relationship between ethical development and sport through rose-colored glasses. After all, if the athlete in question gets away with cheating and continues to do it, most would agree that he or she has certainly regressed morally and will likely pay the price for such regression at some point. Shea's overall point is that sports force most athletes to grow or regress through their interaction with ethical dilemmas. He offers several case studies to illustrate how a number of different ethical questions might affect various athletes (Shea 1996, 156–173).

In addition to the contributions of Fraleigh and Shea, there are at least two other fine works that examine the ethical status of sport, both of which provide complete discussions on some of the more pressing ethical questions faced by athletes. The first is Osterhoudt's *The Philosophy of Sport*, which contains several essays from leading sport philosophers that analyze a number of ethical issues. In "The Ethics of Competition and Its Relation to Some Moral Problems in Athletics," for instance, James Keating discusses the differences between play, a fun activity with no material reward except pleasure, and athletics, featuring contests in which one tries to better oneself by winning, and asks which one is better for an individual and for society. Keating sees the value of both and is careful to emphasize that each has its own set of ethical standards that should not be misapplied to the other. For instance, it is permissible to hit an opponent in athletics as long as the rules stipulate that it is acceptable. By contrast, play has few if any formal rules, and since there is no importance placed on victory, any violence would seem immoral (Osterhoudt 1985, 157–175). Other scholars address questions such as whether competition is good or bad, whether sport functions as a hegemonic social construction that reenforces the values of dominant groups or as a democratic process that allows those values to be challenged by the masses, whether or not it is healthy to break rules and question the decisions of officials, whether or not it is proper to view sport as an outlet for aggression or as an arena in which it is appropriate to practice imposing one's will on others in preparation for a world in which one must do just that to get ahead, and whether gambling has positive or negative effects on sports spectators.

*Philosophic Inquiry in Sport*, edited by R. Scott Ketchmar, William Morgan, and Klaus Meier, contains a fascinating section called "Fair Play, Sportsmanship and Cheating," in which several scholars debate two critical questions: What is the ethical status of sportsmanship? What are the moral effects of competition? On the subject of the former, one might want to contrast Keating's essay "Sportsmanship as a Moral Category," which debunks the notion that sportsmanship should be viewed as a moral component to sports, and Peter Arnold's "Three Approaches Toward an Understanding of Sportsmanship," which argues that sportsmanship is a vital moral component in sport because it celebrates important values such as fairness, it results in respect for oneself and one's opponent, and it fosters good feelings between competing teams. Regarding the effects of competition, Fraleigh's "Why the Good Foul Is Not Good" and Oliver Leaman's "Cheating and Fair Play" make for a study in contrasting views. Fraleigh holds that competition can be good as long as all of the rules of a game are observed. No rules can be broken because, unlike in society where rules do oppress some people, all of the rules in sport apply equally to all and are fully accessible to all participants. On the other hand, Leaman contends that we have been too hard on cheating in the past and that most of the things we consider to be cheating are acceptable. Leaman attempts to support his highly questionable argument by advancing the notion that, as long as the cheater understands the potential consequences of his or her actions, it is all right for him or her to try to get away with any behavior that might result in winning. Leaman's view is quite Machiavellian and is somewhat disconcerting. It is not what we want to believe, but as anyone who follows the National Hockey League would have to admit, this view probably characterizes the attitude of many professional athletes. Ketchmar, Morgan, and Meier also include sections that analyze ethical considerations regarding gender and racial issues in sport, and the use of performance-enhancing drugs. A final section on the ethical dilemmas faced by hunters makes for interesting reading.

## THE AESTHETICS OF SPORT

Ketchmar, Morgan, and Meier's *Philosophic Inquiry into Sport*, Hyland's *Philosophy of Sport*, and Osterhoudt's *The Philosophy of Sport* are three sources to which one can turn for diverse ideas on whether or not sport is art, or if sport at least has aesthetic qualities. In Ketchmar, Morgan, and Meier's work, scholar David Best contributes an essay entitled "The Aesthetic in Sport," in which he argues that some sports are purposive, having no artistic value because they are only concerned with winning and utilitarian ends such as scoring a goal, while others are aesthetic in that some form of artistic display is integral to the activity. Gymnastics would be an example of an aesthetic sport. Though he concedes that purposive sport can have some aesthetic movement, Best argues that a sport such as football need not involve artistry as long as the touchdowns are scored and victory is achieved. The author further insists that neither purposive nor aesthetic sports are art because they do not engage larger "life issues," such as those inherent in politics, religion, economics, and social dilemmas (Ketchmar, Morgan, and Meier 1995, 377–390). Best's argument is much like that of German philosopher Georg W. F. Hegel who, according to Osterhoudt's "An Hegelian Interpretation of Art, Sport, and Athletics," believed that sports could not be considered art because "they have no purpose greater than themselves" (Osterhoudt 1985, 352). Hegel conceded that sport has been consistently abused as "a chauvinistic, cultural, economic, historical, military, natural scientific, pedagogical, political, psychological and social instrument" (Osterhoudt 1985, 352). Yet, these uses are written off as abusive applications of athletics that have no basis in art, which by nature should not be overtly exploitive in a quest for material reward. In any event, such applications do not prove that sport has any inherent relation to art anyway. Also chiming in to agree that sport is not art is Christopher Cordner, who argues in "Grace and Functionality" that "the concept of art is distinguished from that of sport by the presence of internal ends in the former and the absence of such in the latter" (Ketchmar, Morgan, and Meier 1995, 447). Part of these internal ends is art's continual concern over what it means to be an artist and what the function of art is in society. This critical, meta-artistic character is, for Cordner, missing in sport, which exists not to debate the role of art or to produce graceful movement, but to produce points, wins, victories, fame, money, medals, honor, and any number of other material rewards. For Cordner, like Best and Hegel, sport is not art for the same reason a romance novel is not considered serious literature: It is designed for external reward without addressing important external issues, and it does not address serious questions concerning the nature of art.

Still, other scholars believe that if sport is not fully art, it at least has artistic elements. Paul G. Kuntz's "The Aesthetics of Sport," for instance, argues that both sport and art rely on performance to be considered successful. This performance requires an audience whose reception of the action often determines the success or failure of the venture in both an economic and artistic sense. In addition, this performance usually takes place in a special venue in which the audience is drawn into a unique world that creates what Kuntz calls a "symbolic reality." This reality, either in a play or in a sporting event, is meant to have some emotionally pleasing effect on the audience (Osterhoudt 1985, 306–307). Hyland argues that sport and art are closely related because they have the same "stance," that of responsive openness. This means that both art and sport can involve actors that improvisationally respond to important human issues such as dealing with time constraints, coping with rules and authority figures, learning to be an individual within a community structure that calls for each person to behave in sanctioned ways, knowing how and when to take risks, understanding the meaning of loyalty, achieving self-respect, and displaying sacrifice (Hyland 1990, 118–120). Finally, Joseph Kupfer argues in "Sport—The Body Electric" that, no matter what their external aims, both purposive and aesthetic sports have "inherent dramatic possibilities and qualities that make these activities eligible for aesthetic attention and serious axiological inquiry" (Ketchmar, Morgan, and Meier 1995, 447). These qualities include the development of tension, the element of uncertainty that keeps audiences at a play or game on the edge of their seats, and a final resolution to the action that provokes significant emotional response on the part of those who care about the outcome. For Kupfer, however, the most important thing is the permanency of that resolution. For the author argues that with both good art and great games there is the potential that the action might become part of a nation's collective consciousness, thereby becoming part of what defines that nation's view of itself (Ketchmar, Morgan, and Meier 1995, 397–400).

Interestingly, there do not seem to be many sport philosophers who contend that sport is art. However, Francis W. Keenan takes a good stab at it in "The Athletic Contest as a Tragic Form of Art." Keenan basically argues that some athletic contests do satisfy all six of the Aristotelian elements for a tragedy. For Keenan, the most important of these is plot. Much like Kupfer, Keenan argues that many sporting events start with a conflict, build with tension to some climactic moment, and end with a resolution that inspires a cathartic reaction for those in the audience. Certainly, it seems that this can be true. A great baseball game, for instance, often captivates the viewer until a decisive home run or error decides the game. Fans of the Boston Red Sox will not likely forget their reaction in the wake of Bill Buckner's error against the Mets in the 1986 World Series. Keenan also makes a good case for the presence in sport of the other five elements, character, thought, diction, music, and spectacle. Certainly, sporting contests feature several characters that perform the action. Often, we can identify with one or more of these characters and his or her behavior in the game, and his or her treatment by other characters is something that can affect us emotionally. Rebellious teenagers, for example, might respond to Dennis Rodman's ejection from a game. Keenan even argues that a game can have a tragic hero, whose flaw costs the team the game. By identifying with this athlete's plight, the audience can experience catharsis. In regard to thought, Keenan argues that a game offers athletic action that speaks for itself, evoking any number of serious thoughts from an audience. A particularly brutal football tackle, for instance, might make a viewer consider the concept of pain and how it operates in human lives. Diction and music are essential elements of many athletic contests, in which players communicate in what is often specialized language and in which music is used both to start the game with the national anthem and to pump the crowd up to support the home team. Finally, the mere fact that we often refer to games as sporting *events* is indicative of their status as significant societal spectacles. Spectacle refers to the effect of an event's overall ambiance on the viewer. Perhaps nothing illustrates how the Aristotelian concept of spectacle works in sport better than a college football game between two big rivals. Here, the viewer does not just experience a game. He or she is swept away by the sights, sounds, and smells of pregame tailgate parties, frolicsome students, beautiful cheerleaders, militaristic bands that blast powerful fight songs, and the raucous cheers of the crowd. Even the weather can play a crucial role. Thus, a viewer is emotionally moved not just by the game, but by all of the trappings that surround it. Anyone who has watched Michigan play Ohio State, Auburn play Alabama, or Yale play Harvard might understand how spectacle operates in sport. In any case, Kennan's essay is well written, and though it is certainly possible to point out how athletic contests often fail to meet some of the Aristotelian criteria for a tragedy, the essay is both thought provoking and convincing. Those interested in other articles that discuss sport's relationship to art might consult *The Journal of the Philosophy of Sport*, which sometimes contains articles on that subject.

## SPORT AND POLITICAL IDEOLOGY

Another topic that has drawn the interest of some scholars is the relationship between a nation's political ideology and its philosophic approach to sports. In *More than a Game: Sports and Politics*, Martin Barry Vinokur affirms that "sports have been used for nation-building and political integration by governments. The significance and conduct of a national sports system reflects the political system of that country rather than individual effort. For example, Romania's total control of, and subsidization of, its sports goals are also highly political goals" (Vinokur 1988, 18). Vinokur goes on to show how sports in several different countries are shaped by the political agenda of their governments. His discussions of sport in Romania and the former East Germany are particularly good. Perhaps his best chapter involves a comparison between sport in Eastern Europe and the West. Generally, Vinokur concludes that Eastern European sport, especially as it existed in East Germany and the Soviet Union, has been characterized by massive youth sport activities whose purpose is to identify young talent; a highly structured, governmentally controlled framework that works to train that talent for the good of the state; an emphasis on scientific research as a way of fostering superior athletic performance; and special schools and other privileges for athletes, whose sole jobs are to bring glory to the nation by winning international competitions (Vinokur 1988, 104). Such political goals would explain the vast amounts of money and effort that such countries put into training athletes. On the other hand, Western countries such as the United States reflect their more democratic political leanings in their attitudes toward sport. These attitudes result in sports that are local instead of national in focus and that are controlled by parents or local authorities as opposed to authoritative governments. In addition, there are massive secondary school sport programs, college programs that feature both varsity and intramural sports, international sporting efforts that are, to a great extent, privately funded, informal and amateur competition, and professional leagues (Vinokur 1988, 107). Thus, for Vinokur, sport in Eastern Europe and China has reflected the authoritarian, Communist aims of the governments in those regions, while Western sport has reflected an emphasis on individual development and commercial enterprise, both of which are highly valued in democratic governments. Perhaps the greatest difference is that authoritarian governments tend to fund sport so that its top athletes can bring prestige to the state, while democratic governments tend to rely on diverse elements from the private sector to fund a variety of different types of sport for a variety of different types of athletes. Of course, as evidenced by American efforts in the 1996 summer Olympic games, this does not mean that democratic nations are not interested in glory. They just finance their prestige differently.

Another detailed book on the subject is William Morgan's *Leftist Theories of Sport: A Critique and Reconstruction*. The book is broken up into three sections. The first is dedicated to explaining how traditional leftist theories of sport pervert what is truly good about sport. The basic thrust of Morgan's argument is that leftist ideologies such as communism inevitably associate sport with work. Eventually, such association leads to sport workers who labor in service to the state. At the opposite end of the spectrum is what Morgan calls hegemonic sport, a system that he criticizes severely in the second section of the book. According to Morgan, hegemonic sport is similar to leftist sport in that it ties sport together with work. The main difference is that the athlete-worker in a hegemonic system is working for a dominant overclass whose financial interests and social and political values drive organized sport: "More specifically, hegemony refers to all the ways in which the dominant class extends its sphere of influence over other classes and social groups" (Morgan 1994, 70). That sphere of influence includes sport. Of course, it might be argued that this process does allow athletes to better themselves financially, but Morgan insists that, while a few athletes do benefit in both the leftist and hegemonic systems, many more are hurt and the masses are deprived of what is truly good about sport: its liberating quality that allows for maximized personal fulfillment. Morgan's third section is dedicated to exploring how governments can implement a philosophy that will emancipate sport from its control by selfish parties who, in the name of external, material rewards, corrupt its capacity to act as an agent of freedom in people's lives. His solution, which he calls a "New Left Theory" of sport, is that all agents that currently exercise formal control over sport must be swept aside in favor of voluntary practice communities, which would exist to ensure that athletic opportunity exists for the internal betterment of participants rather than the external reward of controlling bodies. These communities would be purely voluntary, open to all players regardless of class, race, gender, or religion, have the goal of providing a sporting experience that benefits everyone on a personal level, and would not be subsidized by any outside agents. As Morgan comments, "If membership in such a community stands for anything, it stands for a shared dedication to the good of the kind of life embodied in sport, and the standards of excellence, values, and virtues that are an integral part of that life" (Morgan 1994, 236). While Morgan's argument is idealistic, and he is unclear about defining just how one achieves internal goodness through sport, his book is well written and worth reading, especially if one wants to understand the down side of liberal and hegemonic philosophies of sport.

A third book, John Hoberman's *Sport and Political Ideology,* is dedicated to discussing how political systems have impacted sport philosophies in the twentieth century. Hoberman covers several topics, including liberal Eastern European philosophies of the 1930s, Christian fatalism that held sway in both Western Europe and the United States in the 1920s and 1930s, aristocratic vitalism that was popular in England and France in the 1920s, radical disillusionment, and postmodern neo-Marxist theories of sport. Most of the book, however, deals with fascism, especially as it existed in Nazi Germany; Marxism, especially as it evolved in the former Soviet Union and East Germany; and Maoism. One of the best chapters outlines key differences between fascist and Marxist views of sport. Essentially, "the fascist leader is, in short, an athlete, whether sexual or equestrian. In either case, he takes pride in the act of mastery itself" (Hoberman 1984, 58). Sport is just another vehicle through which one can prove one's superiority, as well as that of one's nation and way of life. In a sense, then, the fascist athlete is a political athlete, competing to advance himself or herself within the state and the reputation of the state within the world. This philosophy was employed by Nazi Germany, which saw itself as a nation of heroic athlete-warriors that was endowed by nature with superior qualities. As Hoberman writes, "The dream of dynamic virility, prominently featuring the perfected body as a symbol of force, has been a theme of every fascist culture. Fascism has always incorporated a cult of virility. It is well known that the Nazis promulgated a 'virile' ideal of the Aryan warrior, and the Nazi art demonstrated a fascination with the ideal body type" (Hoberman 1984, 84). By contrast, Marxist doctrine rejected the myth of the political athlete and instead focused on two divergent athletic types that reflected different aspects of the ideology. The first is commonly referred to as the Stakhanovite worker, a man or woman who ideally played sports as a means for relaxing and gearing up for work in the labor force. The Workers Sport Movement was designed to break down barriers of class and to counter the fascist emphasis on competition for personal, material ends. As Hoberman writes, the Stakhanovite worker was "the heroic record-breaker that vastly overfills the production quota" (Hoberman 1984, 69). This Marxist model was popular in the 1930s, but eventually gave way to the Stalinist athlete of the 1950s, whom Hoberman describes as "the daring long-distance aviator who brings glory to the Socialist state" (Hoberman 1984, 69). For Stalin, sport had less of an economic function and more of a political one. It was a vehicle by which the state could make its name. Thus, the Stalinist philosophy of sport took the Soviet Union in the direction of Nazi Germany, establishing athletics as a vehicle by which to bring glory to the state. This, of course, is the central tenet of the athletic philosophies of authoritarian governments.

The authoritarian philosophy of athletes acting as soldiers of the state found its extreme application in East Germany, where a reliance on chemical technology allegedly made for the best mechanized athletes that science could produce. Hoberman dedicates an entire section of his book to East German philosophies of sport and concludes that "if East German sport culture has not become robotics, it nonetheless retains an alien and even disturbing ambiance" (Hoberman 1984, 213). Of course, much of this philosophy has been modified because of the reunification of the Germanies and by greater scrutiny on the part of athletic governing bodies such as the International Olympic Committee. Still, the East German athletic machine is an excellent example of how political ideology influences a nation's sporting philosophy, and Hoberman's chapter does justice to the topic. In addition, Hoberman provides an interesting analysis of how Maoist ideology impacted athletic philosophy in the People's Republic of China (PRC) until well into the 1980s. Hoberman argues that the Maoist philosophy shared with Marxism the desire that sport be used for the collective good. However, Maoist sport ideology was most recognizable because of its rules of strict etiquette that had to be followed by its athletes. Competition was seen as essentially harmful unless it could engender good feelings of friendship and camaraderie between the workers of the state. The Maoist athlete, then, could never be rude, overly aggressive, or lose ungracefully (Hoberman 1984, 222). Naturally, this has changed a great deal in recent years as China has undergone some political alterations, but Hoberman's analysis entertainingly points out how traditional Maoist athletes played havoc on the highly competitive international scene for years because they refused to take part in accepted athletic behaviors like engaging in physical contact with opponents.

Without question, this should be an area that intrigues scholars of sport philosophy over the next several years, and this should result in more scholarship regarding the relationship between a country's athletic philosophy and its political ideology. Political changes such as the reunification of East and West Germany, the break up of the Soviet Union, the return of Hong Kong to the People's Republic of China, and internal changes within the PRC will no doubt alter the governmental philosophies and sporting practices in those countries. Already, several professional sports leagues have developed in Russia, reflecting capitalism's impact on the region. Again, those interested in current information on this issue should consult the *Journal of the Philosophy of Sport*.

## SPORT AND RELIGION

Closely related to the philosophy of sport is the relationship between sport and religion. Anyone who has witnessed the way America responds to the Super Bowl must admit that the rituals and emotional fervor associated with the game border on religious practice. Over the last decade, scholars have penned several fantastic books that explore religious aspects of sport. Basically, the works concentrate on answering two main questions: Is sport a religion? How does traditional religious practice operate in sport? The first question has inspired heated debate. Stephen J. Overman not only denies that sport is a religion, but maintains that nothing has perverted sport in the United States more than religion. In an excellent book entitled *The Influence of the Protestant Ethic on Sport and Recreation*, Overman argues that sport can, in fact, have a spiritual function for participants:

The antithesis of the prevailing sports ethos would be activity that emphasizes playing and competing for the pure pleasure of the experience; stifling the cognitive functions during play in a Zen-like effort to get wholly into the flow; playing the game for the sake of the game, with no other goal in mind; playing without awareness of self or audience; attempting to break records not for personal glory but for the sense of excellence that accompanies the extension of human limits; focusing on the present and cherishing the moment in human movement; and finally, refusing to appropriate sport to the various agendas of the nonplay world. In this sense, sport can recapture a sense of the religious, which is where we begin the journey of the Protestant ethic. (Overman 1997, 352–353)

For Overman, however, this spiritual potential has been muted because America's traditional adherence to the Protestant ethic has combined with a capitalist economy to irrevocably associate sport with work. Overman's argument is essentially that sport has been objectified as a commodity of labor, something which we have viewed as work which must be engaged successfully if we are to achieve external rewards. Early in the country's history, the reward may have been the maintenance of the body as a temple for the Holy Spirit. In contemporary America, it might be an athletic scholarship or large signing bonus. In any case, it is always something material and outside the body that deprives an individual of the true spiritual benefits of sport. As Overman writes, "The virtues inherent in the Protestant ethic have been misapplied to sport and recreation" (Overman 1997, 352).

Another good work comes in the form of a special edition of *The South Atlantic Quarterly*. Edited by James Fisher, *Real Sports* contains a number of fine essays, some of which reject the notion of sport being a religion. For instance, Kenneth Parker's "Never on a Sunday: Why Sunday Afternoon Sports Transformed Seventeenth-Century England" is an entertaining and eye-opening essay that contends that not only is sport not a religion, but that the mixing of sport and religion has always been dangerous. Parker recounts how individual sporting behaviors, specifically one's adherence to or rebellion against Charles I's policy of allowing some athletic activity on the Sabbath, became one way of determining who was a Royalist and who was a "Protestant rebel" in seventeenth-century England. While Parker hardly suggests that a disagreement over sports on the Sabbath was a major cause of the Protestant rebellion of 1649, he makes it clear that it was a significant issue that further exacerbated tension between those loyal to Charles I and those who would side with Oliver Cromwell. As Parker concludes, "In an age when many would like to ignore or discount the power of religious conviction to shape individuals and nations, we would do well to remember the seventeenth-century English conflict over Sunday afternoon recreations" (Fisher 1996, 361). Interestingly, there are a few essays in the volume that, while not stating outright that sport is a religion, do at least admit that it can have spiritual significance for many participants. For example, Philip Deloria's "'I am of the Body': Thoughts on My Grandfather, Culture and Sports" discusses the belief of many Native American religions that wisdom proceeds from the body and that physical activity is a type of religious experience: "My grandfather's sports experience became intertwined with his personal sense of spirituality and his place as an Indian in America. He made those connections in explicitly familial terms, looking back to his father and grandfather and finding in his physicality not simply performance or pleasure but a way of serving, a special gift that informed his intellect, spirituality and moral sensibility" (Fisher 1996, 335–336). Not all of the essays in *Real Sports* deal specifically with sport as religion, but anyone interested in the topic should consult the volume. Its essays are well written, provocative, and touch upon our perceptions of why sports have a spiritual function in our lives.

An essay that is more open to the religious aspects of the sporting experience is Carloyn Thomas's "Sports," located in Peter Van Ness's *Spirituality and the Secular Quest*. The book is a compilation of several quality essays that examine how humans use secular activities to gain a sense of spiritual fulfillment. Thomas argues that sport is particularly effective in this quest because it is by nature a malleable entity that athletes can mold into their own unique sports world. Within this subjective world, the sporting participant finds several important spiritual benefits. As Thomas describes the power and attraction of such a world, "Sport, like a book, a script, a score, or a canvas, is inert until defined or interpreted by the acts of a participant. Sport is not unlimited; individuals bring their own limitations and thereby structure sport in their own image. Sport is, essentially, amoral and does not generate values; we each bring our values to sport and make it as worthy as we are. Hence, the athlete becomes largely responsible for defining his or her own 'world for the moment'" (Van Ness 1996, 502). One of the most important aspects of this condition is that the athlete can, to some extent, fashion his or her own identity. Thomas believes that "in subtle and overt ways, individuals seek to identify their own uniqueness—their selfhood—and to measure themselves against the world in the hope of coming to know who they are" (Van Ness 1996, 505). Practically speaking, this can be observed in an athlete's consistent encounters with adversity. The athlete's conception of self will hinges, to some degree, on his or her ability to overcome setbacks. A person who consistently runs from such challenges may unwittingly define himself or herself as a quitter.

A second function of the sport world is that it allows athletes to find meaning in life, answering the larger question of why we are here. This, of course, is usually one of religion's chief functions. Examples of how it works in the sports world can be seen in people that simply order their lives around projects in sports, the completion of which gives them a sense of having done something meaningful, or in the person who sees athletic activity as somehow serving others. Thomas also points out that participation in sports rescues some people from a sense of alienation that the author sees as being central to the postmodern condition. From this point of view sports are seen as a medium that allows us to spiritually reconnect with other people and thereby rescues us from "daily, routine, and utilitarian activities" (Van Ness 1996, 507). Just as important is the idea that sport can reconnect us with our own bodies, allowing us to become fully aware of ourselves physically in an age where technological comfort has come to dominate our lives and has alienated us from intimate knowledge of our bodies. Thomas refers to this as knowing the "body as subject," a condition where "the athlete not only has a body but is her or his body" (Van Ness 1996, 510).

For some athletes, the sport world functions as a place of meditative tranquility. It is, for instance, a place of escape from the rigors and pressures of everyday life: "Left behind are the pressures of school, work, family, finance, and interpersonal relationships" (Van Ness 1996, 507). Instead, the athlete concentrates on the game at hand. For others, sport is an arena in which one can find meaning by seizing control over his or her destiny. The control may last only a moment, but the desire for such control of our fate is the very thing that religion tries to give us. For some athletes, this may manifest itself in the desire to leave a mark, to make oneself significant by becoming part of history by executing some spectacular athletic feat. Still, for other athletes, the spiritual element of the sport world might exist as the antithesis of order. The sport world might function as a place where they can become spiritually reinvigorated by taking risks that demand that they intellectually and physically rise to new levels of performance. As Thomas writes, "Intentional and planned risk demands all the qualities most valuable in life: intelligence, skill, intuition, subtlety, and control. Sports provides a place where people can dominate fear and passion; a place where adventure and purpose and commitment can remove a sense of dread that might otherwise prevail. The element of risk can turn a weekend hobby into a small-scale model for living, a life within a life" (Van Ness 1996, 508). Perhaps no image better sums up Thomas's argument about the spiritual nature of the sport world. It is a world within our workaday world, one in which we can experience some of the basic functions that we might get from traditional religion: emotional solace, spiritual renewal, a sense of who we are, exhilaration, connection, and order. Thomas is careful to point out that this sport world is not religion in the traditional sense of the word because it has no connection to the supernatural realm, has no god, and offers no hope of sending its participants to heaven or to another, better world. Her work, however, is a good example of how humans sometimes perceive sport as having a religious function.

The three best books that tackle the question of whether sport is a religion are Charles Prebish's *Religion and Sport: The Meeting of Sacred and Profane*, Shirl Hoffman's *Sport and Religion*, and Michael Novak's *The Joy of Sports*. The first two books contain several essays that reflect a range of views about sport's capacity to act as a religion, including a few that completely reject the notion that sport and religion could ever be synonymous. For example, Joan Chandler's "Sport Is Not a Religion" contends that sport could never be considered a religion because it cannot lead to one's spiritual salvation. As Chandler writes, "Sport per se cannot tell us where we came from, where we are going, nor how we are to behave while we are here; sport exists to entertain and engage us, not to disturb us with questions about our destiny" (Hoffman 1992, 59). Prebish agrees with Chandler but is careful to point out that sport and religion have always played into each other. In "Religion and Sport: Convergence or Identity," Prebish chronicles how religious organizations such as Campus Crusade for Christ, Athletes in Action, and Fellowship of Christian Athletes and evangelists such as Billy Graham and Billy Zeioli have used sport to spread the gospel and to reach a large segment of an American society that loves its games. He also includes a fascinating discussion about how religious schools such as Notre Dame and Brigham Young University used sports, especially football, to garner prestige and wealth. Finally, he includes several excerpts from athletes and coaches describing how they used their faith to either improve their performance or help them through rocky times in their careers (Prebish 1993, 46–58).

Still, Prebish agrees that sport is not a religion in the traditional sense of the word. His opening chapter, "Religion: Approaches and Assumptions," discusses the four Cs that define a traditional religion: creed, code, cultus, and community. In traditional Christianity, the creed would be the Bible, the code would be the rules for human behavior set forth in that holy book, the cultus would be the rituals and ceremonies held sacred by Christians, and the community would be the churches into which Christian believers organize themselves. Prebish argues that sport does not meet these criteria. Instead, he concludes that sport may qualify as what some theologians call an emergent religion. According to Prebish, the four main qualities of an emergent religion are that it appear at a time of cultural instability, that it is unique or unusual, that it is oriented toward a better future, and that it has charismatic leadership (Prebish 1993, 16). The author considers how sport measures up to these criteria at length and concludes that "if sports can bring its followers to an experience of the ultimate, and this experience is expressed through a formal series of public and private rituals requiring a symbolic language and space deemed sacred by its worshipers, then it is both proper and necessary to call sport a religion" (Prebish 1993, 74).

Prebish's argument is intriguing and well worth reading, but one is left wondering if sport really meets the four criteria of an emergent religion. Clearly, the last half of the twentieth century has been turbulent. Massive changes in social mores, politics, religion, gender roles, demographics, economics, and technology have many Americans unsettled. In addition, sport when considered as a religion is certainly unusual. With Michael Jordan, Bret Favre, Eric Lindros, and a host of other heroes, sport clearly has its share of charismatic subdeities. But what about the ultimate deity? According to Prebish, the ultimate deity is the athlete, who gets as close to heaven on earth as one can through sport. According to Prebish's "An Existential Phenomenological Analysis of Sport as Religious Experience," an athlete can attain "transcendence" through athletic competition. This is a state where the athlete is in perfect physical, emotional, and cerebral harmony with the world and with him or herself. It is this state of transcendence that brings about happiness and that signifies a truly religious experience (Prebish 1993, 143). This experience sounds nice, but it comes across as being somewhat elusive if not fully unattainable. Also, if this is as good as it gets, how much should we really value sport as an emergent religion? Finally, Prebish never explains how sport is oriented toward a better future. Is his view that we will all somehow become better people through transcendent athletic experience? I hope not. Many of us who do not enjoy such sporting epiphanies on a regular basis will be left in a spiritual deep freeze.

In *The Joy of Sports*, Michael Novak reiterates Prebish's argument that sport is not a religion in the traditional sense of the word. However, Novak does not see sport as an emergent religion as much as he does a civil religion that operates in America as a vehicle by which we celebrate our ethnic myths. For instance, Novak argues that baseball celebrates the Anglo-American myths of rugged individualism and agrarian ideals on which our country was founded. Novak cites the beauty of the green grass of the baseball diamond within the modern steel and cement structures of the city as being symbolic of pastoral America and argues that the batter's confrontation with the pitcher is representative of the spirit of individualism that made America great. As the author writes, "In those nations where, in various forms, individualism and personal honor and the dignity of a man alone are deeply cherished, baseball elicits a responsive chord" (Novak 1994, 59). Novak further argues that football celebrates our more modern corporate myth. In football, men work together, each player being a key cog in a larger machine. If the machine is to work, each specialized part must perform. The emphasis is on community well-being as opposed to individual achievement: "Football exemplifies the strategies, the tactics, the crushing disappointments and the explosive 'scores' that constitute our working lives" (Novak 1994, 81). Perhaps Novak's most interesting assertion is that basketball celebrates African-American myths, especially ones that involve the relationship of African Americans with white society. Specifically, Novak says that basketball is a form of jazz to African Americans, an art form that represents the improvisational nature of their experience in a country where they have often had to feel their way past white barriers to political, economic, and social progress: "One 'puts on' the man. One 'puts a move on' him. The man has no right to know one's inner thoughts, desires, plans, schemes, intentions" (Novak 1994, 114).

Shirl Hoffman's *Sport and Religion* contains two essays that back up Novak's argument that sport is a civil religion in America. Joseph Price's "The Super Bowl as Religious Festival" contends that football's big game plays out two dominant American myths. The first is the spirit of conquest and domination that has defined the American ethos from the beginning. This is seen within the game as two teams armed with the best weapons thus far created by American technology execute a military-like plan to wage war on each other, battling for the other's territory in a series of violent altercations. The second reflects our penchant to see ourselves as innocent and pure, even though we define ourselves through conquest. Price analyzes the half-time extravaganza, which often features some light, whimsical number such as a Disney production aimed at children, as evidence for this assertion. He concludes that "as a cultural festival, it commands vast allegiance while dramatizing and reinforcing the religious myths of national innocence and apotheosis" (Hoffman 1992, 15). Like Price's essay, James Mathisen's "From Civil Religion to Folk Religion: The Case of American Sport" holds that sport has, in fact, operated as a civil religion in the United States. However, Mathisen contends that America has become too much of a diverse nation of skeptics to support sport as civic religion any longer. There are too many scandals, million dollar athletes with whom the fans cannot identify, and teams that have no loyalty to cities that have supported them for years. Instead, he says that sport has now become a folk religion, one in which pockets of Americans celebrate what is good about the country by lionizing individuals as opposed to sports themselves. Mathisen profiles Vince Lombardi to support his argument, pointing out that Lombardi embodied traditional values such as hard work, determination, sacrifice, and victory that are highly prized by Americans (Hoffman 1992, 26–30). Perhaps the popularity of the mild-mannered, humble, well-educated Mia Hamm might be a good example of a contemporary folk hero, an athlete who embodies what we want to believe about ourselves.

Interestingly, Novak also argues that sport acts as a secular religion in America in that we use it to celebrate our deepest national passions and values, as well as to play out our most pressing concerns. For instance, Novak writes that Americans want order and stability in their lives, and through sport we are able to transform regular time and space into sacred time and space, a uniquely spiritual world in which we can escape our usual problems and fashion a subjective experience that is healing for us (Novak 1994, 140–144). This, of course, is very close to Thomas's argument about our ability to merge into a spiritually uplifting sport world. Novak also believes that sports help us to fill our need for intimacy, allowing us to make meaningful connections with others: "The point of team sports is to afford access to a level of being not available to the solitary individual, a form of life ablaze with communal possibility" (Novak 1994, 149). In addition, sports provide the opportunity for people to attach their loyalty to things outside of themselves. This is important. We want to believe in something greater than ourselves. This is one of religion's most powerful lures, and it is one of the foremost reasons that a spectator becomes a fan. According to Novak, a sports team can provide spiritual uplift not only for individuals, but for entire cities and states, which often develop positive or negative identities based on the performance of sport teams: "Around Pittsburgh we went for decades without a winner in anything; inferiority matched the mood of the region. When the Pirates burst through as world champions, followed later by the Steelers, their success released pleasant feelings of vindica- tion, and grounded a rectification of reality" (Novak 1994, 151). Yet another spiritual need answered by sport is our desire to test ourselves, to find our limits and possibilities through competition. Novak refers to this as *agon*, a conflict that allows us to sharpen our abilities and spiritual faith (Novak 1994, 156). Novak introduces several other characteristics of the sporting experience that afford us spiritual growth and that qualify sport as a secular religion. Those interested in Novak's notion that sport is a secular religion might also want to consult his article "The Natural Religion" that appears in Hoffman's *Sport and Religion*. The article nicely sums up Novak's views: "To have a religion, you need to have a way to exhilarate the human body, and desire, and will, and the sense of beauty, and a sense of oneness with the universe and other humans. You need chants and songs, the rhythm of bodies in unison, the indescribable feeling of many who together 'will one thing', as if they were each members of a single body. All of these things you have in sport" (Hoffman 1992, 41).

Allen Guttmann echoes Novak's sentiments from a slightly different angle in "From Ritual to Record." Guttmann points out that in many societies throughout history sport was synonymous with a religious happening. The Greek Olympic festival, for instance, honored Zeus. The Pythian festival at Delphi paid homage to Apollo. Every two years the Isthmian games at Corinth and the Nemean contests at Nemea were conducted as tributes to Poseidon and Apollo, respectively. Guttmann includes many other examples of how various peoples have used sport as a religious celebration throughout the course of history, before convincingly arguing that contemporary sport does not do this. Instead, in America we play to honor our countries, cities, towns, schools, ourselves, and the process of capitalism. In short, we have made what was religious in the supernatural sense into a secular religion of which we are the center of worship: "The bond between the secular and the sacred has been broken, the attachment to the realm of the transcendent has been severed. Modern sports are activities partly pursued for their own sake, partly for other ends which are equally secular" (Hoffman 1992, 149–150).

While there is healthy disagreement among scholars as to just what sport and religion mean to each other, most scholars admit that sport is not a religion in the same way that Christianity, Judaism, and Islam are. Sport does not, for instance, tell us where we came from or why we are here. It does not get us into heaven. Thus, another key question that sport philosophers and theologians have addressed is how does traditional religion function within the sporting context. A number of academics and athletes give the researcher a variety of answers to that question. A fascinating book is Ellen Dugan's *This Sporting Life, 1878–1991*, which contains an essay by Harvey Green entitled "Rational Muscle Culture." Green shows how, by examining the development of photography, one can better understand how vital sport and religion have always been to each other in the United States. Green's essay proves that when photography was developed for popular use around the turn of the century, both sporting and religious communities used it for promotional purposes. Interestingly, both the church and the old town teams had the same idea to associate themselves with each other so as to make themselves look better. Green shows several pictures with entertaining captions used by churches to promote the idea that the best Christians were fun-loving folks who excelled at sport, keeping their bodies in shape out of respect for God. In addition, he analyzes several photos used by sporting clubs and businesses that are clearly meant to promote the idea that sports participation is closely connected to spiritual health and good Christian character (Dugan 1992,15–25). While Green's essay reveals the intimate connection between sport and religion during a specific time in American history, Robert J. Higgs's *God in the Stadium: Sports and Religion in America* is the ultimate authority on how both informal and organized sport and a variety of American religious practices have been entangled from the colonial period to the present. Higgs's work is a fabulous read that actually traces how religion and sport have vitally impacted each other's growth at every stage of American history. Topics of interest include how the Puritans used sport, how Native Americans have used sport, the relationship between sport and religion on the ever-expanding American frontier of the eighteenth and nineteenth centuries, the role played by sport in religious revivals, how colleges designed to train ministers have used sport, the intersection of sport and religion during wars, the differences between how various ethnic groups used sport in conjunction with religious practice, how the industrial revolution changed the way Americans viewed both sport and religion, and the complex factors that influence the relationship between sport and religion today.

In his final chapter, Higgs explores how modern athletes use religious practice in sport. To be sure, the rituals are highly divergent. Several books exist that chronicle the variety of approaches that religious athletes take to sport. Rick Arndt's *Athletes Afire* is one of several books on the market that compiles the personal stories of athletes who bring their faith to the field. A common thread that links most of the stories is that most of the athletes seem to use their faith to help them alleviate stress and pressure. Former baseball player Wayne Gross's writing is typical of that found within Arndt's work: "Instead of wavering so much and worrying about slipping and this and that, I know that I'm doing the best I can for the Lord. The Holy Spirit helps me in simple everyday situations and decisions; I say, 'Lord, through your Holy Spirit tell me which way to go,' and there's just a confidence and a peace that comes when I'm making the right decision" (Arndt 1985, 158). Hoffman's "Evangelicalism and the Revitalization of Religious Ritual in Sport" confirms that many athletes use religious ritual in sport not to try to win or gain unfair advantage, but to resolve spiritual problems presented by their sports participation. Hoffman includes examples of athletes who explain in their own words how they use their faith to help them deal with having to hit another player or even hurt another player even though it might be within the rules and what the game requires. In addition, the essay features professional athletes discussing how they use their faith to help them account for things like making a lot of money and having fame and gaining stature through the conquest of others, things which most religions stand against. Many of the athletes Hoffman features actually get over that hump by saying that the money, fame, and prestige that comes from winning actually helps them spread their religion so that they can, in particular, reach more kids (Hoffman 1992, 119–121). While some may look askance at millionaire athletes who take this position, it is, along with using sport to help them face pressure, perhaps the sentiment most commonly expressed by athletes about their use of faith in sport. Those interested in reading further on this subject might search Prebish's *Sport and Religion: The Meeting of Sacred and Profane* for Lori Rotenberk's "Pray Ball," an essay that contains several examples of how different athletes use sports to spread the gospel, or one of several biographies written by Christian athletes. Some recent ones include David Bannon and Joe Pellegrino's *Safe at Home*, Gary Carter and Ken Abraham's *The Gamer*, A. C. Green's *Victory*, Neil Lomax's *Third and Long*, and Reggie White's *In the Trenches*.

Despite the sentiments just expressed, it is clear that athletes do use their faith to help them win games. Both Hoffman and Rotenberk recount the stories of victorious athletes thanking God for answering their prayers for a championship or, even more humorous, of boxers thanking God for allowing them to smash an opponent. Some scholars have speculated that this sort of entanglement between sport and religion distorts the true nature of both. In "The Emergence of Born Again Sport," W. W. Aitken contends that the idea of invoking religious ritual to change the outcomes of games actually belittles them, while mistakenly reinforcing the notion that sport is something sacred in itself: "'Born Again Sport' has contributed to the ongoing process of secularization by reducing religion to magic where secularization is interpreted in the deeper philosophical sense as a reduction of sensitivity to the sacred or supernatural" (Prebish 1993, 208). In "The Spirit of Winning: Sports and the Total Man," Carol Flake charges that using prayer to secure victory and material reward is an outright abuse of religion. When surveying the behavior of Christian athletes, coaches, and administrators over the last few decades, she writes "Christian athletes, like the new evangelical activists and the Christian capitalists, were not prepared to wrestle against the principalities and powers; they were too eager to bear the banners and wear the uniforms of success" (Hoffman 1992, 174). In a similar manner, James T. Baker's "Are You Blocking for Me, Jesus?" drives home the point that mixing religious ritual with competitive sports tends to associate religion with winning at all cost, greed, sensual fulfillment, self-interest, and material gain, while linking sport to spiritual fulfillment. Baker's essay is both amusing and poignant in its descriptions of comical attempts that have been made, mostly by evangelists and coaches, to turn sports, mostly football, into religious motifs for a living faith. As Baker concludes, "Despite some admirable efforts—and some not so admirable—past motifs to make football a motif for the faith have fallen somewhere between faintly amusing and hilarious. Or, if you take them seriously, between vaguely threatening and downright sinister. They have all missed the goal by yards" (Hoffman 1992, 189).

Most scholars agree that trying to mold sport and traditional religious ritual into a new faith always amounts to what Baker calls "a theology of failure." Still, most also agree that many athletes do need some form of religious ritual to combat stress, deal with personal problems that affect performance, and to compete consistently under the watchful eye of the public. Mari Womack's "Why Athletes Need Ritual: A Study of Magic Among Professional Athletes" outlines a number of different types of rituals that athletes go through, from uttering the Lord's Prayer to putting on their socks a certain way, all of which reveal the fact that athletes desperately want to rely on something larger than themselves, be it God or fate, to control their destiny. Womack contends that athletes, like all people, lack faith in themselves for a number of reasons. They rely on ritual to help them focus, to threaten another team (remember Al Hrabosky's mad Hungarian routine), to cope with stress, to establish identity, to interact with teammates, to deal with the unknown, and to motivate themselves (Hoffman 1992, 200). Whatever the reason, it is difficult for anyone who has seriously played a sport not to identify with Womack's argument.

Thus, the question remains: Are there ways to use religion in sport in healthy ways that help the athlete, that do not belittle religion, and that do not exaggerate either the negative qualities of sport or its importance as a religious entity? A few scholars offer helpful answers. Denise Lardner Carmody expresses the views of many sport philosophers when she argues in "Big Time Spectator Sports: A Christian Perspective" that we must learn to castigate perversions of religious doctrine as they exist in sport, while celebrating the beauty of God's handiwork that one sees in sport. For while big-time sports in particular involve many unsavory practices, they also feature the human body at its most realized state in terms of physical stature and performance (Hoffman 1992, 105–111). Robert Feeney and Thomas Ryan take Carmody's argument a bit further. In *A Catholic Perspective: Physical Exercise and Sports*, Feeney contends that sport, or at least physical activity, should be used by all people to make their body into a healthy, clean temple in which both the mind and spirit can flourish for the glory of God. This, of course, is simply the Greek version of the whole man with a Christian twist to it. Feeney writes that "a sound body in a sound mind is an ideal which can make a person worthy of the description once applied to St. Thomas Aquinas, 'an orderly exposition of what a man should be, delightful to God and man.' Sports and physical exercise can perfect the body as an instrument of the mind and help the mind in the search and communication of the truth" (Feeney 1995, 22). The nice thing about Feeney's view of sport is that it includes everyone as a participant. The same is true of Ryan's *Wellness, Spirituality and Sport*, in which the author says that the combination of a healthy body, mind, and spirit promoted by sport can help the athlete attain spiritual wellness so that he or she might commune effectively with God, carrying out one's life with divine purpose: "In seeking wellness we will no longer be content with the minimum but will seek to maximize our use of God's gifts" (Ryan 1986, 56). Perhaps the article that captures the interaction of sport and religion at its best is Hal Higdon's "Is Running a Religious Experience." Higdon argues that running represents mostsporting experiences in that it can be an intense, meaningful, beneficial religious activity even though it is not a religion per se. Higdon discusses a wide range of spiritual interpretations of runners, each of which is singular but no less or more valuable than any of the others. For some, running is a way of pleasing God; for others it is a way of communing with nature; for some it is a way of attaining knowledge of the self; still, some runners claimed to have experienced the Zen-like transcendence spoken of by Prebish earlier in this chapter (Hoffman 1992, 77–83). Higdon's main point is that the extent to which sport is a religious activity depends on the participant. Significantly, Higdon, Ryan, Feeney, and Carmody all agree with scholars such as Overman, Thomas, Aitken, Flake, and Baker in making it clear that the extent to which this activity is positive depends on its focus on individual improvement and well-being and not on external, material rewards for an athlete, religious organization, school, or business. Those researchers interested in finding other recent perspectives about the relationship between sport and religion might consult such journals as *American Heritage, American Scholar, Banner of Truth, Christian Century, Christian Education Journal, Commentary, Ethics, Faith and Philosophy, Humanist, Journal of Religion, Journal of Ritual Studies, Journal of Thought, Judaism: A Quarterly of Jewish Life and Thought, Maclean's, Philosophical Review, Philosophy Today, Quest, Religion and American Culture,* and *Religious Studies,* all of which periodically contain articles that examine some aspect of the relationship.

## BOOKS FOR THE CURRICULUM

Finally, those interested in developing a class on either the philosophy of sport or sport and religion might find several texts helpful. David Vanderwerken's *Sport in the Classroom: Teaching Sport-Related Classes in the Humanities* contains pedagogical rationales and syllabi for several different classes that philosophy professors have offered at universities across the county. The syllabi are particularly useful because they contain suggested texts and assignments. Donald Chu's *Dimensions of Sport Studies* also contains suggested methods for teaching courses in sport philosophy, as well as a short history of the discipline. Perhaps the best textbook for the philosophy of sport would be Ketchmar, Morgan, and Meier's *Philosophic Inquiry in Sport*, which is equipped with summaries, review questions, and activity projects, as well as being broad enough to cover most of the field's main issues and branches. Osterhoudt's *The Philosophy of Sport* would also be a good text that offers discussions of most of the current views on the vital issues driving the field. Both Hoffman's *Sport and Religion* and Prebish's *Religion and Sport: The Meeting of Sacred and Profane* would be excellent texts for a course in sport and religion. Robert Higgs's *God in the Stadium: Sports and Religion in America* would be especially good for such a religion class or for a course in American History or American Studies. Hopefully, these books will inspire more texts that will expand our knowledge of how sport operates in the philosophical and religious realms as we move into a new millennium.

## REFERENCES

### Books

Arndt, Richard. *Athletes Afire*. South Plainfield, NJ: Bridge Publications, 1985.

Arnold, Peter J. *Sport, Ethics and Education*. Herndon, VA: Cassell, 1997.

Bannon, David, and Joe Pellegrino. *Safe at Home*. Chicago: Moody Press, 1992.

Barry, Michael. *Playing Dirty*. New York: St. Martin's, 1983.

Baum, Gregory, and John Coleman. *Sport*. Edinburgh, UK: T&T Clark, 1989.

Berlow, Lawrence. *Sports Ethics: A Reference Handbook*. Santa Barbara, CA: ABC/CLIO, 1994.

Black, William T. *Mormon Athletes II*. Salt Lake City, UT: Deseret Books, 1982.

Bradley, Joseph. *Ethnic and Religious Identity in Modern Scotland: Culture, Politics, and Football*. Aldershot, UK: 1995.

Callois, Roger. *Man, Play and Games*. New York: Free Press, 1961.

Carter, Gary, and Ken Abraham. *The Gamer*. Dallas: Word Publications, 1993.

Cashmore, Earnest. *Making Sense of Sport*. New York: Routledge, 1996.

Chu, Donald. *Dimensions of Sport Studies*. New York: John Wiley & Sons, 1982.

Cooper, Andrew. *Playing in the Zone: Exploring the Spiritual Dimensions of Sport*. Boston: Shambhala, 1998.

Cottrell, Stan. *No Mountain Too High*. Old Tappan, NJ: F. H. Revell, 1984.

Dugan, Ellen, ed. *This Sporting Life, 1878–1991*. Atlanta, GA: High Museum of Art, 1992.

Eitzen, Stanley. *Fair and Foul: Beyond the Myths and Paradoxes of Sport*. Lanham, MD: Rowman and Littlefield Publishers, 1999.

Feeney, Robert. *A Catholic Perspective: Physical Exercise and Sports*. Forest Grove, OR: Aquinas Press, 1995.

Fisher, James T., ed. *Real Sports: Special Issue of the South Atlantic Quarterly*. Durham, NC: Duke University Press, 1996.

Fraleigh, Warren P. *Right Actions in Sport: Ethics for Contestants*. Champaign, IL: Human Kinetics Books, 1984.

Green, A. C. *Victory*. Lake Mary, FL: Creation House, 1994.

Guttmann, Allen. *The Erotic in Sports*. New York: Columbia University Press, 1996.

Herrigel, Eugen. *Zen in the Art of Archery*. New York: Pantheon Books, 1971.

Higgs, Robert J. *God in the Stadium: Sports and Religion in America*. Lexington, KY: University of Kentucky Press, 1995.

———. *Sports: A Reference Guide*. Westport, CT: Greenwood Press, 1982.

Hoberman, John. *Sport and Political Ideology*. Austin, TX: University of Texas Press, 1984.

Hoffman, Shirl J., ed. *Sport and Religion*. Champaign, IL: Human Kinetics Books, 1992.

Hubbard, Steve. *Faith in Sports: Athletes and Their Religion on and off the Field*. New York: Doubleday, 1997.

Huizinga, Johan. *Homo Ludens: A Study of the Play Element in Culture*. Boston: Beacon Press, 1960.

Hyland, Drew. *Philosophy of Sport*. New York: Paragon House, 1990.

Johnson, Elliot. *Hope in Suffering: Letters from Peter with Application to the Coaching Profession*. Grand Rapids, MI: Full Court Press, 1993.

Jones, Donald J. *Sport Ethics in America: A Bibliography*. New York: Greenwood Press, 1992.

Ketchmar, R. Scott. *Practical Philosophy of Sport*. Champaign, IL: Human Kinetics Books, 1994.

Ketchmar, R. Scott, William Morgan, and Klaus Meier, eds. *Philosophic Inquiry in Sport*. Champaign, IL: Human Kinetics Books, 1995.

Ladd, Tony, and James Mathisen, eds. *Muscular Christianity: Evangelical Protestants and the Development of American Sport*. Grand Rapids, MI: Baker Books, 1999.

Lomax, Neil. *Third and Long*. Old Tappan, NJ: F. H. Revell, 1986.

Lumpkin, Andrea. *Sports Ethics: Applications for Fair Play*. St. Louis, MO: Mosby, 1994.

Mechikoff, Robert A., and Steven Estes. *A History and Philosophy of Sport and Physical Education: From Ancient Greece to the Present*. Madison, WI: Brown & Benchmark, 1993.

Mihalich, Joseph C. *Sport and Athletics: Philosophy in Action*. Totawa, NJ: Rowan & Littlefield, 1982.

Morgan, William J. *Leftist Theories of Sport: A Critique and Reconstruction*. Urbana. IL: University of Illinois Press, 1994.

Novak, Michael. *The Joy of Sports*. Lanham, MD: Hamilton Press, 1994.

Oates, Joyce Carol. *Ox Boxing*. Garden City, NY: Dolphin/Doubleday, 1982.

Osterhoudt, Robert G., ed. *The Philosophy of Sport*. Springfield, IL: Charles C. Thomas, 1985.

———. *The Philosophy of Sport: An Overview*. Champaign, IL: Stipes, 1991.

Overman, Steven J. *The Influence of the Protestant Ethic on Sport and Recreation*. Brookfield ,VT: Avebury Press, 1997.

Pirsig, Robert. *Zen and the Art of Motorcycle Maintenance: An Inquiry into Values*. New York: Morrow, 1974.

Postow, Betsy. *Women, Philosophy, and Sport: A Collection of New Essays*. Metuchen, NJ: Scarecrow Press, 1983.

Prebish, Charles S. *Religion and Sport: The Meeting of Sacred and Profane*. Westport, CT: Greenwood Press, 1993.

Prosek, James. *The Complete Angler: A Connecticut Yankee Follows in the Footsteps of Walton*. New York: HarperCollins, 1998.

Ryan, Thomas. *Wellness, Spirituality and Sports*. New York: Paulist Press, 1986.

Shea, Edward J. *Ethical Decisions in Sport: Interscholastic, Intercollegiate, Olympic and Professional*. Springfield, IL: C. C. Thomas, 1996.

Shields, David Lyle. *Character and Moral Development and Physical Activity*. Champaign, IL: Human Kinetics Books, 1995.

Slusher, Howard. *Man, Sport and Existence: A Critical Analysis*. Philadelphia, PA: Lea and Febiger, 1967.

Stowers, Carlton. *Real Winning: Faith in the Lives of Thirteen Great Athletes*. Waco, TX: Word Books, 1986.

Thomas, Carolyn E. *Sport in a Philosophic Context*. Philadelphia, PA: Lea & Febiger, 1983.

Vanderwerken, David. *Sport in the Classroom: Teaching Sport-Related Courses in the Humanities*. Rutherford, NJ: Farleigh Dickinson University Press, 1990.

Vanderwerken, David, and Spencer K. Wertz, eds. *Sport Inside Out: Readings in Literature and Philosophy*. Ft. Worth, TX: TCU Press, 1985.

Van Ness, Peter, ed. *Spirituality and the Secular Quest*. New York: Crossroad, 1996.

Vinokur, Martin Barry. *More Than a Game: Sports and Politics.* Westport, CT: Greenwood Press, 1988.

Wertz, Spencer K. *Talking a Good Game: Inquiries Into the Principles of Sports.* Dallas, TX: Southern Methodist University Press, 1991.

White, Reggie. *In the Trenches.* Atlanta, GA: Thomas Nelson Publishers, 1996.

Wilson, John. *Playing by the Rules: Sport, Society and the State.* Detroit, MI: Wayne State University Press, 1994.

Zeigler, Earle. *Physical Education and Kinesiology in North America: Professional and Scholarly Foundations.* Champaign, IL: Stipes, 1994.

## Journals

*American Heritage* (Harlan, IA)
*American Scholar* (Washington, D.C.)
*Banner of Truth* (Carlisle, PA)
*Christian Century* (Chicago, IL)
*Christian Education Journal* (Deerfield, IL)
*Commentary* (New York, NY)
*Ethics* (Chicago, IL)
*Faith and Philosophy* (Wilmore, KY)
*Humanist* (Amherst, NY)
*Journal of Religion* (Chicago, IL)
*Journal of Ritual Studies* (Pittsburgh, PA)
*Journal of the American Academy of Religion* (Whittier, CA)
*Journal of the Philosophy of Sport* (Champaign, IL)
*Journal of Thought* (San Francisco, CA)
*Judaism: A Quarterly of Jewish Life and Thought* (New York, NY)
*Maclean's* (Toronto, Ontario, Canada)
*Philosophical Review* (Ithaca, NY)
*Philosophy Today* (Chicago, IL)
*Quest* (Champaign, IL)
*Religion and American Culture* (Bloomington, IN)
*Religious Studies* (New York, NY)

# 8

# Sport and Popular Culture

What is popular culture? In *An Introduction to Popular Theory and Popular Culture*, John Storey submits several definitions. Popular culture simply refers to anything that has mass appeal within a society; it is available to all members of a society and therefore stands in contrast to elite or high culture; it is profoundly ideological and quite complex, so much so that it is used by those in power to bolster their advantages and by those on the margins to fight oppression; postmodern theorists contend that it is the phenomena that describes the end of absolute value, a condition that results in the obliteration of the distinction between high and low culture, revealing in its rubble this catch-all thing called popular culture. He finally concludes that "what all these definitions have in common is the insistence that whatever else popular culture might be, it is definitely a culture that emerged following industrialization and urbanization" (Storey 1998, 17). Theorist Tony Bennett is even less optimistic: "As it stands, the concept of popular culture is virtually useless, a melting pot of confused and contradictory meanings capable of misdirecting inquiry up any number of theoretically blind alleys" (Storey 1998, 1). Clearly, the main problem is popular culture's breadth. It is a vast and nearly all-encompassing domain. For instance, when it comes to literature, we think of a comic book being part of popular culture, while we consider a Don DeLillo novel to be part of the literary realm of "art." In reality, however, DeLillo's work is part of mass culture, as are the works of Jane Austen, Charles Dickens, William Shakespeare, and Oscar Wilde, many of which appear in various forms on the silver screen from time to time. Perhaps the better question, then, is what *is not* popular culture? Nevertheless, for the purposes of simplicity and organization, I have divided this chapter into five sections, all of which profile works that deal with aspects of sport that do not neatly fit into the boundaries of traditional disciplines. The five sections include academic works on sport as popular culture; investigational works, mostly by sports writers or social critics, that promise inside looks at sporting institutions and practices; works on film studies, sports photography, popular art and architecture; books that discuss the importance of sports' language within the larger society; and general interest works that deal with a veritable hodge-podge of topics.

## CRITICAL WORKS ON SPORT AND POPULAR CULTURE

That there are so many fine academic studies dedicated to popular culture is indicative of both a rise in interest in the subject among scholars and a new acceptance of its legitimacy as an academic discipline within the halls of colleges and universities. It seems that, as with all new disciplines, dedicated practitioners of popular studies have sought to establish an impressive body of theory from which to survey the field. Why theory equates with significance or why it makes an area of study legitimate is hard to say. Still, that seems to be the case, and there are several quality theoretical works available for those investigating the intersection between sports and popular culture. General theory books include Arthur Asa Berger's *Popular Culture Genres*, Diane Crane's *The Production of Culture*, and Paul Du Gay's *Production of Culture/ Cultures of Production*, all of which either have sections dedicated to sport or include some discussion of how we can learn about our culture by analyzing the methods by which we construct sport. Other theory readers focus more intensely on athletics. For example, David Rowe's *Popular Cultures: Rock Music, Sport and the Politics of Pleasure* contains an informative chapter that details how political ideology has shaped organized sport in the United States over the last fifty years. One of the most unique volumes on the subject is *Sport and Postmodern Times*, edited by Genevieve Rail. She includes essays on the potential uses of virtual sport, on using sport as the basis for New Age religious practice, on sport as a social construction whose best use is the deconstruction of gender norms, on sport as the perfect medium for illustrating how our existence is best defined as fluid, chaotic hypertext rather than any kind of stable text, and on the postmodern nature of the sports bar and other sporting venues. Article titles include "(Ir)Relevant Ring: The Symbolic Consumption of the Olympic Logo in Postmodern Media Culture," "Colonizing the Feminine: Nike's Intersections of Postfeminism and Hyperconsumption," and "Seismography of the Postmodern Condition: Three Theses on the Implosion of Sport." As one might imagine, it takes a while to wade through these rather complicated essays, but the journey is worth it for those who want to get a good idea of what postmodernism is, what its theoreticians think about sport, and why we will be in serious trouble as a society if we ever fully embrace chaos, valuelessness, and meaninglessness as the postmodernist suggests. Rail's work is best read hand in hand with *Coroebus Triumphs: The Alliance of Sport and the Arts*, edited by Susan Bandy. It is full of essays that approach sport from more familiar historical and cultural perspectives and covers such topics as the importance of sport to various ethnic groups over the twentieth century, the importance of athletic language to everyday life, the role of sports heroism in contemporary society, and how we can use sport literature and film to analyze any given society.

In most of the books available on sport as popular culture, authors attempt to use athletics as a lens through which to examine the political, social, and religious trends in society. For instance, Nathan Aaseng's *The Locker Room Mirror: How Sports Reflect Society* takes the reader inside the most private domain of the athlete. The view is not pleasant. Aaseng shows us how the values of the locker room—hypermasculine posturing and womanizing, obsession with winning and self-promotion, drug abuse, hidden rage, and fear of failure—drive sport because they define us as a culture. They are what make us do what we do, but we never talk about them, remaining content to see the pleasant surface as opposed to the seamy underside of sport and life. *SportsCult*, edited by Randy Martin and Toby Miller, is also illuminating in this regard. The authors include several essays that force the reader to confront the darker side of sport and life in the contemporary period. They are particularly concerned with how sport acts as a kind of cult with different faces that represent divergent groups whose lives are in some significant way controlled by athletic participation or spectatorship. Daniel Ginsberg's *The Fix Is In: A History of Gambling and Game Fixing Scandals* is a more entertaining book than the others, but its message is no more uplifting when one realizes that the longest American marriage on record is that between sport and corrupt gangsters and hucksters. Even Stephen Lowe's *The Kid on the Sandlot: Congress and Professional Sport, 1910–1992* reads as a sad catalogue of legislative actions that have helped to squeeze amateurism, free-spiritedness, and playfulness out of our games, leaving us with unhealthy conceptions of sport that are continually perpetuated throughout the realm of popular culture.

On the positive side, Neil Shumsky's *American Cities: A Collection of Essays* contains selections by authors that, in part, detail how sport has contributed to the growth of American cities since the nineteenth century. Perhaps the most engaging text on sports and popular culture is Michael Oriard's *Reading Football: How the Popular Press Created an American Spectacle*. Oriard provides a convincing argument that highlights the power of newspapers, journals, and juvenile literature in making football into the quintessential American game. His work is characterized by impeccable research and a balanced point of view, one that leaves us with an appreciation for sportswriters and football, while still allowing us to see the harmful attitudes toward gender, race, and class that were part of football's rise to prominence on college campuses in the 1920s. By contrast, Allen Guttmann's *The Erotic in Sports* is a captivating book that deals frankly with the fact that sport, from nude wrestling in Ancient Greece to American football in modern times, has been so attractive to us on a deeper psychic level because it has always featured erotic elements. In any given age, Guttmann argues, we can learn about our sexual values and views on gender by studying the erotic qualities of our sports. Two more sober, yet optimistic studies are Peter Williams's *The Sports Immortals: Deifying the American Athlete* and Richard Cashman's *Paradise of Sport: The Rise of Organized Sport in Australia*. The first explores how Americans have always felt an intense desire to make sports stars into larger-than-life cultural icons, heroes that could be worshiped because they embodied all the traits Americans so admired. Williams shows how few heroes have ever come close to truly being like the demigods Americans wanted them to be, but he does not blame the athletes or the public. It is clear that he still believes in heroes, but his book cautions us that the world of popular culture is nothing if not hyperbolic and shallow, one whose images should be examined for what they say about us but never believed for what they seem to be. Cashman's argument is much the same, but he focuses his discussion on Australian sports history, proving that many Western nations have watched their sports undergo the same paradoxical processes of advancement and degeneration under capitalism and under the lights of the ever-present media.

Some scholars have narrowed their lens to focus on specific issues or athletes. The relationship between sport and gender, and its development within the complex popular culture of American society, is a hot topic. For instance, Laurel Davis's *The Swimsuit Issue and Sport: Hegemonic Masculinity in Sports Illustrated* is a feminist analysis of America's most respected sports magazine. Davis concludes that its controversial swimsuit edition, which features nearly naked women modeling the latest beach fashions, represents much of popular culture's insistence that women should be viewed not as athletes, but as sex objects whose most important athletic acts are to contort their bodies suggestively for the male gaze. Alan Klein offers another indictment of the patriarchy in his *Little Big Men: Bodybuilding Subcultures and Gender Construction*, in which the author shows how traditional masculine expectations embedded in sport hurt men as well as women. Wanda Wakefield's *Playing to Win: Sport and the American Military, 1898–1945* is less judgmental than either Davis or Klein's books. The author does, however, provide a thorough and intriguing analysis of how sport has been used by the American armed services to teach their fighting men about manhood and what it means to be a warrior. Other authors have written fabulous works that show how and why famous athletes became icons. For instance, Elliott Gorn's *Muhammad Ali: The People's Champ* is a fascinating read that explains not only why Ali was popular with blacks, but also why he became a hero for many whites in the 1970s. Equally as good as Gorn's study is Jules Tygiel's *Baseball's Great Experiment: Jackie Robinson and His Legacy*. Tygiel recounts the story of Jackie Robinson's assault on the color line, why it succeeded when so many other attempts had failed, and what baseball's acceptance of a black player meant to Americans.

Naturally, there are several other books on baseball, since it is an important piece of American popular culture. One of the best is James Vlasich's *A Legend for the Legendary: The Origin of the Baseball Hall of Fame*, in which the author discusses the social and political factors that led to the construction of the great hall in Cooperstown, New York. It is a critical book, but it is also an uplifting celebration of baseball and its centrality to Americana. Richard Skolnik's *Baseball and the Pursuit of Innocence: A Fresh Look at the Old Game* is a delightful commentary on the American insistence that, no matter how many times baseball gives itself black eyes with punches made of strikes, labor wars, and spoiled athletes, the game still embodies the best of what the nation wants to be: rugged, pastoral, simple, direct, democratic, and fiercely independent. In *Batboys and the World of Popular Culture,* Neil Isaacs echoes these sentiments by calling on a number of former batboys, whose stories are both vastly entertaining and revealing about how important the game was to those boys and to the fans who watched the games they worked. A less pleasurable work is *Baseball in 1989: Players vs. Owners*, by David Pearson, whose sharp research and prose reminds us that conflict, labor, and law most accurately define sport's place within popular culture in the 1990s.

Many writers have chosen to focus on the relationship between the ultimate force in popular culture, the media, and sport. The most frequent topic is the beast itself, television. One of the most complete works is Benjamin Rader's *In Its Own Image: How Television Has Transformed Sports,* in which the author poses a logical, well-supported argument that television, while helping to facilitate some positive changes, such as the promotion of women's sports, has largely been a corrupt force that has perverted the way we think about athletics. According to Rader: "While the value of this participatory revolution in sport cannot be denied, much has been lost. Televison, more than any other single force, has transformed spectator sports into trivial affairs. No longer are sports as effective in enacting the rituals embodying traditional American values, and no longer do they evoke the same intensity, the same loyalty, the same commitment" (Rader 1984, 210). In *Sport: Money, Morality and the Media*, Richard Cashman comes to the same conclusions about the effects of television on British sport. However, he is even more insistent than Rader that these negative consequences are moral in nature. To Cashman, television has meant an increase in materialism for materialism's sake, gambling, rowdyism, the glorification of winning at the expense of sportsmanship, and the perversion of education and the amateur ideal. Fellow British scholar Garry Whannel echoes Cashman's beliefs in *Fields in Vision: Television Sport and Cultural Transformation*, in which he concludes his analysis of the BBC's role in the evolution of British sport and society by arguing that capitalistic monetarism, bolstered across the globe by a rise in conservative leadership in the 1980s, has lead to a cult of individualism and personal gain: "Sports now stress the need to be businesslike and efficient, offer sites for the celebration of corporate capitalism, provide executive boxes and hospitality tents to serve the needs of commercial sponsors, and in general have become prime sites for the construction and reproduction of an entrepreneurial culture" (Whannel 1992, 208).

Whannel's study has a less severe tone than Cashman's work and thus falls more in line with works by other recent authors. For instance, Lawrence Wenner has edited a fine volume of essays that, through rigorous academic methods and sober language, discuss how sport is shaping society and how its present state is simply an accurate reflection of what values now hold sway in society. In *Media, Sport and Society*, Wenner features essays on how television networks determine what they will cover, studies of why people watch certain sports, and several case studies relating how networks formulate diverse marketing strategies to hook different cross-sections of their large audience. Wenner's own essay, "The Super Bowl Pre-game Show: Cultural Fantasies and Political Subtext," is a clever piece that shows quite neatly how artificial sport has become in its current pre-packaged state, as well as commenting on what our acceptance and desire for this condition says about contemporary American culture. Wenner's work complements Aaron

Baker and Todd Boyd's *Out of Bounds: Sports, Media and the Politics of Identity*, a collection of essays that explore the ways in which media contributes to the construction of racial, ethnic, gender, and nationalistic identity. Again, the essays are thought provoking and well written. Selections include Ava Rose and James Friedman's "Television Sports as Mas(s)culine Cult of Distraction," which explains how media moguls deliberately package sporting events to bolster traditional masculine ideals, and Todd Boyd's "The Day the Niggaz Took Over: Basketball, Commodity Culture, and Black Masculinity," in which the author looks at how the sports world capitalizes on and subtly reinforces the nation's fear of black masculinity. One other noteworthy book on the relationship between sports and television is Danta Quirk's *Television Sports Rights*, in which the author draws an illuminating picture of television's cultural power. Particularly riveting is the ease with which television drives university athletic departments, often shaping school policies and changing educational practices to suit its needs.

## SPORTSWRITERS AND INVESTIGATIONAL WORKS

The number of works by and about sportswriters reveals how influential those unique scribes have been over the course of this century. James Reisler's *Black Writers/Black Baseball: An Anthology of Articles from Black Sportswriters Who Covered the Negro Leagues* is a fantastic compilation of articles from some of the best American writers you have never heard of unless you are a huge fan or an academic who has done research into the history of "Negro Weeklies" or black baseball. Featured writers include Joe Black of the *Amsterdam News*; Sam Lacy of the *Baltimore Afro-American*; and Wendell Smith, the legendary writer from the *Pittsburgh Courier* who led the crusade against professional baseball's color line that eventually culminated in Jackie Robinson's contract with the Brooklyn Dodgers. Shelby Strother's *Saddlebags: A Collection of Columns and Stories* and Glenn Stout and David Halberstam's *The Best American Sportswriting of the Century* include not only articles from black writers, but material from many of the great scribes who dominated the golden age of American sports and who had such a powerful role in making the myths that defined American sports into the contemporary era. For a look at the best sportswriting of the last two decades, one should consult Stout's series entitled *The Best American Sportswriting of the Century*. It has been produced since the early 1980s on an annual basis and regularly features the best writing of each year. Another unique book is Oliver Trager's *Sports in America: Paradise Lost*, which is a fascinating collection of sports stories that recount all of the nasty things that have happened in the realm of athletics just since 1985. Unfortunately, it is a large book, its size underscoring both the sheer volume of corruption in sports in only ten years, and our endless fascination with it. A more positive reading experience is gained via Richard Orodenker. *The Phillies Reader* is an entertaining collection of articles on the Philadelphia Phillies during the last forty years; it is noteworthy because the articles are written by some of the best American writers of the post-World War II era. Such notables as Roger Khan,

Robert Creamer, and Ira Berkow are featured, and their biting prose reveals how much our attitude about sport has changed since the 1940s.

Orodenker is the sole author of his other book, *The Writer's Game: Baseball and Writing in America*, a collection of analytical essays in which he discusses the lives, styles, and significance of baseball's legendary writers. Roger Khan, Ring Lardner, Jimmy Cannon, and Red Smith are just a few of the men whose careers are examined by the author, whose smooth prose makes the book a short, enjoyable read for anyone who wants to understand what these journalists did for the world of sport. By contrast, Mark Inabinett focuses on the story of one writer, Grantland Rice, in his *Grantland Rice and His Heroes: The Sportswriter as Mythmaker in the 1920s*. Inabinett's effort is another fun read that reinforces that power that writers such as Smith wielded in the days before television. In many ways, these writers were bigger than the sports they covered and were responsible not only for millions of fans falling in love with the games and the players, but for creating myths that contemporary sports and athletes could never match. Bruce Evensen's *When Dempsey Fought Tunney: Heroes, Hokum and Storytelling in the Jazz Age* is a well-researched, entertaining book that explains how sportswriters were used to publicize events, shift public opinion, and create heroes in the 1920s and 1930s. Like the books by Orodenker and Inabinett, Evensen's book is humorous, nostalgic, and generally positive. Thus, it stands in contrast with many of the works by contemporary newspaper writers. For instance, long-time-sportswriter/ESPN college football guru Gene Wojciechowski's *Pond Scum and Vultures: America's Sportswriters Talk about Their Glamorous Profession* stands out as a sign of the times. It is a collection of stories by modern writers that reflect the sordid nature of their business and the corrupt world of sport that they cover. Drugs, sexual liaisons, greed, betrayal, insincerity, and many other forms of decadence are the chief subjects of the book, which, as an important popular culture artifact, shows just how much American views and expectations of spectator sports have changed over the years.

There are several good books that, while not the products of rigorous academic research, are nevertheless worth reading. Usually these works take the forms of light, journalistic investigations into some aspect of sport that provide the reader with an inside look at a team or athlete. Many of these books are dedicated to examining the importance of sport in a certain region or to a group of people. For instance, anyone who wants to understand the power of football in the American South should not miss H. G. Bissinger's *Friday Night Lights: A Town, a Team and a Dream*. It is the story of Permian High School football, its players, and the team's place as centerpiece of the social and political scenes in Odessa, Texas. It is fascinating to read about the players, fourteen- to eighteen-year old boys who are treated as little gods in a town where one's relationship to the football team often determines one's economic viability and certainly one's social standing. Season tickets are passed down in wills, players are given excessive privileges, and, from September to December, the mood of the town is largely determined by what the gridiron heroes do on Friday night. A similar book is Stephen Wild's *The Lions of Swinton*, the story of one of the oldest teams in one of England's oldest rugby leagues. Like Bissinger's book, it is as much the story of a region and its love and need for sport as it is the story of specific players or matches in which the team engages. Though lacking depth, another noteworthy piece that bears some resemblance to the works of Bissinger and Wild is David Paul Press's *A Multicultural Portrait of Professional Sports.* Press focuses on the contributions that various ethnic groups have made to professional sports over the last half century and what those contributions have meant to those groups.

Two other books that focus on place are Carl Prince's *Brooklyn Dodgers: The Bums, the Borough, and the Best of Baseball* and Leo Trachtenberg's *The Wonder Team: The True Story of the Incomparable 1927 New York Yankees.* The first is a heart-warming reminiscence about baseball in Brooklyn in the 1940s and 1950s. The book features a great deal of commentary from Brooklyn fans, most of whom were just kids or young adults when the team abandoned its legions of loyal fans for the West Coast in the late 1950s. It is the passion and the depth of feeling of these voices that arrest the reader, who cannot help but be impressed at how much it mattered to some folks that a baseball team changed its place of business forty years ago. It had been a rallying point for the borough, the one thing with which every racial and ethnic group identified, the one thing that made them all proud to be from Brooklyn. By contrast, Trachtenberg's piece is a less emotional celebration of the Yankee juggernaut of 1927. The author concentrates on the colorful personal lives of the players who made that team one of the best, and the tales that make up the book provide an entertaining glimpse of life in New York City during the Roaring Twenties just before the bottom fell out of the stock market in October 1929.

Other authors focus on particular sports. Todd Crosset's *Outsiders in the Clubhouse: The World of Women's Professional Golf* takes the reader on a journey with the players of the Ladies Professional Golf Association, where one experiences the pressure of the tour, the boredom the players combat during the long periods when they are not golfing, the discrimination faced by women golfers, and the difficulty of being a male reporter covering elite female athletes. Gerald Early's *The Muhammad Ali Reader* is a compilation of articles about the charismatic pugilist; the essays focus on what he meant to different Americans throughout the 1960s and 1970s and indirectly provide a glimpse of the bizarre business of professional boxing and the shady characters that power its engine. Chris Mortenson's *Playing for Keeps: How One Man Kept the Mob from Sinking Its Hooks into Professional Football* is a fascinating look at the always unspoken of and uneasy alliance between professional football and the underworld. More specifically, it is the story of FBI agent George Rudolph, whose investigation and apprehension of crooked sports agents Norby Walters and Lloyd Bloom may have saved the NFL from unwanted intrusions by organized crime. Walters and Bloom had, with the aid of several mobsters, made an unsuccessful attempt to gain a foothold in professional sports in the late 1980s. Mortenson's revelation of their story provides an intriguing look into the sometimes sinister cultural forces that are always at work to influence sports. Another work along these lines is Mel Levine's *Life in the Trash Lane: Cash, Cars, and Corruption.* A former sports agent, Levine relates several lurid tales detailing the exploits of sports agents in the 1980s. Though Levine is given to hyperbole, his book is worth reading, especially for those who want to get a good look at some of the nastier ways sport actually operates in our society. Sex, drugs, political corruption, greed, false images made for public consumption, and the duplicitous nature of most sports agents and their horrible effects on athletes and professional sports are Levine's themes.

Two other books of interest, Christine Ammer's *Southpaws & Sunday Punches: And Other Sporting Experiences* and Gary Bender's *The Call of the Game,* focus on what sport means to individual Americans. Ammer's book relates the unique activities of different athletes and is perfect for illustrating the diversity of American sportspeople. The best thing about the book is that it focuses on the athletic pursuits of average American citizens and is therefore perfect for the researcher who wants to get a feel for the many ways that sport operates in American culture. While Ammer relates the stories of what sport means to several people, Bender's book is the story of his own journey across the country in 1983. A schoolteacher, Bender decided to take a year off and attend sporting events in the United States. His book records his feelings about the World Series, the Super Bowl, Olympic trials, bowling tournaments, minor league baseball, and almost every other major or minor sporting event that one might want to see. It is a fun book, valuable for any sports fan that has ever dreamed about living out this fantasy and for any student who wants to know what sport means to individual Americans.

## SPORTS FILMS AND OTHER VISUAL ARTS

Perhaps the best way to examine sport is through its visual representations. Television is by far the most dominant medium today, but radio, film, cartoons, photography, painting, and drawing should not be neglected. There have, of course, been many good sports films over the last few decades. *Field of Dreams* (1989), *Major League* (1989), *Eight Men Out* (1988), and *The Natural* (1984) are just a handful of good baseball movies from the 1980s that explore or in some way reveal important facets of American culture. Football films include *Everybody's All-American* (1988) and *The Program* (1994), while *Blue Chips* (1994) and the acclaimed *Hoop Dreams* (1995) exposed the underside of the glitzy world of college basketball. The best bibliography of sports films is Harvey Zucker's *Sports Films: A Complete Reference Guide.* Though it does not cover the films of the 1990s, it has thorough listings and complete annotations for hundreds of films before 1990. Another helpful bibliography is Judith Davidson's *Sport on Film: The North American Society for Sport History Guide.* Academic book-length studies on film are not as plentiful as one would hope. Most writing on the subject is in the form of journal articles and can be accessed through journals such as *Aethlon, The Journal of American Culture, The Journal of Popular Culture, Film & History,* and *Images: A Journal of Film and Popular Culture.* Still, a few fine books exist, mostly on baseball. Among them are Gary Dickerson's *The Cinema of Baseball: Images of America, 1929–1989,* Robert Edelman's *The Great Baseball Films,* Hal Erickson's *Baseball in the Movies: A Comprehensive Reference, 1915–1991,*

Howard Good's *Diamonds in the Dark: America, Baseball, and the Movies*, and Deborah Tudor's *Hollywood's Vision of Team Sports: Heroes, Race, and Gender*. For those interested in a broader overview of several sports, there is Karl Raitz's *The Theater of Sport,* a fascinating book that examines how different sports are purposefully staged as theatrical events designed to produce specific cathartic responses in different audiences, and Mark Wallington's *Portrayal Changes of the American Athlete in Popular Film*, a neat little study that examines the evolution of the American athlete in film from a simple hero who is all things to all people to a complex human being who often struggles to understand himself and his world. Of course, one should be careful not to miss out on Wiley Umphlett's two pioneering works, *Mythmakers of the American Dream: The Nostalgic Vision in Popular Culture* and *The Movies Go to College: Hollywood and the World of the College-Life Film*, both of which contain thorough examinations of film and other popular culture artifacts.

*Mythmakers of the American Dream* is a particularly interesting work because Umphlett provides analyses of cartoons, comic strips, and other forms of pop art that until recently have been largely ignored in academic circles. The recent appearance of a few other books dedicated to matter formerly relegated to the land of "trivia" marks the slow recognizance by scholars that all of the minutiae of popular culture carries a certain degree of importance. After all, generations of kids have grown up on comic books, *The Simpsons* is the most popular show on television, and both Speed Buggy and Speed Racer make auto racing a staple of the Nickelodeon television network. Lamar Sparkman's *The Cartoon World of Lamar Sparkman: His 40-Year History of Sports, 1947–1987* is a compilation of sports cartoons drawn, of course, by Sparkman, perhaps the greatest sports cartoonist ever. Steven Moore's *Revolution in the Bleachers: More Sports Cartoons* is another fine look at the rich material sport has afforded some of the nations leading humorists, while Wayman Spence's *The Satirical World of Jose Perez* reveals the potential political power of the artist and his or her sometimes poison pen.

Photographs, illustration, and paintings are also critical artifacts for students of sports in popular culture. Those interested in photography should consult Robert Riger's *The Sports Photography of Robert Riger*, Mike Shield's *Never, Never Quit: A Photographic Celebration of Courage in Sports*, and Ruth Silverman's *Athlete: Photographs (1860–1986)*, all of which feature classic sports photos, which most casual sports fans would recognize, and rarely seen shots of scenes that bear testament to America's love of sport. If you prefer the brush to the lens, Reilly Rhodes's *Sport in Art From American Museums: The Director's Choice* and Michael D'Orso's *Pumping Granite: And Other Portraits of People at Play* contain beautiful sports paintings as well as biographical lists of museums that feature such paintings. Of course, Leroy Neiman's *Winners: My Thirty Years in Sports* remains the standard by which all books on sports art will be judged. Two other books of interest are Geoffrey Ward's *Baseball: An Illustrated History* and a work put out by Dover Publications entitled *Sports: A Pictorial Archive of Contemporary Illustrations*, both of which feature illustrations that allow the student of popular culture a vehicle by which to gauge the ever-changing relationship between Americans and their games.

## THE LANGUAGE OF SPORT

While the popularity of sport hinges on its visual representations and aesthetic appeal, part of its charm has to do with its unique linguistic systems. What would a trip to the ball yard be without a round of "Take Me Out to the Ball Game" wherein we all affirm that "it's one, two, three strikes, you're out," a phrase that a teacher might just as well use the next afternoon to tell a student that he has just used his last chance to pass a test and must repeat a class? This kind of influence of sporting vernacular on American patterns of speech has been the subject of a number of books. One is Robert Palmatier's *SportsTalk: A Dictionary of Sports Metaphors*, in which the author catalogues thousands of our everyday expressions that are rooted in our games. For instance, the term "above board" springs from poker playing in the 1600s, a game in which one had to keep his hands above the board table or be accused of cheating. "Call off your dogs" comes from fox hunting. We owe "flash in the pan" to faulty discharges experienced by hunters in the early 1800s; "in the nick of time" to eighteenth-century British soccer in which the goals were marked by cutting notches on a stick, the last of which was called the nick of time; "nip and tuck" to fencers who nipped at each other with their tucks (swords); and "right up your alley" not to boxing but to baseball.

Palmatier's work is fascinating, and there are several others like it that are just as good. Lawrence Franks's *Playing Hardball: The Dynamics of Baseball Folkspeech* and David Nathan's *Baseball Quotations: The Wisdom and Wisecracks of Players, Managers, Owners, Umpires, Announcers, Writers and Fans of the Great American Pastime* are heavenly reads for baseball junkies. If there is a baseball phrase for which you want an origin, or if you just want to relive some of the great quips of baseball lore, these are the books for you. Both books reveal just how much baseball has impacted our language and culture, but America's diamonds have not been the only sphere of such influence. Jonathon Waterman's *The Quotable Climber: Literary, Humorous, Inspirational, and Fearful Moments of Climbing* is both an anthology of great stories about the outdoors and a provocative look at how our relationship with nature has changed our language, encouraging us among other things to "hang in there" and "stick with it." Lafe Locke's *The Name of the Game: How Sports Talk Got That Way* gives us the history of sports talk on a sport-by-sport basis. Celine Gendron's *Acrosport: Acronyms Used for Sport* is a unique little book that explains what all those acronyms we see really mean. Peter Berlinson's *The Sports Page: Quotations on Baseball, Football, and Other Sports* shows us how great sports scribes such as Damon Runyon, Grantland Rice, and Ring Lardner have woven sports and their own prose into our linguistic quilt. Timothy Considine's *The Language of Sport* is much like Palmatier's work but contains longer explanations of terms and phrases and is more precise about how and why they operate today, while George Plimpton's *Sports Bestiary* provides a humorous slant on the language of sport.

Again, all of the works remind us of the importance of sports in our world, while forcing us to rethink our patterns of speech to analyze just how charged they are with sports talk.

## MISCELLANEOUS WORKS ON SPORT AND POPULAR CULTURE

Because popular culture is so vast and its relationship with sport so complex, it is difficult to fully categorize all of the material available on the subject. There are a number of works on the market that must be classified as general interest books. They deal with a wide range of important and interesting topics. For instance, there are two excellent books that deal exclusively with how one can use the Internet to conduct sports-related research. One is Terry Fain's *A Pocket Tour of Sports on the Internet* and the other is Bob Temple's *Sports on the Net*. Both offer detailed instruction on how to find information on current sports news, past events, recreational opportunities, or fantasy sports. In addition, they are a good source for hundreds of the most-used sports web sites. Fain's edition is particularly good because it is organized on a sport-by-sport basis and therefore gives the reader a quick way to find many sites for most of the major and minor sports played in North America.

While the Internet has established itself as the most fascinating way to surf the sports world, there remain many quality print reference guides that are indispensable for the sports enthusiast. For those who like to visit the ballparks and stadiums of America, there is Will Balliet's *USA Today Sports Atlas*, a detailed work that profiles hundreds of destinations for sports spectators. For more active participants, there is Chelsea Mauldin's *Fodor's Great American Sports and Adventure Vacations*, a hefty volume that examines a plethora of outdoor activities, and Patrick Phillips's *Developing with Recreational Amenities: Golf, Tennis, Skiing, Marinas*, a work full of instruction and advice on how to find and use the best sports equipment. Joy Standevan and Paul DeKnop's *Sports Tourism* and Richard Whittingham's *Rand McNally Sports Places Rated: Ranking America's Best Places to Enjoy Sports* address the concerns of both the athlete and the fan by providing several suggestions for sports vacations. Whether your cup of tea is a weekend of baseball at Wrigley Field in Chicago or a mountain climbing trip in Colorado, both of these books will have something for you. Frank Hoffman's *Sports and Recreation Fads* is a fun book for those who would like a refresher course on what sports fads were hot over the last few decades and what cultural factors gave rise to their popularity. Of course, Hoffman's work is also designed for those who would like to take advantage of the latest sports crazes.

Other fine reference materials on popular culture include Nancy Herron's *The Leisure Literature: A Guide to Sources in Leisure Studies, Fitness, Sports, and Travel*, Jonathon Fraser Light's *The Cultural Encyclopedia of Baseball*, Vincent Sparano's *Complete Outdoors Encyclopedia*, Jennifer Swan's *Sports Style Guide and Reference Manual: The Complete Reference for Sports Editors: Writers and Broadcasters*, and Gerald Tomlinson's *Speakers Treasury of Sports Anecdotes, Stories and Humor*. The books by Herron and Sparano are well-written, exhaustive resources that not only contain a great deal of information about sporting opportunities in this country, but also provide complete bibliographic listings of other articles, books, and videos that one might access. Light's work is a delight for baseball fanatics, while Swan's is a must for anyone affiliated with the sports media. Tomlinson's book is a hilarious romp through the world of sports; it features stories, mostly anecdotal tales, from a variety of fans, players, coaches, and writers.

Those interested in sports nicknames and traditions should consult Kathlyn Gay's *They Don't Wash Their Socks: Sports Superstitions*, Joanne Sloane's *College Nicknames: And Other Interesting Sports Traditions*, or Chuck Wielgus's *From A-Train to Yogi: The Fan's Book of Nicknames*. Of these, the most basic is Wielgus's work, which is evidently intended for young adult audiences. Sloane's book is a must for all fans of college sports or for any pop culture connoisseur who wants to know what a Georgetown Hoya is, why the Michigan Wolverines have striped helmets, or why Penn State insists on sporting its "vanilla" uniforms in an age of flashy new logos. Gay's book is one of the more entertaining works one could peruse on popular culture. It is a full account of some of the strangest and most disquieting superstitions of American athletes. She features stories of athletes who do silly things, like wearing the same socks all week, and tales that are quite disturbing, such as those about athletes who are slaves to harmful rituals like vomiting before every game. It is a light-hearted book, but it has serious implications for the culturally minded student. After all, one must ask why Americans have so many superstitions and examine what they reveal about us and how we need and use sport on fundamentally spiritual levels.

There are a few other general interest works available. Andrew Kaplan's *Careers for Sports Fans* provides several creative suggestions for those passionate spectators who want to find a way to turn their enthusiasm into a rewarding job. One such profession might be as a peddler of sports collectibles. Two writers, John Bloom and Theodore Hake, give readers an inside look at this industry that, over the last decade, has exploded in the United States. In *A House of Cards: Baseball Card Collecting and Popular Culture*, Bloom invites the reader into the baseball card industry for a glimpse of how it works, who controls it, and why card collecting continues to be a mania that grips many Americans. In contrast, Hake's *An Illustrated Price Guide to Non-Paper Sports Collectibles* discusses life on the side of the collectibles industry that eschews cards and posters for traditional art; sports equipment such as autographed jerseys, bats, or racquets; and other more expensive artifacts. Finally, Jeremy Feinberg's *Reading the Sports Page: A Guide to Understanding Sports Statistics* is a quality book for beginning fans who want to understand sports and why statistics, a separate language unto itself, are such a vital part of the sports world.

Another important way that sport is represented within popular culture is seen in juvenile literature. I should probably say juvenile texts, since the marketing of sports films, such as Disney's *Mighty Ducks* series, *Little Giants, The Sandlot*, and *Little Big League*, have proven to be so profitable, and since the sale of sports merchandise, such as shirts, replica jerseys, key chains, hats, and posters, is increasing at a dizzying pace. I trust, however, that the visibility of these things is such that they need not be given more than a mention in this chapter. Indeed, I will not discuss the explosion of player biographies and stories of championship seasons that seem to be aimed at adolescent audiences. There are simply too many of those works to include, and their existence and whereabouts is well known. Instead, I will focus a short discussion on a few books that might be of interest to scholars of popular culture and, more particularly, for educators. For instance, there are a number of fine books for teachers who want to use sport as a way to interest their students in literature and writing. Arnold Adoff's *Sport Pages*, Lillian Morrison's *The Break Dance Kid: Poems of Sport, Motion and Locomotion*, and R. R. Knudson and May Swenson's *American Sports Poems* are all superb collections of sports poems that would be perfect for introducing young readers to the often dreaded topic of poetry. David Friend's *Baseball, Football, Daddy and Me* fulfills the same function for very young audiences, while Robert Lypsyte's *Assignment Sports* and Lance Gentile's *Using Sports for Reading and Writing Activities: Middle and High School Years* are perfect for those who teach English or journalism to secondary school students. Because Gentile is a teacher who has experimented with most of his suggestions and Lypsyte a noted sports journalists, both books are very practical.

There is no shortage of books for teachers of science, psychology, and history. Science teachers might try Robert Gardner's *Experimenting with Science in Sports*, a book that contains all sorts of relatively simple indoor and outdoor experiments students can conduct in the context of sports. Another unique book that uses sports to bridge the gap between students and the study of science is George Coulter's *Science in Sports*. Like Gardner's book, this one introduces experiments and hands-on activities that allow the students to gain access to science by physically engaging their natural world. Other good science books are Ian Graham's *Sports*, Neil Duncanson's *Sports Technology*, which uses sports to help students understand computers among other things, and Ron Schultz's *Looking Inside Sports Aerodynamics*. Psychology books include Missy Allen's *Dangerous Sports*, Lowell Dickmeyer's *Winning and Losing*, Robert Ross Olney's *Imaging: Think Your Way to Success in Sports and the Classroom*, and Nate Zinsser's *Dear Dr. Psych*. The books by Dickmeyer and Olney are especially good for coaches who want their charges to have positive sporting experiences and for guidance counselors looking for unique ways to get uninspired students interested in school. Finally, history teachers might be interested in Robert B. Lyttle's *The Games They Played: Sports in History*, a work in which the author uses sport to discuss how Americans have lived for four centuries. Other history books include Don Wulffson's *How Sports Came To Be*, which includes discussion of the various social, political, and economic factors that led to the development of several sports; Hank Nuwer's *Sport Scandals*, which is the perfect book with which to introduce children to the fact that sport and its heroes should not be blindly idolized; Herbert Kamm and Willard Mullin's *The New Junior Illustrated Encyclopedia of Sports*; and Norman Barrett's *Sport: Players, Games and Spectacles*, in which the author tries to help students understand why sports are so popular today and why this has both positive and negative implications for the United States.

Finally, when it comes to articles about sport as popular culture, there are several important journals that regularly feature well-researched articles on the subject. Two of the best are *Aethlon*, a quarterly dedicated to the study of sports literature and text, and *The Journal of Sport History*. Other academic journals that frequently include articles in which an author uses sport to take a closer took at culture are *Australian Magazine, China Sports, Film & History, Images: A Journal of Film and Popular Culture, Journal of American Culture, Journal of American Folklore, Journal of Canadian Studies, Journal of Latin American Studies, Journal of Popular Culture, Journal of Ritual Studies*, and *Sports in Japan*. For a larger list of related periodicals, one might consult the master list of sports periodicals in Appendix 2 of this volume, the sports database SPORTSDiscus, or the website for *Sportsjones* magazine at www.sportsjones.com.

How far can scholars go in their study of popular culture? When it comes to sports, there seem to be no signs of limits emerging even on the most distant horizon. Video games get more realistic every year, making virtual sport an inevitable topic as we enter the twenty-first century. Sports participation has gone through the roof. Televised sport threatens to overwhelm us. Americans with satellite service can now literally watch every game staged by Major League Baseball, the National Hockey League, the National Football League, and the National Basketball Association. ESPN has three versions of itself, including the Classic Sports Network, which rebroadcasts sporting events of yesteryear just in case the present inundation is not enough. All the while, we are bombarded with highly suggestive advertisements that advance any number of agendas. What does all of this say about us? What does this kind of saturation and intense marketing do to children? How has this mega-business approach to athletics changed sport in the minds of Americans and where will it take them in terms of sports spectatorship, participation, and sponsorship? How can we harness the power of popular culture and ensure that we make the most of our sporting institutions? All of these questions beg to be analyzed and will no doubt occupy academicians, journalists, and others as we play our way into a new millennium.

## REFERENCES

### Books

Aaseng, Nathan. *The Locker Room Mirror: How Sports Reflect Society*. New York: Walker and Co., 1993.

Ammer, Christine. *Southpaws & Sunday Punches: And Other Sporting Experiences*. New York: Dutton, 1993.

Baker, Aaron, and Todd Boyd, eds. *Out of Bounds: Sports, Media and the Politics of Identity*. Bloomington, IN: University of Indiana Press, 1997.

Balliett, Will. *USA Today Sports Atlas*. New York: H. M. Gousha, 1993.

Bandy, Susan, ed. *Coroelous Triumphs: The Alliance of Sports and the Arts*. San Diego, CA: San Diego State University Press, 1984.

Bender, Gary. *The Call of the Game*. Chicago: Bonus Books, 1994.

Bergen, Ronald. *Sports in the Movies*. New York: Proteus Books, 1982.

Berger, Arthur Asa. *Popular Culture Genres*. Newbury Park, CA: Sage Publications, 1992.

Berlinson, Peter. *The Sports Page: Quotations on Baseball, Football and Other Sports*. White Plains, NY: Peter Pauper Press, 1996.

Bissinger, H. G. *Friday Night Lights: A Town, a Team and a Dream*. New York: Harper-Collins, 1990.

Bloom, John. *A House of Cards: Baseball Card Collecting and Popular Culture*. New York: Dover Publications, 1989.

Cashman, Richard. *Paradise of Sport: The Rise of Organized Sport in Australia*. Oxford: Oxford University Press, 1995.

————. *Sport: Money, Morality and the Media*. Kensenton, Australia: New South Wales University Press, 1981.

Considine, Timothy. *The Language of Sport*. New York: Facts on File, 1982.

Crane, Diana. *The Production of Culture*. Thousand Oaks, CA: Sage Publications, 1997.

Crosset, Todd. *Outsiders in the Clubhouse: The World of Women's Professional Golf*. Albany, NY: State University of New York Press, 1995.

Davidson, Judith A. *Sport on Film: The North American Society for Sport History Guide*. Metuchen, NJ: Scarecrow Press, 1993.

Davis, Laurel. *The Swimsuit Issue and Sport: Hegemonic Masculinity in* Sports Illustrated. Albany, NY: State University of New York, 1997.

Dickerson, Gary. *The Cinema of Baseball: Images of America, 1929–1989*. Westport, CT: Meckler, 1991.

D'Orso, Michael. *Pumping Granite: And Other Portraits of People at Play*. Lubbock, TX: Texas Tech University Press, 1994.

Du Gay, Paul. *Production of Culture/Cultures of Production*. Thousand Oaks, CA: Sage Publications, 1997.

Early, Gerald. *The Muhammad Ali Reader*. Hopewell, NJ: Ecco Press, 1998.

Edelman, Robert. *The Great Baseball Films*. Secaucus, NJ: Carol Publication Group, 1994.

Erickson, Hal. *Baseball in the Movies: A Comprehensive Reference, 1915–1991*. Jefferson, NC: McFarland, 1992.

Evaleen, Hu. *A Level Playing Field: Sport and Race*. Minneapolis, MN: Lerner Publishing, 1995.

Evensen, Bruce. *When Dempsey Fought Tunney: Heroes, Hokum, and Storytelling in the Jazz Age*. Knoxville, TN: University of Tennessee Press, 1996.

Fain, Terry. *A Pocket Tour of the Internet*. San Francisco, CA: Sybex Press, 1995.

Feinberg, Jeremy. *Reading the Sports Page: A Guide to Understanding Sports Statistics*. New York: New Discovery Books, 1992.

Franks, Lawrence. *Playing Hardball: The Dynamics of Baseball Folkspeech*. New York: P. Lang, 1983.

Gay, Kathlyn. *They Don't Wash Their Socks: Sports Superstitions*. New York: Walker, 1990.

Gendron, Celine. *Acrosport: Acronyms Used for Sport*. Gloucester, ON: Sports Information Resource Office, 1993.

Ginsberg, Daniel, ed. *The Fix Is In: A History of Baseball Gambling and Game Fixing Scandals*. Jefferson, NC: McFarland, 1995.

Good, Howard. *Diamonds in the Dark: America, Baseball, and the Movies*. Lanham, MD: Scarecrow Press, 1997.

Gorn, Elliott. *Muhammad Ali: The People's Champ*. Urbana, IL: University of Illinois Press, 1995.

Guttmann, Allen. *The Erotic in Sports*. New York: Columbia University Press, 1996.

Hake, Theodore. *An Illustrated Price Guide to Non-Paper Sports Collectibles.* York, PA: Hake's American & Collectible Press, 1986.

Herron, Nancy. *The Leisure Literature: A Guide to Sources in Leisure Studies, Fitness, Sports, and Travel.* Englewood, CO: Libraries Unlimited, 1992.

Hicks, Peter. *Sport and Entertainment.* New York: Thomas Learning, 1995.

Hoffman, Frank. *Sports and Recreation Fads.* New York: Harrington Park Press, 1991.

Inabinett, Mark. *Grantland Rice and His Heroes: The Sportswriter as Mythmaker in the 1920s.* Knoxville, TN: University of Tennessee Press, 1994.

Isaacs, Neil D. *Batboys and the World of Popular Culture.* Jackson, MS: University of Mississippi Press, 1995.

Johnson, Don, ed. *Coroebus Triumphs: The Alliance of Sports and the Arts.* San Diego, CA: San Diego State University Press, 1988.

Kaplan, Andrew. *Careers for Sports Fans.* Brookfield, CT: Millbrook Press, 1991.

Klein, Alan. *Little Big Men: Bodybuilding Subcultures and Gender Construction.* Albany, NY: State University of New York Press, 1993.

Levine, Mel. *Life in the Trash Lane: Cash, Cars, and Corruption.* Plantation, FL: Distinctive Publications, 1993.

Light, Jonathon Fraser. *The Cultural Encyclopedia of Baseball.* Jefferson, NC: McFarland, 1997.

Locke, Lafe. *The Name of the Game: How Sports Talk Got that Way.* White Hall, NY: Betterway Publications, 1992.

Lowe, Stephen. *The Kid on the Sandlot: Congress and Professional Sport, 1910–1992.* Bowling Green, OH: Bowling Green University Press, 1995.

MacCambridge, Michael. *The Franchise: A History of Sports Illustrated Magazine.* New York: Hyperion, 1997.

Manchel, Frank. *Great Sports Movies.* New York: Franklin Watts, 1980.

Martin, Randy, and Toby Miller. *SportsCult.* Minneapolis, MN: University of Minnesota Press, 1999.

Mauldin, Chelsea. *Fodor's Great American Sports and Adventure Vacations.* New York: Fodor's Travel Publications, 1994.

Melville, Thomas. *Cricket for Americans: Playing and Understanding the Game.* Bowling Green, OH: Bowling Green University Press, 1993.

Moore, Steven. *Revolution in the Bleachers: More Sports Cartoons.* New York: Collier Books, 1991.

Mortenson, Chris. *Playing for Keeps: How One Man Kept the Mob from Sinking Its Hooks into Professional Football.* New York: Simon & Schuster, 1991.

Nathan, David, ed. *Baseball Quotations: The Wisdom and Wisecracks of Players, Managers, Owners, Umpires, Announcers, Writers and Fans on the Great American Pastime.* Jefferson, NC: McFarland, 1991.

Neiman, Leroy. *Winners: My Thirty Years in Sports.* New York: H. N. Abrams, 1983.

Palmetier, Robert. *Dictionary of Sports Idioms.* Lincolnwood, IL: National Textbook Co., 1993.

———. *SportsTalk: A Dictionary of Sports Metaphors.* New York: Greenwood Press, 1989.

Oriard, Michael. *Reading Football: How the Popular Press Created an American Spectacle.* Chapel Hill, NC: University of North Carolina Press, 1993.

Orodenker, Richard, ed. *The Phillies Reader.* Philadelphia: Temple University Press, 1996.

———. *The Writer's Game: Baseball and Writing in America.* New York: Simon & Schuster, 1996.

Pearson, David. *Baseball in 1989: Players vs. Owners.* Bowling Green, OH: Bowling Green State University Press, 1993.

Phillips, Patrick. *Developing with Recreational Amenities: Golf, Tennis, Skiing, Marinas.* Washington, D.C.: Urban Land Institute, 1986.

Plimpton, George. *A Sports Bestiary.* New York: McGraw-Hill, 1982.

Press, David Paul. *A Multicultural Portrait of Professional Sports.* New York: Marshall Cavendish Corp., 1994.

Prince, Carl. *Brooklyn Dodgers: The Bums, the Borough, and the Best of Baseball.* New York: Oxford University Press, 1996.

Quirk, Danta. *Television Sports Rights.* Hartsdale, NY: Q.V. Publishers, Inc., 1986.

Rader, Benjamin. *In Its Own Image: How Television Has Transformed Sports.* New York: Free Press, 1984.

Rail, Genevieve. *Sport and Postmodern Times.* Albany, NY: State University of New York Press, 1998.

Raitz, Karl. *The Theater of Sport.* Baltimore, MD: Johns Hopkins University Press, 1995.

Reisler, James. *Black Writers/Black Baseball: An Anthology of Articles from Black Sportswriters Who Covered the Negro Leagues.* Jefferson, NC: McFarland, 1994.

Rhodes, Reilly. *Sport in Art from American Museums: The Director's Choice.* New York: Universe Press, 1991.

Richardson, Allen. *Sports.* Princeton, NJ: Peterson's Books, 1993.

Rigby, Julie. *Sports.* Lincolnwood, IL: VGM Career Horizons, 1995.

Riger, Robert. *The Sports Photography of Robert Riger.* New York: Random House, 1995.

Rosenbloom, Joseph. *The World's Best Sports Riddles and Jokes.* New York: Sterling Publishing, 1988.

Rowe, David. *Popular Cultures: Rock Music, Sport, and the Politics of Pleasure.* Thousand Oaks, CA: Sage Publications, 1995.

Shields, Mike. *Never, Never, Quit: A Photographic Celebration of Courage in Sports.* Lombard, IL: Great Quotations Publications Co., 1987.

Shumsky, Neil, ed. *American Cities: A Collection of Essays.* New York: Garland, 1996.

Silverman, Ruth. *Athletes: Photographs (1860–1986).* New York: Knopf, 1987.

Skolnik, Richard. *Baseball and the Pursuit of Innocence: A Fresh Look at the Old Game.* College Station, TX: Texas A&M University Press, 1994.

Sloan, Joanne. *College Nicknames: And Other Interesting Sports Traditions.* Northpoint, AL: Vision Press, 1993.

Sparano, Vincent T. *Complete Outdoors Encyclopedia.* New York: St. Martin's, 1998.

Sparkman, Lamar. *The Cartoon World of Lamar Sparkman: His 40-Year History of Sports, 1947–1987.* Tampa, FL: Hillsboro Printing, 1994.

Spence, Wayman. *The Satirical World of Jose Perez.* Waco, TX: WRS Publishing, 1996.

*Sports: A Pictorial Archive of Contemporary Illustrations.* New York: Dover, 1989.

Standevan, Joy, and Paul DeKnop. *Sport Tourism.* Champaign, IL: Human Kinetics Books, 1999.

Storey, John. *An Introduction to Popular Theory and Popular Culture.* Athens, GA: University of Georgia Press, 1998.

Stout, Glenn, and David Halberstam, eds. *The Best American Sportswriting of the Century.* Boston: Houghton-Mifflin, 1999.

Strother, Shelby. *Saddlebags: A Collection of Columns and Stories.* West Bloomfield, MI: A&M Publishing, 1991.

Swan, Jennifer, ed. *Sport Style Guide and Reference Manual: The Complete Reference for Sports Editors, Writers and Broadcasters.* Chicago: Triumph Books, 1996.

Temple, Robert. *Sports on the Net.* Indianapolis, IN: Que Publications, 1995.

Tomlinson, Gerald. *Speaker's Treasury of Sports Anecdotes, Stories and Humor.* Englewood Cliffs, NJ: PrenticeHall, 1990.

Trachtenberg, Leo. *The Wonder Team: The True Story of the Incomparable 1927 New York Yankees.* Bowling Green, OH: Bowling Green State University Press, 1995.

Trager, Oliver. *Sports in America: Paradise Lost.* New York: Facts on File, 1990.

Tudor, Deborah. *Hollywood's Vision of Team Sports: Heroes, Race, and Gender.* New York: Garland Press, 1997.

Tygiel, Jules. *Baseball's Great Experiment: Jackie Robinson and His Legacy.* New York: Oxford University Press, 1997.

Umphlett, Wiley. *The Movies Go to College: Hollywood and the World of College-Life Film.* Rutherford, NJ: Fairleigh Dickinson University Press, 1984.

———. *Mythmakers of the American Dream: The Nostalgic Vision in Popular Culture.* Lewisburg, PA: Bucknell University Press, 1983.

Vlasich, James A. *A Legend for the Legendary: The Origin of the Baseball Hall of Fame.* Bowling Green, OH, Bowling Green State University Press, 1990.

Wakefield, Wanda Ellen. *Playing to Win: Sports and the American Military, 1898–1945.* Albany, NY: State University of New York, 1997.

Wallington, Mark. "Portrayal Changes of the American Athlete in Popular Film." M.A. thesis, University of Florida, 1993.

Ward, Geoffrey. *Baseball: An Illustrated History.* New York: Knopf, 1994.

Waterman, Jonathon, ed. *The Quotable Climber: Literary, Humorous, Inspirational, and Fearful Moments of Climbing.* New York: Lyons Press, 1998.

Wenner, Lawrence, ed. *Media, Sport and Society.* Newbury Park, CA: Sage Publications, 1989.

Whannel, Garry. *Fields in Vision: Television Sport and Cultural Transformation.* New York: Routledge, 1992.

Wielgus, Chuck. *From A-Train to Yogi: The Fan's Book of Nicknames.* New York: Perennial Library, 1987.

Wild, Stephen. *The Lions of Swinton.* Manchester, England: Swinton Press, 1998.

Williams, Peter. *The Sports Immortals: Deifying the American Athlete.* Bowling Green, OH: Bowling Green University Press, 1993.

Wittingham, Richard. *Rand McNally Sports Places Rated: Ranking America's Best Places to Enjoy Sports.* Chicago: Rand McNally, 1986.

Wojciechowski, Gene. *Pond Scum and Vultures: America's Sportswriters Talk about Their Glamorous Profession.* New York: Macmillan, 1990.

Zucker, Harvey Marc, ed. *Sports Films: A Complete Reference Guide.* Jefferson, NC: McFarland, 1987.

## Juvenile Books

Adoff, Arnold. *Sports Pages.* New York: Lippincott, 1986.

Allen, Missy. *Dangerous Sports.* New York: Chelsea House, 1993.

Barrett, Norman. *Sport: Players, Games and Spectacle.* New York: F. Watts, 1993.

Coulter, George. *Science in Sports.* Vero Beach, FL: Rourke Publications, 1995.

Dickmeyer, Lowell. *Winning and Losing.* New York: F. Watts, 1984.

Duncanson, Neil. *Sports Technology.* New York: Bookwright Press, 1992.

Friend, David. *Baseball, Football, Daddy and Me.* New York, Puffin Books, 1992.

Gardner, Robert. *Experimenting with Science in Sports.* New York: F. Watts, 1993.

Gentile, Lance. *Using Sports for Reading and Writing Activities: Middle and High School Years.* Phoenix, AZ: Oryx Press, 1983.

Graham, Ian. *Sports.* Austin, TX: Raintree Steck and Vaughn, 1995.

Kamm, Herbert, and Willard Mullin, eds. *The New Junior Illustrated Encyclopedia of Sports.* Indianapolis, IN: Bobbs-Merrill, 1986.

Knudson, R. R., and May Swenson, eds. *American Sports Poems.* New York: Orchard Books, 1988.

Lypsyte, Robert. *Assignment Sports.* New York: Harper & Row, 1984.

Lyttle, Richard. *The Games They Played: Sports in History.* New York: Atheneum, 1982.

Morrison, Lillian. *The Break Dance Kid: Poems of Sport, Motion and Locomotion.* New York: Lothrop, Lee and Shepherd, 1985.

Nuwer, Hank. *Sport Scandals.* New York: Watts, 1994.

Olney, Robert Ross. *Imaging: Think Your Way to Success in Sports and the Classroom.* New York: Atheneum, 1985.

Schultz, Ron. *Looking Inside Sports Aerodynamics.* Santa Fe, NM: John Muir Publications, 1992.

Wulffson, Don. *How Sports Came to Be.* New York: Lothrop, Lee & Shepard Books, 1980.

Zinsser, Nate. *Dear Dr. Psych.* Boston: Little, Brown & Co., 1991.

## Journals

*Aethlon: The Journal of Sport Literature* (Johnson City, TN)
*Australian Magazine* (Sydney, Australia)
*China Sports* (Beijing, China)
*Film & History* (Cleveland, OH)
*Images: A Journal of Film and Popular Culture* (Kansas City, MO)
*Journal of American Culture* (Bowling Green, OH)
*Journal of American Folklore* (Bowling Green, OH)
*Journal of Canadian Studies* (Ottawa, Ontario, Canada)
*Journal of Latin American Studies* (Oxford, England)
*Journal of Popular Culture* (Bowling Green, OH)
*Journal of Ritual Studies* (Pittsburgh, PA)
*Journal of Sport History* (University Park, PA)
*Sports in Japan* (Tokyo, Japan)

# 9

# Sport and Psychology

Sports psychology has informally existed as long as humans have engaged in sport and physical activity. Participants in sports from horse racing to rounders, or in physical work from farming to wood chopping, have always had to use the mind to battle fatigue, fear, anxiety, and pain. Sportspersons have had to figure out the tendencies of opponents, while developing strategies to cope with their own weaknesses. Coaches and trainers have always had to motivate athletes, help them adjust to hostile fans, bad weather and other environmental stimuli, and steer them through both inner turmoil and conflicts with teammates. Still, it was not until the nineteenth century that researchers began to develop sports psychology as a formal discipline. Many books on sports psychology start with a chapter that outlines the relatively brief history of the field, whose value has only come to be fully appreciated by sporting and academic communities in the last half of the twentieth century. Bryant Cratty's *Psychology in Contemporary Sport* offers a concise, informative overview of the field's historic foundation. Cratty breaks up his discussion into four distinct periods: colonial American views on psychology, the formation of sports psychology in the mid-nineteenth century, developments from 1900–1950, and the evolution of the field from 1950–2000. This method allows the reader to become acquainted with the most important developments and trends that characterized each epoch. Items of special concern include the ramifications of the early American tendency to intertwine psychology and religion, specifically Christianity, as well as nineteenth-century developments in motor psychology, the study of the benefits of play, behaviorist theory, cognitive theory, and psychological testing procedures designed for athletes. In addition, Cratty analyzes early twentieth-century international research on the psychological aspects of athletic performance and the late twentieth-century emphasis on creating organizational structures, both in academe and in the professional arenas of business and medicine, intended to solidify sport psychology's reputation as a discipline worthy of serious study and as a professional field that greatly enhances the sporting experience for athletes, coaches, and fans (Cratty 1983, 8–22). Recent scholarship emerging from these organizational structures has concentrated on several different areas. These include the study of coaches, children's sports, ethical questions and theoretical issues that drive the field, team sports, strategies for athletic preparation, aggression and violence, gender concerns, international perspectives, curricular possibilities, and issues that are currently hot in the field such as the psychology of sports spectators and the public's psychological need for heroes.

## COACHING AND PSYCHOLOGY

Stories of Little League coaches screaming at umpires or teaching young football players to hit with their helmets have become all too familiar to many Americans and are only two of the reasons why scholars have addressed the psychological needs and duties of coaches. In *Psychology in Contemporary Sport: Guidelines for Coaches and Athletes*, Cratty introduces at least eight important characteristics a coach should exhibit in order to facilitate the stability and success of his players. According to Cratty, a coach must display both discretion and good timing in his judgments. A coach must know when to discipline his team and when to nurture it; he must know which players he needs to coddle and which kids need a swift kick in the rear from time to time. In addition, a coach must be in command of himself, denying any selfish displays of emotion in favor of actions that meet the emotional needs of the team. A basketball coach who blows up at an official at the wrong moment and earns a critical technical foul can be just as detrimental to his team's psyche as a great play by the other team. A coach must also be a fair, considerate moderator of team disputes, being careful to smooth over conflicts between team members so that the team can function as a unit and to enact consistent punishments when necessary. Flexibility is another key characteristic. Often, coaches need to exhibit authoritarianism, intellectualism, sensitivity, and creativity within the span of a one-hour practice. Because their role is so demanding, coaches should seek to make themselves into well-rounded teachers who can not only teach the finer points of their sport, but who can also communicate verbally and emotionally with students on a number of issues, especially issues surrounding each player's emotional state at any given point in the season. Like most teachers, it is also important that coaches come to grips with the fact that they will not be liked by all team members and that there will be times when no one is seemingly in their corner. The mark of a good coach is that he can maintain psychological balance during these times, continuing to do what is good for the team despite internal pressures and external disapproval. Finally, it is important that a coach has a realistic psychological appraisal of himself. He must take all precautions to make sure that his players see him as a fair and competent leader. Cratty suggests that a coach tape games and practices and critique his own performances, paying special attention to how his players react to his actions. (Cratty 1983, 241–243). Cratty also provides some exercises that coaches might undertake to help ensure that they exhibit these eight characteristics while under great stress.

The *Handbook for Youth Sport Coaches*, edited by Vern Seefeldt, does a nice job of describing the multiple roles a youth coach has to play to ensure that her individual players have positive sporting experiences and that her team is a fun and productive outlet for the children. In the chapter entitled "Your Role as a Youth Sports Coach," Daniel Gould argues that the two most important qualities of a youth coach must be that she is a good organizer and an effective teacher. She must make sure that practices are held at clearly designated times and locations as well as ensuring that both parents and players are informed in advance of any team activity. As a teacher, she must not only impart instruction on how to play the game, but must also administer some important lessons that many sports psychologists feel young people need to learn early in their sporting careers. These include the idea that, while it is permissible to play to win, winning is not the most important thing. Instead, helping and encouraging one's teammates while striving to improve one's own game should be emphasized. Also critical is the idea that physical fitness should be emphasized as much as exploits within the game. Coaches are also instrumental in delivering lessons on fairness, having a good attitude and sportsmanship. In addition to roles as organizer and teacher, a coach can create a psychologically pleasant atmosphere for children by being a firm but fair disciplinarian, a friend who listens to the player's feelings, a conservative medical consultant who consistently tries to anticipate and prevent player injury, and a motivator who takes the time to administer to the unique psychological needs of all of her charges (Seefeldt 1987, 20–25).

Frank Ryan's *Sport Psychology* echoes some of Gould's and Cratty's sentiments but also discusses a few other psychological duties that coaches must undertake to be successful at the college level. First, a college coach must understand the pressure on his administration both to field a winning team that makes money and showers positive publicity on the school, and to run a tight academic ship in which all of the players graduate. All of a coach's decisions must be made with an eye toward this precarious balance. A coach must take into account that college presidents and athletic directors get fired or rehired in part on the basis of successful athletic teams. Dealing with the pressure that comes from fulfilling this dual role of businessperson and educator is the prime psychological challenge for college coaches. Second, a college coach must deal with stress that comes from blending the demands of powerful alumni with the overall goals of the program. Alumni dollars help to fuel college sports, and although their demands can be selfish and contrary to producing winning teams or educated students, the coach must find a way to placate them. A third character trait essential for the successful college coach is a pleasant personality. He has to be able to win over key alumni, assure an often skeptical administration, and inspire confidence in his team and the fans. Of course, organization is the string that ties these three duties together. Above all, a coach must delegate responsibility to qualified assistants and budget his time wisely to meet his many demands (Ryan 1981, 85–94).

## MOTIVATION

One of a coach's most important functions is to figure out what motivates her team. Sports psychologists have established several motivational strategies that can be used during a season to inspire an athlete or a team. In *Motivation: Implications for Coaching and Teaching,* Albert Carron argues that at least four strategies can be used alternatively by coaches to motivate a team. The first involves a reward system in which, for best results, the coach gives out rewards or punishments on a small scale. For instance, a coach might reduce the number of postpractice sprints if her team puts forth an extraordinary effort during the practice, or she might hand out a player of the game award to inspire players to play at the top of their game. Carron writes that "it is important to identify the specific behaviors which are critical, to set up a token rewards system in which an appropriate behavior leads to a specific reward, to outline this clearly to the group, and then, to consistently follow the program through to completion" (Carron 1984, 14). A second motivational strategy involves setting goals that are attainable but that will require a top notch effort from each team member. If possible, it is desirable to let the team set its own goals, encouraging members not only to set overall goals for a season, but to set subgoals that can serve as encouragement as the team plows its way through a long campaign. For instance, a team might set as its long-term goal to win a conference championship, but it could also have short-term goals such as beating an arch rival, defending their home court, or winning a preseason tournament. A third motivational tool is social reinforcement, which often comes in the form of praise from the coach. Carron points out that this can only work if the athlete respects the coach and truly desires her praise, if the praise is given sincerely, and if the coach uses the tool consistently without overusing it. Finally, it is important for a coach to be an organized leader who convinces the players that they can grow personally and that the team can blossom under her tutelage. As Carron writes, "There is little doubt that participants are most satisfied, most motivated and most productive in an environment which is most characterized by warmth, positivism, respect, and support from their coach or teacher and in which the opportunity for personal growth and skill learning is maximized" (Carron 1984, 42). Carron also discusses some of the pitfalls associated with each motivational strategy.

Mark Anshel's *Sport Psychology: From Theory to Practice*, Steven Brennen's *Competitive Excellence: The Psychology and Strategy of Team Building,* and Rainer Martens's *Coaches' Guide to Sport Psychology* all contain informative sections on motivational strategies for coaches. Generally, each agrees that a coach must continually utilize several of these techniques throughout the course of a long season, being careful to pick her strategy based on the psychological mood and emotional make-up of her team.

One of the more provocative books on the subject of sports psychology for coaches is Shane Murphy's *Sport Psychology Interventions*. Murphy discusses three main areas in which coaches must display keen psychological insight if they are to be successful. The first is the selection of players for the team and, once the team is set, the placement of players in the roles that best maximizes their ability.

Often, a coach's success in this area depends on his ability to understand which of his athletes can handle leadership roles, which need to start, and which can function well in specialized roles. In addition, a coach needs to consider the level of competition at which his athletes are playing. In youth sports, for instance, the selection of players for certain roles is different than in college sports in which the coach often needs to win to keep his job. A second area of intervention is athletic skill training. Here, a coach needs to understand how each of his players respond to his coaching style. Some players will need a more authoritarian approach. Others will respond to a more democratic, conversational style in which the player and coach can talk about goals and expectations. Finally, a coach needs to be an effective strategic planner in at least two ways. He needs to be able to make decisions during the game that reflect an accurate understanding of his players' psychological needs. For example, it would be appropriate for a football coach to try a complicated trick play if his team's confidence is soaring as the result of several perfectly executed plays. However, the same trick play could be a disaster to a team whose psyche is shaken after several miscues. In addition, a coach needs to consider his team's emotional needs when he handles off-the-field planning. For instance, a coach might not want to plan a schedule that puts a young team in the precarious position of playing several road games in front of hostile crowds (Murphy 1995, 161). It is important to note that, whether engaging in intervention or motivational techniques, a coach must always consider the unique background of each player before making any decision that would impact that player as an athlete or as a person. In *Social Psychology in Athletics*, Cratty points out that a coach must not only consider the athlete's social, economic, political, religious, educational, and family background when he coaches that athlete, he must also take into account what sport psychologists call Attribution Theory. This simply means that a coach must find out to what factors an athlete attributes his or her success or failure so that he can base his decisions on a realistic view of the player's mind set (Cratty 1981, 129–131). After all, if a player attributes her success to pregame prayer, the coach will want to take that player's religious beliefs and practices into consideration when making decisions that would affect her daily schedule or role on the team. It might not be a good idea, for instance, to make such a player practice on Sunday morning if it would interfere with religious services.

## AGGRESSION

Another topic that has drawn the attention of sports psychologists is the place of aggression and violence in sport. In recent years, scholars have diligently sought to provide definitions for the term *aggression*. In *Psychological Dynamics of Sport*, Diane Gill asserts that there are four characteristics of aggression in sport. The first is that aggression can only be measured in terms of actual action. "Aggression is behavior. Aggression is not an attitude, emotion, or motive" (Gill 1986, 195). In addition, aggressive acts are those that are intentional, those that are directed at living beings as opposed to inanimate objects, and those that, through either verbal or physical assault, involve some type of intended harm to another person (Gill

1986, 195). While the definition seems sound, it is possible to challenge Gill on certain points. For instance, one wonders if a person's hostile attitude can in fact be seen as a type of aggression, especially if that hostility is manifested in the player's body language. Also, it seems as though aggression against nonhuman objects is possible. For instance, when a hockey player whacks his stick against the opposition's net because he is frustrated, his action could be construed by opposing players as an act of aggression, one that says "this time I hit the net, next time it will be one of you." In *Social Psychology in Athletics*, Cratty expands Gills's definition by introducing three categories of aggression. The first is instrumental aggression, in which the behavior is intended to procure material rewards that do not include the suffering of others. The second is hostile aggression, where the goal is to purposefully inflict injury on another player. Closely related is psychological aggression, where the specific goal is to mentally punish one's opponent (Cratty 1981, 160). Still, problems exist. After all, instrumental aggression hardly seems negative on the surface. Should not players aggressively pursue trophies and championships? Is not aggression permissible as long as both sides can actively access its potential benefits in an environment in which both agree to participate under established rules that sanction a certain amount of aggression? *Sport Psychology: An Analysis of Athlete Behavior*, edited by William Straub, includes an essay entitled "Understanding Aggressive Behavior and Its Effects upon Athletic Performance," written by John Silva, which attempts to answer these questions. The author argues that when defining aggression, it is necessary to distinguish between aggressive and assertive behavior. According to Silva, "Proactive assertion has been defined as the heightened physical behavior that is goal directed in nature. Proactive assertion requires the expenditure of unusual effort and energy. There is, however, no intent to harm or injure another person" (Straub 1980, 179). By contrast, aggressive behavior is that which is designed to inflict physical or psychological pain or injury. That winning the game or some other noble goal is part of the aggressive act does not matter. It is still unacceptable aggression if there is any willingness to cause pain or suffering for the opponent. Still, as Silva admits, "The sport setting is perhaps the only social setting where both aggressive and proactive assertive behaviors occur with regularity" (Straub 1980, 179). It is often hard to tell where assertiveness ends and unwarranted aggression begins. As a result, scholars such as Cratty have pointed out that most sports psychologists now realize that each situation must be examined individually to determine whether a player's behavior was acceptable. Thus, while sometimes seen in a negative light, "the term aggression should be viewed in a flexible manner, reflecting behaviors that are situationally specific" (Cratty 1981, 161).

Indeed, most scholars seem not to view aggression as being entirely positive or negative. Instead, researchers such as Dorcas Susan Butt see aggression as something that is socially sanctioned by the public as long as it does not spill into overt, gratuitous violence. For Butt and others, it is essential that athletes behave aggressively. The key, however, is that they control their aggression, using it to defeat opponents in socially acceptable ways instead of launching into violent tirades or behaviors that are not needed to win the game and that are destructive both to opponents and themselves. In *The Psychology of Sport: The Behavior, Motivation, Personality and Performance of Athletes*, Butt states that "it is essential to all athletes that aggression be controlled and channeled into skill in the sport" (Butt 1987, 17). She goes on to describe six types of aggression in which the athlete must engage if she is to be successful. The first is called trait aggression, which refers to the athlete's use of biological traits to gain competitive advantage. For instance, since body checking is a sanctioned part of hockey, a 6'4", 235 lb. left wing would be missing an incredible opportunity not to use his size to physically intimidate a smaller forward. The second type of aggression is socialized aggression, in which certain types of aggressive behaviors are not only within the rules, but are actually expected. This is often seen in hockey where players are expected to fight, and where backing away from violent confrontation can lead to a player's dismissal. Closely related is game aggression. This involves sports such as football where a team literally cannot win unless it physically punishes the other team. Strategic aggression is a part of most team sports. It simply refers to the fact that many coaches will implement physical aggression as part of a game plan that relies on intimidation to achieve victory. Again, this is only acceptable for Butt because society says it is all right. Perhaps the most common type of aggressive behavior is situational aggression, in which a player retaliates violently to a perceived act of aggression. Nowhere is this more obvious than when a batter charges the mound because he feels the ninety-mile-an-hour fastball that just plunked him was intentionally thrown at his head. The idea is that if the batter does not charge the mound, he will have given the pitcher a mental advantage, and he will have lost face with teammates and fans. Finally, postgame aggression is common to both players and fans who, aggravated by the events of the game, take out their frustrations on opposing players, officials, or visiting fans. A player punching a reporter or the highly publicized soccer riots in Europe, Brazil, and other areas of the globe where soccer stirs deep national passions are good examples of this type of aggression. According to Butt, the athlete who can push the limits of what is acceptable in each of these six categories will likely have a good chance to be successful. "Such an individual is readily adaptable to a society and/or to a situation in which aggression is socially sanctioned" (Butt 1987, 17). While not all sports psychologists agree with Butt's conclusion that this type of aggression is permissible as long as society tolerates or enjoys it, her six categories and general conclusions do seem to fit American sports today.

No matter what position a scholar takes on the use of aggression in sport, most books on sport psychology have tried to address the causes of aggression. Gill outlines three major theories that have traditionally been used to explain aggression. The first set is loosely termed instinct theories. These theories stipulate that aggression is simply an innate response that is ingrained in the human animal. Gill describes both psychoanalytic theories, which stem from Freudian research and contend that aggressive actions occur when the death instinct innate to all humans is turned outward toward other individuals, and ethological theories, which attempt to explain human aggression by drawing comparisons to the behaviors of other instinctual animals. A second group of perspectives is called drive theories. The best known drive theory is the frustration-aggression hypothesis, which states that there is an aggression drive that always stems from frustration of some sort and that all frustration ends in some type of aggression. The hypothesis has since been modified to account for the fact that most people have experienced frustration without acting out aggressively to vent that frustration. Gill discusses Leonard Berkowitz, for instance, who has concluded that frustration is important to aggressive behavior only in that it creates a readiness for anger that may result in aggressive actions. Yet a third theoretical school of thought, referred to as social learning theory, says that whether or not that readiness results in aggressive behavior depends upon how the player in question has been socially conditioned to respond to frustration. Social learning theorists contend, then, that athletic aggression hinges on what a player has observed over his playing career and whether or not past aggressive actions have been positively rewarded (Gill 1986, 197–200). A variety of scholars have advanced different explanations for aggression, most of which would fall under the social learning theory umbrella. For instance, in "Violence in Sports: Its Causes and Some Solutions," Jerry Freischlag and Charles Schmidke write that relaxed social mores are a significant contributor to aggression in contemporary American sport, in which fans are conditioned to revel in bone-crushing hits or breathtaking crashes in auto racing. They also contend that the media encourages violence by glamorizing it in order to make money. They specifically assert that the media attempts to exploit regional, ethnic, religious, political, or racial divisions in order to create rivalries that benefit both the sport and its accompanying media outlets. Finally, they say that most kids learn that aggression and violence are acceptable responses by watching their adult heroes. Every time Dennis Rodman pushes an official, for example, a certain number of kids are encouraged to think that is the cool, manly way to behave (Straub 1980, 161–163).

In *The Handbook of Research on Sport Psychology*, Robert Singer advances the notion that aggression can stem from spectator expectations, the fear that an opponent might gain an advantage by striking the first blow, or, in the case of male athletes, from the desire to prove one's manhood in ways deemed appropriate by society (Singer 1993, 370–375). A final explanation is offered by Peter Cataldi in an article entitled "Sport and Aggression: A Safety Valve or a Pressure Cooker." Cataldi analyzes the notion that aggression exists as a catharsis, a purging of frustration and repressed anxiety. He does an excellent job of explaining what instinct, drive, and social learning theorists have had to say on the matter and eventually concludes that, while there does seem to be some level of emotional cleansing with some aggressive acts, "the cathartic explanation of aggression is, at best, naive and simplistic, and, at worst, deleterious to the progress of the state-of-the-art because of its very problem of pervasiveness" (Straub 1980, 200).

For those interested in the causes and potential effects of aggression, Britton Brewer and Judy Van Raalte's *Exploring Sport and Exercise Psychology*, Richard Cox's *Sport Psychology: Concepts and Applications*, John Kremer's *Psychology in Sport*, and Arnold LeUnes's *Sport Psychology: An Introduction* all contain chapters that discuss current research on the subject. While most refuse to condemn or uphold aggression absolutely, each offers some suggestions as to how coaches, parents, and athletes can either minimize or control aggression. Likewise, in *Psychology in Contemporary Sport*, Cratty offers no less than seventeen suggestions about how to curb aggressive behavior in team sports. Some ideas include precontest meetings between players, coaches, and sports psychologists to make sure players can talk about any anger they might be harboring; quick disciplinary action for any player who aggressively tries to harm another player; and heightened crowd control to prevent spectators from inciting violence in the game (Cratty 1983, 108–109). Freischlag and Schmidke suggest that sports promoters could encourage more families to attend games because more families usually means less violence. They also advocate pregame handshakes, media coverage that plays down rivalry, and public address announcers who do not work spectators into a frenzy (Straub 1980, 164). While the enactment of some of these ideas may help, one has to wonder if instinctual theorists were originally correct in their assertion that aggression is part of the human condition, one that we like, and one that will not go away because down deep few of us really want it to go away. Do we secretly like rivalry? Is there some part of us that is not only fascinated with but also enjoys violence? Psychologically, do we love sport because it allows us to legally express anger, brutality, and deep-seated desires to conquer others and assert our will? As debates about family values, America's moral condition, and the nation's crime problem continue to heat up, aggression in sport will certainly continue to be an important topic as sport psychologists grapple with these and other questions whose answers would help us to better understand our attraction to and revulsion of aggressive behavior.

## ETHICAL CONCERNS

One of the major tasks for researchers and practicing psychologists has been to establish a code of ethics that is specifically designed for sports psychology. In *The Ethics and Practice of Applied Sport Psychology*, Robert M. Nideffer argues that a complete code of ethics should define the responsibilities of a practitioner and the level of competence necessary to enter the field. In addition, such a code should make clear exactly what the moral and legal obligations of a sports psychologist are in regard to confidentiality, the welfare of the patient, public statements, testing procedures, and professional relationships. Nideffer provides a good overview of each of these issues and explains many of the ethical precepts of the current code adopted by the American Psychological Association (APA) (Nideffer 1981, 9–16). His book is replete with case studies that force students to deal with difficult but common ethical dilemmas faced by sports psychologists. In addition, the author makes it clear that anyone who wants to study or practice the psychology of sport must be familiar with some of the theories from which ethical standards spring. As Nideffer writes, "It is difficult to imagine a sport psychologist being able to function consistently in an ethical and competent way, without having some theoretical framework that guides his/her practice" (Nideffer 1981, 17). One of the best books on sports psychological theory is Brewer and Van Raalte's *Exploring*

*Sport and Exercise Psychology*. The authors provide solid discussions on the purpose of ethical codes, the specifics of the APA code, and historical ethical standards in the field of sports psychology. In doing so, Brewer and Van Raalte analyze the two main theories that have dominated ethical concerns in the field. The first is consequentialism, which asserts that the consequences of an action determine whether or not it is an ethical action. Generally, this means that if an action produces happiness for an individual or team it is probably an ethical, moral action. If similar actions produce a sense of well-being for a group of people over an extended period of time then one can be relatively sure of its moral rightness. Thus, a sports psychologist must seek to adopt policies that have been proven to promote happiness and psychological satisfaction for athletes. As Brewer and Van Raalte write, "If it can be shown that a particular action produces the greatest good for the greatest number, then people should engage in that action. Ethics codes are rules that are based on past experiences" (Brewer and Van Raalte 1996, 437). To many sports psychologists, consequentialism is problematic because of its failure to account for the fact that happiness for an individual or team often comes at the expense of the happiness of other players and teams. How can such happiness or the acts that inspired it be called moral? A second line of theory is called deontology, which holds that ethical standards must spring from an immutable foundation of truth. For deontologists, ethics do not exist as a set of behaviors that make people happy. On the contrary, ethics refers to the process by which any action is compared against an ideal set of standards. A sports psychologist might pick *The Holy Bible*, Kant's *Grounding for the Metaphysics of Morals*, or any other set of principles from which to construct ethical standards. No matter what type of theoretical approach a practitioner takes, it is necessary to have a firm understanding of how to integrate their preferred theoretical philosophy with ethical practice. For instance, a sports psychologist with consequentialist leanings might have trouble dealing with an athlete who is happy even though he won a big tennis match by cheating. Brewer and Van Raalte include several case studies in which students can practice applying their philosophical convictions to ethical situations (Brewer and Van Raalte 1996, 430–445).

Those looking for an analysis of the major ethical issues facing sports psychologists today should read Michael Sachs's "Professional Ethics in Sport Psychology" in Singer's *Handbook of Research on Sport Psychology*. Sachs discusses eight different dilemmas, including how to deal with the intimacy factor in sports psychology where counseling often takes place one-on-one in the privacy of a locker room or team offices. He specifically mentions some techniques a team psychologist can adopt to make sure that, while he is being supportive of the player's needs, he is also maintaining a professional posture that will protect himself from any accusations of sexual harassment. In addition, Sachs discusses issues of competency, such as how sports psychologists can avoid legal problems that might result from stepping beyond their limitations in trying to help an athlete. Certification is the key issue here, and the author discusses how the certification process can impact a practitioner's career. Sachs also tackles ethical issues that come into play when practitioners counsel athletes from other cultures, the expectations and mores of which that practitioner might be unfamiliar. Issues of confidentiality, supervision, payments, and marketing are all covered in the essay. For instance, Sachs addresses whether or not vital information should be released to parents of child athletes, whether it is advisable to allow a coach or friend to supervise a session with an athlete, whether it is ethical to allow third parties to pay for an athlete's treatment, whether or not that third party should be notified of the athlete's condition, and what steps should be taken by practitioners to avoid charges of false advertising. Sachs concludes by speculating about future ethical directions in the field. Sachs writes that "issues encompassing certification, confidentiality, intimacy and marketing will be raised in our evolving field in years to come" (Singer 1993, 930).

One of the most pressing issues that Sachs does not discuss is how sports psychologists can work to promote morality through athletic experience. In *Character Development and Physical Activity*, David Lyle Light Shields asserts that sport ought to have moralizing effects that teach participants fair play and sportpersonship, while enhancing character development. Shield's book is valuable because it traces several theories that sports psychologists have used over the last century to examine whether or not sport really has a moral function. He discusses the psychoanalytic belief that sport has no intrinsic moral value. It is merely one medium through which children develop a sense of morality by integrating instinct with societal demand. Conversely, those who ascribe to the moral trait approach believe that morality can be shaped by sports. For these theorists, morality is not consistent. Different activities have the potential of driving home a number of different values. Thus, by participating in a certain athletic environment for a long period of time, an athlete may indeed be inculcated to moral maxims played out within that sporting arena. A third theory, the structural developmental approach, posits that athletics contributes to moral development only in that it is part of what is called equilibration, a process by which children assimilate actions going on around them and then integrate the moral ramifications of those actions into existing belief structures. As new stimuli are confronted and either rejected or accepted, the child's sense of what is moral gradually changes. Sports can play a key part in this process if it provides consistent stimuli that is accepted by the child (Shields 1995, 25–30). Social learning theory insists that sport shapes morality only when it is valued by a culture. Thus, advocates of this point of view think that sports are tremendously influential in the United States today where $300 million sports stadiums are routinely erected in cities faced with large debts and a myriad of social ills. Hoffman's empathy-based theory of morality states that sport can have a moral function only if it inspires some type of empathetic reaction in the participant. If through an athletic experience a player gains insight by identifying with the plight of another, moral development has taken place. Kohlberg's theory of moral development posits that each individual evolves through six stages of moral development. During each stage, athletic participation has the potential to affect the individual's moral growth. For instance, at stage three a person is highly influenced by social units such as the family. If a person's parents happen to attach a great deal of importance to auto racing, its children might be morally influenced by that which they see at the race track or from broadcasts of auto races. Recently, theorists such as Carol Gilligan and Nancy Chodorow advanced the idea that moral development is closely related to conceptions of care and justice. They argue that a child's sense of morality depends on how she feels she is being cared for and whether or not she is being treated fairly. Sports, as an important part of many children's lives, can have far-reaching effects on morality. Norma Hahn's model of interaction morality asserts that the interaction of five major concepts are at the essence of moral formation. These include moral balance, dialogue, truth, and secondary moral structures and levels. Shields does a superb job of explaining each of these concepts and how athletics can be an important facet to an individual's moral development as he experiences the interaction described by the theory.

Another model of moral development is offered by James Rest's model of moral action. Rest argues that in response to any action a person must "interpret the situation and action possibilities, form a moral judgment about what should be done, choose a value to seek through action, and carry out the intended act" (Shields 1995, 82). Naturally, sport can play a key part in a person's moral journey because participants are constantly confronted with difficult questions. For instance, a question such as should a player cheat to win if she can get away with it is a sufficient catalyst for moral development. Shields not only explains how each of these theories of moral development work, but also provides analysis that explains the positive and negative aspects of each theory. Shields even advances a theory of his own, a twelve-component model of moral action, which expands Rest's model by adding three variables, contextual factors, personal competencies, and ego processing (Shields 1995, 20–85).

It is interesting that after surveying all of the theories that attempt to explain the relationship of sports and individual morality, Shields is not fully able to answer the question "Does sport build character." Though he includes a section in which he quotes philosophers and social commentators that espouse varying points of view, Shields echos most scholars by asserting that sport has the potential for developing both positive and negative character traits. Whether one learns responsibility, teamwork, cooperation, self-esteem, loyalty, courage, and self-sacrifice as opposed to winning at all costs, bending the rules for one's own purposes, intimidation, humiliating one's opponent, or how to impose one's will through violent means depends on a number of factors. These include a player's religion, the coaches' attitudes, parental values, and the approach of the administrators who run the sport. Shields lists several recommendations that coaches, parents, athletes, and administrators might follow to ensure that, if sport does have a moral component, it will be beneficial to all participants. Some of these suggestions include regular meetings between coaches and parents at the high school level or lower to discuss how the players are progressing morally and the implementation of programs that would train coaches, athletes, and administrators to use techniques that might facilitate moral growth in sport (Shields 1995, 222–224). William Duquet, Paul De Knop, and Livin Bollart's *Youth Sport: A Social Approach*; Frank Smoll and Ronald Smith's *Children and Youth in Sport: A Biopsychosocial Perspective*; and Maureen Weiss's "Teaching Sportsmanship and Values," located in Seefeldt's *Handbook for Youth Sport Coaches*, all reflect on how sport can be used to develop desired morals in young participants. Weiss's essay is particularly good for those seeking suggestions on how to shape sporting experiences for kids in such a way that they promote moral growth.

## TEAM SPORTS

In recent years, sports psychologists have produced significant research that specifically deals with team sports. In *Psychology of Team Sports*, Hans Schellenberger provides a solid overview of what sports psychologists have traditionally thought about key issues in team sports. These include team chemistry, factors that motivate individual players within a team context, and a variety of social-psychological concepts that impact each player on a team. As Schellenberger writes, "Performance in team sports is determined by the interaction of physical characteristics, co-ordination, technique, and tactics with psychological factors, images, operations and states; and by external conditions, such as the development in international and national standards. Cultural upbringing is just as important as physical training. An analysis of this relationship makes it easier to understand training and competition processes" (Schellenberger 1990, 10). According to Schellenberger, the most pressing concern for any team is cohesiveness, an intangible condition by which a team of individual players comes together as a powerful unit. In *Psychological Dynamics of Sport*, Gill writes that "anyone who has been involved in any team sport knows the value of cohesiveness"(Gill 1986, 226). Gill analyzes Carron's conceptual system for cohesiveness, which asserts that environmental factors, personal factors, leadership factors, and team factors all combine to make a disparate or cohesive team. Environmental factors are dominated by the player's feelings about the team or organization. Personal elements involve things such as contract satisfaction and whether or not the player feels like he is getting enough playing time. Leadership concerns usually involve the player's relationship with coaches and team captains. Team aspects of cohesion also include confidence in the team and happiness with team goals and orientations. According to the model, team cohesion is always tenuous because all of these factors must be relatively stable for nearly all of the players. If one star or a small group of role players is significantly dissatisfied, then team cohesion will be elusive (Gill 1986, 227). In "Group Structure and Group Performance," D. Stanley Eitzen argues that, in addition to factors stipulated in Carron's model, there are at least four other aspects to team cohesion. The most important is what Eitzen refers to as homogeneity of team members. This is basically the idea that, though there can be great cultural diversity within a team, there must be some common bond that is stronger than each player's unique values and which powerfully draws the players together as a team. Other elements of cohesion include racial harmony, a lack of managerial turnover, and minimal player turnover. The last two loom as important for maintaining team morale, since most players respond favorably when team administrations go out of their way to keep well-liked coaches and players in place (Straub 1980, 417–420). Those looking to find suggestions as to how coaches can develop a cohesive team might read Terry Orlick's *In Pursuit of Excellence: How to Win in Sport and Life Through Mental Training*, or Jim Blackburn's "Systematic Program for the Development of Staff Cohesion," which is located in Linda Bunker, Robert Rotella, and Ann Reilly's *Sport Psychology: Psychological Considerations in Maximizing Sports Performance*. Orlick's book focuses on strategies designed to help coaches and athletes work together to promote team unity. Blackburn's article does an effective job of outlining ways that a head coach or administrator can ensure that large coaching staffs work together. Well-defined job descriptions, support systems for coaches' families, fairness in selecting coaches for specific duties or promotions, clinics that promote professional growth, increased wages and responsibility for assistant coaches, and a myriad of communication exercises are all part of Blackburn's recipe for a unified coaching staff (Bunker, et al. 1985, 93–100).

It should be noted that not all scholars believe that cohesion is vital to team success. In "Cohesiveness and Performance in Sport Teams," Gill concludes that, while cohesiveness can be important to team success, a unified team does not necessarily make for a winning team. In addition, in many cases it is winning that makes for team cohesion as opposed to cohesion resulting in on-field victories. Gill points out that talent, luck, and injuries are all important factors to a team's success and mentions several studies that cite examples showing that cohesion is not as important as many other factors that contribute to a team being a winner or a loser (Straub 1980, 421–429). One such factor is how being part of a team motivates individual athletes to give their best performances. In *Motivation: Implications for Coaching and Teaching*, Carron argues that a team's season often hinges on whether or not it can psychologically bring out the best in all team members. In all, Carron issues eight conclusions about the relationship between the team and each of its players. These include the ideas that "the presence of others influences motivation and performance," "the presence of others is relaxing in highly stressful situations," and "the group's goals and successes and failures influence an individual member's level of motivation" (Carron 1984, 69–70). Another major element of team success is leadership. Cratty's *Psychology in Contemporary Sport* and Gordon Russell's *The Social Psychology of Sport* comment on leadership as a key component of team competition. Cratty's work analyzes the main characteristics of a quality team leader. His discussion is interesting in that he analyzes the roles that should exist for elected team captains as well as the vital roles of natural team leaders, players who are respected as leaders without official status. Perhaps Cratty's most provocative conclusion is that any team leader's main goal is to make sure that there are no victims or oppressors on the team and that each member feels like an appreciated member of the squad. According to the author, "The victim-oppressor roles may likewise permeate the team's hierarchy—that is, one individual's victim may become still a third member's oppressor, as the hostility experienced is redirected toward another" (Cratty 1983, 275). Russell concludes that a leader can only fulfill this function if he can master two key duties—instrumental functions, in which he performs well in games and practices and enhances the play of others, and expressive functions, in which he makes sure that each player can speak his mind in any situation (Russell 1993, 111). Russell's work also explains four theories of sports leadership. The trait approach asserts that some players are biologically destined to lead others. The situation approach says that a good leader is one that can handle a particular situation. Thus, each team member must lead at some point during a season. Just who will lead depends on the situation the team is facing at the time. The transactional approach holds that a leader is someone who can accurately reflect and advance the philosophies of his teammates. Finally, sociometry contends that leaders should be selected on the basis of players' responses to carefully worded questions, such as "Who would you go to for advice on a personal problem?" The answers to several such questions would be analyzed, and the player whose name was mentioned the most as an answer to the questions would be elected captain (Russell 1993, 98–102).

## THE PSYCHOLOGY OF INDIVIDUAL ATHLETES

Despite recent interest in team sports, most current research in sports psychology has examined how individual athletes psychologically prepare for competition. Gill's research has revealed that an athlete's personality characteristics have a great deal to do with how he should prepare for competition. The athlete must first understand himself in order to combat the psychological pitfalls he faces before and during competition. Gill analyzes several theories developed by psychologists to explain the relationship between personality and performance. For instance, Sheldon's Constitutional Theory holds that a person's body shape and other physical characteristics actually determine personality. Conversely, psychodynamic theories stipulate that an athlete's personality develops over time as he resolves important conflicts. Trait theories argue that an athlete is guided by one or two dominant personality traits and that all his actions can be understood by considering those traits. Social learning theorists hold that an athlete has no concrete personality that determines his actions, but that each situation can trigger a wide range of personality traits. Finally, the dominant contemporary theory is the interactionist approach, which posits that a player's personality is constantly being reshaped via the interaction of dominant traits with new situations (Gill 1986, 24–30). For example, a player may be very aggressive until he delivers a particularly vicious hit that severely injures another player. At that point, the player might have to readjust his aggressiveness, either becoming less aggressive because of empathy for the victim or more aggressive because he enjoys the feelings of power that came from dominating another person. Either way, the reaction would inform the sports psychologist about the athlete's personality and would alert both the athlete and coach as to what would have to be done to help the player. After all, if he could no longer be aggressive he would not be a very effective player, but too much aggression could lead to problems with violence both on and off the field. The goal of the sports psychologist would be to make sure that, no matter what the athlete's reaction, he is given ample help to move to a position that he can live with and that is not dangerous to others. Gill's discussion of how sports psychologists use these theories to help players develop healthy personality traits that allow them to have a positive experience in sports is first rate. While Gill leaves the debate open as to the overall effects of sport on a player's personality, she generally concludes that sport seems to have the potential for improved physical and emotional health for participants.

One of the most important reasons for understanding an athlete's personality is to help her deal with stress and anxiety. Researchers have posited several reasons why players feel stress. Gill provides interesting commentary on how an athlete's stress can depend on her personality type. For instance, if her personality is guided by a dominant trait, such as shyness, she will likely have a problem dealing with situations in which she is thrust into the limelight. Conversely, the interactionist approach would indicate that the same athlete could also be influenced by whether or not her home life is happy or troubled. Gill also distinguishes between general stress, in which an athlete feels nervous before any competition, and specific anxiety, in which an athlete responds to certain types of situations. Again, Gill uses the personality theories previously described to account for this (Gill 1986, 74–75). In *Psychology in Contemporary Sport*, Cratty writes that fear is the main cause of athletic stress. Fear of losing, for instance, is a huge roadblock for many players: "Male athletes may feel that a loss will somehow brand them as less than a man. Many female athletes, also, simply do not wish to lose, as their self-concept is that of a winner. A loss would seriously interfere with this positive picture of them-selves" (Cratty 1983, 125). For some players, winning is such an important component to their identities that they fear being labeled as losers, failing their teammates, or getting rejected by coaches, friends, and family. Others fear pain or injury, especially if they have already incurred a painful setback in the past. Still others fear aggression itself. According to Cratty, "Some athletes harbor anxieties about the outcomes of their aggressive behavior. They may fear that they will produce real injury to their opponent or to their teammates in practice" (Cratty 1983, 126). Finally, many players suffer anxiety over playing in front of a live audience. Cratty devotes an entire chapter to the effects of an audience on different types of athletes and offers several thought-provoking discussions on playing in front of family, friends, hostile crowds, abusive crowds, and home crowds that expect victory. Other books offering valuable contributions for understanding the causes of stress in athletic competition include Stuart Biddle's *European Perspectives on Exercise and Sport Psychology*, Richard Butler's *Sport Psychology in Action*, and Robert Grant's *The Psychology of Sport: Facing One's True Opponent*.

Several scholars have written about a multitude of methods introduced by sports psychologists to help athletes combat anxiety. David Cook's "Sport Psychology and Christianity: A Comparison of Application," located in Linda Bunker, Robert Rotella, and Ann Reilly's *Sport Psychology: Psychological Considerations in Maximizing Sports Performance*, provides an excellent discussion on how some athletes use spiritual faith to reduce stress. James Bennett and James Pravitz have written a fascinating book entitled *The Profile of a Winner: Advanced Mental Training for Athletes*. The book explains several methods for combating stress, but the best two sections are on mental programming strategies and imaging. The former involves using a five-step method to integrate established goals into the subconscious mind. The steps include scheduling mental programming (repeating your goals to yourself out loud) at least twice a day, creating a nonthreatening environment in which one feels comfortable to program oneself, using positive affirmations, using creative energy to deliver those affirmations, and using emotion to make oneself believe the affirmations (Bennett and Pravitz 1987, 77). Imaging refers to the process by which an athlete uses her imagination to reinforce desired patterns of behavior. Imaginary scenes of pleasant things can be used to relax before a big game or visualization techniques can be employed to help the athlete focus on exactly what she wants to do during that game. For instance, a basketball player might visualize how she will defend an opposing player's best move. The authors even discuss an advanced technique called triple imagery, in which an athlete can visualize different images at once, moving fluidly between them so as to visualize the entire game (Bennett and Pravitz 1987, 287–306).

One of the most comprehensive books that deals with stress reduction for athletes is Cox's *Sport Psychology: Concepts and Applications*. He profiles several strategies commonly used by athletes to fight anxiety and improve performance. One such technique is Edmond Jacobson's Progressive Relaxation Procedure. This involves the athlete lying down in a completely comfortable position so that all tense muscles can relax. The procedure must be repeated every day until the athlete can literally lapse into a fully relaxed position in only a few minutes. While this method deals exclusively with physical relaxation, autogenic training relies on a series of mental exercises to enhance muscle alacrity. Closely related is the traditional concept of meditation, in which an athlete relaxes his body by conditioning his mind to believe certain things. Cox also discusses biofeedback, in which highly sophisticated instruments are used to help athletes control excessive stress. The author also devotes several pages to hypnosis, explaining different ways the procedure can be used and discussing the pros and cons of using it as a method of stress reduction. According to those who practice hypnosis, its value is that it promotes relaxation by allowing the athlete to deal with deep problems that he is otherwise afraid to tackle. According to Cox, the jury is still out as to the effectiveness of hypnosis. Some practitioners view it as a way to help athletes resolve their most fundamental conflicts; detractors point to the fact that it dangerously disturbs the athlete's deepest thought and invites forth issues with which the player may not be ready to grapple (Cox 1994, 155–161). The McClelland-Atkinson model of achievement motivation asserts that any stress reduction techniques should be aimed at helping players over the long run, insisting that short-term solutions are merely stop gap measures that might actually make the athlete's stress more acute. This model introduces the fear of failure (FOF) construct that is designed to help athletes maximize internal motivation while overcoming external fears. By contrast, the fear of success construct (FOS) attempts to help athletes surmount fears of inflicting pain on opponents and other factors that make players feel guilty about winning. Several other theories arise from the belief that the best way to combat anxiety is to build an athlete's self-confidence. Cox discusses Bandura's Theory of Self-Efficacy, which says that the creation of reasonable goals that can be reached over time by an athlete will make him believe that he can succeed. This belief will reduce stress levels because the player will be able to tell himself that he has always succeeded in the past and, therefore, will likely succeed this time as well. Of course, this can also lead to overconfidence and fails to account for the fact that the player is bound to fail several times during his athletic career. Harter's Competence Motivation Theory attempts to address these shortcomings by insisting that stress can be reduced if an athlete is able to improve basic skills on a consistent basis. In the Harter model, winning does not come into play. A player gains confidence and becomes less worried over competition because, even if he does lose, he knows that he is improving and will likely play better than he did in his last game. Nicholls's developmentally-based theory of perceived ability is similar to the Harter model in that it emphasizes the importance of physical abilities, teamwork, and other skills not related to winning. The idea is that if the player has an overall good feeling about himself as a player, teammate, and person, he probably will not suffer as much stress. Finally, Vealey's sport specific model of sport confidence attempts to relieve athletic stress by encouraging players to realize what their dominant personality traits are in regard to sports, so that they can develop a way of approaching sports that is healthy and works to reduce stress. Again, Cox does a wonderful job of explaining each of these stress reduction techniques, and his work is a good primer for anyone interested in the subject.

Scholars have also written extensively on what happens to athletes when they are unable to successfully cope with stress. As Butt writes, "Stress in sport is both physical and psychological. It is easier, however, to chart the physical injuries that cause young athletes to leave the arena than it is to chart psychological injuries which also may be disabling" (Butt 1987, 198). In Shane Murphy's *The Achievement Zone: 8 Skills for Winning All the Time from Playing the Field to the Classroom*, Al Petitpas and Steven Danish include an article entitled "Caring for Injured Athletes" that deals with how athletes cope with the psychological effects of athletic injury. The authors deal with the profound sense of grief felt by injured players, identity loss, separation and loneliness, fear of uncertainty as to whether they will be able to play again, and loss of confidence, offering case studies that allow readers to fully examine the psychological ramifications of each problem. In addition, Petitpas and Danish discuss fourteen different treatments used by practitioners to help injured athletes battle through tough times. Other works that discuss the subject include Lew Hardy's *Understanding Psychological Preparation for Sport: Theory and Practice of Elite Performers* and Singer's *Handbook of Research on Sport Psychology*. Those interested in athletic burnout can consult either Cox's *Sport Psychology: Concepts and Applications* or Robert Weinberg and Daniel Gould's *Foundations of Sport and Exercise Psychology*. Cox provides the reader with a clear understanding of the conditions that result in burnout. These include coach-applied pressure, unrealistic goals that cannot be reached, peer pressure, extended exposure to unreasonable pressure, fear of failure, or any other negative experience that transforms sports from enjoyable play to taxing work (Cox 1994, 376–379). Weinberg and Gould focus on methods of combating burnout, explaining how practitioners can help athletes construct short-term goals, communications exercises, and relaxation breaks designed to enliven the athletic process for the player.

Those interested in the psychological reasons behind drug and alcohol abuse by athletes might look at Singer's *Handbook of Research on Sport Psychology*. Singer examines the reasons for drug use, including pain reduction, rehabilitation, relaxation, weight control, and heightened energy, as well as the psychological consequences of drug abuse. These include an increased fear of failure, physical weakness, lowered self-confidence, and extreme perfectionism. Naturally, the author analyzes several methods of treatment and includes sections discussing what parents, coaches, and athletes can do to both prevent and overcome drug problems. Significantly, Singer devotes an entire section to steroids and other performance-enhancing drugs. Weinberg and Gould also deal with the subject, providing a complete list of performance-enhancing drugs and their common side effects. In "Hypnosis," William P. Morgan explains how practitioners can use hypnosis to heal those with drug addictions. Morgan extends his analysis to show how hypnotic theory can be applied to eating disorders (Singer 1993, 259–261). Petitpas and Danish also provide a thorough discussion of eating disorders, focusing on psychological causes and potential treatments.

Before leaving the topic of mental strategies for athletic preparation, it is necessary to mention Anschel's *Sport Psychology: From Theory to Practice*. The book is a must read for anyone who desires to understand how many of the theories spoken of in this section can actually be used. It is also useful for anyone who wants to understand the qualities of successful, elite athletes, allegedly the qualities that treatment seeks to produce. Interestingly, these include the following behaviors: reserving energy for games as opposed to practices, feeling confident with complex game plans, being able to make adjustments during games, remaining alone and silent before contests so as to be able to focus on the game, not worrying about the opponent, being nervous and tense so as to maintain an emotional edge for the game, being able to maintain composure when things go wrong, being able to practice things over and over, being able to accurately assess individual and team performance, withstanding poor officiating, handling the pressure of the game's final stages, not giving up, and overcoming questionable tactics of the opposition (Anshel 1997, 30–33). While some of these might seem questionable to readers, Anshel's book looms as an important tool that can help students and practitioners gain a better sense of what types of characteristics a psychologically healthy athlete might have and how to use current psychological treatments to help athletes attain them.

## GENDER AND SPORTS PSYCHOLOGY

In the late 1980s, gender, and to a lesser extent race, emerged as important topics in the field of sports psychology. Some works exist on the psychological study of male athletes. One of the earliest works to focus on men's experience in sport is *Jock: Sport and Male Identity*, by Donald Sabo and Russ Runfola. Though the authors' conclusions are somewhat overstated and the book relies too much on the personal experiences of the authors and a few subjects, the work is useful because it introduces many of what have become the central themes of scholarship dealing with men's psychology and sport. The first theme is that sports propagate a masculine identity that calls for men to prove themselves by hurting other men. Thus, sport, through its insistence that men conquer each other to win games, contributes to a larger masculine process by which men learn to see each other as enemies and through which men become increasingly alienated from each other. The second theme is that sports often require violent acts, excessive training, the use of performance-enhancing drugs, and predatory attitudes that estrange men from themselves, causing them to adopt harmful identities that work toward their psychological undoing. The third theme is that sport conditions men to fulfill roles that no longer need to be filled in contemporary society. Specifically, sport allegedly encourages men to develop as physical warriors as opposed to cerebral, cooperative teammates, a role that might help men more easily fit into their postmodern society. The following quote captures the overall tone of the authors:

However, to the extent that the ethos of athletic competition and excellence is associated with the ideology of male supremacy, sexual potency, and a desire for power, sports legitimize a social hierarchy in which men enjoy greater status than their female counterparts. In a way sadly consistent with Hobbesian legacy, sports encourage men to forever compete with one another, never trusting and never feeling, and to regard women as frail underlings who are far removed from the panoply of patriarchal pugnacity and privilege. Evidence mounts that competition has lost its functional effectiveness in both personal and social life. The interpersonal anomie of modern culture and pressing economic, political and ecological problems beckon the birth of a new ethos of cooperation. (Sabo and Runfola 1980, 334–335)

Though Sabo and Runfola dismiss too easily the importance of competition in modern life, their ideas have, in part, inspired two decades of psychological writing along the same lines. One of the most prolific writers on the subject is Michael Messner, a scholar who, though actually trained as a sociologist, contributes enormously to the arguments surrounding the effect of sport on the male psyche. One of his best works is *Sex, Violence and Power in Sports: Rethinking Masculinity,* a work he co-authored with Sabo. Messner reiterates many of Sabo and Runfola's original points but provides much more evidence in support of those arguments. In addition, Messner offers compelling discussions on the relationship between male sports participation and homophobia, sex, pain, and power. He is particularly concerned with how sports, in his view, impair men's relationships with women. The book contains an entire section called "Sexuality and Power," in which Messner and Sabo discuss how sports encourage young men to see women as sex objects to be conquered. Messner concludes that "using women as objects of sexual conquest is important for gaining status in the male peer group, but also tends to impoverish young males' relationships with females" (Messner and Sabo 1994, 47). Messner ends the book with a suggested eleven-step process intended to help men use sport to promote their own psychological health. Some of the steps include resisting locker-room sexism, refusing to participate in violent sports, working for gender equity by supporting women's sports, being advocates for minority athletes, and pushing for public discussions of men's sporting experience (Messner and Sabo 1994, 214–216).

It is interesting that many of the works that deal with men and sport specifically tend to focus on how men need to redefine their sporting practices to gain psychological stability. Very few works seem to concentrate on how many men continue to use sport in very healthy ways. Perhaps this indicates that the field is only in its infancy or perhaps this is indicative of how recent scholarship tends to focus on abuses that need to be solved. In any event, there are a few other works that deal strictly with men that might be of use to a researcher. Messner's *Power at Play: Sports and the Problem of Masculinity*, Jeff Benedict's *Public Heroes, Private Felons: Athletes and Crimes Against Women*, and Brian Pronger's *The Arena of Masculinity: Sports, Homosexuality, and the Meaning of Sex* all discuss how contemporary male sporting practices lead to the abuse of women and gay men, as well as to the psychological instability of men in general. *Sex, Violence and Power in Sports: Rethinking Masculinity* also contains a section called "Marginalized Men," which discusses how the psychological identities of young African-American males are influenced by sport. Roscoe C. Brown's "The 'Jock Trap'—How the Black Athlete Gets Caught" is part of Straub's *Sport Psychology: An Analysis of Athlete Behavior* and reiterates Messner's claim that sport has psychologically steered some African-American males toward an unhealthy identity based solely on athletic ability that is doomed to fade with age, often leaving the athlete emotionally bankrupt (Straub 1980, 300–303). Those wishing to read about how sport can positively impact the male psyche might try David Friend's *Baseball, Football, Daddy and Me* or Donald Hall's *Fathers Playing Catch with Sons: Essays on Sport*, neither of which is very academic, but both of which are uplifting and likely to strike a chord with the millions of boys who benefitted from sports when they were growing up.

Some scholars have concentrated specifically on women's sporting experience to examine facets of the relationship between sports and women's psychological development. Greta Cohen's *Women in Sport: Issues and Controversies* covers several aspects of women's sporting experience, including chapters on how media portrayals of female players affect the psyche of women athletes, how nutrition affects psychological readiness, how women can reconcile competition with cooperative instincts, how women with disabilities can use sport, and how women can help girls move beyond early childhood stereotypes that impede athletic participation. Another good work is Robert Mechikoff's *Sport Psychology for Women*. This book covers how women can use sport to develop leadership skills, to strengthen their connections with other women, and to develop a healthy identity. Mechikoff also devotes several chapters to analyzing what women can do to overcome some of the psychological obstacles unique to them in sport. For instance, he discusses how women can reconcile aggression with the traditional female role of nurturer. Most books on the sports psychology of women athletes are positive and upbeat, insisting that participation in sports is helpful in nearly all ways to psychological stability and that participation in some physical activity is a must for all women. In addition, most books are dedicated to pinpointing potential psychological problems for women in sport and introducing ways of combating those problems. Other books that might be of interest include Ann Hall's *Feminism and Sporting Bodies: Essays on Theory and Practice*, Pamela Creedon's *Women, Media and Sport: Challenging Gender Values*, and Margaret Costa's *Women and Sport: Interdisciplinary Perspectives*.

There are a few other works that address issues that pertain to both men and women. Thelma Horn's *Advances in Sport Psychology* contains an essay by Diane Gill entitled "Gender and Sports Behavior." Students hoping to understand the two main approaches of sports psychologists to the study of gender should consult this article. The first is the Sex Differences Approach, which concentrates on how biological differences between males and females impact the psychological benefits that each sex gets from sport and account for the psychological problems that each sex faces. The second is the Gender Construction Approach, which asserts that the notions implanted in girls and boys by society as to what it means to be male or female are what determine each child's psychological stance toward sport. Most of the current research follows the Gender Construction Approach. For example, the essay also features a clear explanation of the Bem Sex Role Inventory (BSRI) and the Minnesota Multiphasic Personality Inventory (MMPI), two examples of how sports psychologists have attempted to measure an athlete's perception of gender to account for how socially constructed definitions of gender impact athletic performance. Gill includes examples of sex difference research as well and ends with a plea to sports psychologists to consider both biological and social factors when conducting further research, insisting that "we should consider biological factors as part of the dynamic, social process within sport" (Horn 1992, 157).

Researchers hoping to gain an understanding of how sports psychologists have reconstructed views of gender to make sense of the relationship between sport and gender throughout history should read Carole Ogelsby and Karen Hill's "Gender and Sport." The article is located in Singer's *Handbook of Research on Sport Psychology* and discusses gender and sport in four distinct periods. The prehistory discussion features such topics as goddess worship, Amazon mythology, and little known facts about gender relations. The section on ancient history concentrates on men's use of sport for military training and women's use of sport within the domestic sphere. The section "Near History" covers historical events that impacted the relationship of gender and sport from the mid-1800s to the contemporary women's movement. Finally, most of the discussion centers around the "Now and Future" period in which men and women must, according to the authors, redefine current conceptions of gender as they operate within the sporting context in order to remove sport from its destructive historical patterns and transform it into an activity that promotes the following values for both men and women: interdependence, innovation, care for oneself and one's opponent, nonviolence, and an emphasis on improving one's life in the holistic sense as opposed to winning (Singer 1993, 723–724). Like all of the works in the Singer handbook, this essay offers an extensive bibliography to anyone interested in reading about how historical conceptions of gender and sex have impacted the psyche of male and female athletes.

Another significant work is Butt's *Psychology of Sport: The Behavior, Motivation, Personality and Performance of Athletes*. Butt analyzes seven major role strains that men and women share because of their participation in sport and includes a few more psychological challenges that are unique to women athletes. The first of the psychological roadblocks common to men and women is the conflict between the need for individual achievement and the necessity of cooperation to ensure team harmony. This is especially difficult in a society that bestows awards and scholarships on the basis of individual statistics. A second problem occurs when an athlete does not have the personality traits to match societal expectations. For instance, when a male player is passive, nonaggressive, and shies away from contact, he will often be branded a "sissy" or some other derogatory term that indicates that his sporting performance has shown him to be less than manly. Other conflicts include dealing with failure, coping with the loss of athletic skills, balancing other priorities with athletic endeavor, handling overload that can cause burnout, and coping with physical injury and pain. Butt's analysis is compelling, and though the author admits that further research on how to cope with these problems is vital, she does suggest a few techniques that athletes might use to conquer them (Butt 1987, 117–122). Butt also analyzes some of the problems that are unique to female athletes, including how women engaged in sports traditionally perceived as masculine can cope with a lack of societal acceptance and how women can resolve the tension between playing out desired sporting roles of aggression and competitiveness and living out expected female roles of passivity, gentleness, and sensitivity. Butt introduces five templates into which women athletes often try to fit in order to resolve this tension: (1) the feminine type, in which a female athlete will display aggressive tendencies on the court but revert to traditionally feminine behaviors off the court; (2) the hysteric type, in which a female player conforms to female stereotypes both on and off the court to gain societal approval; (3) the instrumental type, in which the player renounces all traditionally feminine ways of being and becomes a true "jock" in every sense of the word; (4) the liberated type, featuring a woman who might be traditionally feminine or athletic in the masculine sense at any moment simply depending on what pleases her and is generally regarded as the most healthy template, largely because it resists being labeled a template or type; rather, it features independence of societal restriction and an emphasis on individual responsibility and accomplishment; and (5) the image maker, who goes out of her way to make a statement with her behavior. This type of athlete is problematic because she is clearly independent but is also a show-off who is willing to exploit athletic popularity to gain personal power. Butt, of course, does a credible job of analyzing each of these templates, providing examples of how each can be beneficial and harmful and describing the process by which most female athletes find some stable identity by at least sifting through the first three types on a journey to the liberated type (Butt 1987, 124–129).

## INTERNATIONAL PERSPECTIVES

For those interested in gaining access to international scholarship in sports psychology, there are several well-written, informative sources. One of the best is Sidonio Serpa's *International Perspectives on Sport and Exercise Psychology,* in which the author explains the growth of sport psychology as a distinctly international discipline.

The official recognition of sport psychology as a new field of applied psychology finally took place after the First World Congress of Sport Psychology, which was held in Rome in 1965. It was really the beginning of a new era! Not only research and practical intervention but also scientific international cooperation developed. National and international societies appeared, and journal on this topic began to be published. The development of this new sport science also originated new fields of research corresponding to social and scientific concerns. Schilling (1992) notes how new tendencies appear in each World Congress since the heterogeneous program in Rome where 216 papers from 27 countries were presented. Social psychology of sport in Washington, performance enhancement in Madrid, personality in Prague, children in sport in Ottawa, motor learning in Copenhagen, and welfare and exercise in Singapore seem to be, according to Schilling, the most popular topics along with the world congresses. Meanwhile, a "common stream" concerning motor learning, social-psychological issues, coaching and performance enhancement have been keeping the place in the conference rooms. In 1993 Lisbon received 628 participants in the 8th World Congress of Sport Psychology coming from 43 countries of the five continents. A total of 409 scientific contributions were presented and the previous research tendencies were confirmed. (Serpa 1994, xviii)

The book contains articles from leading scholars in several countries and addresses such topics as cognition and decision making, integrated approaches to sport psychology, group dynamics in sport, gender and socio-cultural perspectives, health and wellness, and motivation.

John Kremer's *Psychology in Sport* features a unique look at British perspectives on many of these same issues, while Jitendra Mohan's *Psychology of Sports: The Indian Perspective* offers several intriguing essays that give the Western reader a broader understanding of the field. Stuart Biddle's *European Perspectives on Exercise and Sport Psychology* is notable for its focus on psychological factors that influence recreational athletes and those in fitness programs rather than on professional athletes or players who are involved in highly competitive sports. The following example of Biddle's writing on the relationship between exercise and a person's mood is typical of the work:

Further evidence for the idea that exercise helps people maintain a constant positive mood state comes from Germany. Abele and Brehm (1993) have made a useful distinction between physical activities that create an equilibration effect on mood and well-being, (that is, these activities return mood to a median level and provide a relaxation function), and activities that create a disequilibration effect, (that is, create short-term disturbance and recovery, sometimes seen in people's quest for excitement). These authors suggest that exercise can have an equilibration effect, while competitive sports activities have a disequilibration effect. Adele and Brehm (1993) present evidence to support their theoretical position from many studies that have not appeared in the English language psychology literature. Their work suggests that alternative measurements of mood must be made and that we must not confine ourselves to exercise studies in assessing the psychological effects of activity. (Biddle 1995, 56)

Some scholars from the United States also include chapters on international research in their books. One of the best is Singer's *Handbook on Sports Psychology,* which contains chapters on current research in France, Germany, Australia, the former USSR, China, and Japan. In addition, Butt's *Psychology of Sport: The Behavior, Motivation, Personality and Performance of Athletes* ends with a chapter on the importance of international cooperation to the future of the field. Butt concludes that cross cultural perspectives will be important not only because scholars can learn so much from one another, but because increased international competition will necessitate that coaches, trainers, administrators, and sports psychologists understand the psychology of athletes from all over the world (Butt 1987, 272).

## FUTURE INVESTIGATIONS

The field's recent international growth is indicative of the fact that sport psychology is a young, burgeoning discipline in which scholars admit that they have just scratched the surface in terms of producing research in any given area. Several scholars have speculated as to what the hot areas of research will be as sport psychology continues to grow both as an academic discipline and as professional practice. In "Exercise and the Quality of Life," Bonnie G. Berger and Adrian McInman write that exercise psychology, particularly for middle-aged adults and senior citizens, will be of prime concern to practitioners. "Exercise is associated with psychological well-being in members of the 'normal' population. We emphasize that considerable research is needed to investigate exercise guidelines to maximize the changes in anxiety, stress, depression, and anger that have been reported by many exercisers" (Singer 1993, 730). Singer argues in "The Future of Sport and Exercise Psychology" that in an effort to produce quality research, sports psychologists will specialize in one of seven different research areas: youth sport, group dynamics, learning processes, counseling, psychometrics (psychological testing and diagnosis), performance enhancement and well-being (wellness and the quality of life). In addition, Singer says that sport psychologists will likely take on one of seven professional roles from which they will conduct research. These include scientist, scholar-educator, counselor, performance-enhancement consultant, psychodiagnostician, spokesperson, and health promotion specialist. Singer provides some interesting speculation as to just what sports psychologists will do in each of these research and professional roles (Brewer and Van Raalte 1996, 454–455). In *Sports Psychology: From Theory to Practice,* Anshel says that in an attempt to produce more accurate research, sports psychologists will become more multidisciplinary, relying on history, biology, physical education, anthropology, and business to help them redefine existing theories and to create new knowledge that will improve the field. In addition, Anshel explains the necessity for sports psychologists to take on dual roles of researchers and public servants, making sure to reach out to their respective communities with usable information that everyone can understand. He provides several suggestions as to how this can be done. (Anshel 1997, 385–390). Jeffrey Goldstein's *Sports, Games and Play: Social and Psychological Viewpoints* contains two excellent essays that tackle two relatively new issues. In "The Development of Make-Believe Play," Lonnie Sherrod and Jerome Singer offer a fascinating analysis on how make-believe play can be used by athletes of all ages to enhance athletic performance. The authors also show how by understanding how make-believe play works, sports psychologists can develop techniques that could potentially make sports and exercise a healthier experience for all participants (Goldstein 1989, 8–11). In "Personality and Change in the American Sports Scene," Thomas Tutko examines the public need for athletic heroes, offering insight into why fans follow sports and why fans misbehave (Goldstein 1989, 111–123). Gordon Russell's *The Social Psychology of Sport* dedicates an entire chapter to our psychological need for heroes, including discussion about how a society gains psychological satisfaction by creating and destroying its heroes, how the media impacts our perception of the heroic, and how variables such as race, gender, and age affect our conception of what a hero should be like (Russell 1993, 126–145). Russell also features an excellent chapter on spectatorship and crowd behavior in which he examines a variety of potential motives that turn people into fans (Russell 1993, 237–265).

There is every indication that sports psychology will continue to be a rather expansive field as it enters the next century, a field that is not afraid to broach new topics and innovative techniques to push the boundaries of our understanding. One book that does this is Michael Murphy and Rhea White's *In the Zone: Transcendent Experience in Sports*, in which the authors attempt to explain some of the psychological implications of being in a zone, focused, in sync, in a rhythm, or in some transcendent state in which we perform at optimal levels in what can seem like an out-of-body experience. Murphy and White tackle such topics as ecstasy, feelings of immortality, psychokinesis, altered perceptions of time and space, and the spiritual elements of athletic experience. Their concern is that "there is some degree of blindness and fear about these things, an avoidance of the spirit in athletics. And this can be as destructive to enjoyment and adventure as inflated claims or solemn incantations" (Murphy and White 1995, 6). They even offer a rather specific mind/body training program. The book is notable for its method of explaining concepts such as out-of-body experiences in language that is easy to understand, discussing previous scholarship on the concept, and then introducing a few personal testimonies from athletes who have allegedly had such episodes. Far from being purely speculative, the book contains a bibliographic list of over 1,500 entries and is a fabulous source of research material.

Another book that pushes the boundaries is Allen Guttmann's *The Erotic in Sports*, which asserts that we must understand the psychological satisfaction we derive from the erotic nature of athletic activity if we are to fully benefit from sports. Guttmann's book is a fascinating read that includes chapters on sport as an important erotic activity in antiquity, the Middle Ages, the Renaissance, and in the modern period, as well as an in-depth exploration of how erotic athleticism is ingrained in American popular culture. Guttmann concludes that "men's and women's sports experiences can be and often have been suffused with a sense of erotic pleasure. The Greeks who gathered at Olympia for the athletic festivals in honor of Zeus and Hera were candid about this pleasure. Perhaps, after two millennia of disavowal and denial, it is time for us to be as candid as they were" (Guttmann 1996, 172). Guttmann's work allows the reader to do just that.

Perhaps a final future direction of the field will be a continued attempt by professors to ensure the validity of sport psychology as a unique, valid discipline by securing its place in the university curriculum. Donald Chu's *Dimensions of Sport Studies* and David Vanderwerken's *Sport in the Classroom: Teaching Sport-Related Courses in the Humanities* both introduce methods by which a professor might conduct a class in sports psychology. Chu's work outlines subject matter for several potential courses, while Vanderwerken's book features an essay by Wayne A. Burroughs entitled "Sport and Psychology: An Applied Approach," in which the author provides several syllabi for various courses, complete with rationale, selected readings, and assignments. Vanderwerken also includes an essay by Goldstein entitled "Teaching Sport Psychology from a Humanist Perspective," which discusses how to teach sport psychology on both the graduate and undergraduate levels (Vanderwerken 1990, 205–210). Of special interest to academicians will be how to conduct more research on the psychology of race, class, ethnicity, gender, and sexual orientation as each intersects with sporting experience and how to work such research into classroom pedagogy. Those interested in these and other current trends in sports psychology can consult a number of quality academic journals. *American Journal of Family Therapy; Canadian Journal of Experimental Psychology; International Journal of Sports Psychology; Journal of Applied Sports Psychology; Journal of Athletic Training; Journal of Leisure Research; Journal of Physical Education, Recreation and Dance; Journal of Social Psychology; Journal of Sport and Exercise Psychology; Journal of Sport Behavior; Perceptual and Motor Skills; The Physician and Sports Medicine; Professional Psychology; Psychological Reports; Psychology Today; Research and Practice; Research Quarterly for Exercise and Sport; Sports Psychology;* and *Teaching of Psychology* all contain recent scholarship on the pressing issues in the field.

## REFERENCES

### Books

Anshel, Mark. *Sport Psychology: From Theory to Practice*. Scottsdale, AZ: Gorsuch Scarisbrick, 1997.

Baker, Aaron, and Todd Boyd. *Out of Bounds: Sports, Media and the Politics of Identity*. Bloomington, IN: Indiana University Press, 1995.

Bell, Keith. *Winning Is Not Normal*. Austin, TX: Keel Publications, 1982.

Benedict, Jeff. *Public Heroes, Private Felons: Athletes and Crimes Against Women*. Boston: Northeastern Press, 1997.

Bennett, James, and James Pravitz. *The Profile of a Winner: Advanced Mental Training for Athletes*. Lansing, NY: Sport Science International, 1987.

Biddle, Stuart. *European Perspectives on Exercise and Sport Psychology*. Champaign, IL: Human Kinetics Books, 1995.

Brennen, Steven. *Competitive Excellence: The Psychology and Strategy of Team Building*. Omaha, NE: Peak Perfection Publishing, 1995.

Brewer, Britton, and Judy L. Van Raalte. *Exploring Sport and Exercise Psychology*. Washington, D.C.: American Psychological Association, 1996.

Bronsen, Hugo. *Sports and Psychological Influences: Index of Modern Authors and Subjects with a Guide for Rapid Research*. Washington, D.C.: Abbe Publishers Association, 1994.

Bull, Stephen, ed. *The Mental Game Plan: Getting Psyched for Sport*. London: Sports Dynamics, 1996.

Bunker, Linda, Robert Rotella, and Ann Reilly. *Sport Psychology: Psychological Considerations in Maximizing Sports Performance*. Ann Arbor, MI: McNaughton and Gunn, 1985.

Butler, Richard. *Sports Psychology in Action*. Boston: Butterworth-Heinemann, 1996.

Butt, Dorcas Susan. *Psychology of Sport: The Behavior, Motivation, Personality and Performance of Athletes*. New York: Van Nostrand Reinhold, 1987.

Carron, Albert. *Motivation: Implications for Coaching and Teaching*. London, ON: Sports Dynamics, 1984.

———. *Social Psychology in Sport*. Ithaca, NY: Mouvement Publications, 1980.

Chu, Donald. *Dimensions of Sport Studies*. New York: John Wiley & Sons, 1982.

Coakley, Jay. *Sport in Society: Issues and Controversies*. St. Louis, MO: Times Mirror/Mosby College Publications, 1986.

Cohen, Greta, ed. *Women in Sport: Issues and Controversies*. Newbury Park, CA: Sage Publications, 1995.

Cooper, Andrew. *Playing in the Zone: Exploring the Spiritual Dimensions of Sport*. Boston: Shambhala, 1998.

Costa, Margaret. *Women and Sport: Interdisciplinary Perspectives*. Champaign, IL: Human Kinetics Books, 1994.

Cox, Richard. *Sport Psychology: Concepts and Applications*. Madison, WI: Brown & Benchmark Publications, 1994.

Cratty, Bryant. *Psychological Preparation and Athletic Excellence*. Ithaca, NY: Mouvement Publications, 1984.

———. *Psychology in Contemporary Sport: Guidelines for Coaches and Athletes*. Englewood Cliffs, NJ: PrenticeHall, 1983.

———. *Social Psychology in Athletics*. Englewood Cliffs, NJ: PrenticeHall, 1981.

Creedon, Pamela, ed. *Women, Media and Sport: Challenging Gender Values*. Newbury Park, CA: Sage Publications, 1994.

Dalloway, Marie. *Reflections of the Mental Side of Sports*. Phoenix, AZ: Optimal Performance Institute, 1994.

Dieter, Hackfort, ed. *Psycho-Social Issues and Interventions in Elite Sports*. New York: P. Lang, 1994.

Duquet, William, Paul De Knop, and Livin Bollart. *Youth Sport: A Social Approach*. Brussels: VUB Press, 1993.

Fixx, James. *Maximum Sports Performance*. New York: Random House, 1985.

Friend, David. *Baseball, Football, Daddy and Me*. New York: Penguin, 1992.

Fuoss, Donald. *Effective Coaching: A Psychological Approach*. New York: John Wiley & Sons, 1981.

Gavin, James, and Nettie Gavin. *Psychology for Health Fitness Professionals*. Champaign, IL: Human Kinetics Books, 1995.

Gill, Diane. *Psychological Dynamics of Sport*. Champaign, IL: Human Kinetics Books, 1986.

Goldstein, Jeffrey H., ed. *Sports, Games and Play: Social and Psychological Viewpoints*. Hillsdale, NJ: L. Erlbaum Associates, 1989.

Grant, Robert W. *The Psychology of Sport: Facing One's True Opponent*. Jefferson, NC: McFarland, 1988.

Greenspan, Emily. *Little Winners: Inside the World of the Child Sports Star*. Boston: Little, Brown & Co., 1983.

Guttmann, Allen. *The Erotic in Sports*. New York: Columbia University Press, 1996.

Hall, Ann. *Feminism and Sporting Bodies: Essays on Theory and Practice*. Champaign, IL: Human Kinetics Books, 1996.

Hall, Donald. *Fathers Playing Catch with Sons: Essays on Sport*. New York: Dell, 1986.

Hardy, Lew. *Understanding Psychological Preparation for Sport: Theory and Practice of Elite Performers*. New York: John Wiley & Sons, 1996.

Hemeny, David. *Sporting Excellence: What Makes a Champion*. London: Collinswillow, 1991.

Horn, Thelma S., ed. *Advances in Sport Psychology*. Champaign, IL: Human Kinetics Books, 1992.

Kirschenbaum, Daniel. *Mind Matters: Seven Steps to Smarter Sports Performance*. Carmel, IN: Cooper Publications, 1997.

Kremer, John. *Psychology in Sport*. Bristol, PA: Taylor and Francis, 1994.

Leohr, James. *Mental Toughness Training for Sport: Achieving Athletic Excellence*. Lexington, MA: S. Greene Press, 1986.

LeUnes, Arnold D. *Sport Psychology: An Introduction*. Chicago: Nelson-Hall, 1996.

Llewellyn, Jack. *Psychology of Coaching: Theory and Application*. Minneapolis, MN: Burgess Publishing Co., 1982.

Martens, Rainer. *Coaches' Guide to Sport Psychology*. Champaign, IL: Human Kinetics Books, 1987.

Mechikoff, Robert. *Sport Psychology: The Coach's Perspective*. Springfield, IL: C. C. Thomas, 1983.

————. *Sports Psychology for Women*. New York: Harper & Row, 1987.

Messner, Michael. *Power at Play: Sports and the Problem of Masculinity*. Boston: Beacon Press, 1992.

Messner, Michael, and Donald Sabo. *Sex, Violence and Power in Sports: Rethinking Masculinity*. Freedom, CA: The Crossing Press, 1994.

Mitchell, Perry J. *In the Zone: It Happens in Sports—How to Make It Happen in Business*. Chicago, IL: Contemporary Books, 1997.

Mohan, Jitendra. *Psychology of Sports: The Indian Perspective*. Delhi: Friends Publications, 1991.

Murphy, Michael, and Rhea White. *In the Zone: Transcendent Experiences in Sports*. New York: Penguin/Arkana, 1995.

Murphy, Shane. *The Achievement Zone: 8 Skills for Winning All the Time from Playing the Field to the Classroom*. New York: G. P. Putnam, 1996.

————, ed. *Sport Psychology Interventions*. Champaign, IL: Human Kinetics Books, 1995.

Nideffer, Robert. *Athletes' Guide to Mental Training*. Champaign, IL: Human Kinetics Books, 1985.

————. *The Ethics and Practice of Applied Sport Psychology.* Ithaca, NY: Mouvement Publications, 1981.

Orlick, Terry. *Coaches Training Manual to Psyching for Sport.* Champaign, IL: Leisure Press, 1986.

————. *In Pursuit of Excellence: How to Win in Sport and Life Through Mental Training.* Champaign, IL: Leisure Press, 1990.

————. *Psyching for Sport: Mental Training for Athletes.* Champaign, IL: Leisure Press, 1986.

Ostrow, Andrew C. *Directions of Psychology Tests in the Sport and Exercise Sciences.* Morgantown, WV: Fitness Information Technologies, 1990.

Pargman, David. *Psychological Bases for Sport Injuries.* Morgantown, WV: Fitness Information Technologies, 1993.

————. *Stress and Motor Performance: Understanding and Coping.* Ithaca, NY: Mouvement Publications, 1986.

Pierce, Alexandra. *Expressive Movement: Posture and Action in Daily Life, Sports, and the Performing Arts.* New York: Plenum Press, 1989.

Pronger, Brian. *The Arena of Masculinity: Sports, Homosexuality, and the Meaning of Sex.* New York: St. Martin's, 1994.

Russell, Gordon W. *The Social Psychology of Sport.* New York: Springer-Verlag, 1993.

Ryan, Frank. *Sports and Psychology.* Englewood Cliffs, NJ: PrenticeHall, 1981.

Sabo, Donald, and Russ Runfola. *Jock: Sports and Male Identity.* Englewood Cliffs, NJ: PrenticeHall, 1980.

Salmela, John. *The World Sport Psychology Sourcebook.* Champaign, IL: Human Kinetics Books, 1992.

Schellenberger, Hans. *Psychology of Team Sports.* Toronto, ON: Sports Books, 1990.

Schubert, Frank. *Psychology from Start to Finish.* Toronto, ON: Sports Books, 1986.

Seefeldt, Vern, ed. *Handbook for Youth Sport Coaches.* Reston, VA: American Alliance for Health, Physical Education, Recreation and Dance, 1987.

Seppo, Iso-Ahola. *Psychology of Sports: A Social Psychological Approach.* Dubuque, IA: William C. Brown Publishers, 1986.

Serpa, Sidonio, ed. *International Perspectives on Sport and Exercise Psychology.* Morgantown, WV: Fitness Information Technologies, 1994.

Sheikh, Anees A. *Imagery in Sports and Physical Performance.* Amityville, NY: Baywood Publication Co., 1994.

Shields, David Lyle Light. *Character Development and Physical Activity.* Champaign, IL: Human Kinetics Books, 1995.

Silva, John, and Robert Weinberg, eds. *Psychological Foundations of Sport.* Champaign, IL: Human Kinetics Books, 1984.

Singer, Robert, ed. *Handbook of Research on Sport Psychology.* New York: Macmillan, 1993.

————. *Peak Performance—and More.* Ithaca, NY: Mouvement Publications, 1986.

Smoll, Frank, and Ronald Smith, eds. *Children and Youth in Sports: A Biopsychosocial Perspective.* Madison, WI: Brown & Benchmark, 1996.

Stein, Murray, ed. *Psyche and Sports.* Wilmette, IL: Chiron Publishers, 1994.

Straub, William F., ed. *Sport Psychology: An Analysis of Athlete Behavior.* Ithaca, NY: Mouvement Publications, 1980.

Ungerleider, Steven. *Mental Training for Peak Performance: Top Athletes Reveal the Mind Exercise They Use to Excel.* Emmaus, PA: Rodale Press, 1996.

Vanderwerken, David. *Sport in the Classroom: Teaching Sport-Related Courses in the Humanities.* Rutherford, NJ: Farleigh Dickenson University Press, 1990.

Weinberg, Robert S., and Daniel Gould. *Foundations of Sport and Exercise Psychology.* Champaign, IL: Human Kinetics Books, 1995.

Williams, Jean, ed. *Applied Sport Psychology: Personal Growth to Peak Performance.* Palo Alto, CA: Mayfield Publishing Co., 1993.

Williams, Jean, Judy Van Raalte, and Britton Brewer, eds. *Exploring Sport and Exercise Psychology.* Washington, D.C.: American Psychological Associates, 1996.

### Journals

*American Journal of Family Therapy* (Boca Raton, FL)
*Canadian Journal of Experimental Psychology* (Winnipeg, Manitoba, Canada)
*International Journal of Sport Psychology* (Rome, Italy)
*Journal of Applied Sports Psychology* (West Lafayette, IN)
*Journal of Athletic Training* (Dallas, TX)
*Journal of Leisure Research* (Ashburn, VA)
*Journal of Physical Education, Recreation and Dance* (Reston, VA)
*Journal of Social Psychology* (Washington, D.C.)
*Journal of Sport and Exercise Psychology* (Champaign, IL)
*Journal of Sport Behavior* (Mobile, AL)
*Perceptual and Motor Skills* (Missoula, MT)
*The Physician and Sports Medicine* (New York, NY)
*Professional Psychology, Research and Practice* (Washington, D.C.)
*Psychological Reports* (Missoula, MT)
*Psychology Today* (Sussex, England)
*Research Quarterly for Exercise and Sport* (Reston, VA)
*Sports Psychology* (Champaign, IL)
*Teaching of Psychology* (Clarion, PA)

# 10

# Sport: Science and Technology

The relationship between sport and science and technology dates back at least to Ancient Greece where physicians, called gymnasts, undertook the task of providing special care for athletes during competitions. During the Renaissance and the Enlightenment, scientists such as Galileo, who developed the first law of motion, and Sir Isaac Newton, who furthered Galileo's findings by explaining the properties of objects in motion, began to lay the groundwork upon which modern science would erect explanations for much of what transpires in sport, from curve balls, to measuring velocity, to figuring out what spin a golfer should put on a wedge shot out of the bunker. Today, we have become so accustomed to watching athletes use the latest technological developments in game equipment and training devices that it is easy to ignore the significance of those highly sophisticated improvements. A mere ten years ago, aging hockey players could not rejuvenate themselves in a hyperbaric chamber, quarterbacks could not talk to coaches via small communicators installed in their helmets, and golfers could not rely on the ten to twenty extra yards afforded by the latest titanium drivers. Advances in computer science and medicine have led to the development of machines that allow Olympic swimmers to analyze every movement they make during a race. If a stroke is even slightly altered from the desired position the computer image will identify it, allowing for immediate correction. Considering the advances in preparatory methods, including weight training and nutrition, it is no wonder that several Olympic swimming records fall every four years. Advances in sports medicine have been just as crucial for both amateur and professional athletes. Fifteen years ago, a knee injury might have meant the end of a professional career. Now, even severely injured knees and ankles can be reconstructed in a short time, allowing the athlete to return to action in only a few weeks in some cases. In addition, health care professionals concentrating in sport medicine have written several works dealing with injury prevention, rehabilitation, and nutrition for athletes of all ages.

This chapter will discuss some of the more significant works that have been penned over the last decade and a half that shed light on the following subjects: the historical relationship between sport, science, and technology; the impact of mathematics, engineering, and the sciences on sport; general concepts in sports medicine; the causes, prevention, and rehabilitation of injuries; the relationship between diet and sports performance; health concerns for women, children, and older athletes; the impact of technology on specific sports and the unique health risks posed by each sport; and legal issues with which those in sports medicine must contend.

## THE HISTORY OF SPORTS AND SCIENCE

Though directed at a high school audience, Robert Sheeley's *Sports Lab: How Science Has Changed Sports* is valuable as a starter book for those investigating historical connections between sport and science. Sheeley highlights several key dates in the development of science and provides short discussions about how each advance impacted the world of sport. For instance, the author chronicles how the invention of the stopwatch and the emergence of other measuring devices in the 1850s ushered in the era of sports records by making it possible to accurately record times of human runners or race horses. In addition, he discusses how the 1948 invention of the aluminum diving board brought diving into a new age in which it could market itself as an entertaining sport worthy of Olympic status. Other key scientific advances analyzed by Sheeley include the first reconstructive knee surgery (1964), the first test that could successfully diagnose the presence of performance-enhancing drugs in an athlete's bloodstream (1969), the development of high-speed photography that traced the arc of a curve ball (1982), and the first operation to actually transplant an entire knee joint (1987). Though his analyses of how these events have impacted sport lack fully documented evidence, his discussions are still compelling and make for a good introduction to the subject.

A more academic book that explains how science has impacted sport over the last half century is Lee Torrey's *Stretching the Limits: Breakthroughs in Sport Science that Create Superathletes.* One might get the impression from the title that the book deals with steroids and the scientific production of synthetic athletes, but that is not the case. Instead, Torrey impressively tackles a number of rather intriguing subjects that might be of interest to the sports scholar. First, he discusses how new technology has resulted in improved sports performance. In basketball, for instance, scientists now use the electroencephalograph (EEG), a device that measures electrical activity in the brain, to help players shoot better free throws. Specifically, the scientist in question, Dr. Daniel Landers of Arizona State University, concluded that one of the keys to shooting better free throws is being able to shut down the left brain through specific concentration techniques (Torrey 1985, 49). In addition, Torrey discusses how scholars have used high-speed photography to figure out how a hockey player can get as much speed on a slap shot as possible. Researchers found that a player's stick actually touches the puck three times during a slap shot, and that technique, not strength or stick speed, is the key to a high velocity shot: "In other words, players who wielded the stick with a certain technique, which optimally exploited the blade's elasticity, produced a faster shot regardless of their strength or the force they applied to the blade" (Torrey 1985, 84).Torrey also discusses how understanding the aerodynamics of a baseball's movement has changed the war between pitchers and batters, and how tennis rackets have been altered because of scientific determinations about the location of the sweet spot of the racket. The rest of Torrey's book is dedicated to analyzing the impact of new forms of training on contemporary athletics, which the author feels have been more important than new sports technology. For instance, Torrey discusses the benefits of plyometrics, a new series of exercises designed to build leg muscles through repetitive long jumps, triple jumps, and hurdle hops, that has replaced laps and other traditional exercises in football, and that has resulted in vastly improved running times for players. Torrey also discusses the development of five new types of exercises that have helped athletes reach new levels of performance. These include isometric exercises designed to stress muscles at a constant length, isotonic exercises in which the muscle is strengthened through weighted resistance, eccentric exercises in which the muscle fibers actually lengthen while contracting, isokinetic exercise which involves gradual resistance that changes to accommodate the strength of the muscle, and neuromuscular facilitation which utilizes repetitive, rhythmic exercises designed to strengthen injured joints (Torrey 1985, 116). Torrey goes on to explain how athletes in several different sports use each of these exercises to prepare for competitions.

One of the most comprehensive books on the history of sport and science is *Sport and Exercise Science: Essays in the History of Sports Medicine*, edited by Jack W. Berryman and Roberta J. Park. The work contains ten methodically researched, well-written essays that essentially allow the reader to trace the evolution of Western medical views on sport and physical activity from Ancient Greece to the contemporary period. For instance, Berryman's "Exercise and the Medical Tradition from Hippocrates through Antebellum America: A Review Essay" is essential reading for anyone who desires to understand fundamental Western views of the body in motion. Berryman examines Hippocrates' "humoral theory" and Galen's "Galenic Medical Theory" to show how each relied on scientific manipulation of what Galen called the "six non-naturals." These were air; motion and rest; sleeping and waking; breathing; eating and anything else that is taken into the body; that which is retained or excreted from the body; and emotion and passion. Classical medical theory dictated that an athlete must follow a highly disciplined regimen to control these six factors in a moderate way. This, in turn, would produce optimal health and athletic performance. Not surprisingly, the athletic-minded Greeks and Romans viewed the relationship between athletes and the non-naturals as one characterized by reciprocity. If moderate attitudes toward the non-naturals improved health and performance, then athletic and physical activity also promoted a healthy relationship with the non-naturals (Berryman and Park 1992, 4–7). The rest of Berryman's lengthy essay shows how scientists in Europe and North America have developed unique views on the relationship between the non-naturals and athleticism based on the unique cultural conditions and the technology and medical knowledge of the day. For instance, the humanist values of the Renaissance spawned the first true self-help guides whose aim was to show the upper class how to use athletics to live longer, healthier lives. Thomas Elyot's *The Castel of Helthe* was published in the 1530s and stressed "regimen as part of the new sixteenth century advice literature" (Berryman and Park 1992, 17). According to Berryman, "Central to the writings on longevity was the belief that any individual who decided to live a temperate life, especially with reforms in their habits of diet and exercise, could extend their longevity in a significant manner. Beginning with the writings of Cornaro in 1558, the non-natural tradition received increasing attention from those wishing to live longer and more healthy lives" (Berryman and Park 1992, 17).

In the nineteenth century, new medical knowledge about alcohol, tobacco, and sexual promiscuity and concerns over developing industry and the emergence of large cities combined with the prevailing Christian code of morality, which viewed the body as a temple to be kept pure for the indwelling of the Holy Spirit, to produce the first medical texts, most of which were as much moral as medical guides. Berryman makes the point that all of the new texts depended on the non-natural tradition. For example, Shadrach Ricketson's *Means of Preserving Health and Preventing Diseases* argued that "people whose inclination, situation or employment does not admit of exercise, soon become pale, feeble, and disordered," and that "exercise promotes the circulation of the blood, assists digestion, and encourages perspiration." Berryman goes on to write that "he also warned of the destructiveness of 'high living and strong drink' and noted that 'idleness and luxury create more diseases than labour and industry'" (Berryman and Park 1992, 37). The essay provides similar commentary for each period of history in which significant social change or medical advancement necessitated changes in how scientists viewed the proper relationship between people and the non-naturals.

Another compelling essay is James Thornton's "'Athlete's Heart': The Medical Debate over Athleticism, 1870–1920," which discusses the debate within the Victorian scientific community in America over whether exercise has redeeming or detrimental effects on the heart. Amazingly, the sentiment against rigorous athletic involvement was great among physicians of the time, even among those who might classify themselves as the pro-athletic doctors. Thornton details, for instance, the fear of "bicycle heart" that gripped overprotective doctors in the 1880s, when, due to several deaths of overzealous bicycle enthusiasts, many physicians deemed it dangerous to engage in any such activity that caused a loss of breath. Bicycling, in particular, became suspect as an activity that threatened one's health: "The greater concern, however, remained the chronic effects of the activity, and physicians discovering hypertrophy in devotees of the wheel were quick to diagnose 'bicycle heart.' Men were actually rejected from military service because they were found to be victims of the complaint" (Berryman and Park 1992, 126). Though part of this apprehension can be attributed to Victorian conservatism regarding anything that involved physical exertion or bodily excitement, part of the problem was that medical science had not done enough studies on strenuous physical exercise to reassure itself as to the safety of the throngs of Americans who began participating in physical activity of all kinds in the late nineteenth century when bicycling, baseball, racing, ice skating, football, and running all flourished. The trepidation on the part of the medical community was so strong that when the first Boston Marathon was run in 1897 the *Journal of the American Medical Association* "stated so bluntly, that heart damage must be a common result of marathoning was "unquestionable"" (Berryman and Park 1992, 126). Thornton goes on to explain that such fear on the part of the medical establishment is what actually prompted the medical studies that would defeat the anti-athletic scientists. For example, when a three-year study of Boston Marathon participants revealed no thorastic damage due to the race, physicians quelled their opposition to running. Studies such as these continued at a breakneck pace into the 1920s until pro-athletic forces finally managed to convince the rank and file in the medical community that, although athletic activity could be abused, it was generally an important part of a healthy lifestyle that should be encouraged to promote hygiene and character development (Berryman and Park 1992, 138). Thornton provides an extensive discussion that details the specific studies and the important social and political reform movements that lead to the victory of pro-athletic forces.

Significantly, many of the reforms that led to greater athletic opportunity for men did not apply to women, who continued to be hampered by the beliefs of the all-male medical establishment until well into the twentieth century. Patricia Vertinsky's "Exercise, Physical Capability, and the Eternally Wounded Woman in Late Nineteenth-Century North America" shows how male fears about female power and social mores that relied on the woman to be the chaste, feminine wife and mother combined with common medical practice to prevent women from taking part in athletics on the basis of alleged physical dangers. Specifically, doctors asserted that women's menstruation symbolized an "eternal wound" that represented female weakness and cast athletics as something whose strenuous nature threatened the already fragile woman. Another part of the theory was that women used up a great deal of energy during menstruation and, because they were believed to have less energy than men anyway, it was necessary to avoid strenuous activity that might impede a woman's ability to function as a mother. According to Vertinski, Herbert Spencer was the leading theorist in this area:

Though males and females both needed physical strength for growth and development, girls developed more rapidly than boys and used up their available strength quota faster. Thus, not only did they start with less strength and lose it more quickly, women were subsequently "taxed" with the special energy demand necessitated by menstruation and reproduction. This tax was a biological one and a social one for women who were obliged to pay the price for the preservation of society. It was a "reproductive sacrifice" that was bound to limit individual development, but that could only be seen as a requirement for the fitness of the race. Thus, Spencer set up the central argument against female emancipation by elucidating the conflict between self-development and reproduction. To social theorists of his ilk, self-development for females could only mean self-sacrifice and this meant spending their cachet of physical and mental energy at the motherhood bank. (Berryman and Park 1992, 191)

Spencer's views combined with medical opinions about women and exercise to relegate women to physical activities that were noncompetitive and only lightly strenuous. As Vertinsky writes, "The demands of periodicity were monthly reminders that women could not, and should not, play the game like men" (Berryman and Park 1992, 200). This, of course, was a legacy that would plague women well into the twentieth century and that has not yet entirely abated.

Berryman and Parks's book also contains essays on nineteenth-century training procedures in Britain and the United States, a history of reforms in women's athletics, the early development of sports medicine in Germany, the misuse of medical "knowledge" in the name of social and political goals over the last two centuries, debates over nutrition, and the history of anabolic steroids in sport. Terry Todd's "A History of the Use of Anabolic Steroids in Sport" is particularly good, but a more complete work on the subject of how athletes have used science to improve performance through chemicals and other synthetic means is John M. Hoberman's *Mortal Engines: The Science of Performance and the Dehumanization of Sport.* Hoberman asserts that the human desire to use stimulants as a means for procuring better athletic performance is nearly as ancient as sport itself. It certainly existed in Ancient Greece and Rome. However, the author contends that modern doping can be traced to the middle of the nineteenth century when views of the human body as a temple given by God began to give way to scientific, materialistic views of the body as something that is not innately holy but is instead just another thing that has evolved in nature for millions of years. The leader in this movement was, of course, Charles Darwin, whose theories, according to Hoberman, separated the human body from the realm of the divine and established it as a kind of machine that could be altered in any number of ways for any number of effects. Hoberman makes it clear that Darwin "did not envision breeding a superior athletic type," something that was "simply beyond Darwin's imagination" (Hoberman 1992, 42). However, his theories clearly advocated the idea that the human body had been consistently altered by nature and could be manipulated by science to achieve desired ends. For many in the mid to late nineteenth century and early twentieth century this meant experimenting with external substances to gain competitive advantage in sports or business. Hoberman chronicles the attempts at "doping" made by several notable figures, including those of author Honoré de Balzac, who wrote his "Treatise on Modern Stimulants" in 1838. In all, Hoberman discusses the historical use of alcohol, opium, morphine, cocaine, other drugs, coffee, tea, sugar, and a variety of other natural substances that were used to improve on the normal actions a human body could perform.

Hoberman argues that the desire to improve athletically combined with the popular existentialist view of man existing in a godless world, where moments of self-realization are the only hope of order or happiness, and the scientific advances of the mid-twentieth century to launch the era of anabolic steroids. Hoberman includes a terrific chapter in which he explains the conditions that led to the development of steroids in the 1950s and the subsequent conditions surrounding the importance of sport in various countries that led to the escalation of steroid use through most of the latter half of the twentieth century. He includes commentary on East German and Soviet medical studies that indicate that steroids are not harmful to athletes as evidence that some countries have in the past been willing to sacrifice the health of their athletes to win athletic contests, which they believed to represent the superiority of their nation's political ideologies and economic systems. "The East Germans claimed to have thoroughly investigated the effects of steroids on the various physiological systems linked to training. 'The results,' they claimed, 'suggest that high-performance training offers medical opportunities that are scientifically well founded and can specify doses without side-effects'" (Hoberman 1992, 286). The author also includes several examples of American athletes' use of steroids to win medals and professional victories in the pursuit of money and other material accolades. He ends his book with a discussion on genetic engineering, the next frontier of athletic enhancement. According to Hoberman, "It is genetic engineering that promises to bring about the most profound biological transformations of the human being, and it is likely that technology will be used to develop athletes before it is applied to the creation of other kinds of human performers" (Hoberman 1992, 286). This is because of the visibility of the athletic arena and the fact that correlations between athletic activity and certain genes are easier to measure than genetic alterations in musicians or poets. Hoberman provides an informative and provocative discussion on the pros and cons of genetic engineering, something that has arrived in full force with the 1997 cloning of sheep in England. Some of the questions he tackles in which sports scholars might be interested include how genetic engineering will affect the integrity of athletic competition, how it will affect the casual athlete, and what side effects it will have on the human race in terms of reproduction, racial and gender classifications, sex roles, class, employment, and religion. Hoberman's skepticism of any form of scientific enhancement of athletes, either through synthetic substances or genetic engineering, is clear throughout the book, but his balanced approach and solid evidence make the work a must read for those interested in the role science will play in sport in the future.

## THE INFLUENCE OF MATHEMATICS, ENGINEERING, AND THE SCIENCES ON SPORT

Scholars in traditional academic disciplines have taken an interest in sport over the last two decades and have written some helpful books for those interested in how mathematics, physics, computer science, engineering, and biology play into athletics. Stewart M. Townend's *Mathematics in Sport* covers a broad range of topics but focuses on how specific mathematical applications are used in running, throwing, jumping, rowing, sailing, and in team sports such as football and baseball. In a chapter that is typical of the book, Townend mathematically explains the inner workings of the famed winged keel, which the Australians used to wrest the America's Cup from the United States in 1983 for the first time in well over a century. Townend provides some mathematical formulas that are somewhat daunting for those who do not hold a Ph.D. in the discipline, but also includes a down-to-earth discussion of the subject in which he explains why the winged keel is so effective. "In practice the presence of the wing tip has a considerable effect on the flow pattern around that portion near the tip since the crossflow force reduces in magnitude toward the tip" (Townend 1984, 120). Townend then goes on to explain, using simple diagrams and reasonably understandable mathematical formulas, how this reduction in magnitude allows the yacht to go faster. Townend uses the same method to explain how one can use math to develop an understanding of how to run faster and more comfortably, how to develop the optimal strategy to row a boat, shoot a basketball, ride a horse or throw the hammer, and how to retain balance when wind surfing.

While Townend's book tends to focus on explaining how one can use math to better one's performance in different sports, Leonid Sadovskii's *Mathematics and Sports* introduces mathematical models that are designed to explain any number of sporting phenomena. Sadovskii writes that a mathematical model "may be geometric figures, number sets, equations, systems of equations, etc, that describe properties of the real object or phenomena under study" (Sadovskii 1993, 8). Generally, models are constructed on the basis of statistical data gathered by mathematicians whose task it is to analyze certain sports. For instance, Sadovskii explains how mathematicians helped to develop mathematical analyses of baseball teams for opposing managers. They compiled all of the "at bats" a player had during the season, analyzed what he did during each at bat against both right-handers and southpaws, at home and away, during the day and under the lights, during different counts, or with men on base, and developed a mathematical formula that would allow a manager to better predict what that batter might do in any given situation. Naturally, the formulas only predict tendencies, but no Major League manager does without the hundreds of computerized printouts that reveal the tendencies of both pitchers and batters in many game situations. Sadovskii explains how this is done for other sports as well, including basketball, football, and hockey. Football is perhaps the sport that relies the most on mathematical formulas, which allow coaches to predict what their opponent might do when they line up in a running formation or when they break into a four wide receiver set. Sadovskii reveals that the National Football League teams could hardly succeed without such models: "One paper contains the analysis of 8,373 games in 56 rounds, including the U.S. National Football League table. It supplies important recommendations on offensive strategy" (Sadovskii 1993, 149). Sadovskii's work also features demonstrations on how individual athletes such as skiers, bowlers, pentathletes, or surfers can use mathematical models to improve their performances. Though he includes some complicated mathematical formulas and jargon, the book is generally readable and could be helpful for those interested in the intersection of mathematics and sport.

The books available on physics and sport are somewhat similar to those in the field of mathematics in that they focus on using mathematical formulas to explain sporting phenomena. However, works such as Sharon Blanding's *What Makes a Boomerang Come Back: How Things in Sports Work* also provide fascinating scientific explanations for why things happen in sports. For instance, the author dedicates an entire chapter to explaining why a knuckle ball knuckles. She concludes that the pitch's movement hinges on its slow speed and the interaction between the wind and the raised stitches of the ball. Also included are the findings of Dr. Robert Watts, a Tulane University mechanical engineer who developed a computerized program that predicts what a knuckle ball will do depending on how it is thrown (the grip), the wind, the temperature, the barometric pressure, and the moment of release. "According to this model, knuckle balls should become less lively as temperatures rise" (Blanding 1992, 6). The author goes on to use theories of physics to explain how a pitcher should vary his grip based on wind conditions and the angle at which he releases the ball relative to the ground. In addition, Blanding analyzes the shape of a football, its usual trajectory, wind resistance, and a player's mechanics to explain how a quarterback can throw a spiral every time he goes back to pass. Both sports scholars and weekend duffers might want to consult the chapter on golf, in which the author explains the physics of putting. The findings of Brian W. Holmes, a physicist from San Jose State University, are of special interest. They include the premise that "if a ball is rolling without slipping, it must be moving at 5.34 feet per second or less to be captured. Otherwise, it has enough velocity to sustain a straight-line path across the top of the hole"(Blanding 1992, 149). Accordingly, putters have been modified to allow golfers to control the speed at which they hit the ball. Likewise, irons, and especially drivers, have been modified as physicists have developed formulas that predict how shaft flexibility and club head formation impact how far a player can hit a ball. Among other things, the author includes a structural analysis of how a golfer can use basic concepts of physics to develop her model golf swing. The book also features chapters on shooting a basketball, throwing darts, skiing, karate, surfing, tennis, billiards, diving, and bicycling. Other books on physics that may be of interest include Angelo Armenti's *The Physics of Sport* and Peter Brancazio's *Sport-Science: Physical Laws and Optimal Performance*, both of which are similar in content and method to Blanding's book.

Another fascinating book is Steve Haake's *The Engineering of Sport,* which contains a series of essays that explain how engineers impact the sports world. For instance, one essay in aerodynamics analyzes how a cyclist's posture and position in regard to other riders effects aerodynamic drag and the speed at which that cyclist can ride. An essay in biomechanics features a discussion on how body weight influences ski jumping performance and how size considerations determine how manufacturers make skis. The book contains an entire section on design, which features essays on how engineers have developed tennis rackets that maximize a player's chances for hitting the ball on the sweet spot, how they have made significant improvements to poles for pole vaulting and bicycle frames for racing bikes, and how they have designed shuttlecock hitting machines that allow for optimal training of badminton players. Other essays of interest cover the mechanics of kicking in sports; how scientists have reengineered sports equipment, including sailing masts, golf balls, archery bows and arrows, fishing gear, bicycle chains, and artificial turf, to improve user performance, along with analyses of motion in various sports, and design improvements that account for vibrations in golf clubs and baseball bats. One of the more interesting essays is entitled

"Engineering 'Feel' in the Design of Golf Clubs." The authors define "feel" as the feelings of comfortableness or uncomfortableness that golfers have when they swing the club and impact the ball. An accelerometer was attached to the shaft of a golf club to measure the vibration levels felt by several golfers who took part in the study. The vibration felt by each golfer indicated how his club would have to be modified in terms of length, shaft flexibility, and head weight in order to give that golfer the best feel possible. The authors conclude that such measurements of vibration "can assist equipment designers in engineering 'feel' in the design of golf clubs" (Haake 1996, 337).

James Mason's *Modern Sports Administration* contains an excellent chapter entitled "Computer Applications in the Administration of Sports" that elucidates the important connections between the field of computer science and sports. Mason describes how colleges and professional teams use computer programs for ticketing, financial management, budget analysis, sports information, facility scheduling, recruiting, scouting, game analysis, concession management, strength training, and medical and injury reporting to run their businesses. Of special interest is his discussion of how reliant coaches are on computer programs for scouting opponents, evaluating talent, and developing game plans. This is particularly true of football. As Mason writes:

Before computers, coaches would spend days breaking down films of an upcoming opponent, analyzing the game tendencies and getting the information to their players by Wednesday, three days before the game. Now, with the use of computerized game packages, the coaching staff gets the information in time for Monday practice, which saves two days. The team has the information two days earlier, and it frees the coach to do more coaching. In fact, it is almost like having another coach. Not only is more information gathered more quickly, with more coaching time available, but through computer analysis, one can predict the offensive tendencies of the opposing team with about 85 percent accuracy. Every football team that has played in the last five Super Bowls used computer technology. (Mason 1988, 233)

Perhaps the best feature of the chapter is that it ends with a comprehensive list of scholarly articles on the subject of how computers are being used by athletes, coaches, and managers in sport. In all, Mason profiles over fifty articles, providing the researcher with a healthy list of leads on the subject that include a short explanation of exactly what each article covers. One article that Mason does not mention is V. Kleshnev's "The Application of Computer Technologies to the Management of Sport Specific Training in Rhythmic Sports," which is located in Victor Rogozkin and Ron Maughan's *Current Research in Sports Sciences: An International Perspective*. Kleshnev focuses less on team sports and more on how computer technology can be used by individual athletes. His analysis of how rowers can use computer training programs to improve on technique, for example, is quite complete. Generally, Kleshnev concludes that "it is possible to improve the quality and stability of rowing motions more effectively with CARE [the computer-aided rowing exerciser], when the rowers can see on a computer display the level of rowing motion stability, force and power curves for each stroke and can compare them with patterns of skilled rowers" (Rogozkin and Maughan 1996, 145). Rogozkin and Maughan also include an essay entitled "A Computer System for Analysis and Correction of Antioxidant Intake," which shows how computers are being used to create improved diets for athletes.

## SPORTS MEDICINE

Though closely tied to sports medicine, the specific field of biology certainly impacts the sports world in its own right, especially in the area of genetics research. Robert M. Malina's *Sport and Human Genetics* is an informative book that explains several ways in which genetics affects athletic performance. One of the best chapters is D. F. Roberts "Genetic Determinants of Sports Performance," which discusses how important factors in athletic performance such as aerobic power and capacity, and motor development are influenced by complex genetic codes that make up each athlete. Significantly, Roberts concludes that, while genetic composition is important to body size, motor skills, and endurance, there is no one-to-one correspondence between one's genes and one's ability in any of these three areas: "Certainly there is chromosomal influence, but in most of the variables reviewed the genetic contribution is likely to be multifactorial. The characteristics of adult athletes derive from events during the growing period; there is evidence that genetic control operates throughout the whole process of growth, and performance may be seen as the outcome of interaction between genetic predisposition and environmental modifications" (Malina 1986, 121). Roberts believes that the key to figuring out just how much genes do control athletic performance will come through the study of isolated moments of peak athletic performance, in which the essence of a player's natural ability can be medically reviewed. Other essays of interest in Malina's text include his own "Genetics of Motor Development and Performance," Claude Bouchard's "Genetics of Aerobic Power and Capacity," and Napoleon Wolanski's "Heredity and Psychomotor Traits in Man," all of which discuss how genetic make-up impacts an athlete's physical size, dexterity, cardiovascular power, and endurance, as well as the strength of his or her heart and lungs. Overall, the book contains eleven well-researched essays that are easy to follow and that contain sizable bibliographies.

Genetics research is just a small part of sports medicine, a large field that has come to play an increasingly important role in the lives of athletes, coaches, and teams, whose success often lies in the ability of a medical staff to keep players healthy and to rehabilitate injured players. Since the field is so broad and somewhat complex because it is laden with highly professional language that eludes those who do not possess an M.D., it is helpful for the researcher to consult one of several fine introductory books on the subject. A good starter book is Larry Kettlekamp's *Modern Sports Science*, which provides short, easily read discussions on such topics as how muscles work, what joints do, the relationship between energy and nutrition, sports training methods, sports injury and rehabilitation, drug use, and sports psychology. The book is written for a high school audience but might be valuable to anyone initially trying to come to grips with important subjects, definitions, and practices within the field of sports medicine. Another excellent primer is Robert E. Sallis's *Essentials of Sports Medicine,* which contains a series of essays written by doctors, most of whom are members of medical school faculties across the United States. Medical topics include cardiology, hematology, infectious disease, pulmonary concerns, general medicine, the female athlete, the pediatric athlete, and drugs and sports. Under each topic are several essays that address how medical procedures in each of the areas affect athletes. For instance, the cardiology section contains essays on hypertension, cardiac rehabilitation, and arrhythmia. A second section entitled "Musculoskeletal Topics" includes essays on preventing and treating injury to various parts of the body. Sections on the shoulder, elbow, wrist, hand, head, spine, knee, hip, ankle, and foot feature essays on how to diagnose injury, what injuries are most common to certain sports, and what medical science is doing to help athletes protect their bodies and heal injuries faster. The strength of the book is threefold. It is comprehensive, its essays are well written and supported by the latest medical knowledge, and because it is written for the undergraduate student and general public, it makes some relatively difficult material easy to understand. John Bloomfield's *Science and Medicine in Sport* is similar to Sallis's book but adds chapters on several other issues, including disabled athletes, the effects of environmental stress on athletes, medical considerations in aquatic sports, and situations that confront a team physician. The book also includes a section on "Special Medical Considerations" in which various physicians discuss causes and current treatments of specific medical conditions, including epilepsy, diabetes, and eating disorders, that negatively impact athletic performance. One of the best chapters, written by Dr. A. R. Morton, is on asthma. It includes commentary on what asthma is, several ways that it affects athletes, potential strategies for minimizing those effects, special diets and exercise techniques designed to reverse exercise-induced asthma, and special training techniques for asthmatic athletes of all ages and all participatory levels. Like Sallis's work, the Bloomfield text also contains a complete section on how to prevent and treat common sports injuries. Bloomfield does include some unique topics in chapters focusing on dental problems, abdominal disorders, and pelvic injuries.

   *The History of Exercise and Sport Science*, edited by John D. Massengale and Richard A. Swanson, has chapters that discuss current research on motor behavior, sport and exercise psychology, exercise physiology, and the historical relationship between sport and medical science throughout the twentieth century. One of the book's best chapters, however, is on the future direction of sports science. Written by the editors, the chapter focuses on sports medicine and explains why the field will likely fragment into several subfields as doctors and medical professors continue to produce new knowledge. As evidence of this, Massengale and Swanson introduce a chapter on biomechanics, a relatively new field that draws on the knowledge and methods of several established disciplines. Written by Jerry Wilkinson, the chapter explains the history of biomechanics, what it is, and how it has changed over the last two decades. According to Wilkinson, biomechanics is a subdiscipline that borrows from physics, biology, physiology, and engineering to create a holistic approach to measure human movement (Massengale and Swanson 1997, 447). The ultimate goal of this new subdiscipline is to fully understand how the human body moves and under what conditions it best operates so that medical personnel can work with athletes to create those conditions.

Further evidence that Massengale and Swanson are on the right track with their theory of specialization is seen in books such as Roger Bartlett's *Introduction to Sports Biomechanics*, which is dedicated to fully explaining all eight of the major parts of the biomechanical process. The first of these is anatomical issues, which include the planes and axes of human movement, the function of the skeleton, how muscles work, and the importance of joints and soft tissues to movement. The second chapter deals with kinematic or movement principles that guide the field. These include linear motion, angular motions, and rotational motion. The third chapter is angular kinetics, which explains how gravity, friction, and other physical forces effect bodily motion. Fourth is fluid mechanics or energetics, which explains aquatic movement, the types of energy our bodies use, how energy is transferred to our vital organs during athletic competition, and how we can alter this transfer so as to maximize our energy levels. The fifth chapter explains how scientists engaged in biomechanical research use cinematography and video analysis to record and analyze athletic movement in order to diagnose mechanical problems. The sixth chapter profiles new technology that allows doctors to measure the external force acting upon an athlete's body as he or she performs, thus making it possible to deduce whether or not the athlete is undergoing too much stress on any given body part. Chapter seven explains electromyography, the electronic process by which muscle tension is measured. Finally, the last part of the biomechanical process involves new technological techniques such as electrogoniometry, through which the actual movement of joints can be studied. Bartlett's final chapter contains several other new forms of technology that allow scientists to study how the body moves, so that they can better protect it against the wear and tear of athletic competition.

Another book that bears out the specialization thesis is Jack H. Sandweiss's *Biofeedback and Sports Science*. Sandweiss defines biofeedback as a series of processes dedicated to measuring the vital signs of the body as it progresses through a range of movements and does a fine job of explaining just how these processes allow scientists to help athletes train more effectively. For instance, he describes how electromyographic feedback, loosely defined as that which comes from electronically monitoring various body parts during exercise to establish the power and direction of muscle movements, can be used to make sure an athlete is using his or her muscles properly (Sandweiss 1985, 9). Conversely, thermal feedback involves the measurement of skin temperature to detect whether or not an athlete is suffering from hypertension, circulatory deficiencies, or excess stress. Electrodermal feedback measures the electrical activity in the skin during exercise to analyze the stress level under which the athlete is operating. Through seven chapters, Sandweiss profiles several types of biofeedback and their various uses. According to the author, no matter what method of biofeedback is used, they are all uniquely valuable because they are fast and effective: "Even though clinical biofeedback involves an enormous number of relevant variables, the fact remains that with suitable instrumentation and a skilled biofeedback therapist, most patients can learn to alter physiological functioning within a short time" (Sandweiss 1985, 13). For athletes, this can be crucial when trying to break out of a slump and find that winning form before the big game. Sandweiss also includes a great chapter on applications of biofeedback within sporting contexts, in which he demonstrates how an athlete can use biofeedback techniques to monitor his or her own progress during athletic competition, light exercise, or rehabilitation.

## INJURY PREVENTION AND-REHABILITATION

Without doubt the lion's share of books that examine the relationship between sports and science concentrate on medical knowledge and technological advances that help athletes both prevent and rehabilitate athletic injury. There are several excellent books dedicated to explaining how athletes, coaches, and trainers can employ sports medical knowledge to enhance the training process. One of the best is Daniel D. Arnheim's *Essentials of Athletic Training*. The text boasts chapters on assessment procedures and techniques; environmental concerns, including how athletes can prepare for hyperthermia; hypothermia; high altitudes or air pollution; and special techniques that coaches and trainers can use to minimize the chance of athletic injury. The latter chapter contains Arnheim's "Ten Cardinal Conditioning Principles," which include instructions on how to adopt a proper warm-up routine; how to decide which training programs are best for any athlete based on sport, age, condition, and ability; how to help the athlete learn self-motivation techniques; and how to develop relaxation exercises that serve to rejuvenate the athlete. Other key concepts include a gradual improvement schedule, the regulation of timing and intensity, and a plan to develop the athlete's strength and endurance so that he or she can work to capacity during each workout (Arnheim 1995, 68). Arnheim's work also contains several review questions and case studies, making it the ideal classroom text for introductory courses on sports training and injuries. Those who like Arnheim's book might also want to consult *Principles of Athletic Training,* written by Arnheim and William E. Prentice. This large, comprehensive work contains twenty-six chapters that are broken into five sections; (1) "Injury Prevention," which concentrates on nutritional considerations and protective devices; (2) "Basic Foundations of Sports Trauma," which explains how to diagnose and provide initial treatment to several sports injuries; (3) "Management Skills," which instructs trainers on how to deal with emergency procedures, drug use, and rehabilitation practices; (4) "Specific Sports Conditions," in which the authors discuss how to prevent and treat common injuries in various sports; and finally (5) "Athletic Training Administration," a must read for managers of athletic training facilities because it discusses key aspects of program operation, including legal issues, insurance requirements, and budgetary and safety concerns.

Those specifically interested in how modern technology, especially advances in chemistry, has led to improved methods in athletic training, should consult Robert Goldman and Ronald Klatz's *The "E" Factor: The Secrets of New Tech*

*Training and Fitness for the Winning Edge.* The authors spend two full chapters discussing the dangers associated with anabolic steroids and recreational drugs such as marijuana, cocaine, and alcohol. Overall, these chapters are clear and disturbingly insightful, but the best chapter is on "Nutritional Ergocentric Aids," natural substances that can greatly enhance athletic performance if administered properly. For instance, the authors discuss the value of baking soda as a substance that, when taken under the right conditions, can significantly reduce the build-up lactic acid in runners: "When highly trained half-milers took sodium bicarbonate shortly before their time trials, their times improved by almost three seconds." Other studies have suggested that "taking baking soda after a hard, intense workout may speed muscle recovery by helping lactic-acid-loaded blood to return to its normal neutral condition" (Goldman and Klatz 1988, 8). Goldman and Klatz also explain the potential benefits of sodium phosphate, several vitamins and minerals, water, sports drinks, and specialized diets to athletes. Another chapter entitled "Keeping the Edge/Longevity and the Athlete" explains what happens to an athlete's body as it ages and suggests some steps for players who want to better protect themselves as they get older. For instance, the authors explain how one can use antioxidants such as vitamin C or Hydergine to combat the effects of free radicals, negative chemicals that are capable of deforming large cells and preventing them from functioning as they should. They also discuss new techniques being used to stimulate an athlete's DNA, and the use of drugs such as Ubiquinone that stimulate human immunological systems so that athletes can perform at optimum levels for a longer period of time. Their description of aspirin in the battle against aging is eye-catching: "Aspirin can be listed in the category of wonder drugs. It relieves muscle aches, offers relief from arthritis pain and headaches, and has been a mainstay of medical practice since the turn of the century. Now recent studies indicate that it may extend life-span" (Goldman and Klatz 1988, 28). Goldman and Klatz also include chapters on how to use various kinds of exercise equipment, the pros and cons of eight different diagnostic muscle-training systems, and an evaluation of electronic treatments for sports injuries.

There are literally hundreds of books that focus on how athletes can prepare specific parts of their bodies for competition. Works exist on the feet and ankles, the knee, the back, and nearly every other part of the body that must be ready for athletic endeavor. One of the more interesting is Donald Loran's *Sports Vision*, a book dedicated to explaining how new technology has allowed the athlete to maximize visual potential. Notable chapters include "Sports for the Visually Impaired," "Sports Vision Correction," and "Eye Injuries in Sport," but the best essay is Bradley Coffee and Alan Reichow's "Visual Performance Enhancement in Sports Optometry," which details several new techniques used to improve athletic vision. For instance, Visual Acuity Training and Dynamic Visual Acuity Training are designed to enhance the athlete's ability to focus on motion and detail. Accommodative-Vergence Facility Training, which is especially valuable for players in fast moving team sports such as hockey and football, improves the athlete's ability to rapidly adjust focus on shifting targets. Sight is also the key to balance in sport, and Vergence Stability Training helps athletes develop the ability to quickly adjust to changing spatial relationships so that they can maintain control of their bodies under intense game conditions. Visual Spatial Perception Training, in which athletes view shifting targets through prisms and lenses, is another method designed to help athletes maintain balance and control. Coffee and Reichow also describe techniques designed to improve the speed at which one adjusts to changes on the visual landscape, eye-hand coordination, and peripheral vision (Loran 1995, 163–173). Other books dealing with vision and other specific body parts are listed in the bibliography following this chapter.

Those interested specifically in a book on injury assessment should consult James M. Booker and Gary A. Thibodeau's *Athletic Injury Assessment*, a book dedicated to explaining exactly what causes injuries, what the body goes through in its response to injury, and what should be done at each stage of this response. The book's key chapter is "The Body's Response to Trauma and Environmental Stress," in which the authors suggest several medical procedures that might facilitate the healing process as the body responds to injury. For instance, the primary stage usually involves swelling and bleeding, which must be contained by the trainer so as to prevent further damage to the injured area. The second phase involves both inflammation and infection. According to Booker and Thibodeau, "Athletic trainers can greatly affect this phase of the athletic injury cycle." Generally, a trainer has three goals: "To localize the extent of the injured area, to rid both the body as a whole and the injury site of waste products resulting from the initial trauma and secondary response, and to enhance healing" (Booker and Thibodeau 1994, 116). The authors discuss how to diagnose and treat damaged tissue and broken bones, as well as how to handle an athlete who faints from pain or loss of function. They then provide a detailed account of how wounds heal and what trainers can do to facilitate the healing process depending on the injury. The book is also notable for its valuable chapters on osteology, the study of skeletal structure; anthrology, the study of athletic impact on joints; myology, the impact of physical activity on skeletal muscles; and neurology, the impact of the nervous system on athletic performance. A similar book in layout and content is *Sports Injuries and Their Treatment*, edited by Basil Helal, J. B. King, and W. J. Grange. It contains discussions on many of the same topics tackled by Booker and Thibodeau but includes a unique chapter on how athletes can adopt specific procedures to prevent both extrinsic injuries, such as turf toe or facial lacerations, and intrinsic injuries, such as torn ligaments. Helal, King, and Grange also include essays that effectively address psychological aspects of recovering from injury and strategies for dealing with unconscious patients.

There are several other fine books that discuss rehabilitation techniques for injured athletes. One of the more intriguing works is Marc Chasnov's *Healing Sports Injuries: A Hands-On Guide to Restorative Massage and Exercise*. Chasnov, a physical therapist who has worked with several Olympic athletes, explains how various massage therapies can be used to help heal injuries to the neck, shoulders, back, abdomen, hip, knee, elbow, wrist, foot, and ankle. According to the author, one of the prime benefits of massage is that it relaxes the injured area, allowing the patient to get much needed sleep: "Massage, when applied properly, uses a smooth, steady, and rhythmical pressure on the body. The effect is a strong hypnotic, relaxing feeling that is not unlike rubbing a baby's back to help him or her sleep or petting a dog to keep it calm" (Chasnov 1988, 49). Massage also helps to increase circulation, allowing blood and lymph, the clear fluid that removes waste products from the body, to flow into the injured area to speed up the healing process. Massage also helps to rejuvenate muscles: "Restorative massage works directly on muscles by stimulating inactive muscles and compensating in part for inactivity due to illness or injury" (Chasnov 1988, 51). Chasnov also includes an interesting chapter on the effect of posture on the rehabilitation process. He explains how sloped shoulders, a head that leans forward, a back that arches, hyper-extended knees, and flat feet can all put so much strain on other parts of the body, including injured areas, that it makes it difficult for injuries to heal quickly or correctly. In addition, poor posture also leaves an athlete more susceptible to injury as he or she gets older: "By sixty years of age, years of neglect, tight imbalanced muscles, and poor exercise habits cause pain and loss of function. We may have to fight so hard to stand upright or hold our head up that the majority of our body's energy is used simply fighting gravity" (Chasnov 1988, 22–23). At the end of the chapter, Chasnov leaves the reader with various strategies designed to improve posture as a means of bettering athletic performance.

James R. Andrews and Gary Harrelson's *Physical Rehabilitation of the Injured Athlete* has two unique chapters. The first examines how therapists use modalities in rehabilitation. Modalities refer to the use of cold, heat, electricity, compression, and massage to treat an injury. They are vital because they comprise a great part of the initial care an athlete receives for an injury. The authors are very specific about when each modality should be used and provide explicit instructions on various types of each modality, being careful to stress the pros and cons of using each type on certain injuries. Another distinctive chapter discusses various aquatic rehabilitation techniques. These include warm-up exercises for those trying to revive unused muscles; lower body exercises for the knee, ankle, back and hips; upper body exercises for the shoulders, elbows, and wrists; and an assortment of other exercises specifically designed to rehabilitate certain injuries. The chapter contains several excellent case studies to show students and athletes how and when to use aquatic rehabilitation and a sample exercise program. All of the chapters in the book are followed by complete bibliographies that will be invaluable to those interested in the subject.

Perhaps the most comprehensive of all books on the rehabilitation of sports injuries is *Rehabilitation Technique in Sports Medicine*, edited by William E. Prentice. Overall, the book contains twenty-six essays written by some of the top medical school professors in the United States and covers just about every topic a student might wish to research. One notable chapter, Janine Oman's "Isokinetics in Rehabilitation," discusses the use of isokinetic exercise in the rehabilitative process. Isokinetic exercise is defined as movement that takes place at a consistent rate with varying resistance (Prentice 1994, 86). Its many uses are perfectly described by Oman, who concludes that the chief advantage of such activity is that it allows each athlete to work on his or her unique injury at his or her own pace

(Prentice 1994, 86). Mike Voight and Steve Tippett provide an equally detailed analysis of plyometrics, a set of exercises designed to combine strength with speed to produce powerful muscle tissues and strong joints that can resist injury. Prentice includes his own chapter on closed-kinetic chain exercises, which are primarily intended to strengthen muscles by immobilizing them during exercise. Closed-kinetic exercises for the lower body would include mini-squats and leg presses, while upper body activities might take the form of push-ups. Voight and Tippet analyze the impact of each type of closed-kinetic exercise on several different types of injuries. Other chapters that stand out are Prentice's "Proprioceptive Neuro-muscular Facilitation Techniques," which profiles a series of exercises for the spinal chord intended to stretch and relax muscles; Prentice's "Pharmalogical Considerations in a Rehabilitation Program," which weighs the pros and cons of using chemical therapies such as cortisone shots to heal injuries; and Dan Hooker's "Back Rehabilitation," which gives those with chronic back pain a good summary of strategies that they can use to protect their backs during exercise.

Two other works that might be of interest to students of sports injuries are Werner Kuprian's *Physical Therapy for Sports* and James Garrick's *Peak Condition: Winning Strategies to Prevent, Treat and Rehabilitate Sports Injuries*. The former makes the distinction between passive and active treatments and discusses how each can be applied to any number of common injuries. Passive treatments are those that do not require exertion by the athlete. Massages, modalities, and electrotherapy would be examples of passive treatments. Other treatments would be hydrotherapy and balneotherapy, both of which use water to heal injuries. Kuprian's discussion of the various uses of both therapies is excellent. An active treatment, by contrast, involves the athlete's physical engagement in exercises such as weight lifting, stretching, and isokinetic movements. Kuprian dedicates several chapters to explaining how both active and passive treatments can be jointly used to heal various injuries. Similarly, Garrick's book is a functional book whose intent is to help injured athletes administer their own rehabilitation. Like Kuprian, he covers injuries to nearly every body part.

## NUTRITION

Most of the books already mentioned have chapters that discuss how to develop nutritional plans that will promote maximum performance, prevent injuries, and facilitate the rehabilitation process. For instance, Arnheim and Prentice's *Modern Principles of Athletic Training*, Goldman and Klatz's *The "E" Factor: The Secrets of New Tech Training and Fitness for the Winning Edge*, and Garrick's *Peak Condition: Winning Strategies to Prevent, Treat and Rehabilitate Sports Injuries* all have chapters on the importance of an athlete's diet. There are at least three other works that discuss specific nutritional issues that are pertinent to athletes. One is Victor Rogozkin and Ron Maughan's *Current Research in Sports Sciences: An International Perspective*. The authors feature two essays on the subject of nutrition. One is Nikolai Volkov's "Ergocentric Effects of the Creatine Supplementation During the Training of Top-Class Athletes," in which the author concludes that the addition of creatine supplements to an athlete's diet will increase that athlete's total store of energy (Rogozkin and Maughan 1996, 171). The other is H. J. Engels's "Metabolic and Ventilatory Effects of Caffeine during Light Intensity Exercise in Trained and Sedentary Low Habitual Caffeine Users." Engels concludes that "caffeine intake one hour prior to exercise results in an enhanced fractional contribution of fat for energy and exerts a mild thermogenic effect during constant load light intensity exercise" (Rogozkin and Maughan 1996, 330). Thus, in small amounts, caffeine can have beneficial effects on athletic performance.

Frank Brouns's *Medicine and Sports Science* contains eleven essays that examine how different types of diets affect the chemical composition of an athlete's body during competition. For instance, E. F. Coyle's "Carbohydrate Feedings: Effects on Metabolism, Performance and Recovery" discusses the benefits to cyclists of loading up on carbohydrates before competition. Coyle concludes that "carbohydrate is the most important nutrient to cycling performance. The energy from carbohydrate can be released within exercising muscles up to three times as fast as energy from fat (Brouns 1991, 12). Coyle describes a strategy for consuming the proper amount of carbohydrate before competition. P. W. R. Lemon's "Does Exercise Alter Dietary Protein Requirements?" examines the importance of proteins to athletic success, concluding that "although protein provides a small percentage of total exercise energy, the absolute increase [in exercise] could affect protein needs. At least four separate lines of evidence collected over the past 20 years indicate that endurance exercise does increase protein need" (Brouns 1991, 31). Lemon also produces some guidelines about how athletes can safely use protein supplements to ensure that they have enough energy resources to compete. A third essay of interest is R. A. Anderson's "New Insights on Trace Elements, Chromium, Copper and Zinc, and Exercise," which analyzes the importance of those three elements to athletic endeavor. Anderson writes that "these trace elements play key roles in energy production and utilization and are therefore of utmost importance in exercise performance" (Brouns 1991, 53). He explains how strenuous exercise leads to significant losses of the elements and supplies some strategies for supplementation for both highly competitive and recreational athletes. Other essays in the book discuss the effect of vitamins on exercises, how an athlete should resupply fluids and energy sources during competition, and the best way to construct a diet that minimizes excess weight gain.

Another book of interest for students researching the complex relationship between diet and performance is Constance Kies's *Sports Nutrition: Minerals and Electrolytes*. The work contains twenty-four essays, most of which deal with the effects of iron and calcium on exercise and strenuous athletic competition. For instance, J. L. Beard's essay "Iron Deficiency Affects Exercise and Exercise Affects Iron Metabolism: Is This a Chicken and Egg Argument?" argues that iron supplements are a must for every athlete because not only does iron deficiency hamper performance, but strenuous activity continually saps iron from the body (Kies 1995, 44). Kies's essay, "Dietary Calcium and the Bioavailability of Iron in Physically Active Adults," shows that an athlete must cultivate a diet that ensures a balance between iron and calcium: "The best overall outcome should occur with the feeding of a calcium supplemented, high iron diet. This diet promoted good apparent iron absorption and good calcium retention" (Kies 1995, 117). Kies gives examples of different types of diets that were examined to see which would yield the best balance between iron and calcium and concludes by recommending a very specific diet for athletes. Other essays in the book deal with such topics as the effects of minerals and electrolytes on athletic performance, the importance of incorporating magnesium and potassium into a diet, and the special iron and calcium needs of disabled athletes.

## WOMEN, CHILDREN, AND OLDER ATHLETES

Over the last decade, a number of books have been written to specific groups of people, including women, children, and older athletes. In addition, some quality efforts have attempted to describe the impact of science and technology on certain sports. Two of the best works to tackle the special needs and challenges of female athletes are Michelle Warren and Mona Shangold's *Sports Gynecology: Problems and Care of the Athletic Female* and Shangold's *The Complete Sports Medicine Book for Women.* The former covers issues that confront female participants at every stage of their lives but has two particularly good sections that offer recommendations for pregnant athletes and athletes who are going through menopause. The authors stress the importance of light exercise for pregnant women, highlight specific dangers associated with highly stressful endeavors, recommend several activities, and issue a list of guidelines meant to foster healthy athletic participation. For instance, they write that "regular exercise is preferable to intermittent activity," that "women should avoid exercise in the supine position after the first trimester," and that "women should be aware of decreased oxygen available for aerobic exercise during pregnancy. They should be encouraged to modify the intensity of their exercise according to maternal symptoms" (Warren and Shangold 1997, 130). The authors also instruct athletes at menopause how to develop a diet and exercise regimen, providing suggestions as to how these women can use aerobic exercise, strength training, flexibility exercises, and hormone replacement therapy to combat the physical effects of menopause as well as depression. *The Complete Sports Medicine Book for Women* is also quite comprehensive, featuring chapters on nutrition, drugs, the weather, injury prevention, gynecological concerns, choosing the right equipment, and protecting one's hair and skin. The work contains two especially good chapters on issues facing young girls at the age of puberty and older women. Shangold is careful to stress the importance of exercise to young girls, listing several benefits of sports participation. She also discusses some of the problems girls have with sports during puberty, especially those associated with menstruation. Shangold examines several medical guidelines developed to help girls continue to enjoy athletics during this time, including ways of dealing with irregular periods and awkwardness, which sometimes prompt girls to quit playing. Shangold also stresses the importance of exercise for older women as a means of slowing the aging process and promoting both psychological and physical health. She includes recommended diets and exercise regimens that would be appropriate for older women.

Robert K. Kerlan's *Sports Medicine in the Older Athlete* is the best book for those looking for a comprehensive study of most of the issues that confront older athletes. One of the many informative articles is Jack Wilmore's "The Aging of Bone and Muscle" in which the author argues that the most important thing for aging athletes to do is to keep working their muscles and joints. He makes the distinction between aging and disuse: "Much of what had previously been considered aging is now regarded as functional disuse. With aging, muscle undergoes a reduction in size, and consequently strength, which is related to a loss of muscle fibers. Exercise training can increase the size and strength of the trained muscles." He also notes that "exercise training appears to attenuate the normal decreases in bone with aging and can even lead to small increases in bone density and mass" (Kerlan 1991, 241–242). Kerlan includes a number of essays that explain exactly how older athletes should go about the business of keeping themselves healthy through athletic endeavor. For instance, several authors discuss the benefits of participating in sports such as rowing, rock climbing, golf, tennis, cycling, swimming, skiing, and running. Other subjects include how athletes can use exercise to combat arthritis, to improve circulation and cardiovascular health, to strengthen the spine, to increase bone strength and flexibility, and to promote a psychological sense of well-being. Cheryl Rock's "Nutrition of the Older Athlete" provides a complete overview of how older athletes can develop a diet that is based on their individual needs and strengths.

Bruce Reider's *Sports Medicine: The School-Age Athlete* and Dov B. Nudel's *Pediatric Sports Medicine* are two of the best books available that examine how sports medicine has enhanced our understanding of the problems and needs of child athletes. Reider's work is the most comprehensive work on the subject. It is composed of thirty-five essays, all of which address a unique aspect of the adolescent sporting experience. A section entitled "The Foundations of Sports Medicine" contains essays on strength training, endurance training, flexibility training, nutrition, ergocentric aids for children, and modalities in rehabilitation of injuries to children. "Common Sports Injuries" includes chapters that give coaches and trainers an idea of how to treat injuries to children. A third section, "Sport-Specific Sports Medicine" contains twelve chapters that examine common injuries associated with different sports and the unique physical challenges that confront young athletes in each sport. For instance, in the chapter on baseball, William Jay Bryan describes several techniques young pitchers can use to improve their arm strength when they move from the Little League diamond to the regulation-sized field. Reider's essay on football examines several stretching exercises in which a young player should engage to avoid injury and to protect developing muscles, bones, and joints. Nudel's book features a chapter by Lyle J. Micheli entitled "Sports Injuries in Children and Adolescents," which explains the injuries to which children are most susceptible and which gives the coach or trainer several tips on how to prevent and treat those injuries. Other chapters of interest include John R. Sutton's "Drugs in Sports," which explains the effects of certain drugs on child athletes; Yasoma B. Challenor's "Exercise and Sports for the Handicapped Child," which provides detailed exercise plans for children suffering from any number of physical disabilities; Leonard Epstein's "Exercise in the Treatment of Obese Children;" Rod Dishman's "Pediatric Sports Psychology;" and Nudel's "Sports in Children with Cardiovascular Disease." Both books have extensive bibliographies and provide commentary that is highly readable and utilitarian.

## SCIENCE AND SPECIFIC SPORTS

A number of books exist that deal exclusively with technological advances and medical concerns in specific sports. Typical of the genre is Barry Jordan's *Medical Aspects of Boxing,* which contains twenty-four essays written by physicians that have studied boxing injuries. Subjects include the history of medical treatment of boxing injuries; medical arguments for not participating in boxing; new technology that has made boxing safer; the role of the ringside physician; recommended physical conditioning practices; the dangers of doping; common brain, facial, and dental injuries; cardiovascular and abdominal problems; AIDS; and strategies for injury prevention. Other noteworthy books in the genre that discuss the same topics for other sports include A. J. Cochran and M. R. Rarraly's *The Science of Golf II: Proceedings of the 1994 World Science Congress of Golf,* Bjorn Ekblom's *Soccer,* Edward Muller's *Science and Skiing,* and Timothy Noakes's *Running Injuries: How to Prevent and Overcome Them.*

Finally, those interested in the legal aspects of sports medicine should consult Letha Y. Hunter-Griffin's *Athletic Training and Sports Medicine,* which contains an excellent chapter entitled "Legal Responsibilities in Sports Medicine" that uses case studies to examine liability issues, negligence, and various torts that impact the sports physician. Since the book is designed as a textbook for undergraduate use, it contains review questions, summaries, and extensive bibliographies for those who want to read more about the legal concerns of those involved in sports medicine as doctors, trainers, researchers, or teachers.

Students, practioners, or researchers who want to stay abreast of current information in any of the fields of sport science and technology should consult the following scholarly periodicals, all of which regularly contain well-researched, academic articles that reflect the newest insights and discoveries: *American Journal of Drug and Alcohol Abuse; American Journal of Physics; American Journal of Physiology; American Journal of Public Health; American Journal of Science; American Journal of Sports Medicine; Canadian Journal of Applied Psychology; Canadian Journal of Public Health; Chronicle of Higher Education; Genetics; Health; Issues in Science and Technology; Journal of Applied Sport Science Research; Journal of Athletic Training; Journal of Heredity; Journal of Nutrition; Journal of Physical Education, Recreation and Dance; Journal of Recreational Mathematics; Journal of Strength and Conditioning Research; Journal of the American Medical Association; The Physician and Sports Medicine; Physics Today; Research Quarterly of Athletic Training; Scientific American; Sport*

*Science Review; Sports Medicine Digest; Technology Review;* and *Women's Sport and Fitness.*

## REFERENCES

### Books

Abdenour, Thomas. *Sports Injury Care.* Boston: Jones & Bartlett Publications, 1993.

Andrews, James R. *The Athlete's Shoulder.* New York: Churchill Livingstone, 1994.

Andrews, James R., and Gary Harrelson. *Physical Rehabilitation of the Injured Athlete.* Philadelphia, PA: Sauders, 1998.

Armenti, Angelo. *The Physics of Sport.* New York: American Institute of Physics, 1992.

Arnheim, Daniel R. *Essentials of Athletic Training.* St. Louis, MO: Mosby, 1995.

Arnheim, Daniel R., and William E. Prentice. *Principles of Athletic Training.* St. Louis, MO: Mosby, 1993.

Atko, Viru A. *Adaptation in Sports Training.* Boca Raton, FL: CRC Press, 1995.

Bar-Or, Oded, ed. *The Child and Adolescent Athlete.* Cambridge, MA: Human Kinetics Books, 1996.

———. *Exercise and the Female—A Life Span Approach.* Carmel, IN: Cooper Publishing, 1996.

Bartlett, Roger. *Introduction to Sports Biomechanics.* New York: E. & F. N. Spon, 1997.

Bartone, John C. *Science and Medicine of Sports.* Washington, D.C.: Abbe Publishers, 1984.

Berryman, Jack W., and Roberta J. Park. *Sport and Exercise Science: Essays in the History of Sports Medicine.* Urbana, IL: University of Illinois Press, 1992.

Blanding, Sharon L. *What Makes a Boomerang Come Back: How Things in Sports Work.* Stamford, CT: Longmeadow Press, 1992.

Bloomfield, John. *Science and Medicine in Sport.* Cambridge, MA: Blackwell Scientific Publications, 1995.

Bompa, Tudor. *From Childhood to Champion Athlete.* Carmel, IN: Cooper Publications, 1995.

———. *Periodization of Strength.* Carmel, IN: Cooper Publications, 1993.

———. *Power Training for Sport.* Carmel, IN: Cooper Publications, 1993.

Booker, James M., and Gary A. Thibodeau. *Athletic Injury Assessment.* St. Louis, MO: Mosby, 1994.

Bowers, Richard. *Sport Physiology.* Dubuque, IA: William C. Brown Publishers, 1992.

Brancazio, Peter. *SportScience: Physical Laws and Optimal Performance.* New York: Simon & Schuster, 1984.

Bronson, Hugo. *Sports and Anabolic Steroids: An Index of Modern Information.* Washington, D.C.: Abbe Publisher's Association, 1985.

———. *Sports and Athletic Injuries: Medical Subject Analysis and Research Index with Bibliography.* Washington, D.C.: Abbe Publisher's Association, 1985.

Brouns, Frank. *Medicine and Sports Science.* Basel, Switzerland: Karger, 1991.

Burke, Edmund, and Jacqueline Berning. *Training Nutrition.* Carmel, IN: Cooper Publishing, 1996.

Butts, Nancy K. *The Elite Athlete.* Champaign, IL: Life Enhancement Publications, 1987.

Caine, Dennis. *Epidemiology of Sports Injuries.* Champaign, IL: Human Kinetics Books, 1996.

Cantu, Robert C. *ACSM's Guidelines for the Team Physician.* Philadelphia, PA: Lee and Febiger, 1991.

Carr, Gerald C. *Mechanics of Sports: A Practitioner's Guide*. Champaign, IL: Human Kinetics Books, 1997.

Chasnov, Marc. *Healing Sports Injuries: A Hands-On Guide to Restorative Massage and Exercises*. New York: Fawcett-Columbine, 1988.

Coates, Joseph. *The Highly Probable Future: 83 Assumptions about the Year 2025*. Bethesda, MD: World Future Society, 1989.

Cochran, A. J., and M. R. Farrally. *Science and Golf II: Proceedings of the 1994 World Science Congress of Golf*. New York: E. & F. N. Spon, 1994.

Costill, David. *Inside Running: Basic Sports Physiology*. Carmel, IN: Cooper Publishing, 1986.

————. *The Making of Motion Video*. Carmel, IN: Cooper Publishing, 1989.

De Mestre, Neville. *The Mathematics of Projectiles in Sport*. New York: Cambridge University Press, 1990.

Ekblom, Bjorn. *Soccer*. Boston: Blackwell Scientific Publications, 1994.

Figelman, Alan. *Keeping Young Athletes Healthy*. New York: Simon & Schuster, 1991.

Flood, Dennis. *Practical Math for Health Fitness Professionals*. Champaign, IL: Human Kinetics Books, 1996.

Fox, Edward L. *The Physiological Basis of Physical Education and Athletics*. Philadelphia, PA: Saunders College Publications, 1988.

Gallaspy, James B. *Signs and Symptoms of Athletic Injury*. St Louis, MO: Mosby, 1995.

Garrick, James. *Peak Condition: Winning Strategies to Prevent, Treat and Rehabilitate Sports Injuries*. New York: Crown, 1986.

Gisolfi, Carl, David Lamb, and Ethan Nadel, eds. *Exercise and Older Adults*. Carmel, IN: Cooper Publishing, 1995.

Goldman, Robert, and Ronald Klatz. *The "E" Factor: The Secrets of New Tech Training and Fitness for the Winning Edge*. New York: William Morrow, 1988.

Haake, Steve. *The Engineering of Sport*. Brookfield, VT: A. A. Balkema, 1996.

Halloran, James. *Current Issues in Sport Science*. Schorndorf, Germany: Hofman, 1996.

Hatfield, Frederick. *Ultimate Sports Nutrition*. Chicago: Contemporary Books, 1987.

Hawkey, Roy. *Sport Science*. London: Hodder & Stoughton, 1991.

Hawkins, Jerald D. *The Practical Delivery of Sports Medicine Sciences: A Conceptual Approach*. Canton, OH: PRC Publications, 1993.

Hay, James. *The Biomechanics of Sports Techniques*. Englewood Cliffs, NJ: PrenticeHall, 1993.

Helal, Basil, J. B. King, and W. J. Grange, eds. *Sports Injuries and Their Treatment*. Cambridge: Chapman and Hall, 1986.

Hoberman, John. *Mortal Engines: The Science of Performance and the Dehumanization of Sport*. New York: Free Press, 1992.

Holtz, Jerry B. *Sports Performance—Analysis, Skills, Conditions, Training and Human Factors: Index of New Information with Authors and Subjects*. Washington, D.C.: Abbe Publishers Association, 1991.

Huizenga, Robert. *You're OK, It's Just a Bruise: A Doctor's Sideline Secrets about Pro Football's Most Outrageous Team*. New York: St. Martin's, 1994.

Hunter-Griffin, Letha Y., ed. *Athletic Training and Sports Medicine*. Park Ridge, IL: American Academy of Orthopedic Surgeons, 1999.

Hyde, Thomas. *Conservative Management of Sports Injuries*. Baltimore, MD: Williams & Williams, 1997.

Johnson, Robert. *Current Review of Sport Medicine*. Philadelphia, PA: Current Medicine Publications, 1994.

Johnson, William E. *Concepts of Human Movement*. Dubuque, IA: Kendall Hunt Publishing, 1991.

Jordan, Barry, ed. *Medical Aspects of Boxing*. Boca Raton, FL: CRC Press, 1993.

Kent, Michael. *Oxford Dictionary of Sport Science and Medicine*. New York: Oxford University Press, 1994.

Kerlan, Robert. *Sports Medicine in the Older Athlete*. Philadelphia, PA: W. B. Saunders, 1991.

Kettlekamp, Larry. *Modern Sports Science*. New York: William Morrow, 1986.

Kies, Constance V., ed. *Sports Nutrition: Minerals and Electrolytes*. Boca Raton, FL: CRC Press, 1995.

Klawans, Harold L. *Why Michael Couldn't Hit, and Other Tales of the Neurology of Sports*. New York: W. H. Freeman, 1996.

Knight, Kenneth. *Cryotherapy in Sport Injury Management*. Champaign, IL: Human Kinetics Books, 1995.

Komi, Paavo V. *Strength and Power in Sport*. Boston: Blackwell Scientific Publications, 1992.

Kuhn, Harold W., ed. *Classics in Game Theory*. Princeton, NJ: Princeton University Press, 1997.

Kuprian, Warner J. *Physical Therapy for Sports*. Philadelphia, PA: Saunders, 1995.

Kurz, Thomas. *Science in Sports Training: How to Plan and Control Training for Peak Performance*. Island Pond, VT: Stadium Press, 1991.

Lamb, David, Howard Knuttgen, and Robert Murray, eds. *Physiology and Nutrition for Competitive Sport*. Carmel, IN: Cooper Publishing, 1994.

Loran, Donald. *Sports Vision*. Boston: Butterworth-Heinemann, 1995.

Luckstead, Eugene F. *Medical Care and the Adolescent Athlete*. Los Angeles: Practice Management Information Corp., 1993.

Malina, Robert M., ed. *Sport and Human Genetics*. Champaign, IL: Human Kinetics Books, 1986.

Marder, Richard. *Sports Injuries of the Ankle and Foot*. New York: Springer, 1997.

Martire, Joseph. *Imaging of Athletic Injuries: A Multimodality Approach*. New York: McGraw-Hill, 1992.

Mason, James G. *Modern Sports Administration*. Englewood Cliffs, NJ: PrenticeHall, 1988.

Massengale, John D., and Richard A. Swanson. *The History of Exercise and Sport Science*. Champaign, IL: Human Kinetics Books, 1997.

McKeag, Douglas B. *Primary Care Sports Medicine*. Dubuque, IA: Brown & Benchmark, 1993.

McLatchie, G. R. *The Soft Tissue: Trauma & Sports Injuries*. Boston: Butterworth-Heinemann, 1993.

Merrill, Robert A. *Your Injury: A Common Sense Guide to Sports Injuries*. Indianapolis, IN: Master's Press, 1994.

Micheli, Lyle. *The Sport Medical Bible*. New York: Harper Perennial, 1995.

Morgan, Lyle. *Homeopathic Treatment of Sports Injuries*. Rochester, VT: Healing Arts Press, 1988.

Mottram, David R. *Drugs in Sport*. New York: E. & F. N. Spon, 1996.

Muller, Edward. *Science and Skiing*. New York: E. & F. N. Spon, 1997.

Murray, Robert, and David Lamb, eds. *Recent Advances in the Science and Medicine of Sport*. Carmel, IN: Cooper Publishing, 1997.

Nickel, David. *Acupuncture for Athletes*. New York: Holt, 1987.

Noakes, Timothy. *Running Injuries: How to Prevent and Overcome Them*. New York: Oxford University Press, 1996.

Nudel, Dov B. *Pediatric Sports Medicine*. New York: PMA Publications, 1989.

Paciorek, Michael, and Jeffrey Jones, eds. *Sports and Recreation for the Disabled*. Carmel, IN: Cooper Publishing, 1994.

Potparic, Olivia. *A Dictionary of Sports Injuries and Disorders*. New York: Parthenon Publications Group, 1996.

Prentice, William. *Rehabilitation Techniques in Sports Medicine*. St. Louis, MO: Mosby, 1994.

Reichow, Alan W. *Sports Vision*. Santa Ana, CA: Optometric Extension Program, 1993.

Reider, Bruce. *Sports Medicine: The School-Age Athlete*. Philadelphia, PA: Saunders Press, 1991.

Reilly, Thomas. *Biological Rhythms and Exercise*. Oxford: Oxford University Press, 1996.

———. *World Congress of Science and Football*. New York: E. & F. N. Spon, 1993.

Ritter, Merrill. *Your Injury: A Common-Sense Guide to Sports Injuries*. Carmel, IN: Cooper Publishing, 1987.

Robinson, Nikki S. *A Bibliography of Strength and Basic Muscle Function in Sport and Industry*. Iowa City, IA: University of Iowa Press, 1987.

Rogozkin, Victor, and Ron Maughan. *Current Research in Sports Sciences: An International Perspective*. New York: Plenum Press, 1996.

Ruud, Jaime S. *Nutrition and the Female Athlete*. Boca Raton, FL: CRC Press, 1996.

Sadovskii, Leonid. *Mathematics and Sports*. Providence, RI: American Mathematical Society, 1993.

Sallis, Robert E. *Essentials of Sports Medicine*. St. Louis, MO: Mosby, 1997.

Sammarco, James G. *Rehabilitation of the Foot and Ankle*. St. Louis, MO: Mosby, 1995.

Sandweiss, Jack H. *Biofeedback and Sports Science*. New York: Plenum Press, 1985.

Seiderman, Arthur. *The Athletic Eye: Improved Sports Performance Through Visual Training*. New York: Hearst Books, 1983.

Shangold, Mona, ed. *The Complete Sports Medicine Book for Women*. New York: Simon & Schuster, 1992.

Sharkey, Brian. *Fitness and Health*. Champaign, IL: Human Kinetics Books, 1997.

Sheely, Robert. *Sports Lab: How Science Has Changed Sports*. New York: Silver Moon Press, 1994.

Shepherd, Roy. *Physical Activity, Training and the Immune Response*. Carmel, IN: Cooper Publishing, 1997.

Snyder, Ann. *The Influence of Exercise and Nutrition on Health*. Carmel, IN: Cooper Publishing, 1997.

Stainback, Robert. *Alcohol and Sport*. Champaign, Il: Human Kinetics Books, 1997.

Teitz, Carol, ed. *The Female Athlete*. Rosemont, IL: American Academy of Orthopedic Surgeons, 1997.

Townend, Stewart. *Mathematics in Sport*. New York: Halstead Press, 1984.

Torrey, Lee. *Stretching the Limits: Breakthroughs in Sport Science that Create Superathletes*. New York: Dodd, Mead, 1985.

Viru, A. A. *Adaptation in Sport Training*. Boca Raton, FL: CRC Press, 1995.

Wade, Michael G. *Introduction to Kinesiology: The Science and Practice of Physical Activity*. Madison, WI: Brown & Benchmark, 1995.

Warren, Michelle P., and Mona Shangold. *Sports Gynecology: Problems and Care of the Athletic Female*. Cambridge, MA: Blackwell Scientific Publications, 1997.

Wells, Christine. *Women, Sport & Performance: A Physiological Perspective*. Champaign, IL: Human Kinetics Books, 1991.

Williams, Clyde. *Food, Nutrition, and Sports Performance: An International Scientific Consensus*. New York: E. & F. N. Spon, 1992.

Wilmore, John. *Physiology of Sport and Exercise*. Champaign, IL: Human Kinetics Books, 1994.

Zachazewski, James E. *Athletic Injuries and Rehabilitation*. Philadelphia, PA: Saunders, 1996.

Zagelbaum, Bruce. *Sports Opthamology*. Cambridge, MA: Blackwell Scientific Publications, 1996.

## Journals

*American Journal of Drug and Alcohol Abuse* (New York, NY)
*American Journal of Physics* (Amherst, MA)
*American Journal of Physiology* (Bethesda, MD)
*American Journal of Public Health* (Washington, D.C.)
*American Journal of Science* (New Haven, CT)
*American Journal of Sports Medicine* (Waltham, MA)
*Canadian Journal of Applied Physiology* (Champaign, IL)
*Canadian Journal of Public Health* (Ottawa, Ontario, Canada)
*Chronicle of Higher Education* (Washington, D.C.)
*Genetics* (New York, NY)
*Health* (San Francisco, CA)
*Issues in Science and Technology* (Richardson, TX)
*Journal of Applied Sport Science Research* (Champaign, IL)
*Journal of Athletic Training* (Dallas, TX)
*Journal of Heredity* (Buckeystown, MD)
*Journal of Nutrition* (Bethesda, MD)
*Journal of Physical Education, Recreation and Dance* (Reston, VA)
*Journal of Recreational Mathematics* (Kettering, OH)
*Journal of Strength and Conditioning Research* (Champaign, IL)
*Journal of the American Medical Association* (Chicago, IL)
*The Physician and Sports Medicine* (Minneapolis, MN)
*Physics Today* (College Park, MD)
*Research Quarterly of Athletic Training* (Reston, VA)
*Scientific American* (New York, NY)
*Sport Science Review* (Champaign, IL)
*Sports Medicine Digest* (Van Nuys, CA)
*Technology Review* (Cambridge, MA)
*Women's Sports and Fitness* (Boulder, CO)

# 11

# Sport and Sociology

It was not necessary to be a sports fan in the summer of 1998 to appreciate the powerful role that sport plays in the lives of most of the people on this little planet. Entire nations in Europe, Africa, the Far East, and South America sat glued to the television or bent collective ear to the radio to follow the exploits of their teams at the World Cup Soccer tournament in France. When the French won the deciding match in a shocking upset of Brazil, the celebrations in the streets of Paris were larger than those that followed the end of World War II. In America, the Mark McGuire home run watch of the summer of 1998 was upstaged only by the illicit oval office activities of President Bill Clinton. All that actually happened was that a man hit more baseballs out of the park in one season than any other person in the game's history. No one found a cure for cancer or AIDS. Peace was not achieved in the Middle East. Not a single state budget was balanced. Yet people wept openly in the stadium and in homes throughout America. Announcers cried on national television, and the country stopped to pay homage to the big slugger. Why do we care so much about sport? What functions do sports have in our society? How do they reveal our values and national identity? These are some of the questions that sociologists have tried to answer since 1899 when Thornstein Veblen's landmark book, *The Theory of the Leisure Class*, appeared on the academic scene and laid the foundation for the discipline we now know as sociology. Over the last century, sports sociologists have dedicated themselves to studying the operation of games and athletics in society. In 1953, Frederick Cozens and Florence Strumpf published *Sports in American Life*, a work which set the stage for several books that would examine the critical role of sport in the history of the American people. In 1976, the *Review of Sport and Leisure* became the first academic journal devoted to the sociology of sport and was followed by *The Sociology of Sport Journal* in 1984. In 1978, the North American Society for the Study of the Sociology of Sport was founded, and two years later the group had its first conference. Such conferences and journals have encouraged young scholars to make their mark in the field, and since 1980, many excellent books and articles have been written on the social aspects of sport in America and throughout the world. In this chapter, I will profile the best of these works and discuss what some of the top authorities in the field have had to say about the most pivotal topics in the world of sports sociology. General definitions of the field and descriptions of what sports sociologists do will be featured, as will discussions of the various theories and paradigms from which such scholars work. The relationship between sport and social values will be examined, with particular emphasis paid to how American sport reveals the true nature of the country, especially what it values in terms of morality and ethics. One of the most interesting parts of sports sociology is the study of fans and heroes. What drives a person to be a fan? What does a fan get in exchange for his loyalty? What constitutes a sports hero, and why do we look to sport, of all things, for heroic models? What kind of sports subcultures exist around the world and why do they develop? All of these questions will be explored.

## SPORTS SOCIOLOGY: AN OVERVIEW

One of the best books to consult for an explanation of the sociology of sport is still Donald Chu's *Dimensions of Sport Studies*, first published in 1982. According to Chu, sports sociology has two levels of concern. One is the macrolevel, which deals with large-scale social systems and their relations. For instance, the political function of sport in various societies in terms of the transmission of values and beliefs, the promotion of ideologies, and the use as political tools by presidents and other officials are at issue. Other macrolevel concerns of sports sociologists are sport and religion, including such issues as spiritual awareness through sport and the formation of religious sports groups such as Athletes in Action; sport and education, featuring such topics as the effect of sports on high school students; sport and race; and sports and sexism. By contrast, microlevel concerns tend to focus on small social systems. Common research areas include team dynamics, group interaction among players and fans, socialization, morale, aggression, and delinquency. Mainstream research questions might include how leadership skills emerge from sport, how sport socializes boys and girls into certain behavioral templates, how sport affects self-perceptions, how sport affects community morale and behavior within any given community, how sport relates to character, how sport relates to violence, or how sports impact the behavior of children. The sociology of sport, then, is not a simple, narrow field. It deals with a wide range of topics, covering anything that might shed light on how sport functions politically, economically, socially, religiously, educationally, and morally in any given society. It is a huge field with ever-expanding parameters. For a complete discussion on the evolution of the field from the publication of Veblen's text to the present, one might consult John D. Massengale and Richard Swanson's *The History of Exercise and Sport Science*. Chapter four of that text is "Sport Sociology," a complete history of the field before it was considered a field compiled by noted scholar George Sage.

Almost all sociology books, especially introductory texts, deal with all of the previously mentioned topics that define the discipline. Still, it seems as though most texts are especially strong in one area or another. For instance, Timothy Curry's *Sports: A Social Perspective* features a tremendous chapter on the relationship between sport, social class, and mobility. Among other things, Curry concludes that, while sports have no inherent class elements, they are used by the upper class to cement its own social prestige. In addition, despite the occasional exception exemplified by a boxer such as Mike Tyson, who rose from illiteracy and poverty to be a multimillionaire, the only reason sport leads to upward mobility is because it is tied to education. Being a good player means getting a scholarship to college and often a degree that pushes the athlete up the social and economic ladder (Curry 1984, 85). By contrast, Stanley Eitzen and George Sage's *Sociology of North American Sport* has three unique chapters that stand out even in a book of considerable quality. The first is on children and sport and focuses on why kids like sports; when sports are healthy or unhealthy for children; what sports should do for young adults; how sports contribute to the socialization process for boys and girls; and the effect of families, peers, coaches, schools, and the media on children's participation in sport. Not surprisingly, it seems as though the media often has the biggest effect on children's perception of sports. This is a shame since media portrayals of sport tend to focus on playing for fame, money, and power; lavish rewards for outrageous behavior a la Dennis Rodman; and the importance of winning as the ultimate goal of any sporting experience. A second chapter of note is on the reasons behind substance abuse and violence in sport among players and fans, while the final chapter of the book, "Contemporary Trends and the Future of Sport in North America," is fascinating because it analyzes demographic trends and technological innovation to predict how sports will function early in the next century. Among the more significant prognostications is the resurgence of baseball and the ascendency of soccer because of the rising number of Asian and Hispanic Americans who have long-standing relationships with those sports.

John Loy, Gerald Kenyon, and Barry McPherson's *Sport, Culture and Society: A Reader on the Sociology of Sport* is organized in three parts. The first traces the history of sport sociology and attempts to forge a definition of sport that would hold in any culture. Generally, Loy agrees with Conrad Vogler and Stephen Schwartz, who, in *The Sociology of Sport: An Introduction,* contend that sport is structured, has formal rules, allows the participant a separation from the rigors of daily life, requires increased responsibility to teammates, involves competition, operates out of history and tradition, and has pleasure and fun as its main goal. This would be different from athletics, which has a focus on winning for external rewards. Both these authors and Chu seem to see athletics as an advanced or perhaps corrupted form of sport, one based on conquest for social, political, or economic gain. The second section of the Loy text addresses individual concerns that athletes have in different societies. For instance, Walter Kroll's "Multi-Variate Analysis of the Personality Profiles of Championship Czechoslovakian Athletes" shows that sports participants in that country have their personalities shaped by the sports they play and the success or failure they have in those sports. Other essays cover the ways that team dynamics affect individual players, the way institutions affect an athlete's athletic experience, and the reasons behind the development of sport subcultures, which, not surprisingly, center around the fact that the needs of players or spectators are not being met by mainstream athletic organizations. Finally, part three focuses on how factors external to sport impact the way sport is played in any society. Education systems, government, churches, technology, and the media all have a huge impact on an individual's sporting performance. Curiously, the family is not discussed, perhaps indicating its increasingly marginalized position in Western society.

Other useful textbooks include Howard Nixon and James Frey's *A Sociology of Sport;* Barry McPherson, James Curtis, and John Loy's *The Social Significance of Sport: An Introduction to the Sociology of Sport*; and Peter McIntosh's *Sport in Society*. Nixon and Frey's work is noteworthy for its sections on the role of sport in the socialization process for girls and boys and on the role sport plays for those engaged in socially deviant behaviors. Usually, this involves player violence and fan misbehavior of all kinds. McPherson and company have put together a tremendous text. Some of the strongest chapters are as follows: "Sport, Socialization, and the Family," "Sport, Law, and Politics," "Sport and the Economy," and "Sport and the Mass Media," all of which zero in on some of the key issues that impact sport in society. Civil Rights Law, antitrust law, public policy formation at grass-roots levels, gambling, the loss of amateurism in high school and college, and the relationship between the power of television to affect change in sports and the insatiable hunger of people for sport are all covered. Finally, McIntosh's book has an entire section dedicated to the factors that will influence how sport is played in the next century. Not surprisingly, technology, politics, changing demographics, urbanization, the physical fitness movement, and the conflict between amateurism and professionalism should define sport in the years to come. Technology is especially noteworthy. It boggles the mind to think of the effects that gender and genetic selection and cloning could have on sports. Just as the chemical supplement Creatine may have helped McGuire break Roger Maris's record, perhaps techniques in genetic selection will help a child of today hit 200 home runs tomorrow. Technology promises to change sport drastically, but will it be for the better?

Other books that help define what sport sociology is include Susan Greendorfer and Cynthia Hasbrook's *Learning Experiences in the Sociology of Sport*, which contains several exercises on how to do sociological research in any of the areas of sociological inquiry mentioned so far in this chapter; Sage's *Handbook of Social Science of Sport;* and Paul Redekop's *Sociology of Sport: An Annotated Bibliography*. The latter is invaluable for the beginning researcher because it contains hundreds of fairly current resources in the field with complete annotations. Sage's work also has an excellent bibliography in addition to six well-researched chapters on various topics in sport sociology, the best two of which are on cross cultural and cross national analyses of games and the effect of social expectations on the practice of sports in any given society.

Those interested in sociological theory should start with two well-written books that allow even those who are uninitiated in the rigors of theoretical jargon to understand the various paradigms out of which sociologists do much of their research. Wilbert Marcellus Leonard's *A Sociological Perspective of Sport* has the most comprehensive chapters on descriptions and explanations of actual theories. Leonard spends a great deal of time discussing four main theoretical schools that have informed much of contemporary research. The first is evolutionary theory, which, having its roots in Darwinism, suggests that sport is best explained by analyzing how a society or a segment within a society responds to new cultural stimuli. Changes in technology, politics, or in the climate cause people to adjust their ways of life. Their sports will reflect this, and the result will be that the sports that come to the fore will be the ones played by those who have secured power by best adapting to the changes. On the other hand, cyclical theorists, such as historians Oswald Springer and Arnold Toynbee, contend that societies go through measurable patterns as they rise and fall. The nature of sports will be determined by where a society is in this progression. Conflict theory, rooted in Marxist ideology, is the idea that various parts of any society are in constant conflict with most of the other parts of that society. Social arrangements are derived by the constant exploitation of one group by another. Thus the National Football League might be explained as the natural result of a capitalist society in which the many workers and fans who pay for the lavish lifestyles of the few players in the league are exploited by wealthy team owners who, by controlling the capital, continually work to perpetuate the league's dominance through control of the media, thereby securing their power and the servile status of the masses. Finally, there is functionalist theory, perhaps the most popular school of thought among current researchers. This idea is that most societies want to maintain a certain level of comfort and for that to happen most of its major groups must remain relatively satisfied. When any significant group becomes dissatisfied, it launches some type of campaign to throw the society into tumult. To reestablish the balance, the society must accommodate this group to some degree. In doing so, the society changes a little bit. For instance, the civil rights movement of the 1960s changed America, which had to meet demands of African Americans and women if it was to maintain its balance. This changed sports dramatically as black players began to integrate and then dominate many professional and college sports, and Title IX legislation forced schools to give female athletes previously unheard of opportunities. Leonard's discussion of these theories is quite clear, but he does not stop there. He also introduces the reader to theories that explain fan loyalty, fan and player violence, and group behavior.

Once one has finished the Leonard text, it is advisable to move on to *Sport and Social Theory*, edited by Roger Rees and Andrew Miracle. The book contains no less than twenty-one chapters that, for the most part, are theoretical analyses by various sociologists. These essays, then, are examples of how to apply the various theories described by Leonard. For example, in "Small Groups and Sport: A Symbolic Interactionist Perspective," Gary Fine uses one type of functionalist theory to explain why members of teams behave the way they do in certain situations. In "Athletes and Higher Education: A Conflict Perspective," Stanley Eitzen uses elements of several conflict theories to show how the various forces that run college sports, including administrators, alumni, faculty, fans, media, parents, and players, keep the current system in place with little change despite much needed reform. A helpful feature of this book is that several of the essays are followed by a rebuttal, which offers reasons why the theory in question fails to fully explain the sporting practice and offers an alternative theoretical reading. Other important chapters include Gerald Kenyon's "The Significance of Social Theory in the Development of Sport Sociology," in which the author traces the rise and fall of theoretical approaches that have dominated the field, and Gunther Luschen's "The Practical Uses of Sociology of Sport: Some Methodologies," in which the author gives some practical advice for budding scholars who are just starting to put their theories to the test. His warning to keep one's research practical and effective and one's language comprehensible is laudable and should be heeded by academicians everywhere.

Two other notable books on theories that guide the discipline are Grant Jarvie and Joseph Maguire's *Sport and Leisure in Social Thought* and Eldon Snyder and Elmer Spreitzer's *Social Aspects of Sport*. The latter discusses functionalist and conflict theories but also does a nice job explaining exchange theory, the idea that sport can only be explained as a give-and-take relationship, which both demands certain sacrifices of participants and grants some significant rewards to them, and symbolist interaction theory, where sport is viewed as something used by players to symbolize some part of their identity. Jarvie and McGuire have penned a more traditional theory book in which they explain the main suppositions of theories of cultural pluralism, classical Marxism, feminism, modernism, postmodernism, and dependancy theory. The authors then show how each of these contributes to our understanding of sport and its complex functions in regard to gender, race, class, economics, politics, religion, and philosophy.

## SPORT AND SOCIAL VALUES

The point of theory, of course, is to provide ways of understanding what sport means in any given culture. One thing that most scholars agree on is that we can study sport to understand the fundamental values of a society. After all, most people work because they have to work. Sport, however, is what we choose to do, and as our preferred activity, we put much of what we hold dear into our games. Robert Simon sees sport as an essentially noble activity, one in which we find the best of humanity. In the sports arena we display out best side and often work to resolve key ethical issues facing our community. In *Fair Play: Sports, Values and Society*, Simon writes that "sports properly conducted provide values of enduring human significance. Through sport we can learn to overcome adversity and appreciate excellence. Through sports we can develop and express moral virtues and vices and demonstrate the importance of such values as dedication, integrity, fairness, and courage" (Simon 1991, 200). In their *Social Aspects of Sport*, Snyder and Spreitzer agree with Simon that sport is indeed a great place to study cultural values but are not as positive as Simon is about what one might find when examining sporting practice. Through Simon's rose-colored lenses, one gets the idea that sport is the best thing we have to offer our children as a moral training ground, but Snyder and Spreitzer are much more cautious. While they admit that sport has great potential as a forum for character development, they acknowledge that it often works the other way as well, acting as a repository for all manner of antisocial and deviant behavior. For these two authors, the main point is that sport is a mirror of social values. It is not as effective as Simon would have us believe and should only be studied because it is a reflection of larger behavioral trends.

Most scholars have combined these ideas when trying to determine the functions of sport in society. That is, they believe that sport does reflect dominant themes in any culture, but that sport is not a mere reflective pool. It is affective and capable of producing great changes in social values. For instance, Norbert Elias and Eric Dunning contend in *Quest for Excitement: Sport and Leisure in the Civilizing Process* that sport primarily has two functions. One is as a safety valve for pent up aggression. The other is as a way to relieve boredom. Both suppositions are rooted in what philosophers such as Richard Rorty call the postmodern condition. The idea is that contemporary existence is, for most people, devoid of meaning. It is workaday, full of trivial activity that has no ultimate meaning. In the absence of transcendent truth, people look to sport to provide excitement to their lives. A man may have a dead-end job, endless bills, and belong to a church that espouses doctrine in which, in his heart of hearts, he does not really believe, but he can always look forward to the tailgating, the bands, the cool air, and victory for his alma mater on college football Saturday afternoons. Likewise, the violence on the gridiron and his boisterous rooting in the stands can help him blow off some steam, taking out his frustrations of daily living by joining fellow alums in chants and taunts that rub it in the face of the other team. Elias and Dunning see this as a decent alternative to walking into a post office with an m-16.

Conversely, Bero Rigauer in *Sport and Work* views sport as just another form of work. We work at sport in order to get rewards. No matter how old you are, no matter what country you are from, the work for rewards system stays constant. Rigauer feels that we do not really want it to be this way, but economic and political factors force us to take part in this repressive athletic system. "Quite apart from the considerations of class or social status, the ability to achieve can become a constituent element of individual social status. Differing economic and material preconditions are not the point. Simultaneously, a system of behavior which is based on achievement coerces its members into conformity to the existing framework of social behavior" (Rigauer 1981, 77). Whether one is competing for the United States with its systems of democracy and capitalism or for a communist or socialist country, one must win in order to achieve social status, political privilege, and economic opportunity. Even little children fall into this category. Some gain status in school and even full scholarships to colleges for their athletic feats, while others are ostracized for their inability to compete. The point is that all athletes are commodities whose sports participation must exist within larger systems that determine the worth of their sporting experiences.

Still, while this seems true in part, this theory certainly leaves a great deal unexplained. For instance, is a forty-year-old man skiing for fun really working to improve his position politically? Are a group of girls playing pick-up basketball really carving out some deeply important social hierarchy? Probably not. Jay Coakley, for example, believes that many sporting experiences are exercises in work, but not for the purpose of improving one's position within societal frameworks. In *Sport in Society: Issues and Controversies*, he asserts that sport can also be an effective site for reform, a place where, because of its status as a special, almost ideal oasis in the desert, problems that plague society are not tolerated. For instance, racism is a huge problem in America, and there has been significant action to fight racism over the last half century. But nowhere has the progress been as great as in sport. Minority players dominate and are often revered by all Americans, and when some racist action is perpetrated in the sports world, quick and decisive action is taken. Often this corrective action leads to calls for an end to racism throughout society. Remember when Al Campanis, an administrator for the Los Angeles Dodgers, said that there were so few blacks in management positions because they lacked the mental necessities to do the job? He was fired the next day and programs went into place to boost minority hiring. The next year, more minorities were hired in baseball than ever before, and several other nonsport companies looked to Major League Baseball as a model of how to diversify their workforces. According to Coakley, this reform potential is perhaps the best quality of sport, and it results from the expectation of people that sport be pure and free from so many of the problems that infect our world.

Taking the opposite viewpoint, Richard Gruneau's argument in *Class, Sport, and Social Development* is no less effective. He contends that, far from being a place where the seeds of social reform are nurtured, sport is a place where deviant behavior is not only tolerated but expected. It is a place where players and fans can safely engage in taboo acts that would never be tolerated in polite society. Football players, for instance, can hit each other as hard as they can with their bodies, helmets, or pads. Hockey players routinely smash each other with sticks and fighting remains an attraction for fans. Swearing is considered manly, threats are part of the game, intimidation is a must, and showing off to the point of narcissistic self-absorption is par for the course. In the stands, fans scream obscenities, make nasty gestures, drink too much, and exhibit antisocial behaviors that would be grounds for dismissal at any workplace in the country. Gruneau writes that "profane play is one of the few ways in which any one human agent can challenge the forces of repression" (Gruneau 1983, 150). Of course, this profane play is not necessarily noble. In fact, it often features human nastiness in the form of racist, sexist, or otherwise obnoxious acts that are not tolerated in the civilized world of rules. For example, treating a female coworker as a sex object would not be permissible, but ogling the cheerleaders at the football game is expected.

Clearly, sport has a broad array of functions in society, and no two sport sociologists agree on just what sport means in any given culture. Two fine books show the contrast nicely. In *Play, Games and Sports in Cultural Contexts*, Janet Harris and Roberta Park argue that sport is meaningful for several reasons. First, sport reinforces the importance of revered rituals and traditions by consistently reenacting them. The coin toss before a football game or the meeting of umpires at home plate to explain the ground rules before a baseball game emphasizes our love of fair play and justice. The constant deferment to the officials by players shows our love for rules and order. Secondly, sport is a great place for enculturation, a place to show young people how to behave in society, what is valued, and what kinds of behaviors are rewarded or punished. Finally, sport is also a prime area for acculturation, a safe place in which members of one culture can learn to respect the ways of other cultures. All of this presumes the idea that there is a purpose to living, that life means something, and that sport can help a person figure out what he or she should do in life. By contrast, John Gibson's *Performance Versus Results: A Critique of Values in Contemporary Sport*, is written from the view of a postmodernist who believes that life is essentially meaningless and that the best we can do is cope with our abysmal condition by immersing ourselves in pleasant and momentary illusions. Sport is one of the most pleasant illusions, a very subjective world in which one can yell, scream, cheer, or play in a self-imposed vacuum. As long as a season or league or game continues, the illusion that there is something to be gained, be it a trophy, a championship, or the simple satisfaction of winning, is maintained. As soon as the experience is over, one is again immersed in the meaninglessness of existence. Thus, you have the phenomena of the four-season sport fan, who drifts from baseball to football to basketball to hockey, following the exploits of favored teams as one temporal world blends into another. It is scary when one thinks of how many people live this way in America, primarily because of the underlying unbelief that informs the entire process. Imagine living in a world where the majority of people really do not believe anything and are forced to placate themselves with sports and other social constructions intended to give temporary relief from an existential world.

## SPORT IN AMERICA

Naturally, there is considerable debate about what sport means to Americans. One thing that all scholars agree on is that sport is an American obsession. In *America's Obsession: Sports and Society since 1945*, Richard Davies makes it clear that television, increased leisure time, and an ever-expanding economy have led to the pre-eminence of sport on the American social landscape. National holidays seem to revolve around sports. Universities are known for their athletic prowess more than their academic successes. Nearly everyone plays something and, more than anything else, to be American means to be an athlete. Davies explores how this obsession has developed since World War II. Two other books are good sociological studies that speak to this obsession. One is Charles Euchner's *Playing the Field: Why Sports Teams Move and Cities Fight to Keep Them*. Euchner profiles Los Angeles, Baltimore, and Chicago, analyzing why these cities either did or did not spend hundreds of millions of dollars to build new stadiums for their teams. He concludes that sport is so important in America that for a city to lose one of its teams is to be disgraced, to become a second-class city with no soul. Thus, cities dig huge financial holes for themselves by overspending on the new palatial ball parks of the 1990s. The other work is a dissertation by Michael Kelsey entitled

*The Cultural Geography of Sports Halls of Fame.* Kelsey discusses why certain halls were erected at certain locations, and his study bears witness to our obsession with sport because we have erected impressive shrines to our athletic past lest we forget our traditions as memories fade.

There seems to be little doubt about the centrality of sport to the American experience. But what exactly does sport do for us? According to several of the essays and poems in Peter Stine's *Sports in America*, sport has the unique function of reminding Americans of their heritage. In particular, it reminds us of the frontier spirit that we like to associate with being American. In the face of increasing comfort, sports speak to the values of hard work and sacrifice. In an age of soft words and careful actions designed not to compromise one's place on the corporate ladder, sports feature bravado, confidence, and individual achievement. It harks back to a time when men were men in the most mythical sense of the word. A segment from a poem by Keith Taylor, entitled "Hockey: An Apology" captures this spirit:

Gentle people in warmer places see the fights and inflated salaries. They will not believe the stories about fights my grandfather witnessed in Edmonton generations before anyone out there could afford to go pro. There and then fights lasted an hour, stained the ice red. The audience stayed quiet in the stands, grimacing as if in church. Police carted the players off and penned them up until they all cooled down. Farm kids, I'd like to say, from cold places. They all became good fathers and never beat anyone. (Stine 1995, 93)

Though this is a Canadian reference, its sentiment meshes very well with American myth. Its message that sport is a place where we keep alive the old ways, which were better than revisionist historians would have us believe, is one that strikes a chord in American hearts.

Both Howard Nixon and A. Bartlett Giamatti, the former commissioner of baseball and president of Yale University, believe that sport is important to Americans because it represents our attempt to forge something ideal in the midst of a chaotic and often unpleasant world. Nixon contends in *Sport and the American Dream* that this world is one which we desperately want to keep pure, purging it of greed, corruption, and every form of loathsome behavior that we detest so much in our daily lives. However, he is realistic, and much of his book is dedicated to explaining why sport has ceased to be a comfort for many Americans, who used to look at games such as baseball as being the best of what we had to offer in American culture. He warns us to be especially aware of greed, pride, and excessive consumerism, all of which he views as perversions of what can be a place of tranquility and nobility. Giamatti's *Take Time for Paradise: Americans and Their Games* echoes these warnings. Still, the author spends most of his short treatise explaining one of the main reasons why Americans love sport. Sport allows us to play out the essential feature of American democracy, the conflict between individual rights and community need. Our country has prospered because we have created and nurtured a way of living that allows for ample individual freedom and self-development within an overall structure that calls for each of us, through taxes, military service, and a hundred other activities, to behave in ways that help keep the state healthy and powerful. Our games are characterized by exercises in balance between being an individual player who wants to showcase her own abilities and being a player who is part of the team. The beauty of sport, like the beauty of America, is that for the team to do well all of its parts must prosper. It is a wondrous reciprocity that defines us as Americans and that is the defining characteristic of our sports. Richard Lipsky's *How We Play the Game: Why Sports Dominate American Life* is not quite as eloquently crafted as Giamatti's work, but the sentiments are largely the same. Lipsky, a fine writer in his own right, contends that we love sports because they allow us to celebrate the defining ideas of American life. These include democratic structures with room for authoritarianism when it is needed, fairness in the context of chance, individual worth alongside the importance of community, logic coupled with emotion, and predictability coupled with the unexpected. Sport is never one thing; it is, instead, all things American at the same time.

Taking a different path, more along the avenue of a cultural studies approach, some scholars argue that sport must be understood in terms of its relationship to gender, race, class, and age. In *Sport and Play in American Life: A Textbook in the Sociology of Sport*, for example, Stephen Figler and Gail Whitaker explore, among other things, how the use of sport changes with age for the average American. When one is a child or an adolescent, sport is primarily used as a means of socialization. In college, sport can be a means of socialization, fitness, or business, particularly if one is on scholarship. Adult sport usually concerns fitness, pure recreation, or business ventures, while sport for the senior citizen is often about the prevention of muscular deterioration. By contrast, Donald Mrozek's *Sport and American Mentality, 1880–1910* focuses on sport as inexorably tied not only to economic development and concerns over public health, but also to gender anxiety. Particularly, much of sport can be explained as men's attempts to establish themselves as real men and to maintain traditional gender norms and spheres. Certainly, this can be seen today in sports such as football and in the rising conflict between men and women's sports on college campuses. Then there is Sage's *Power and Ideology in American Sport: A Critical Perspective*, in which the author takes a Marxist approach to American sport, contending that more than anything else sport is a center for class conflict. Our games consist of rich people and other folks with economic or political leverage maintaining athletic systems that will allow them to get more power or at least to keep what they have got. The masses fund the system in hopes that they might break through into the ranks of the elite one day or because they can gain recognition even if it is only vicariously through the victories of their chosen team.

William Baker's *Sports in Modern America* and Steven Riess's *City Games: The Evolution of American Urban Society and the Rise of Sports* are two quality works that provide competing explanations of why Americans love sport. Riess believes that sport is essentially a by-product of urbanization and thus is really a celebration of the excitement of the city. Both sports and cities celebrate fast-paced life and excitement. Teams represent cities, and people love going to a game in part because it means experiencing the flavor of the city. On the other hand, essayist

Bill Broeg argues in Baker's book that people like sport because it allows them to separate themselves from the concerns of daily life. In an essay entitled "The Impact of Sports on Americans," Broeg writes that "whether saddled with an unpleasant or monotonous job, confined by a barely tolerable marriage or the pangs of four-wall loneliness, or weighted down by ill health, financial worries, or family problems, too many people need relief" (Baker 1981, 1). Of course, both views can be true. People do love the excitement of dining at the Inner Harbor in Baltimore and then ambling over to Camden yards for an Orioles game. Americans like to be in the center of the action. Of course, when they have had enough of the center, they like to head for the margins, and where better to do that than in front of the tube watching golf, tennis, or baseball while lounging on the couch far away from the deafening roar of the city.

Noted sports researcher Richard Lapchick, who has crusaded for reform in college athletics for years, views sport as a place where American reform initiatives originate and often come to fruition. In both *Fractured Focus: Sport as a Reflection of Society* and *Sport in Society: Equal Opportunity or Business as Usual?* Lapchick shows how racism, sexism, academic fraud, lack of diversity, gambling, and drugs have infected sports just as they have polluted society at large. However, it also becomes clear that the appearance of these ugly things in the supposedly pristine world of athletics, especially college athletics which we still want to believe is more innocent than the world of professional sports, is often the cause of small reformation movements. Lapchick and several top researchers in the field discuss how these reforms have worked in both college and professional sport and debate how far we still have to go as a nation to fully correct the problems. William Dudley's *Sports in America: Opposing Viewpoints* features essays in which top scholars debate what sport practitioners can do to help curb some of America's most serious problems. Reforming college sports so that they serve the interests of all students and not just scholarship athletes, funding children's sports that teach the benefits of cooperation instead of competition, using sports as a platform to fight racism and sexism, and using professional sports as a stage on which to model noble instead of ignoble behavior are the key topics upon which these thinkers expound.

Finally, Randy Roberts and James Olson's *Winning Is the Only Thing: Sports in America since 1945* and Allen Guttmann's *A Whole New Ball Game: An Interpretation of American Sports* capitalize on the postmodern spirit of the age. Roberts and Olson contend that in the absence of any true religious belief, Americans have adopted sport as their unofficial secular religion. One might not be able to go to heaven, but one can surely attain victory, a type of momentary salvation that rescues one from the sea of meaningless action that defines daily living. Naturally, the power of a victory wears off, so one must continually seek spiritual uplift through sports participation, be it as a player or as a spectator. The writers point out that rituals such as tailgate parties have come to define American existence; they are sacred rituals that make life worth living. Guttmann essentially agrees with this. He suggests that most of the problems that plague society will continue to plague sport. So, the only alternative is to accept it and get out of sport what you can. After all, he contends, anything that can make one happy and better one's life for a while is good. The two works are well written and well reasoned, but their best quality is that they make the reader question fundamental values. Do you believe in truth, in God, in heaven? Is there a point to life? In the end, one's view of sport is closely tied to how one answers these questions. Writers such as Guttmann and Roberts and Olson make one think.

Those interested in what particular games mean to Americans might start with J. Bowyer Bell's *To Play the Game: An Analysis of Sports*. Bell says that games fall into four categories. The first is primitive games, loosely defined as those which are often limited to a single, spontaneous act, are not recorded, and do not result in rewards. Aside from the most simple children's games, little of this type of activity remains today. The second category involves tribal games. These are more structured contests designed to prepare men for war or hunting season or some other task important for tribal survival. The third category includes communal games, organized contests that link one community with another. A good example would be the old-time baseball games held between competing towns on special holidays in the nineteenth century. Still, records are not kept and the players are not trained professionals as they are in polistic games, those that are played for some tangible reward, usually money, in front of large audiences. Finally, for the truly advanced and powerful society, there are imperial games, those that embody the highest virtues and values of a country and that are used by that country to inculcate those values in people from other countries. Bowyer does not specifically attempt to describe where the United States is on this four-step scale, but it seems obvious that we continue to dabble in all four areas. Little children often play primitive games such as paddle ball or skimming rocks. We do not move in tribes, but we certainly view sport as being a way to prepare our kids for future challenges. High school football, especially in the South, is a good example of communal sport. Most major college and professional sport is decidedly polistic, and like many countries, we have been known to use sport, especially Olympic sport, to advance political, economic, and social agendas.

But what about specific sports? Wiley Umphlett's *American Sport Culture: The Humanistic Dimensions* contains a number of essays that comment on why our games touch so many Americans so deeply. Perhaps the best of the essays is by noted theologian Michael Novak, who argues in "American Sports, American Virtues" that baseball, basketball, and football all have a unique relationship with Americans of all ages. Novak contends that baseball represents an agrarian ideal of pastoral simplicity that is still very much with us and that the game's deliberate nature, balanced symmetry, and insistence on fair play and individual worth appeals to American democratic ideals. By contrast, he sees football as reflecting the capitalist spirit of the United States. It is a game of micromanagement, corporate structure, and specialized labor, a game that strongly resembles the corporate jungle where one either conquers or is conquered, and where one's fate is often bound up with the fortunes of one or more individuals over whose actions one has little control. Basketball, according to Novak, is a game that speaks equally to rural and urban America. Rural basketball is much like football with its emphasis on team play and systems of defense, while the urban game is individual, improvisational, and unstructured. It is a game dominated by African Americans and is reflective of a black style that departs from the traditional "white game," which is highly structured and controlled. The "black game" is rhythmic and refuses to be constrained by predefined patterns; it is a political act as much as it is an athletic act (Umphlett 1985, 44–48). Of course, Novak's argument goes much deeper than this, and several other essays in the book are quite valuable for understanding why we have placed such value on certain sports.

Those specifically interested in basketball should look at Lars Anderson and Chad Millman's *Pickup Artists: Street Basketball in America* and Bill Bradley's *Values of the Game*. The two books stand in contrast to each other but are so incisive and aesthetically pleasing that they seem to offer two halves of a complete vision of what the sport means in America today. Bradley, a Princeton graduate and long-time senator from New Jersey, waxes poetic on the best that basketball has to offer the young man or woman who wants to be more than a player of games. His book speaks of discipline, sacrifice, selflessness, respect, passion, resilience, and courage, all of which become part of the true player's personality. These are the things that make for good caretakers of democracy, according to the former all-American. The best thing about the book is that Bradley takes these workaday notions and makes them come alive by weaving in anecdotes from his past in a modest, touching, and sometimes amusing tone. He speaks eloquently about basketball in its ideal form, and he reminds us that even in an age of scepticism we should never stop hoping to construct games that build character. Bradley's book pairs nicely with Anderson's work, a set of earthy tales about what basketball means to urban kids, especially the ones who never make it big but whose dedication to the game never dies. Anderson shows what the sport means to people with otherwise gloomy lives, and his unique focus allows him to get beyond sport as a business or as an arena for building character. *Pickup Artists* is a book for scholars who want to know what shooting hoops all day does for a person with no job and no prospects, who want to know what being a "street artist" means to a man with no chance of ever being a professional athlete.

Other works of a similar ilk include Donald Calhoun's *Sport, Culture, and Personality,* Robert Pankin's *Social Approaches to Sport,* Don Harkness's *Sports in American Culture*, and Mark D. Howell's *From Moonshine to Madison Avenue: A Cultural History of the NASCAR Winston Cup Series.* Calhoun's book offers the most depth. He offers discussions on baseball, basketball, football, soccer, hockey, tennis, and golf, and he sees each sport as representing an important characteristic of the American people. Baseball, for example, stands for individuality, while football shows our love for intimidation, and basketball is about our need for trickery and deception. Harkness's volume contains an essay entitled "Soccer in America: An Old Sport Emerges with New Life," in which Lynn Berling-Manuel argues that while soccer is not doing well as a spectator sport, it is the perfect participant sport for the United States. She contends that the game's emphasis on conditioning and safety, the fact that boys and girls can play together, and the fact that most kids have the physical skills to play effectively until they reach more competitive leagues in high school, combine to make soccer the ideal sport for kids. With the numbers of youth soccer leagues soaring, all indications are that Berling-Manuel is right, or at least on the right track. Considering the fact that it is much less expensive to play than some of the other sports, particularly football, perhaps soccer is the perfect sport for the next century. Pankin's book is a collection of essays that tackle sport from a cultural studies perspective. Each of the essayists looks at how American sports reflect prevailing views on race, gender, class, religion, and other cultural variables that are part and parcel of human existence. As the title would indicate, Howell's work is a general history of NASCAR, the most powerful auto racing organization, in which he explores reasons behind the sport's rise in popularity over the last twenty years. Individualism, hard work, and self-reliance are familiar themes, but his discussion on our fascination with speed and danger, and our need to master technology are insightful and help one understand why auto racing may be the definitive sport of the next century.

## HEROES AND FANS

Whatever sports dominate the twenty-first century, their popularity will likely be driven by the athletic feats and appealing personalities of sports heroes. How one defines a hero depends on many variables, not the least of which are the prevailing norms in any given culture. Still, in *The Social Psychology of Sport*, Gordon Russell lists five classifications of heroes that correspond to basic human values. The first is the Winner, who appeals to us because he gets what he wants and is the best, which is what we want to be. The second is the Splendid Performer, who commands the attention of an audience and appeals to our love of being able to be the center of attention in a way that makes us look beautiful and powerful. The third type is the Hero of Social Acceptability, the girl we admire because she is well liked and has many friends. The Independent Spirit is loved for his ability to stand alone, to forge his way to success independently and often by force of his supreme self-will. Finally, there is the Group Servant, the hero who earns respect for her ability to self-sacrificially help others and promote better conditions for those in her community (Russell 1993, 127). These heroes appeal, then, to our most basic desires. According to Russell, they fulfill three main functions in any society. The first is as a symbol that something ideal can exist and that therefore society can get better. The second is that heroes remind us that valued traits that seem lost in modern society are not dead but can still be very much a part of our world. Ideals such as bravery, servanthood, selflessness, and modesty can exist, and heroes remind us of this. Finally, heroes allow people who might not otherwise interact to forge relationships based on the admiration of the positive traits that they see embodied by the hero. Ideally, this would lead to better people and a more humane society.

Two other scholars have attempted to define the qualities of a sports hero. One is Peter Williams, who, in *The Sports Immortals: Deifying the American Athlete*, argues that most American heroes can be explained by understanding two heroic models. One is the Appolonian model and the other is the Dionysian model. The former is defined as an orderly, reasoned being, who is brave, gentle, strong, stable, and balanced. He is known for consistency, for keeping a level head, and for being a good team player who gladly sacrifices personal goals for the good of the unit. Walter Payton, Don Mattingly, or Joe Dumars come to mind as examples of this type of hero. By contrast, the Dionysian hero is unpredictable, decidedly volatile, and given to extreme highs and lows. He is the wild man, whose antics often endanger his health, but whose dark nature has a strange appeal for many Americans. Dennis Rodman would certainly fall into this category. While there is merit to Williams's argument, one must also pay heed to Dwight Hoover and John Koumoulides who, in *Conspectus of History: Sports and Society*, explain how for most ethnic Americans a hero is someone who represents the larger possibility of transcendence. Men such as Karl Malone, Emmitt Smith, or Alex Rodriguez, who rose to prominence from modest beginnings and attained both material riches and societal respect are seen as beacons in the darkness by young people who believe that they, too, might climb to the top of the ranks some day. Certainly, many young girls feel the same way about Mia Hamm, Bonnie Blair, or Cammie Granato.

Janet Harris disagrees with Hoover, Koumoulides, Williams, and Russell in *Athletes and the American Hero Dilemma*, in which she questions whether it is really possible for heroes to exist in the modern world. Though she concedes that it is still possible, she believes there are several factors that make it very difficult for heroes to exist in the same way they have existed in the past. After all, increased media exposure has made it difficult for athletes to hide their human flaws. When Wade Boggs has an affair or when Dwight Gooden has a drug problem, we know about it. In addition, the amount of money and fame enjoyed by athletes today often alienates some fans, as does the fact that athletes often show no loyalty to their fans. Instead of staying with one team, they will move from place to place depending on which team offers them the most money. Of course, the fact that American leaders such as Bill Clinton have routinely been exposed as being people of low character has created a sense of distrust and even disillusionment on the part of many Americans, whose increased skepticism has made it difficult for the would-be hero. Harris also advances interesting arguments about the effects of technology and political changes on the sports hero. Overall, her book is quite provocative, raising all of the right questions and leaving one to ask oneself what one believes about heroes in modern America.

Two books whose authors believe that it is still possible for heroes to exist are *Small Town Heroes: Images of Minor League Baseball* and *A Farewell to Heroes*, both of which are quite moving in their depictions of what it means to be a hero in the sports world. The former, written by Hank Davis, is a series of character sketches of various personages that make up life in minor league baseball parks and towns. Washed-up big leaguers, hopeful young bucks, female general managers, struggling umpires, loyal fans, bus drivers, and a host of colorful characters are profiled as Davis shows us that heroism is not found in the superhuman athlete, but in the very human person who loves the game of baseball and gives something to it. Whether he is in Ohio, Pennsylvania, Tennessee, Virginia, North Carolina, or Iowa, Davis shows us regular folks who, though they struggle with real problems, behave nobly and with a good heart. *A Farewell to Heroes* is written by Frank Graham, a long-time sports writer, who allows the reader to walk along with him for 300 pages as he reminisces about what his heroes, mostly baseball players from the 1920s and 1930s, meant to him. His good-bye is touching, and his sentiments will no doubt resonate with all but the most jaded fans, reminding us that there is indeed still room for heroes, even under the glare of modern lights.

In *The Social Psychology of Sport*, Russell writes that fans have many reasons for following sports, but most sporting events cater to specific types of spectators. For example, golf attracts a more sophisticated audience than does professional wrestling. Many people attend college football games to tailgate, party, enjoy the spectacle, and see old friends, while most high school football fans are either related to one of the players or are long-time residents of one of the towns involved in the game. However, though Russell believes that fans have several motivations for going to games, he does argue that most fans are linked by their need for catharsis. He contends that most fans are hoping not just to blow off some steam, but to actually have an emotional experience that, if it is not life changing, is at least one that provides the fan with significant psychological leverage to get through another week. Russell is supported here by Lawrence Wenner's "The Audience Experience with Sports on Television," which is located in a book entitled *Media, Sports and Society*, edited by Wenner. He confirms that, above all things, the viewer of televised sport is afforded a more comfortable place from which to engage the event, which becomes an occasion for socialization, relaxation, and, most of all, some type of emotional expenditure (Wenner 1989, 244).

In *Sports, Games, and Play: Social and Psychological Viewpoints*, edited by Jeffrey Goldstein, Thomas Tutko asserts that what sports fans really want is to be a part of all of the positive characteristics that are associated with winning teams. These include ambition, determination, dedication, assertiveness, leadership, respect, grace under pressure, mental toughness, cooperation, and confidence. The main thing, of course, is that fans feel like winners if their team wins. It is not necessarily rational thinking, but it is a powerful attraction for many fans. As Tutko explains, "The paradox of the situation is the common feeling that if we win we are ambitious, determined, dedicated, assertive, and so forth, and this will assure us of success in other aspects of life" (Goldstein 1989, 119).

By contrast, several writers believe that sports fans are not really after vicarious identities as winners. Instead, Janet Podell contends in *Sports in America*, that most fans attend games because several societal taboos are condoned within the context of sports. After all, one can yell obnoxiously at other fans, umpires, and players without anyone batting an eye at such behavior. Hooting at women, drinking excessively, and engaging in all sorts of behaviors that are usually deemed antisocial are condoned at sporting venues. Podell discusses these behaviors but focuses mostly on violence as the chief taboo that is encouraged by the frenzied atmosphere of a major sporting event. Gary Armstrong's *Football Hooligans: Knowing the Score* and John Loy, Gerald Kenyon, and Barry McPherson's *Sport, Culture and Society: A Reader on the Sociology of Sport* both focus on the relationship between sports, fans, and violence. Armstrong analyzes why soccer violence is so common in Europe, while Loy and Kenyon's work contains several essays that provide divergent explanations of why sports fans behave the way they do at various sports in the United States. These explanations not only include a fascination with violence, but also a love for domination and submission, and especially a love for putting ourselves in a position to judge the actions of others. Of course, that is what sports fans do above all else, casting stern judgments on every play, pitch, or shot.

In Simon During's *The Cultural Studies Reader*, Pierre Bourdeau laments, in "How Can One Be a Sports Fan," that there is little rational reason for any adult to attach loyalties to any team or individual. He argues that the connection between fan and team is largely illusory and usually results only in frustration for the fan. Certainly, he has a point. After all, the connection between fan and team only exists because the fan wants it to exist. Even the graduate of a particular college rooting for his or her alma mater is pulling for a team that often has little to do with his or her life. Bourdeau also emphasizes that fans are often associated with bad behavior. Of course, several entertaining books feature authors who, as sports fans, try to answer Bourdeau's argument. In *After All, It's Only a Game*, Willie Morris describes the love he had for sports growing up in Mississippi. Morris features both fiction and nonfiction writing as he describes the importance sports has played in his life as both a sports participant and fan. Steve McKee traveled the country for one year to write *The Call of the Game*, a journal in which he reflects on the joy of being a fan. McKee's journey will no doubt inspire any true fan to hit the road for a game or two. Meanwhile, Mike Lupica's *Mad as Hell: How Sport Got Away from the Fans and How We Can Get It Back* and John Underwood's *Spoiled Sport: A Fan's Notes on the Troubles of Spectator Sports* both chronicle the frustrations that fans have had with sports in the 1990s. These include rising ticket prices, teams that leave town, labor stoppages that interrupt seasons, spoiled players, and rich owners that continually demand that fans sacrifice financially while they get richer. Still, the love that these men have for sports is what drives the books, and both make it clear that sports fans are a noble breed that deserve better than what they are currently getting from the American sports establishment.

## OTHER RESOURCES

Three other books of interest include Alan Ingham and John Loy's *Sport in Social Development: Tradition, Transitions and Transformations*, Robert Griffin's *Sports in the Lives of Children and Adolescents: Success on the Field and in Life*, and Sarah Flowers's *Sports in America*. The first is an intriguing compilation of essays that analyze the roles sports have played and continue to play in the social development of countries around the world. The book is a good one for understanding how sports subcultures develop. These include small pockets of fans or players that use sport as a means of resisting some form of perceived oppression. The wearing of black armbands by African-American athletes in the 1968 Olympics as a way of protesting racial inequality is a good example. The latter two books deal with the effect of sports on the social development of children. Flowers's work is intended for a younger audience, while Griffin's work is a fine piece of scholarship that furthers our understanding of how pivotal sport can be to the success or failures of children on the social front.

Those interested in current articles on the sociology of sport or sport as it relates to social issues might consult any of the following journals: *American Journal of Economics and Sociology, American Sociologist, American Sociology Review, Contemporary Sport, International Journal of Sociology, International Review of Social History, Journal of American Culture, Journal of Popular Culture, Journal of Social Issues, Journal of Socio-Economics, Journal of Sociology and Social Welfare, Ritual Studies,* and *Sociology of Sport Journal.*

As we enter the new century, it seems likely that sport sociologists will continue to focus on the relationship between children and their sports. After all, it is in the lives of children that so many of our most pressing issues forcefully resonate. How will sport impact the way children perform in school or in social situations? What is the role of hero worship in the lives of young people today? How can we use sport to foster values in young boys and girls around the world that might lead to a reduction in ethnic violence, religious intolerance, and discrimination of all kinds that has plagued every country in the world throughout history.

Sociologists will certainly be hot on the trail of answers to these questions, but they will also continue to investigate other controversial topics such as how sport impacts and is impacted by the larger economic, political, religious, and social systems in which it is played, and how new advances in technology will impact the way we play. Of course, scholars will continue to follow the increasingly tenuous relationship between fans and their teams, perhaps focusing on how wealthy professional teams operating within an exploitive system will continue to attract the good favor of financially pressed fans and communities and on how the growing economic gap between the haves and the have nots will affect sporting practice in the United States and around the world. Finally, sports sociologists will be intensely interested in how larger social trends impact athletics. How will changing gender roles and definitions impact sports spectatorship? How will economic distance between classes affect athletic participation? How can an increasingly multicultural society use sport as a way to pave the road toward racial and ethnic appreciation? Will sport be an arena in which we effectively cope with cultural change or will it serve as a mirror that reflects a society being ripped apart by its inability to deal with demographic evolution? One thing is for certain: The obsession that the world has with sport ensures that it will be one of the prime areas in which sociologists examine how world cultures, so long separated by geographic distance, begin the slow process of getting to know each other within a close global community.

## REFERENCES

### Books

Allison, Mona T. *Play, Leisure, and Quality of Life: Social Scientific Perspectives.* Dubuque, IA: Kendall-Hunt 1992.

Anderson, Lars, and Chad Millman. *Pickup Artists: Street Basketball in America*. New York: Verso Press, 1998.

Armstrong, Gary. *Football Hooligans: Knowing the Score*. New York: Berg Publications, 1998.

Baker, William J., ed. *Sports in Modern America*. St. Louis, MO: River City Publishing, 1981.

Bell, J. Bowyer. *To Play the Game: An Analysis of Sports*. New Brunswick, NJ: Transaction Books, 1987.

Benedict, Jeff, and Don Yeager. *Pros and Cons: The Criminals Who Play in the NFL*. New York: Warner Books, 1998.

Bradley, Bill. *Values of the Game*. New York: Artisan Press, 1998.

Calhoun, Donald. *Sport, Culture and Personality*. Champaign, IL: Human Kinetics Books, 1987.

Cashmore, Earnest. *Making Sense of Sport*. New York: Routledge, 1990.

Chad, Norman. *Hold On, Honey, I'll Take You to the Hospital at Halftime: Confessions of a TV Sports Junkie*. New York: Atlantic Monthly Press, 1993.

Chu, Donald. *Dimensions of Sport Studies*. New York: John Wiley & Sons, 1992.

Coakley, Jay. *Sport in Society: Issues and Controversies*. Boston: McGraw-Hill, 1998.

Cozens, Frederick, and Florence Strumpf. *Sports in American Life*. New York: Arno Press, 1976.

Creamer, Robert. *The Quality of Courage: Heroes In and Out of Baseball*. Lincoln, NE: University of Nebraska Press, 1998.

Curry, Timothy. *Sports: A Social Perspective*. Englewood Cliffs, NJ: PrenticeHall, 1984.

Davies, Richard. *America's Obsession: Sports and Society since 1945*. Fort Worth, TX: Harcourt Brace Publications, 1994.

Davis, Hank. *Small Town Heroes: Images of Minor League Baseball*. Iowa City, IA: University of Iowa Press, 1997.

Dudley, William, ed. *Sports in America: Opposing Viewpoints*. San Diego, CA: Greenhaven Press, 1994.

During, Simon. *The Cultural Studies Reader*. New York: Routledge, 1993.

Eitzen, Stanley D., and George Sage. *Sociology of North American Sport*. Madison, WI: Brown & Benchmark, 1997.

Elias, Norbert, and Eric Dunning. *Quest for Excitement: Sport and Leisure in the Civilizing Process*. Cambridge, MA: B. Blackwell, 1993.

Euchner, Charles C. *Playing the Field: Why Sports Teams Move and Cities Fight to Keep Them*. Baltimore, MD: Johns Hopkins University, 1989.

Figler, Stephen K., and Gail Whitaker. *Sport and Play in American Life: A Textbook in the Sociology of Sport*. Madison, WI: Brown & Benchmark, 1995.

Flowers, Sarah. *Sports in America*. San Diego, CA: Lucent Books, 1996.

Giamatti, A. Bartlett. *Take Time for Paradise: Americans and Their Games*. New York: Summit Books, 1990.

Gibson, John H. *Performance Versus Results: A Critique of Values in Contemporary Sport*. Albany, NY: State University of New York Press, 1993.

Goldstein, Jeffrey H., ed. *Sports, Games and Play: Social and Psychological Viewpoints*. Hillsdale, NJ: L. Erlbaum Associates, 1989.

Graham, Frank. *A Farewell to Heroes*. New York: Viking Press, 1981.

Greendorfer, Susan L., and Cynthia Hasbrook. *Learning Experiences in the Sociology of Sport*. Champaign, IL: Human Kinetics Books, 1991.

Griffin, Robert S. *Sports in the Lives of Children and Adolescents: Success on the Field and in Life*. Westport, CT: Praeger, 1998.

Gruneau, Richard. *Class, Sport, and Social Development*. Amherst, MA: University of Massachusetts Press, 1983.

Gutkind, Lee. *The Best Seat in Baseball: But You Have to Stand: The Game as Umpires See It*. Carbondale, IL: Southern Illinois Press, 1999.

Guttmann, Allen. *A Whole New Ball Game: An Interpretation of American Sports*. Chapel Hill, NC: University of North Carolina Press, 1998.

Harkness, Donald, ed. *Sports in American Culture*. Tampa, FL: American Studies Press, 1988.

Harris, Janet C. *Athletes and the American Hero Dilemma*. Champaign, IL: Human Kinetics Books, 1994.

Harris, Janet C., and Roberta Park. *Play, Games and Sports in Cultural Contexts*. Champaign, IL: Human Kinetics Books, 1983.

Hart, Mona, ed. *Sport and the Sociocultural Process*. Dubuque, IA: W. C. Brown Co., 1981.

Hoover, Dwight, and John Koumonlides. *Conspectus of History: Sports and Society*. Muncie, IN: Ball State University Press, 1982.

Howell, Mark D. *From Moonshine to Madison Avenue: A Cultural History of the NASCAR Winston Cup Series*. Bowling Green, OH: Bowling Green State University Press, 1997.

Ingham, Alan G., and John Loy, eds. *Sport in Social Development: Traditions, Transitions, and Transformations*. Champaign, IL: Human Kinetics Books, 1993.

Jarvie, Grant, and Joseph Maguire. *Sport and Leisure in Social Thought*. New York: Routledge, 1994.

Kelsey, Michael. *The Cultural Geography of Sport Halls of Fame*. Manhattan, KS: Kansas State University, 1993.

Klatell, David. *Sports for Sale: Television, Money and Fans*. New York: Oxford University Press, 1988.

Kruckemeyer, Thomas J. *For Whom the Bell Tolls: A Fan's Guide to Economic Issues in Professional and College Sports*. Jefferson City, MO: Kruckemeyer Publishing, 1995.

Lapchick, Richard E. *Fractured Focus: Sport as a Reflection of Society*. Lexington, MA: Lexington Books, 1986.

———, ed. *Sport in Society: Equal Opportunity or Business as Usual?* Thousand Oaks, CA: Sage Publications, 1996.

Leonard, Wilbert M. *A Sociological Perspective of Sport*. New York: Macmillan, 1993.

Lipsky, Richard. *How We Play the Game: Why Sports Dominate American Life*. Boston: Beacon Press, 1981.

Loy, John W., Gerald Kenyon, and Barry McPherson, eds. *Sport, Culture and Society: A Reader on the Sociology of Sport*. Philadelphia, PA: Lea & Febiger, 1981.

Lupica, Michael. *Mad as Hell: How Sport Got Away from the Fans and How We Can Get It Back*. New York: Putnam and Sons, 1996.

Mantle, Mickey, and Robert Creamer. *The Quality of Courage: Heroes In and Out of Baseball*. Lincoln, NE: University of Nebraska Press, 1999.

Massengale, John D., and Richard Swanson. *The History of Exercise and Sport Science*. Champaign, IL: Human Kinetics Books, 1997.

McIntosh, Peter C. *Sport in Society*. London: West London Press, 1987.

McKee, Steven. *The Call of the Game*. New York: McGraw-Hill, 1987.

McPherson, Barry D., James Curtis, and John Loy. *The Social Significance of Sport: An Introduction to the Sociology of Sport*. Champaign, IL: Human Kinetics Books, 1989.

Mergen, Bernard, ed. *Cultural Dimensions of Play, Games and Sport*. Champaign, IL: Human Kinetics Books, 1986.

Morris, Willie. *After All, It's Only a Game*. Jackson, MS: University of Mississippi Press, 1992.

Mrozek, Donald. *Sport and American Mentality, 1880–1910*. Knoxville, TN: University of Tennessee Press, 1983.

Nixon, Howard L., and James Frey. *A Sociology of Sport*. Belmont, CA: Wadsworth, 1996.

———. *Sport and the American Dream*. New York: Leisure Press, 1984.

Pankin, Robert M., ed. *Social Approaches to Sport*. Rutherford, NJ: Farleigh Dickinson University Press, 1982.

Podell, Janet, ed. *Sports in America*. New York: Wilson, 1986.

Rail, Genevieve, ed. *Sport in Postmodern Times*. Albany, NY: State University of New York Press, 1998.

Raitz, Karl. *The Theater of Sport*. Baltimore, MD: Johns Hopkins University Press, 1995.

Redekop, Paul. *Sociology of Sport: An Annotated Bibliography*. New York: Garland Publications, 1988.

Rees, Roger, and Andrew Miracle. *Sport and Social Theory*. Champaign, IL: Human Kinetics Books, 1986.

Riess, Steven. *City Games: The Evolution of American Urban Society and the Rise of Sports*. Urbana, IL: University of Illinois Press, 1991.

Rigauer, Bero. *Sport and Work*. New York: Columbia University Press, 1981.

Rinehart, Robert E. *Players All: Performances in Contemporary Sport*. Bloomington, IN: Indiana University Press, 1998.

Roberts, Randy, and James Olson. *Winning Is the Only Thing: Sport in America since 1945*. Baltimore, MD: Johns Hopkins University Press, 1989.

Russell, Gordon. *The Social Psychology of Sport*. New York: Springer-Verlag, 1993.

Sage, George H. *Handbook of Social Science and Sport*. Champaign, IL: Stipes, 1981.

———. *Power and Ideology in American Sport: A Critical Perspective*. Champaign, IL: University of Illinois Press, 1990.

Simon, Robert L. *Fair Play: Sports, Values and Society*. Boulder, CO: Westview Press, 1991.

Sleap, Michael. *Social Issues in Sport*. New York: St. Martin's, 1998.

Snyder, Eldon, and Elmer Spreltzer. *Social Aspects of Sport*. Englewood Cliffs, NJ: PrenticeHall, 1989.

Stine, Peter, ed. *Sports in America*. Detroit, MI: Wayne State University Press, 1995.

Umphlett, Wiley Lee, ed. *American Sport Culture: The Humanistic Dimensions*. Lewisburg, PA: Bucknell University Press, 1985.

Underwood, John. *Spoiled Sport: A Fan's Notes on the Troubles of Spectator Sports*. Boston: Little, Brown & Co., 1984.

Veblen, Thornstein. *The Theory of the Leisure Class*. New York: Macmillan, 1899.

Vincent, Ted. *Mudville's Revenge: The Rise and Fall of American Sport*. New York: Seaview Books, 1981.

Vogler, Conrad, and Stephen Schwartz. *The Sociology of Sport: An Introduction*. Englewood Cliffs, NJ: PrenticeHall, 1993.

Voy, Robert. *Drugs, Sports and Politics*. Champaign, IL: Leisure Press, 1991.

Wenner, Lawrence A., ed. *Media, Sports and Society*. Newbury Park, CA: Sage Publications, 1989.

Williams, Peter. *The Sports Immortals: Deifying the American Athlete*. Bowling Green, OH: Bowling Green State University Press, 1994.

Wise, Suzanne. *Social Issues in Contemporary Sport: A Resource Guide*. New York: Garland Publications, 1994.

Yankannis, Andrew. *Sport Sociology: Contemporary Themes*. Dubuque, IA: Kendall-Hunt, 1987.

## Journals

*American Journal of Economics and Sociology* (New York, NY)
*American Sociologist* (Morgantown, WV)
*American Sociology Review* (University Park, PA)
*Contemporary Sport* (Amherst, MA)
*International Journal of Sociology* (Armonk, NY)
*International Review of Social History* (New York, NY)
*Journal of American Culture* (Bowling Green, OH)
*Journal of Popular Culture* (Bowling Green, OH)
*Journal of Social Issues* (New York, NY)
*Journal of Socio-Economics* (Macomb, IL)
*Journal of Sociology and Social Welfare* (Kalamazoo, MI)
*Journal of Sport and Social Issues* (Thousand Oaks, CA)
*Ritual Studies* (Pittsburgh, PA)
*Sociology of Sport Journal* (Champaign, IL)

# 12

# Sport and World History

Without question, the history of world sport is an immense topic, especially when one considers the long history of athletics in each country as well as the current issues facing nations around the world. It is hard to think of a more worthwhile subject, especially considering the fury with which sport is pursued around the globe. From the colorful pageantry of bull fighting in Spain, to the heated cricket fields of India, the snowy ski slopes of Germany and Switzerland, the long, dry, overland cross-country routes of Nigeria or Kenya, or the icy fjords on which skaters train in Norway, there can be little doubt that sport plays an integral part in the lives of people everywhere. Of course, the 1980 Olympic boycott by the United States and the separate Olympics held by the Eastern block nations in 1984 remind us that for some time sport has been an important political card played by governments in their attempts to impose ideologies and policies on the rest of the world. Naturally, one cannot overlook the economic impact of sport. One need only examine the mini financial boom experienced by France after the 1998 World Cup of Soccer to realize how important hosting an international competition can be to the fiscal health of any nation. This chapter contains brief analyses of several of the sources produced over the last two decades that deal in one way or another with the place of sport in the international arena. The ways that sport has been shaped by political ideology and governmental policy have been of special interest to scholars, who have penned several quality works that show how sport in most countries has been and continues to be the product of specific political climates and governmental agendas. In addition, many researchers have focused their efforts on how sports have developed in specific countries, often showing how athletics evolved through various time periods because of unique cultural circumstances. While excellent studies have been done on many nations, Great Britain has been a particularly popular subject of scholarly inquiry. Enough good books now exist that students can learn about the practice and significance of sport in every decade of England's history from the Middle Ages to the modern period, and, if they have time or inclination, they can enjoy some fine works about sport in Scotland and Ireland as well. Several English language works exist that profile the sporting practices in other European and non-European countries. These books, though not as numerous as one would like, will also be examined in this chapter.

Sport in the ancient world is another popular topic, and many works can be found in college libraries that discuss the role sport played in Ancient Greece, Rome, and Egypt. These works often rely on eye-witness accounts of athletic contests that were part of the first Olympic games, important political celebrations, or sacred religious festivals and thus make for interesting reading that entertains as much as it educates. Of course, the modern Olympics, as the most prestigious international competition, has been the subject of important research, some of which will be discussed in this chapter. Finally, there are many fine books and articles that do not necessarily fit neatly into a category that will be profiled because they make a significant contribution to advancing the boundaries of knowledge regarding world sport. Subject areas that will be covered include the history of specific sports, such as boxing and soccer, which have had such enormous influence around the world; the anthropology of sport; nationalism; cultural heroes; and social movements that have impacted the way sport has been played in the global arena.

## SPORT IN BRITAIN

There is no shortage of resources when it comes to the history of sport in Britain. One of the better historical works on the modern period is Richard Holt's *Sport and the British: A Modern History*, in which the author recounts the major changes in sporting practices from the Victorian period to the present. Holt spends the first chapter analyzing the social and political conditions that led to a decline of traditional forms of sport that had existed until the mid-1800s. These forms included local games and activities of all sorts, most of which were organized around seasonal festivals and ceremonies. Much of the activity was of an impromptu nature and depended on the inclinations of any given group of folk in any given part of the country. Holt discusses the variety of games played by indigenous populations throughout the loosely knit nation before moving on to show how technological, social, and political changes during the Victorian period would lead to the organization of sport along rigid class lines. The remainder of the book is a fascinating critique of governmental and upper class attempts to co-opt sport as a vehicle for implementing national policy and for maintaining the cultural hegemony of England's most powerful families. Holt also discusses the role of England's burgeoning middle class in the development of sport at the end of the nineteenth century and has especially good chapters on the role that the Church and the public school system played in promoting the notion that sport could be used to mold raw boys into fashionable young gentlemen who were both strong and intelligent, men who would embody the best of Christian character while advancing British interests on the national scene. Nationalism and the role of sport in engendering feelings of national pride is an important subject for Holt, one to which he dedicates an entire chapter in which he discusses the role of sport in generating patriotic feelings at home, as well as its integration as a crucial part of England's foreign policy strategies. The section on how sport was used to foster better relations with Scotland, Ireland, and Wales is particularly good. Of course, Holt also includes a chapter on working class sport and its evolution in the modern era, an evolution closely tied to urban development, capitalism, and the rise of professional sports. The final chapter is an analysis of the effects of these latter two things on sport in contemporary Britain in which the author laments the passing of the amateur ideal so prevalent in the first half of the twentieth century.

Another general history that will make a splash with the reader is Tony Mason's *Sport in Britain: A Social History*. Mason organizes his book by sport instead of by historical periods and in doing so gives the reader detailed analyses of what various sports have meant to the British from the Middle Ages to the modern period. Mason includes meticulously researched chapters on angling, athletics (track and field), boxing, cricket, soccer, golf, horse-racing, lawn tennis, bowling, and rugby, concentrating on how these sports have changed over the years and on why they have taken on special significance in the lives of British subjects at various points in history. The chapter on angling is indicative of the power of Mason's work. One does not normally think of angling as having diverse functions within a society, but Mason shows how the sport has always been culturally important to the English. For instance, Izaak Walton's *The Compleat Angler* reveals that during the Interregnum the banished royalists used fishing not only as a means to survive but as a means to flourish psychologically amidst their severe political losses to the Puritans. During the industrial revolution, doctors and educators championed angling as one of the best ways to maintain good health in the face of worsening urban conditions. In recent times, angling has enjoyed status as both a professional sport and as an important refuge from the hurly burly of modern life. Mason is a good researcher, and he provides solid proof to back up his assertions, most of which are quite eye-opening. The chapters on boxing and football are particularly riveting, providing the reader with keen insight into just how deeply those sports have affected the nation at different times.

Those interested in investigating British sports in the Middle Ages should start with either Teresa McLean's *The English at Play: Sport in the Middle Ages* or John Marshall Carter's *Medieval Games: Sports and Recreations in Feudal Society*, both of which are sure to emerge as classic studies in the field. McLean's work includes chapters on outdoor activities and games, animal sports, hunting and hawking, fishing, tournaments and jousts, house and garden games, board games, folk games, dancing, and drama. While she provides separate discussions on how various components of medieval society played, often spending large sections of the book on upper-class activity, knightly sport, women's games, or sports of the common people, McLean makes it clear that sport during this period should not be romanticized. In fact, she asserts that all medieval sports had three primary characteristics: "They were essentially physical, they were played outdoors out of necessity, not choice, and they were usually played by large teams, often consisting of whole villages and parishes. Most medieval sports were a recreational form of gang warfare, fierce with ancient rivalries" (McLean, 1983, 1). She then goes on to describe several examples of this brutal sporting practice. Perhaps the best facet of the book is that it is well researched and replete with interesting examples that illustrate all of McLean's main points. Whether she is discussing the role of sport in women's lives or a jousting tournament to honor a local lord, the author takes great pains to paint a vivid picture of what the sporting scene must have looked like.

Carter's book is also highly readable and is impeccably researched. He includes chapters on sports in pre-feudal Europe, the perceptions that those who lived in the period had of their sports, sport on the feudal plantation, sport as a means of establishing a reputation, the relationship between the Church and sports in feudal society, how sports and recreations were reflected in medieval art, how sport reflected the violent nature of medieval society, and how sport was used to reaffirm established social orders at the time. This last chapter is probably his best chapter of what is a tremendous overall scholarly effort, but at least three other chapters are also indispensable. The first is the introductory chapter entitled "The Study of Medieval Sports and Recreations, 1927–1991," in which Carter provides the researcher with a short discussion of the available resources on the subject. This chapter provides innumerable leads for anyone embarking on a serious research project. Another helpful chapter is the bibliographic essay located at the back of the book. Here, Carter provides a long annotated bibliography in which he discusses most of the sources he used to write the book. Finally, the chapter entitled "Two Medieval Sportspeople" is fascinating because Carter uses several primary documents to trace the sporting activities of two people for whom sport was a vital part of life. Both accounts give the reader a powerful view of how sport was played during the era and what it meant to the people who played it so passionately.

Neil Tranter's *Sport, Economy and Society in Britain, 1750–1914* picks up the story of British sport in the mid-eighteenth century and traces its development to World War I. Tranter focuses on the impact of urbanization and industrialization on sport, the role of the cultural elite in reshaping sport throughout the nineteenth century, the modern conflict between using sport as a way to either promote individual health and social well-being or simply to make money, and the constant use of sport by those in power to promote distinct ways of looking at gender and class. Tranter's best chapter deals with what he calls the revolution in sport that took place over the course of the nineteenth century. He defines this revolution as the spread of certain sporting practices from local areas to the entire nation and as the change from loosely organized, local games, whose rules were quite flexible, to rule-bound, institutionalized sport that had grand political and social implications. In all, Tranter provides evidence that the spread of sport in this manner was pushed along by six main causes, including rivalries with neighboring towns; the adoption of sport by the public school system because it was viewed as being integral to the education of young men; and the rise of the sporting goods industry, which relied on athletic growth for survival. Also influential was the importance of sports to the upper class as a way to reaffirm its power while at the same time placating the masses of workers that helped to make its fortunes in an industrial society. Of course, middle-class reformers and businessmen who used sport to give their workers a healthy outlet and to give their sons a place to learn Christian values were also a factor in the rise of sport, as was the use of sport by men to reaffirm their masculinity in the face of changing social and political conditions, which saw women knock down some of the barriers that had once been treasured by men as distinctive masculine space in which men could prove their worth apart from women. Tranter concludes his book with an illuminating section in which he speculates on the direction that research on British sport history will take in the next century.

While Tranter focuses on several reasons why folk sport evolved into modern sport, John Hargreaves concentrates on sport's inextricable ties with power in *Sport, Power and Culture: A Social and Historical Analysis of Popular Sports in Britain*. Hargreaves's thesis is that "sports are extremely rich in symbolization and undoubtedly possess the capacity to represent social relationships in a particularly striking, preferred way. We can argue not only that great national sports events take on the character of a political ritual, but also that, for example, school sport and local community sport can function to symbolize or encode preferred views of the social order and thus legitimize power relations" (Hargreaves 1986, 12). Hargreaves then goes on during the course of the book to show how sport has always had a political function in Great Britain. He first analyzes the repression and reform of popular sports during the industrial revolution, mostly as a reaction by middle-class moralists against games such as boxing and cockfighting, which they associated with gambling, drinking, and violence. Hargreaves then turns his attention to examining how the bourgeois model of sport was consolidated by the public schools as a means for bolstering the power of the nation and its ruling classes. Finally, he dedicates several chapters to the evolution of working-class sport and all of the factors that contributed to changes in the ways that commoners played over the nineteenth and twentieth centuries. He concludes the work with chapters on the power of the media in contemporary sport, the role of the modern school system in maintaining physical fitness requirements and amateurism in the face of rampant professionalism, and the continuing use of sport by the government to achieve various aims. In his final chapter entitled "Sport and Hegemony," Hargreaves steps away from his focus on Britain to deliver an insightful commentary on the historical relationship between sport and power and on how that relationship is currently being played out around the globe.

Another work that explains how sport has functioned as a political, economic, and social tool throughout Britain's history is Derek Birley's *Sport and the Making of Britain*, in which the author chronicles the greater implications of English sport from pre-feudal days when Celts, Saxons, Jutes, and other tribes developed distinct sporting traditions to go along with games learned from the Romans, to the missionary spirit that defined the mid-Victorian period, in which sport was used to promote Christian values and English policy around the globe. Along the way, Birley provides some truly insightful discussions about the function of sport under the chivalric code, the sporting habits and experiences of feudal lords and royal princes, the motivations and strategies of the first sporting entrepreneurs and the conditions that allowed them to prosper, aristocratic sporting traditions, the effect of war on sports, the promulgation of various laws meant to curtail or reform sport, athletic activities for women, the importance of sport to commoners from serfs to the working masses who fueled the industrial revolution, and the reasons behind the ascendancy of certain sports at certain periods of British history. One of his best chapters is "Politics and Patrons: 1685–1756," in which he discusses the crucial role played by wealthy landowners in the promotion of sport during that period as a means of keeping the masses at bay while solidifying their own political power and securing a significant amount of social prestige.

Two books that complement each other nicely are Thomas Henricks's *Disputed Pleasures: Sport and Society in Preindustrial England* and J. A. Mangan's *Pleasure, Profit, Proselytism: British Culture and Sport at Home and Abroad, 1700–1914*. As the title would indicate, Henricks's book is broken up into chapters on sport in feudal England; the later Middle Ages, which focuses on sport as an expression of new military organizations and the rise of new status groups; the Tudor period (1485–1603), which focuses on how sport changed as the result of the new middle class and its needs; Stuart England (1603–1714), in which sport became a battle ground for Royalist, French, and Puritan values; and Georgian England (1714–1830), where private property and class concerns redirected sport toward its modern forms. Henricks's work is tied together by his constant pursuit of how sport has been linked with identity, particularly group identity, at various times in English history before the industrial revolution. As the author says, "To speak of sports as identity ceremonies then is to focus on such events as structured, public opportunities for personal and collective expression. In the social sciences, identity refers to the more or less complete, enduring pictures or conceptions of persons (and groups) in society." He further contends that "sports have been vehicles of identity construction and management," and that by analyzing how people have behaved in athletic spheres we can tell a great deal about their self-perceptions at the time (Henricks 1991, 8). The three chapters on Tudor, Stuart, and Georgian England are especially informative because they capture how people from all walks of life used sport to fashion identities that helped them cope with specific religious, political, economic, and social conditions at the time in which they lived.

While Henricks writes about the personal use of sport before the industrial revolution, Mangan's work features a collection of illuminating essays that illustrate the multiple functions that sport performed throughout the eighteenth and nineteenth centuries. For instance, Wray Vamplew's "Sport and Industrialization: An Economic Interpretation of the Changes in Popular Sport in Nineteenth-Century England" shows how new economic realities caused by industrialization changed the nature of popular sport from agrarian outdoor games based on physicality in nature to games such as cockfighting, boxing, darts, and team sports that could be played in the confines of the city and that could accommodate the large numbers of folks who lived there. Another essay, Holt's "Football and the Urban Way of Life in Nineteenth-Century Britain," shows how concerns for class, ethnicity, and geography fueled soccer rivalries in cities and caused the sport to become so ingrained into English tradition that it still remains the country's dominant sport today with rivalries between cities and within parts of cities dating back to the mid-1800s. Still other essays deal with the effects that politics had on sport during the period. Derek Birley's "Bonaparte and the Squire: Chauvinism, Virility and Sport in the Period of the French Wars" discusses how England's wars with France in the early part of the nineteenth century caused the British government to think of sport as a way of training troops and as a way of making its male citizens, especially its young boys, into tough young men that could defend their home soil while ensuring that England would have sufficient military might to advance her interests abroad. Other essays, such as Mangan's "Catalyst of Change: John Guthrie Kerr and the Adaptation of an Indigenous Scottish Tradition" and Gareth Williams's "From Popular Culture to Public Cliche: Image and Identity in Wales, 1850–1914" specifically focus on how and why sport developed in other parts of the United Kingdom, often in resistance to what England was doing. All of the essays are informative and readable, and the bibliographies that follow each are great sources of information on sport in Britain during the eighteenth and nineteenth centuries.

Mangan, along with James Walvin, has edited another book entitled *Manliness and Morality: Middle-Class Masculinity in Britain and America, 1800–1940*, which contains several essays that explain various ways that sport was used to address concerns over male identity during the period. For instance, in "Building Character in the British Boy: The Attempt to Extend Christian Manliness to Working-Class Adolescents, 1880–1914," John Springhill explains how concern on the part of church officials, educators, and social reformers for young men living in squalid, morally questionable urban environments led them to establish athletic programs designed to teach these wayward youth Christian values through sport. Of course, such sports programs did not start with an emphasis on poor young vagrants from the city but originated instead with the sons of the elite. In "Social Darwinism and Upper-Class Education in Late Victorian and Edwardian England," Mangan makes it clear that sport became an essential part of the education of rich boys for two rather conflicting reasons. One is that parents and educators wanted to see Christian values inculcated into their sons; the other is that in a kill-or-be-killed-world, England wanted its boys ready to defend the country at all costs. On the one hand, the ruling class wanted the boys to be moralistic, on the other hand they wanted them to have the capability to inflict violent catastrophe on any foe. Several other articles in the volume reveal how gender concerns, especially masculine insecurity, informed changes in sporting practice both in England and America in the late nineteenth and early twentieth centuries.

There are also several good works that deal specifically with the way Britain used sport as a colonizing tool from the mid-1800s through World War I. Two of the best are *The Cultural Bond: Sport, Empire, Society*, edited by Mangan, and Allen Guttmann's *Games and Empires: Modern Sports and Cultural Imperialism*. In the introduction of his work, Mangan writes that "sport was a major medium for the attempted development of 'character' particularly among those who by virtue of their position in elite society were destined to be the Empire's leaders." In addition, sport functioned as a "vital element to British imperialism" (Mangan,

1992, 3). All of the essays in the book are dedicated to showing how the British used sport to weave their own traditions, myths, and values into other countries on which they had imperial influences. For instance, in "Emancipation, Exercise and Imperialism: Girls and the Games Ethic in Colonial Malaya," Janice N. Brownfoot explains how British authorities used games and sports to inculcate gender norms into the Malayan children as a means of getting them to accept British customs and authority. While the essays in Mangan's book are organized by country, Guttmann breaks his book up into chapters that show how different sports have been used by various colonial authorities to advance imperialist strategies. Guttmann does not limit his analysis to Britain, but he does include two chapters, one on cricket and the other on soccer, to show how the British government used sport to its advantage from 1850–1920. He concludes his book with a discussion of how sport aids the process of cultural imperialism. He concludes that, while a complex combination of factors leads to imperialism, the most accurate way to describe the process is to say that the emotional, psychological, and economic needs of a poor country, which usually has an unstable or weak government, are partially met by a stronger country, which gains significant natural resources or political leverage via its occupation and which ensures its continued exploitation of the smaller, impoverished country by using cultural products like sport to enforce values on the citizens of the smaller country that encourage them to accept imperialist occupation. Like Mangan's book, Guttmann provides the reader with not only a valuable lesson about the power of sport, but also with a document that shows how global relationships have been forged and maintained in the twentieth century.

Finally, there are some good works that have been written about sporting practices in the rest of the United Kingdom. Two of the best are John Sugden and Alan Bairner's *Sport, Sectarianism, and Society in a Divided Ireland* and Joseph M. Bradley's *Sport, Culture, Politics and Scottish Society: Irish Immigrants and the Gaelic Athletic Association.* Bradley's book is an excellent account of the sporting practices that have evolved in Scotland over the last century and a half. He pays close attention to how Irish immigrants to Scotland have forged their own athletic games as a means of resisting both Scottish and English discrimination, and the book is as much a story of the inception and development of the Gaelic Athletic Association as it is the story of sport in Scotland. Sugden and Bairner focus their recitation on the development of sport in Ireland over the last half century. It is an incisive work through which one can understand the causes for division between Northern Ireland and Ireland and for the further subdivisions of class, political affiliations, and religion that plague the region. It is quite fascinating to see how sport has played and continues to play a crucial role in the ever-tenuous relationship between the two lands and the various sects that war within them.

## SPORT IN THE ANCIENT WORLD

One of the more interesting topics in sports history that remains somewhat immersed in shadows is the function of athletics in the ancient world. Of the great civilizations of the past, Greece has received the most attention from scholars.

Waldo Sweet's *Sport and Recreation in Ancient Greece: A Sourcebook with Translations* is the place to start one's research. Sweet features a good introductory chapter on the general history of Hellenic athletics, followed by twenty-three chapters on individual sports and important Greek athletic themes. Running events, diskos, pentathlon, jumping, javelin, wrestling, boxing, pankration, horse racing, and weight lifting are all covered, and he includes chapters on women's sports, training procedures, societal attitudes toward sport, and why many events featured nude participation. Sweet concludes that most Greek competitions, especially the Olympics, were viewed as religious activities. He maintains that because of this "any cheating or other irregularity such as bribery was almost unthinkable; the Greeks regarded such misconduct as sacrilegious" (Sweet 1987, 3). Though other scholars have suggested that Greek sport could be quite mercenary, and though Sweet's assertion that "athletics were more important to the Greeks than to us today" is questionable, Sweet's book is an excellent read. He does a fine job analyzing what each sport meant to different components of Greek society and publishes several personal testimonies from Greek competitors that have survived the years. More than anything else, these passionate writings attest to the importance of sport to the Ancient Greeks.

In *Greek Athletics and the Genesis of Sport*, David Sansone reaffirms Sweet's thesis that sport for the Greeks was primarily a religious experience. Sansone, however, insists that the experience was defined not only by worship of the gods or political leaders, but by worship of the Greeks themselves. Sport was, in effect, a ritual sacrifice to Greek physical beauty and aptitude and to the rituals that defined Greek life. As Sansone writes: "The numerous associations between sport and sacrificial ritual in ancient Greece encourage us in the belief that sport is itself a form of sacrificial ritual. The exhilaration that accompanies sport is precisely parallel to that which accompanies sacrifice: by a traumatic and enervating act, the sacrificer has given birth to renewed life and restored vigor" (Sansone 1988, 130). Sansone dedicates his entire book to analyzing various athletic pursuits to show how this process of sacrifice as renewal worked for different city states within the Hellenic community.

In *Arete: Greek Sports from Ancient Sources*, Stephen Miller departs from the more traditional themes pursued by Sweet and Sansone. While using first-hand accounts to provide the reader with an excellent feel for what Greek competitions and sportsmen must have been like, he concludes his book by arguing quite persuasively that, based on the personal accounts and other primary documents that he uses within the work, Greek sport was actually much like our modern sport. The Olympic games, for instance, were ostensibly to honor the gods. However, in reality they were a forum in which careers were made and broken, in which community reputations were at stake, and in which paid athletes often labored for excessive prizes. Like today, athletes were role models for success. As Lucian, the Greek historian, wrote, "Those who followed learned the lesson of this shortcut to fame" (Miller 1991, 91). Also reminiscent of today is the fact that all of the competitions had sponsors, the foremost of which got the best tickets. According to Pausanias, the Greek writer, "The stadium is a bank of earth on which is a seat for the sponsors of the competition" (Miller 1991, 100). Miller quotes Plutarch, Xenophon, Plato, Euripides, Pollux, Pindar, Aristophanes, and other Greek notables as he makes his case that Greek sport should not be idealized, but instead viewed via a well-focused lens that shows both its noble and ignoble aspects.

Paul Plass makes a similar argument about sport in Ancient Rome in his *The Game of Death in Ancient Rome: Arena Sport and Political Suicide*. Plass describes the multiple functions of Roman sport as practiced by the plebeian and the patrician classes, but he concentrates most of his efforts on meanings of the various arena sports sponsored by the Roman government. These sports included gladiatorial spectacles, chariot races, death struggles between humans and deadly animals, hand-to-hand combat to the death between two humans, and several other games that usually ended in bloodshed and death for one or more of the participants. Two things defined Roman sport: it had to be fast-paced, dangerous, or violent, and it was usually overtly political. For instance, fights between gladiators and chariot races often determined promotion in the ranks of the Roman legions. Fights to the death with another man or an animal often determined whether a slave would live or die. Plass shows how arena sport was used by emperors and other high officials to gauge the mood of Rome's citizens and to test the loyalty of those administrators in charge of carrying out proscribed policy. An opiate for the masses that appeased Roman needs for bloodlust and raw, visceral forms of justice, these sports functioned as a training ground for Rome's armies and a place of spiritual nourishment for a populace trained to believe that extreme competitions and survival of the fittest war games were major factors in making the Roman people strong enough to build and defend an empire.

The study of Roman sport is one of the best topics for illustrating the major problem English-speaking scholars have in their quest to study world sport. Many of the latest and most influential studies are written in languages other than English. For instance some of the best books on sport in Ancient Rome include Cigdem Durusken's *Eskicag 'da Spor*, written in Turkish; Violaine Vanoyeke's *La Naissance des Jeux Olympiques et le Sport dans l' Antiquite* and Jean-Paul Thuillier's *Le Sport Dans la Rome Antique*, both in French; Giovanni Manetti's *Sport e Giochi Nell Antichita Classica*, written in Italian; and German works such as Rigobert Fortuin's *Der Sport im Augusteischen Rom*, Ingomar Weiler's *Der Sport bei den Volkern der Alten Welt*, and Christian Wallner's *Soldaten Kaiser und Sport*. Perhaps the best work of all is Horst Ueberhorst's *Welgeschichte der Leibesubungen* (World History of Physical Education and Sport), a six-volume work written between 1976 and 1986 that is perhaps the only true history of world sport. Whether one wants to know about sport in Rome, the Upper Volta or some of the smaller countries and remote peoples that most of us know nothing about, Ueberhorst's book is the one to consult. Those doing research on sport and world history should keep the limitations of working exclusively with English-language books in mind.

The best overall English reference for Greek and Roman sport is David Matz's *Greek and Roman Sport: A Dictionary of Athletes and Events from the Eighth Century B.C. to the Third Century A.D.* He starts the work with an excellent chapter on the general history of Greek and Roman athletics and follows it with a chapter that profiles ancient literary sources that comment on sport. These sources include works by Greek historian Claudius Aelianus, early Christian writer Eusebius, as well as Herodotus, Juvenal, Cicero, and many others. He then spends 100 pages on a detailed dictionary in which he provides insightful commentary on most of the major figures, events, and individual games that defined Greek and Roman athletics. At the end of the dictionary are excerpts from several personal essays written by ancient chroniclers of sport. These passages feature beautiful writing that captures the essence of Greek and Roman sport. Olympic competitions, road races, wrestling matches, Roman chariot races, and gladiatorial competitions come to life as the words of the past jump off the pages. Of course, like Sweet, Sansone, and Miller, Matz offers an excellent bibliography for anyone interested in pursing further research on the subject.

Two of the best sources on the history of sport in Ancient Egypt are Zaki Ibrahim El Habashi's *Tutankhamun and the Sporting Traditions* and Wolfgang Decker's *Sports and Games of Ancient Egypt*. Decker's study is the most complete history of Egyptian sport. After providing an extensive review of sources for those wanting to study sport in Ancient Egypt on their own, he includes chapters on the way sports were played during the reigns of most of the pharaohs and how and why private citizens participated in athletic events from running, jumping, and ball games, to combat sports and aquatic activities. He also profiles several different types of Egyptian games, but his best chapter is on the importance that sport played in the identity of a king. According to Decker, "The function of the king as guarantor of the life of the underlings entrusted to his care demanded overwhelming physical strength, which was given to him by virtue of his office. The king as unconquerable warrior-hero steps into action when enemies threaten Egypt, but he also performs mighty athletic feats" (Decker 1992, 20). Decker describes in some detail how the role of sport functioned for several kings but maintains that the basic part of the relationship always stayed the same: The king could inspire confidence in his people through his athletic prowess, assuring them that he could do that which he was supposed to do.

Unlike Decker, El Habashi breaks his analysis up into discussions of different periods. The first section of his book is dedicated to giving the reader a general overview of the history of Egyptian sport. In addition, he supplies detailed writing on sport in the predynastic period, the Old Kingdom, the Middle Kingdom, and in the Eighteenth Dynasty of Tutankhamun. The second part of the book covers the life of King Tut, focusing on his sporting practices and the influence they have had on subsequent Egyptian athletics. A novice reader will perhaps be surprised at just how important sports were to the ancient Egyptians, who played constantly as a means of honoring political leaders, gaining social prestige, celebrating sacred rituals, and, first and foremost, having fun. As El Habashi concludes, all Egyptian kings were sportsmen and this had a trickle down effect on the rest of the society. Clearly, King Tut was an avid player: "Representations of Tutankhamun participating in battles and some representations of sporting activities are idealistic, ritualistic, or symbolic. However, we tend to believe that some depict actual participation in sport. Supporting our theory is the fact that a great number of sports equipment and sporting scenes were in his tomb. They far exceed any number discovered in any other king's tomb of the Eighteenth Dynasty" (El Habashi 1992, 152). Like Decker, El Habashi provides the reader with not only a wealth of information, but also a step-by-step account of how he uncovered it. Thus, both books are fine examples of how to pursue work in sport history. Naturally, each includes a complete bibliography.

At least three other noteworthy books exist on sport in the ancient world. The first is Michael Poliakoff's *Combat Sports in the Ancient World: Competition, Violence, and Culture*. Poliakoff does not limit himself to Greece and Rome but instead shows how violent, combat sports have always been central to organized societies. The author, using an impressive array of primary documents, argues that military considerations have been the usual reason given for engagement in sports such as boxing, fighting, or sword play but that the root cause of our continual fascination with these sports is buried deep in the human psyche. His writing is crisp and clean, and his eloquent prose brings to life the importance of individual combat sport in many different societies. A second book is *Essays on Sport History and Sport Mythology*, edited by Allen Guttmann. This work contains several essays that seek to debunk the myths long associated with sport in certain periods. One of the articles is "E. Norman Gardiner and the Decline of Greek Sport," in which Donald Kyle shows that much of the initial scholarship done on the sports of antiquity was incorrectly colored by the prejudices and inaccurate presuppositions of various authors' writings in specific cultural contexts. Kyle does a fine job of showing how Greek sport has been misrepresented over the years in early scholarship and tries to provide information that, to some extent, begins the process of correcting past interpretations. A third book of interest is *Ritual and Record: Sports Records and Quantification in Pre-Modern Societies*, edited by John Marshall Carter and Arnd Kruger. Though the writing is rather ponderous and a bit tough to wade through, the contributors to this volume perform a valuable service to the academic community. Each takes a different time period and shows how we can get a new understanding of how sport was practiced within each age by analyzing how any given society attempted to record its rituals. Dietrich Ramba, for instance, supplies an article entitled "Recordmania in Sports in Ancient Greece and Rome," in which he shows how an analysis of the record-keeping practices allows us to get a better idea of how sports were played.

## INTERNATIONAL GOVERNMENTS AND SPORT

Whether one wants information on ancient societies or on changes in sporting habits in countries over the last two decades, there are several good books that describe the inevitable influence of governmental policy on sport. An excellent survey of how political ideology has informed sport in the twentieth century is provided by John Hoberman in *Sport and Political Ideology*. Hoberman profiles Marxist philosophy, fascism, liberalism, Nazi critiques of sport, the Worker's sport movement, Maoist sport, East German techno-sport and current neo-Marxist ideas.

Not only does he provide good descriptions of these theories, but he also analyzes different countries who actually tried to put these ideas into practice. For instance, he looks at Mussolini's Italy, Hitler's strategies in the 1930 Olympics, and China's evolution from a very passive sporting style under Mao to a more aggressive posture in the last two decades. He also tackles muscular Christianity, the Protestant work ethic, and free market capitalism, arguably the three philosophies that have most influenced American sport in the last century and a half. Overall, Hoberman's book is quite effective because the author's command of his subject and straightforward approach gives even the politically uninitiated reader an understandable description of the dominant ideologies espoused by governments in the twentieth century. He also shows how these ideas have continually shaped and reshaped sports over the last 100 years.

Another fine book that shows how modern governments have relied on sport to promote national interests is Clyde Binfield and John Stevenson's *Sport, Culture and Politics*. Binfield and Stevenson include several insightful essays from top scholars of the international community, and though the book does not cover a lot of countries, it does provide a glimpse into how governments have made sport vital to national policy in countries not often discussed in other books. For instance, Terence Monnington's "Crisis Management in Black African Sport" catalogues a series of strategies taken by African nations hoping to use sport to their advantage in the global arena. Gordon Daniels's "Japanese Sport: From Heian Kyo to Tokyo Olympiad" shows how sport has changed in the land of the rising sun as the Japanese government has evolved from an imperial authority to more of a Western-style democracy with capitalism at its core. Perhaps the best essay is James H. Grayson's "Sport in Korea: Tradition, Modernization and the Politics of a Newly Industrialized State." Grayson smoothly shows how the government of the Republic of Korea has used sport to foster national pride and unity since the inception of the country. As Grayson writes: "Sport is never without political implications. In the case of the Republic of Korea the political use of sport as a conscious government policy has been clear from the very establishment of the state. Government policy toward folk customs and sports has helped to foster a new national pride in the country. Similarly, Korean government support for Western-style sport has not only been used to demonstrate Korea's emergence onto the world stage, but has been part of a long-term diplomatic initiative to gain recognition and support from formerly hostile nations" (Binfield and Stevenson 1993, 167). Like the majority of the essays in the book, Grayson proves his key assertion with timely evidence and clear writing.

For an analysis of how several countries who are major players on the international scene have used sport as a political tool in the last fifty years, one should consult Laurence Chalip's *National Sports Policies: An International Handbook,* which contains essays on the political nature of the sporting strategies of Australia, Brazil, Canada, China, several Communist countries, Cuba, France, Germany, Hungary, India, Japan, Norway, Spain, and Sweden, among others. The essays are quite readable and provide the reader with clearly articulated ideas as to how the various approaches adopted by each country have worked. Though the authors avoid being judgmental, they do provide solid critiques of the policies of each country. For instance, Lamartine DaCosta is careful to give Fidel Castro credit for the fact that his authoritarian use of sport fostered unity within his country as well as respect on the international scene. However, DaCosta is quick to point out that eventually socialism will collapse and that, "although the life span of the socialist system in Cuba cannot be predicted, sports will almost certainly suffer" (Chalip 1996, 134). While one might question whether socialism as it is practiced in Cuba will collapse or simply be reworked, one cannot dispute the powerful evidence presented by DaCosta within the essay that suggests that Cuban sport is almost solely funded by the government and that this has led to little development of sporting infrastructures outside the governmental control. Thus, if the government fails, sport will have to be completely "rebuilt" in that country. This provocative statement is typical of the essays in the book, all of which attempt to pinpoint the weaknesses as well as the strengths of athletic policy in different countries.

Three other works that would interest a scholar working in this area are Eric Dunning, Joseph Maguire, and Robert Pearton's *The Sports Process: A Comparative and Developmental Approach,* Jennifer Hargreaves's *Sport, Culture and Ideology*, and Mike Cronin and David Mayall's *Sporting Nationalisms: Identity, Ethnicity, Immigration and Assimilation*. Dunning, et al. edit a collection of quality essays that analyze the various processes by which sport has evolved in different societies from the ancients to the moderns. The first section of the book is actually dedicated to showing how modern sport relies on the sport of ancient societies both in theory and in practice. The second section describes two distinct processes that the editors seem to see as characterizing the development of sport in this century. The first is the general flow from sport that is firmly controlled by the government, typified by Fascist, Nazi, and Communist models, to sport that is controlled largely by private interests with only loose government regulation. While not insisting that democracy and capitalism are the right frameworks in which to approach sport, the essays certainly make it clear that sport as it is practiced in the United States and much of the West is certainly catching on with the rest of the world, while more authoritarian practices are on the wane. The other process involves a pattern whereby in any society sport starts as personal activities that eventually become important social events and finally evolve into economic and political spectacles. This progression is well documented in the book and is also partly the subject of the Hargreaves study, in which the author features several essays that, while it is not their principle object, substantiate that this progression does indeed exist. The essays in Hargreaves's book also address important issues in contemporary sport and how various countries confront them. For instance, the place of women in sport, youth sport, the problems posed by performance-enhancing drugs, violence, and the role of the media on athletics are all discussed, and one of the strengths of the book is that the reader gets a feel for how different countries are handling these issues. Finally, Cronin and Mayall have edited a quality book composed of nine essays that focus on how sport in North America, Britain, and Australia shapes immigrant and minority group notions of individual and collective identity as they assimilate in the host society or maintain cultural insularity under a policy of multiculturalism. All three books have substantial bibliographies.

Anyone interested in how the government of the United States influences American involvement in global competition should consult either Arthur Johnson and Frey James's *Government and Sport: The Public Policy Issues* or John Wilson's *Playing by the Rules: Sport, Society, and the State*. Both authors include essays that spend a great deal of time on how state and local governments make athletic policies within the country. For instance, Johnson's work has essays on the impact of women's sports on the laws affecting athletics in the country; sports broadcasting regulations and how they affect sport; and how local, state, and federal tax codes affect professional and amateur sports in America. Wilson writes about the role sport plays in the process by which the youth of the country learn what it means to be a citizen. He also analyzes how social reform movements have led to new laws that affect the way we play in this country. Still, both books contain sections on how the American government conducts athletic business in the international arena. Both Wilson and James Nafrziger in his essay "Foreign Policy in the Sports Arena," located at the end of Johnson's work, agree that American politicians have continued to be aware of the power of athletics and, knowing that elections are always just around the corner, continue to initiate policy that puts American athletes in a position to excel in international competitions.

Finally, there are two textbooks designed for undergraduate use that would be good starting places for scholars just getting their feet wet in the area of government policy and sport. One is *Sports Governance in the Global Community*, edited by Janet Parks, Gordon Olafson, Brenda Pitts and David Stotlar. The editors include chapters on policy for international sports governance, the Olympic movement, the international development of sport, the process by which one hosts an international event, the significance of national teams, a history of boycotts and political problems, and the key issues that countries will have to cope with in the early part of the next century. The other book is Ralph Wilcox's *Sport in the Global Village*. Wilcox includes chapters on the role of the media in international sport, the implications of professional participation in the Olympics, the history of sport in South Africa and how sport is being used to change the political and social policies in that country, the role of sport in the new Europe, what sport means to different countries, and how international sporting practices are changing the way that physical educators are implementing school educational programs.

## THE FUNCTIONS OF SPORTS IN THE INTERNATIONAL ARENA

Those looking for information about how sport has operated in different countries over the last century will find that most countries have been the subject of some academic inquiry. Anyone interested in the sporting traditions of Asian and African nations, for instance, might begin their research process with Eric Wagner's *Sport in Asia and Africa: A Comparative Handbook*. Wagner includes an informative summary of the recent history of sport on both continents, followed by essays that comment specifically on sport in the Yemen Arab Republic, Japan,

South Korea, the People's Republic of China, Thailand, the Philippines, Malaysia, Egypt, Botswana, Zaire, Nigeria, and Kenya. While it becomes clear that the athletic history of each country is quite unique, Wagner concludes that sport has taken on several basic functions in all of the countries in question: "Sport is used by many countries as a form of political propaganda to gain prestige and support for the regime in power and its particular social system. Sport is often promoted as a means of advancing health, fitness and preparation for life. Sport can be a form of stability that helps to tie people to their social traditions and can help transmit and inculcate the key values of the society" (Wagner 1989, 9). He also contends that, among other things, sport in these countries has had the function of helping citizens release pent up energy and frustration at social and economic policies, has provided people living in big cities with a way of coping with diversity, and has provided common ground on which any given nation's citizens can learn to relate to each other. Finally, sport has been and continues to be an important avenue by which any gifted member of any society can rise to prominence. Perhaps no other thing so distinguishes the worldwide importance of sport as the fact that in almost every country being an athletic superstar is the fastest and most assured path to wealth and fame.

For researchers who want to focus on Africa, William J. Baker and James Mangan's *Sport in Africa: Essays in Social History* contains several top-notch essays that cover the history of African sport from the pre-colonial to the modern period. One such essay is Sigrid Paul's "The Wrestling Tradition and Its Social Functions," in which the author shows how important wrestling was to establishing one's place in social, political, and economic hierarchies in many pre-colonial African societies. As Paul writes: "A boy exhibiting special wrestling capacities gained high prestige within his family, kinship group, and community. Apart from promoting high rank within the age group and a high prestige within family and community, wrestling efficiency also served the purpose of upgrading individuals singly or collectively to higher status levels on the basis of age" (Baker 1996, 40). Other essays in the volume take on the role of sport in colonial days and include such topics as imperial use of sport to promote order and obedience to colonial dictates, the use of sport to train African soldiers, the use of sport to train hunters in Zimbabwe, and the rise of boxing as a means of resisting colonialist influence. A third section on contemporary trends contains essays that focus on the relationship between gender and sport in Africa, the use of sport by the South African government and those who fought so long to resist its racist policies, the use of sport by the Soviets and other world powers to advance economic interests in Africa, and the meaning of international competitions for modern African countries. A small, but notable book that expands on these last two topics is Sam Ramsamy's *Apartheid: The Real Hurdle*, in which the author recounts the history of sport in South Africa, the use of sport by the government to promote apartheid, and the use of sport by black South Africans and many members of the international community to combat the separatist philosophy.

Two other fine books that demonstrate how these themes play out in the southern portions of the Americas are Joseph Arbena's *Sport and Society in Latin*

*America: Diffusion, Dependency, and the Rise of Mass Culture* and Eduardo
Galeano's *Soccer in Sun and Shadow*. Arbena confesses early in his book that
"assessing sport in Latin America is difficult because the region lacks homogeneity" (Arbena 1988, 138). When one speaks of Latin America, one might be
speaking of the French-, Dutch-, or English-speaking Caribbean; Puerto Rico;
Cuba; Nicaragua; the Dominican Republic; parts of Brazil and Mexico; or several
other places where there are enclaves of "Latin" influence. Of course, the usual
designations for class, racial, and gender differences that affect sport in every
country have to be accounted for as well. The essays in Arbena's collection do a
good job of capturing the main issues and controversies that have defined Latin
American sport during the last 100 years. For instance, Steve Stein's "The Case of
Soccer in Early Twentieth Century Lima" discusses the factors that led to the
establishment of soccer as Peru's national game in the 1920s, while Wagner's
"Sport in Revolutionary Societies: Cuba and Nicaragua" underscores the effect of
political change on sport and the use of sport by those attempting to affect that
change. Other articles deal with the rise of baseball on the Yucatan, sport in
countries under military rule, sport as a means of citizenship in Latin American
countries, and the effect of technological modernization on sport in Mexico.
Galeano, a well-known Uruguayan novelist and historian, weaves 200 anecdotes,
sketches, poems, and short commentaries into a book that traces the importance of
soccer in Uruguay, Brazil, Argentina, and other Latin American countries to its
roots early in the twentieth century. This work is a must for the scholar hoping to
understand the passion for soccer in these regions as well as the political
ramifications of the game for government leaders, players, and spectators.

Turning to Eastern Europe, Robert Edelman's *Serious Fun: A History of
Spectator Sports in the USSR* is a terrific book that chronicles the development of
sport in the former Soviet Union from the time of the early Marxists through the
Stalinist regime, the cold war, and *perestroika*. The most interesting parts of the
book are the sections on Stalin and his insistence that sport be developed as a tool
proving the superiority of the Soviet way of life by promoting Russian athleticism
on the international stage. Edelman unearths several primary documents that give
his accounts of the development of Soviet soccer, basketball, and hockey a
vibrancy that hooks the reader. The story of the rise of the hockey program is
particularly riveting. At almost every step, the Russians took pains to do exactly the
opposite of what they thought the North Americans would do. If Canadians fought
and played a tough dump and chase game, the Russians would play finesse hockey,
featuring pinpoint passing and stylish team play. The idea, as with all Soviet
athletic efforts, was not only to win, but to win in such a way that proved that they
were not only athletically superior to their European and North American
counterparts, but also morally superior to them. Edelman shows conclusively how
the Russians took great pride in being able to win like gentlemen on the ice against
the barbaric capitalists from the West. The author also includes some quality
discussion about spectator sport within the Soviet Union, how television changed
the way the Soviet government conducted sports business, and how the break up
of the Soviet Union has affected sport in the region.

Moving eastward, Zbigniew Chmielewski has penned *Polish Sport*, a short book dealing with the relatively brief history of sport in Poland. Poland as we know it has only been a nation since 1918, and most of its own sporting traditions developed in the last eighty years. Naturally, World War II played a significant part in the development, disrupting sporting practices that had developed since the end of World War I, but also setting the stage for the development of modern sport in Poland. Chmielewski does a credible job of summarizing the history of sport in Poland from 1918 to the present, focusing mostly on Polish efforts to compete in Olympic competitions, while also recounting the formation of new athletic organizations in Poland over the last three decades that have promoted amateur and professional sport in that country. Though a bit dated, Chmielewski's work is still a good one for getting a feel for the political, military, and economic obstructions that have slowed the evolution of sport in Poland. It is a work that is somewhat similar to Richard Holt's *Sport and Society in Modern France*, in which the author gives a well-researched account of the complex twists and turns that sport in France has taken over the last century. To be sure, Holt's effort boasts considerably more information about France than Chmielewski's does about Poland but that is mostly because so much more has happened on the athletic scene in France. In any case, Holt's book is not to be missed by any scholar who is serious about French sport.

Finally, there are two very different works that could be used to gain divergent perspectives on sport in China. The first is a fabulously comprehensive anthology simply titled *Sport in China* that is edited by Howard Knuttgen, Ma Qiwei, and Wu Zhongyuan. The book, compiled in 1990, has about everything any sports historian might want to know about sport in China. Chapter subjects include sport in ancient Chinese culture, the role of sport in modern China, the role of physical education in Chinese schools, the maintenance of competitive sport and amateur sport, advances in sports medicine and technology that are changing the way the Chinese use sport, and detailed time lines that outline the most important dates in Chinese history and the most important athletic moments in the history of the country. The work is both well researched and readable. It is a perfect introduction to Chinese athletics both past and present. Once one has digested *Sport in China*, one might try Jonathon Kolatch's *Is the Moon in China Just as Round? Sporting Life and Sundry Scenes*, the personal recitation of Kolatch's trip to China to investigate Chinese sport. His book is entertaining and gives the reader a personal feel not only for what sport in China is like, but for what it means to be Chinese.

Of course, there are many good books about the history of sport around the world that defy simple classification. One of the better works on sport history is Kendall Blanchard's *The Anthropology of Sport: An Introduction*, in which the author is less concerned with elaborating on specific historic moments in the world of sport as he is with discussing the various paradigmatic frameworks in which sport histories are constructed. For Blanchard, the method is as important as the actual history that is uncovered. In fact, the method often determines the way any given historian will record the history about which he or she is writing. Blanchard lists twelve separate goals of any anthropologist studying sport. These include studying how sport has been defined in as many primitive cultures as possible, analyzing how sport works as a factor in acculturation and cultural maintenance, analyzing the language of sport, treating the role of sport in a multicultural educational environment, and describing the functions of sport with the many subgroups of any society. Still, all of these functions are performed by researchers who approach their subject through a specific world view or paradigm. An anthropologist with devout Christian beliefs might draw very different conclusions from raw data than would an anthropologist who is an atheist. Blanchard defines the beliefs and ideals that guide different paradigms that are frequently adopted by anthropologists and gives several examples of how these paradigms have contributed to our understanding of how sport has operated in countries around the world. Overall, he discusses evolutionism, functionalism, structural-functionalism, cultural materialism, conflict theory, and several postmodern paradigms that currently hold sway in the discipline. The book is thus indispensable for anyone hoping to understand how "history" is produced, and how this production inevitably influences our views on sport.

Another provocative work in this area is *Anthropology, Sport, and Culture*, edited by Robert Sands. The book is organized into five sections. The first, "Theory and Method in Anthropology of Sport," deals with experiential ethnography and paradigms through which to understand cultural performance. The second, "Sport, Culture, Race, and Running," focuses on the cultural differences that distinguish white runners from the champions from Kenya and other African nations, whose recent success has stunned the international running community. The third section, "Sport and Cultural Change," analyzes how megastars such as Michael Jordan, international events such as the World Cup of Soccer, and traditional sporting practices work to promote change across cultures. The fourth and fifth parts, "Sport and Cultural Identity" and "Culture, Sport, and Ritual," examines how athletic rituals and institutions operate in the formation of individual and group identities in the United States and Canada.

One of the better books on sport in Europe is Baker's *Sports in the Western World*. Baker includes a nice chapter on the history of ancient sport and how the sporting habits of Greece and particularly of Rome influenced early athletic rituals in the land that would become Britain. In addition, he provides solid discussions of sports during the Renaissance and the industrial revolution, focusing on the origination of the scholar athlete, Puritan views on sport, and the birth of mass leisure. He dedicates an entire section to the development of team sports in the nineteenth century. While Baker's work leaves off at the end of the nineteenth century, James Riordan and Arnd Kruger's *The History of Worker Sport* covers one of the most important worldwide developments in sports in the early twentieth century. Worker sport swept Europe after World War I as a response to the need of industrial workers to have some form of healthy activity in their lives. As Riordan writes: "The aims of worker sport differed from country to country. All countries agreed, however, that worker sport should give working people a chance to take part in healthy recreation and do so in a socialist atmosphere. It provided an alternative to bourgeois competitive sport, commercialism, chauvinism, and the obsession with stars and records" (Riordan and Kruger 1996, vii). Not surprising, worker sport developed alongside pro-Communist sentiment in Europe and in the United States and emphasized activities such as bicycling and swimming that could be noncompetitive and that could exist apart from the institutionalized framework of team sports controlled by the capitalist elites. The authors include chapters that discuss the diverse nature of worker sport in Germany, France, the Soviet Union, Finland, Austria, Britain, Sweden, Norway, Canada, and Israel and finish with a chapter that discusses the demise of worker sport after World War II.

Scholars who enjoy *The History of Worker Sport* will want to read *Sport and International Politics*, edited by Pierre Arnaud and James Riordan. This collection of well-written and focused essays examines the political implications of athletics over the last century. Essay topics include the effort by Americans to boycott the 1936 Nazi Olympics, the role of fascism in shaping Italian sport, the importance of World War II and the recovery period on governmental use of sport in France and England during the 1950s and 1960s, cold war policy and its effects on the sporting activities of the Soviet Union from 1960–1988, and the use of sport by West and East German governments who, from 1945 to 1990, played a delicate political game as both countries tried to rebuild from World War II in the shadows of the two superpowers and newly formed alliances in Western Europe. The book is complemented nicely by Barry Houlihan's *Sport and International Politics*, which preceded its namesake by four years. Houlihan's work is not as academic as that of Arnaud and Riordan but is still a worthy effort that should not be missed.

For a definitive look at the relationship between sport and nationalist sentiment, one should consult either Mangan's *Tribal Identities: Nationalism, Europe, Sport* or Holt and Mangan's *European Heroes: Myth, Identity, Sport.* The former contains eleven diverse articles on how sport has, especially throughout the twentieth century, been used to foster a sense of national pride in countries vying for attention on the international stage. H. F. Moorhouse's "One State, Several Countries: Soccer and Nationality in a 'United' Kingdom" shows how soccer became the measuring stick of patriotism in Ireland, Scotland, and England after World War I to such an extent that it actually became the activity into which much of the animosity between those countries was channeled. Sorlin Sverker's "Nature, Skiing and Swedish Nationalism" shows how Swedes took advantage of their long winters to develop a national ski program that became the pride of the country, something in which Sweden could be regarded as the best in the entire world. This pervasive desire to be the best and to give one's citizens the feelings of pride and fulfillment that come from being the undisputed leaders in some field seems to be the underlying theme that links all of these essays. It once again underscores the fact that sport is one of the most important symbols of modern life, one which no country can ignore if it wants to be taken seriously.

Of course, one of the central components of national pride is the vast network of myths and tales that romantically define a country's athletic past. That is the topic of Holt and Mangan's *European Heroes: Myth, Identity and Sport.* Their thesis is simple. In every age, each country produces its own heroes, whose exploits subsequently become mythologized. This process slowly begins to define a country's sports history, usually in a way that brings great pride to the nation in question by romanticizing the past and glossing over the more ignominious moments that may have actually defined the country's political, social, religious, or economic history. In some ways, then, sport is the tool by which people make themselves feel better about things. Running away from or at least reinventing one's past is part of sports' therapeutic function. Holt and Mangan include several insightful essays that demonstrate how this process has worked for different European countries over the last two centuries. Siegfried Gerhmann's "Symbol of National Resurrection: Max Schmeling, German Sports Idol" is an excellent example. Gerhmann persuasively argues that the reason Schmeling's popularity reached such dizzying heights in Germany in the 1930s was because Germans were desperately seeking to escape their immediate past, especially their role as an aggressor nation during World War I and their subsequent destruction and humiliation at the hands of Europe and the United States. Schmeling became a symbol of German power, and each victory was used by the government to encourage the German people to look to a future that would feature Germany as a vigorous force instead of a weak failure. Again, all of the essays have a similar theme, and since most of the European countries are covered, the book becomes an important resource for understanding how the mythic potential of sport has markedly influenced the modern world.

## SPORTS AROUND THE WORLD

One of the more surprising things one discovers when researching the history of world sport is how few books are written about the history of specific sports and their function in different countries around the world. When considering the history of sport in the United States, for instance, one is confronted with many books on the history of baseball. But there seems to be very little in the way of good academic works on the history of soccer in England, the history of wrestling in Japan, or the history of skating in any of the Northern European countries. There are, however, at least two books that analyze the impact that one sport has had around the world. In *Boxing and Society: An International Analysis*, John Sugden examines the historical significance that the sport has had throughout Europe and South America. His best chapters are on the importance of boxing in Belfast, Northern Ireland, and the role that boxing has had and the prominence it continues to enjoy in Havana, Cuba. It is perhaps not surprising that most of the articles conclude that the importance for men of maintaining a certain type of masculine identity has been at the heart of boxing's popularity in nearly every society, but Sugden includes several descriptions of boxing matches in different countries that might surprise the reader because they vividly show how boxing's functions have been closely tied to any given country's economic, social, political, and even religious needs. Likewise, in *Blood Sport: A Social History of Spanish Bullfighting*, Timothy Mitchell examines the origins of bullfighting and its gradual adoption by Spaniards as a national sport that would come to have deep spiritual, social, and political meanings that go far beyond the annual running of the bulls in Pamplona.

Another fertile area for aspiring scholars is the Olympics. One would think that the world's foremost international competition would be the subject of a good bit of historical inquiry, but while some quality books do exist about various Olympic games, there is still much work to be done in the area. One of the best books on the subject is Richard Mandell's *The Nazi Olympics*, which recounts the story of the 1936 games held in Berlin. Mandell does a superlative job of showing the reader how Hitler viewed the games and how he attempted to use them not only to display German athletic prowess, but to assure the rest of the world of Germany's status as a genteel, sophisticated nation that could be trusted to take a lead in international politics. Since plans to invade Poland were already part of Hitler's master plan, it was essential that he use the Olympics not only as a stage for promoting Germany as a safe, stable nation that did not harbor nefarious plans for world domination, but also as a strong nation whose military might would have to be respected in the years to come. Mandell's book is the story of how this delicate balancing act unfolded in the summer of 1936. Along the way, the author does a remarkable job of showing what the games meant to the athletes, to the German people, and to the world leaders who watched with bated breath as the games unfolded.

Like the games in Berlin, the 1980 Olympic games was also a competition that drew the attention of the world. Derek Hulme's *The Political Olympics: Moscow, Afghanistan, and the 1980 U.S. Boycott* is a complete account of the events in Afghanistan that led to the U.S. boycott of the games. Hulme also provides quality commentary on the decision-making process that led the United States to boycott the competition and on the political fall-out from the boycott. Other good books on the Olympics include Anthony Mark Jones's *The Olympic Games: Trinidad and Tobago, 1948–1988*, in which the author analyzes the importance of the games to the fledgling Caribbean nation; Rod McGeoch's *Bid: How Australia Won the 2000 Games*, which provides a good inside look at the politics that go into securing an Olympic competition; and Uyv Simson's *The Lords of the Rings: Power, Money and Drugs in the Modern Olympics*, a stunning analysis of how the use of performance-enhancing drugs has impacted recent Olympic competitions. Finally, John Findling's *Historical Dictionary of the Modern Olympic Movement* is an invaluable source of information on just about anything one might want to know about the modern Olympics.

The power of the Olympics as an economic and political force is evident in every competition. Host countries invest hundreds of millions of dollars in hopes that the games will result in improved local infrastructure and long-term financial growth. Of course, all nations revel in the glory of Olympic gold. As the world gradually transforms into a true global community, it is likely that international competitions will increase in importance and that scholars in every country will place more emphasis on the sporting practices of other nations. As various members of a technologically connected world begin to study each other via television and the internet, they will want to know more about heretofore distant peoples whose actions increasingly impact domestic matters. One thing that recent studies have proven is that sports and games, whether informal or highly organized, can be used to understand the hearts and minds of the people who play them. As distance between countries continues to shrink, the study of sport in Africa, Asia, South and Central America, Australia, Northern Europe, the Mediterranean, the Far East, and the Middle East will emerge as the most fertile and important research area for scholars. It will not be long before the average American or European needs to understand the average person from Chad, the United Arab Emirates, or the Philippines.

Scholars searching for current information on the topics covered in this chapter can consult any of the following English-language journals: *American Journal of Ancient History, Canadian Historical Review, Canadian Journal of History, Canadian Journal of Latin American and Caribbean Studies, Central European History, Chinese Studies in History, Comparative Studies in Society and History, International History Review, International Journal of the History of Sport, International Studies, Journal of Asian Studies, Journal of Japanese Studies, Journal of Latin American Studies, Journal of Northeast Asian Studies, Journal of Popular Culture, Journal of Sport and Social Issues, Journal of Sports History, Journal of World History, Modern China, Russian Studies in History, Sociology of Sport Journal,* or *Sport History Review*. Of course, scholars with proficiency in other languages might avail themselves of any of a number of fine international journals that can be accessed on SPORTSDiscus.

## REFERENCES

### Books

Allison, Lincoln, ed. *The Changing Politics of Sport*. Manchester, England: Manchester University Press, 1993.

Arbena, Joseph, ed. *Sport and Society in Latin America: Diffusion, Dependency, and the Rise of Mass Culture*. Westport, CT: Greenwood Press, 1988.

Arnaud, Pierre, and James Riordan, eds. *Sport and International Politics*. New York: E. & F. N. Spon, 1998.

Baker, William. *Sports in the Western World*. Urbana, IL: University of Illinois Press, 1988.

Baker, William, and James Mangan, eds. *Sport in Africa: Essays in Social History*. New York: Africana Publishing, 1996.

Binfield, Clyde, and John Stevenson, eds. *Sport, Culture and Politics*. Sheffield, England: Sheffield Academic Press, 1993.

Birley, Derek. *Sport and the Making of Britain*. New York: St. Martin's, 1993.

Blanchard, Kendall. *The Anthropology of Sport: An Introduction*. Westport, CT: Bergin & Garvey, 1995.

Blein, Neil. *Sport and National Identity in the European Media*. New York: St. Martin's, 1993.

Bradley, Joseph M. *Sport, Culture, Politics and Scottish Society: Irish Immigrants and the Gaelic Athletic Association*. Edinburgh, Scotland: John Donald Publishers, Ltd., 1998.

Brownell, Susan. *Training the Body for China: Sports in the Moral Order of the People's Republic*. Chicago: University of Chicago Press, 1995.

Cantelan, Hart, and Robert Hollands, eds. *Leisure, Sport and Working Class Cultures: Theory and History*. Toronto, ON: Garamond Press, 1988.

Carter, John Marshall. *Medieval Games: Sports and Recreations in Feudal Society.* Westport, CT: Greenwood Press, 1992.

Carter, John Marshall, and Arnd Kruger, eds. *Ritual and Record: Sports Records and Quantification in Pre-Modern Societies.* Westport, CT: Greenwood Press, 1990.

Cashman, Richard. *Paradise of Sport: The Rise of Organized Sport in Australia.* Melbourne, Australia: Oxford University Press, 1995.

Chalip, Laurence, ed. *National Sports Policies: An International Handbook.* Westport, CT: Greenwood Press, 1996.

Chmielewshi, Zbigniew. *Polish Sport.* Warsaw: Interpress, 1990.

Coghlan, John. *Sport and British Politics Since 1960.* London: Falmer, 1990.

Cronin, Mike, and David Mayall, eds. *Sporting Nationalisms: Identity, Ethnicity, Immigration and Assimilation.* Portland, OR: F. Cass, 1998.

Dauncey, Hugh, and Geoff Hare. *France and the 1998 World Cup: The National Impact of a World Sporting Event.* Portland, OR: F. Cass, 1999.

Decker, Wolfgang. *Sports and Games of Ancient Egypt.* Munich: C. H. Beck'sche Verlagsbuchhandlung, 1992.

DeLuca, Jeffrey. *Medieval Games.* Willimantic, CT: J. A. DeLuca, 1995.

Digel, Helmut. *Sport in a Changing Society: Sociological Essays.* Schorndorf, Germany: Karl Hoffman, 1995.

Dublin, Roman. *The Truth about the Lie: Soviet Sports Reality.* Toronto, ON: New Pathway Publishers, 1986.

Duff, Hart-Davis. *Hitler's Games: The 1936 Olympics.* New York: Harper & Row, 1986.

Duke, Vic. *Football, Nationality and the State.* New York: Addison-Wesley, 1996.

Dunning, Eric, Joseph Maguire, and Robert Pearton, eds. *The Sports Process: A Comparative and Developmental Approach.* Champaign, IL: Human Kinetics Books, 1993.

Durusken, Cigdem. *Eskicag 'da Spor.* Istanbul: Eskicag Biliinleri Enstitusu, 1995.

Edelman, Robert. *Serious Fun: A History of Spectator Sports in the USSR.* New York: Oxford University Press, 1993.

El Habashi, Zaki Ibrahim. *Tutankhamun and the Sporting Traditions.* New York: Peter Lang Publishing, 1992.

Findling, John, ed. *Historical Dictionary of the Modern Olympic Movement.* Westport, CT: Greenwood Press, 1996.

Fortuin, Rigobert. *Der Sport im Augusteischen Rom.* Stuttgart, Germany: F. Steiner, 1996.

Galeano, Eduardo. *Soccer in Sun and Shadow.* New York: Verso Press, 1998.

Goltermann, Svenja. *Korper der Nation: Habitusformierung und die Politik des Turens, 1860–1890.* Gottingen, Germany: Vandenhoech & Ruprecht, 1998.

Gratton, Chris, and Peter Taylor. *Government and the Economy of Sport.* Harlow, England: Longman Press, 1991.

Guttmann, Allen, ed. *Essays on Sport History and Sport Mythology.* Arlington, TX: University of Texas at Arlington Press, 1990.

———. *Games and Empires: Modern Sports and Cultural Imperialism.* New York: Columbia University Press, 1994.

Hargreaves, Jennifer, ed. *Sport, Culture and Ideology.* London: Routledge & Kegan Ltd, 1982.

Hargreaves, John. *Sport, Power and Culture: A Social and Historical Analysis of Popular Sports in Britain.* New York: St. Martin's, 1986.

Henricks, Thomas. *Disputed Pleasures: Sport and Society in Preindustrial England.* Westport, CT: Greenwood Press, 1991.

Hoberman, John M. *The Olympic Crisis: Sport, Politics and the Moral Order.* New Rochelle, NY: A. D. Caratzas, 1986.

————. *Sport and Political Ideology.* Austin, TX: University of Texas Press, 1984.

Holt, Richard. *Sport and the British: A Modern History.* New York: Oxford University Press, 1989.

————. *Sport and Society in Modern France.* Hamden, CT: Archon Books, 1981.

Holt, Richard, and J. A. Mangan, eds. *European Heroes: Myth, Identity, Sport.* Portland, OR: Frank Cass Publishers, 1996.

Houlihan, Barry. *The Government and Politics of Sport.* New York: Routledge, 1991.

————. *Sport and International Politics.* Paramus, NJ: PrenticeHall, 1994.

————. *Sport, Policy and Politics: A Comparative Analysis.* New York: Routledge, 1997.

Hulme, Derick L. *The Political Olympics: Moscow, Afghanistan, and the 1980 U.S. Boycott.* New York: Praeger Publishers, 1990.

Jarvie, Grant, and Graham Walker, eds. *Scottish Sport in the Making of a Nation: Ninety Minute Patriots.* Leicester, England: Leicester University Press, 1994.

Johnson, Arthur, and Frey James, eds. *Government and Sport: The Public Policy Issues.* Totowa, NJ: Rowman & Allanheld Publishers, 1985.

Jones, Anthony Mark. *The Olympic Games: Trinidad & Tobago, 1948–1988.* Baratana, Trinidad, W.I.: Educo Press, 1989.

Knuttgen, Howard, Ma Qiwei, and Wu Zhongyuan, eds. *Sport in China.* Champaign, IL: Human Kinetics Books, 1990.

Kolatch, Jonathon. *Is the Moon in China Just as Round? Sporting Life and Sundry Scenes.* Middle Village, NY: Jonathon David Publishers, 1992.

Larson, James. *Global Television and the Politics of the Seoul Olympics.* Boulder, CO: Westview Press, 1993.

Laurence, Geoffrey, ed. *Power Play: Essays in the Sociology of Australian Sport.* Sydney: Hale & Iremonger, 1986.

Lukas, Gerhard. *Der Sport im Alten Rom.* Berlin: Sportverlag, 1982.

MacClancy, Jeremy. *Sport, Identity and Ethnicity.* Oxford, England: Berg, 1996.

Mandell, Richard. *The Nazi Olympics.* Urbana, IL: University of Illinois Press, 1987.

Manetti, Giovanni. *Sport e Giochi Nell Antichita Classica.* Milan, Italy: Arnoldo Mondadori, 1988.

Mangan, J. A., ed. *The Cultural Bond: Sport, Empire, Society.* Portland, OR: Frank Cass & Co., 1992.

————. *Pleasure, Profit, Proselytism: British Culture and Sport at Home and Abroad, 1700–1914.* Portland, OR: Frank Cass & Co., 1988.

————, ed. *Tribal Identities: Nationalism, Europe, Sport.* Portland, OR: Frank Cass & Co., 1996.

Mangan, J. A., and James Walvin, eds. *Manliness and Morality: Middle-Class Masculinity in Britain and America, 1800–1940.* New York: St. Martin's, 1987.

Mason, Tony. *Sport in Britain: A Social History.* New York: Cambridge University Press, 1989.

Matz, David. *Greek and Roman Sport: A Dictionary of Athletes and Events from the Eighth Century B.C. to the Third Century A.D.* Jefferson, NC: McFarland, 1991.

McGeoch, Rod. *Bid: How Australia Won the 2000 Games.* Port Melbourne, Australia: William Heinemann Press, 1994.

McKay, James. *No Pain, No Gain: Sport in Australian Culture.* New York: PrenticeHall, 1991.

McLean, Teresa. *The English at Play: Sport in the Middle Ages.* Windsor Forest, England: The Kensal Press, 1983.

Miller, Stephen, ed. *Arete: Greek Sports from Ancient Sources.* Los Angeles: University of California Press, 1991.

Mitchell, Timothy. *Blood Sport: A Social History of Spanish Bullfighting*. Philadelphia, PA: University of Pennsylvania Press, 1990.

Moya, Frank. *Los Problemas del Deporte y La Politica Deportiva en la Republica Dominicana*. Santo Domingo, Dominican Republic: FORUM, 1988.

Muller, Stefan. *Das Volk der Athleter: Untersuchungen zur Ideologie und Kritik des Sports in der Griechisch-Romischen Antike*. Trier, Germany: Wissenschaftlicher Verlag, 1995.

Olivera, Vera. *Sports and Games in the Ancient World*. New York: St. Martin's, 1985.

Parks, Janet, Gordon Olafson, Brenda Pitts, and David Stotlar. *Sports Governance in the Global Community*. Morgantown, WV: Fitness Information Technologies, 1996.

Peppard, Victor. *Playing Politics: Soviet Sport Diplomacy to 1922*. London: JAI Press, 1993.

Pettavino, Paula. *Sport in Cuba: The Diamond in the Rough*. Pittsburgh, PA: University of Pittsburgh Press, 1994.

Plass, Paul. *The Game of Death in Ancient Rome: Arena Sport and Political Suicide*. Madison, WI: University of Wisconsin Press, 1995.

Poliakoff, Michael. *Combat Sports in the Ancient World: Competition, Violence, and Culture*. New Haven, CT: Yale University Press, 1987.

Polley, Martin. *Moving the Goalposts: A History of Sport and Society since 1945*. New York: Routledge, 1998.

Pound, Richard. *Five Rings over Korea: The Secret Negotiations behind the 1988 Olympic Games in Seoul*. Boston: Little, Brown & Co., 1994.

Powe, Edward. *Combat Games in Northern Nigeria*. Madison, WI: D. Aiki Publications, 1994.

Ramos, Roberto. *Futebol: Ideologia do Poder*. Petropolis, Brazil: Vozes, 1984.

Ramsamy, Samuel. *Apartheid: The Real Hurdle*. London: Shadowdean, Ltd., 1982.

Riordan, James. *Sport, Politics and Communism*. New York: St. Martin's, 1991.

Riordan, James, and Arnd Kruger, eds. *The History of Worker Sport*. Champaign, IL: Human Kinetics Books, 1996.

Sands, Robert R., ed. *Anthropology, Sport, and Culture*. Westport, CT: Greenwood Press, 1999.

Sansone, David. *Greek Athletics and the Genesis of Sport*. Los Angeles: University of California Press, 1988.

Senn, Alfred Erich. *Power, Politics, and the Olympic Games*. Champaign, IL: Human Kinetics Books, 1999.

Simson, Uyv. *The Lords of the Rings: Power, Money and Drugs in the Modern Olympics*. Toronto, ON: Stoddard, 1992.

Stepovoi, Pavel. *Sport, Politika, Ideologiia*. Moscow: Fizkultura i Sport, 1984.

Sugden, John. *Boxing and Society: An International Analysis*. New York: St. Martin's, 1996.

Sugden, John, and Alan Bairner. *Sport, Sectarianism, and Society in a Divided Ireland*. Leicester, England: Leicester University Press, 1993.

Sweet, Waldo. *Sport and Recreation in Ancient Greece: Sourcebook with Translations*. New York: Oxford University Press, 1987.

Thoma, James, and Laurence Chalip. *Sport Governance in the Global Community*. Morgantown, WV: Fitness Information Technologies, 1996.

Thuillier, Jean-Paul. *Le Sport dans la Rome Antique*. Paris: Editions Errance, 1996.

Tomlinson, Alan, and Garry Whannel. *Money, Power and Politics at the Olympic Games*. London: Pluto Press, 1984.

Tranter, Neil. *Sport, Economy and Society in Britain 1750–1914.* New York: Cambridge University Press, 1998.

Ueberhorst, Horst: *Welgeschichte der Leibesubungen.* 6 vols. Berlin: Bartels & Wernitz, 1986.

Vanoyeke, Violaine. *La Naissance des Jeux Olympiques et le Sport dans l'Antiquite.* Paris: Les Belles Lettres, 1992.

Vinokur, Martin. *More than a Game: Sports and Politics.* Westport, CT: Greenwood Press, 1988.

Wagner, Eric. *Sport in Asia and Africa: A Comparative Handbook.* Westport, CT: Greenwood Press, 1989.

Wallner, Christian. *Soldaten Kaiser und Sport.* Frankfurt am Main, Germany: P. Lang, 1997.

Weiler, Ingomar. *Der Sport bei den Volkern der Alten Welt.* Darmstadt, Germany: Wissenschaftliche Buchgesellschaft, 1981.

Wiedemann, Thomas. *Emporers and Gladiators.* New York: Routledge, 1995.

Wilcox, Ralph. *Sport in the Global Village.* Morgantown, WV: Fitness Information Technologies, 1994.

Wilson, John. *Playing by the Rules: Sport, Society, and the State.* Detroit, MI: Wayne State University Press, 1994.

## Journals

*American Journal of Ancient History* (Cambridge, MA)
*Canadian Historical Review* (North York, Ontario, Canada)
*Canadian Journal of History* (Saskatoon, Saskatchewan, Canada)
*Canadian Journal of Latin American and Caribbean Studies* (London, Ontario, Canada)
*Central European History* (Riverside, CA)
*Chinese Studies in History* (Armonk, NY)
*Comparative Studies in Society and History* (Ann Arbor, MI)
*International History Review* (Burnaby, British Columbia, Canada)
*International Journal of the History of Sport* (Washington, D.C.)
*International Studies* (Thousand Oaks, CA)
*Journal of Asian Studies* (Salt Lake City, UT)
*Journal of Japanese Studies* (Seattle, WA)
*Journal of Latin American Studies* (New York, NY)
*Journal of Northeast Asian Studies* (New Brunswick, NJ)
*Journal of Popular Culture* (Bowling Green, OH)
*Journal of Sport and Social Issues* (Thousand Oaks, CA)
*Journal of Sports History* (University Park, PA)
*Journal of World History* (Honolulu, HI)
*Modern China* (Thousand Oaks, CA)
*Russian Studies in History* (Armonk, NY)
*Sociology of Sport Journal* (Champaign, IL)
*Sport History Review* (Champaign, IL)

# Appendix 1

# Important Events in American Sports: 1980–2000

The following dates include events that might be considered to be socially, economically, or politically significant. Thus, many "big games" or records usually deemed important are omitted.

## 1980

Feb. 22   The U.S. Olympic hockey team upsets the Soviet Union en route to the gold medal. The victory signals the beginning of a remarkable period of growth for hockey in the United States.

Apr. 12   Cold war politics rears its ugly head as the United States officially pulls out of the 1980 Olympic summer games in Moscow.

Apr. 21   Rosie Ruiz jumps out of the crowd to "win" the Boston Marathon. Despite an attempt to convince the public that she actually ran the entire race, Ruiz is discredited at the awards dinner in one of the most bizarre episodes in the history of running.

May   3   Genuine Risk becomes the first filly in sixty-five years to win the Kentucky Derby.

## 1981

June  12   Major League Baseball players go on strike over free-agent compensation. The strike causes the cancellation of much of the season and plays a major role in the disillusionment of fans with the national pastime.

**1982**

Nov. 16    The longest strike in NFL history ends after fifty-seven days. A five-year agreement between players and owners marks the end of one of the most bitter work stoppages in league history.

**1983**

Nov. 17    Willie Wilson, Willie Aikens, and Jerry Martin become the first active baseball players to be sent to prison when they are sentenced to three months in jail for attempting to purchase cocaine.

**1984**

Feb. 1    David Stern becomes the fourth commissioner of the NBA. Over the next fifteen years, he will lead the league to unprecedented heights.

Mar. 3    Major League Baseball selects former Olympic president Peter Ueberroth as its sixth commissioner.

Mar. 19    Former Detroit Tiger ace Denny McLain is named on a five-count federal indictment. Charges include bookmaking and intent to distribute cocaine. McLain is later convicted.

Mar. 28    Baltimore Colt owner Robert Irsay becomes public enemy number one in Maryland when he moves the team to Indianapolis in the middle of the night.

**1985**

Feb. 23    Indiana basketball coach Bobby Knight throws a chair across the court in a game at Purdue. The incident draws national attention and raises questions about the role of collegiate sport in American society.

Apr. 2    The NCAA adopts a policy to implement a forty-five-second shot clock for all college basketball games. The NCAA is after faster, more entertaining games that will generate more interest and money.

Apr. 3    In search of more post-season revenue, Major League Baseball expands its championship series from five to seven games.

Apr. 4    Tulane University decides to drop its basketball program after several of its players are indicted in a point-shaving scandal.

June  30    The new Basketball Hall of Fame opens in Springfield, Massachu-
            setts.

Nov.  13    Lynette Woodard makes history when she becomes the first woman
            to play for the Harlem Globetrotters.

## 1986

Jan.  13    The NCAA adopts Proposition 48, establishing minimum grade point
            averages and SAT scores for freshmen who want to participate in
            Division I athletics.

Feb.  28    Major League commissioner Peter Ueberroth suspends seven players
            for one year because they violated the league's drug policy. The
            players are offered a chance to avoid suspension via financial
            donations, but the ruling is representative of a growing concern over
            the influence of drugs in sports.

Mar.  21    Skater Debi Thomas becomes the first black American to win a world
            figure skating championship.

Apr.   2    The NCAA adopts the three-point shot as part of its men's basketball
            games.

June  19    All-American basketball player Len Bias dies of a drug overdose
            only two days after being selected by the Boston Celtics.

July  27    Cyclist Greg LeMond becomes the first American, indeed the first
            non-European, to win the Tour de France.

Aug.   4    The U.S. Football League suspends operation. The league had begun
            play in 1983 in an attempt to create a rival league to the NFL.

## 1987

Feb.  25    Southern Methodist University is given the "death penalty" for
            repeated violations of NCAA rules. The ruling underscores the
            rampant corruption in collegiate football and basketball.

Apr.   8    Los Angeles Dodger executive Al Campanis is fired after making
            racist remarks on network television. Campanis stated that blacks
            lacked the "necessities" to be in managerial positions. Ironically, the
            incident acts as a catalyst for reform that would change the hiring
            practices in professional sports.

June    4    The longest winning streak in track and field history comes to an end in Madrid when Danny Harris beats Edwin Moses in the 400-meter hurdles. Moses had won 122 races in a row.

Sep.   22    The National Football League Player's Association interrupts the season by going on strike to procure greater free agent rights.

**1988**

Jan.   16    CBS-TV fires Jimmy "The Greek" Snyder because of derogatory comments he made about blacks during a Washington, D.C. television interview.

Jan.   22    Seven major league players are declared no-risk free agents as a result of arbitrator Thomas Roberts's collusion ruling in favor of the Major League Players Association. The ruling forced owners to make independent bids for free agent players.

Mar.   15    St. Louis Cardinal owner Bill Bidwell gets clearance to move his team to Phoenix, Arizona.

Aug.    8    Wrigley Field plays host to a night baseball game for the first time in its history.

Aug.    9    Edmonton Oiler star Wayne Gretzky is traded to the Los Angeles Kings for draft picks, players, and $10 million. The trade signifies the beginning of a trend that features small market teams selling stars to large market teams so that they can stay in business. The trend would eventually lead to competitive imbalances in most professional leagues.

Sep.   27    Canadian sprinter Ben Johnson is stripped of his recently won Olympic gold medal after he tests positive for performance-enhancing drugs.

**1989**

Feb.    2    Bill White is selected as the thirteenth president of the National League, becoming the highest ranking black executive in professional sports.

Mar.   22    Pete Rozelle retires as commissioner of the NFL. He is credited with making the NFL into the most profitable professional league in the country.

May    4      Soviet hockey star Alexander Mogilny becomes the second Red Army player to defect to the United States. Within the next few years, the former Soviet players will radically impact the NHL.

June   5      The state-of-the-art SkyDome opens in Toronto. With its cutting edge technology and many amenities, the new home of the Toronto Blue Jays is a forerunner for the new ballparks of the 1990s.

June   19     Oklahoma Sooner football coach Barry Switzer resigns under a cloud of scandal that will eventually put the school's program on probation. Switzer's resignation is symbolic of the 1980s and 1990s when greed and pressure to win causes rampant corruption in college sports.

Sep.   1      A. Bartlett Giamatti, the commissioner of Major League Baseball, dies of a heart attack at his home in Martha's Vineyard.

Oct.   3      Art Shell makes history when he becomes the NFL's first black coach when he takes control of the Los Angeles Raiders.

Oct.   16     The World Series is suspended after an earthquake interrupts game 3 in San Francisco.

Nov.   3      The NBA welcomes its first Russian players, Saunas Marciulionis of Golden State and Alexander Volkov of Atlanta.

Dec.   9      The NHL votes to expand from twenty-one to twenty-eight teams by the year 2000.

**1990**

Mar.   1      Looking to expand profits, the NFL expands its playoff field from ten to twelve teams.

July   19     Baseball star Pete Rose is sentenced to five months in prison for tax evasion. Rose had failed to report income from the sale of baseball memorabilia. He had previously been banned from the game for life for gambling on baseball games.

Oct.   5      NFL Commissioner Paul Tagliabue fines Cincinnati coach Sam Wyche for refusing to allow a female reporter into the locker room.

Dec.   7      The NHL grants franchises to Ottawa, Ontario, and Tampa, Florida.

**1991**

Mar. 23    The NFL expands to Europe, and the World League of American Football plays its first game. The London Monarchs beat the Frankfurt Galaxy 24–11.

May 19    Willie T. Ribbs becomes the first black driver to qualify for the Indianapolis 500.

June 10    Denver and Miami are awarded Major League Baseball franchises. They pay a record $95 million entry fee for the right to play.

**1992**

Jan. 8    The NCAA toughens its requirements for Proposition 48 by raising the number of college preparatory courses and the minimum grade-point average incoming freshmen need to qualify for participation in the various sports.

Jan. 10    The Minnesota Vikings become only the second team in the history of the NFL to hire a black head coach, Dennis Green of Stanford University.

Feb. 9    Basketball star Magic Johnson shocks the world with an admission that he is retiring from the game after being diagnosed with the HIV virus.

Feb. 10    Former boxing champion Mike Tyson is convicted of raping an eighteen-year-old girl.

Sep. 10    A Minneapolis jury declares that the NFL's "Plan B" free agency system is unconstitutional. The ruling clears the way for unrestricted free agency in the NFL, precipitating spiraling ticket prices and player salaries.

Dec. 10    The NHL adds franchises in San Jose, California, and Miami, Florida.

**1993**

Feb. 1    Gary Bettman opens his first term as the commissioner of the NHL.

Feb. 6    Tennis star and author Arthur Ashe dies of AIDS, again bringing the disease to the national stage.

Mar. 10     Minnesota North Stars owner Norman Green finalizes a deal to move the franchise to Dallas, Texas, continuing the long exodus of professional teams in search of more money.

Apr. 30     A deranged Steffi Graf fan stabs tennis star Monica Seles in the back during a match in Hamburg, Germany.

Oct. 6     Basketball star Michael Jordan retires for the first time to pursue a career in baseball.

Nov. 4     The NBA admits Toronto into the fold for a record $125 million entry fee.

Nov. 30     The NFL admits Jacksonville and Carolina for $140 million apiece.

Dec. 17     FOX stuns CBS by bidding the outrageous sum of $1.58 billion for rights to broadcast the NFL for four years. It is widely known that FOX will lose millions on the deal but went forward with the offer anyway because having the NFL on the network was thought to be prestigious enough to warrant the huge financial loss.

## 1994

Jan. 6     Ice skater Nancy Kerrigan is attacked in Detroit, Michigan, after a practice session. It is later revealed that rival Tonya Harding is connected to the attack.

Mar. 16     Ice skater Tonya Harding, famous for her involvement in an assault on rival Nancy Kerrigan, ends her career when she pleads guilty to a felony charge.

July 17     The United States completes its first stint as host of the World Cup of Soccer. The event is so successful that it spawns a new professional league in the United States.

Aug. 12     Major League Baseball announces the strike that will eventually cancel the World Series, bringing baseball's popularity to an all-time low.

Sep. 13     Continuing its spending spree, FOX spends $155 million to broadcast NHL games for four years. The network overbids by at least $60 million.

Sep.  14    As the result of its ongoing war with its players, Major League
            Baseball officially cancels the World Series.

Dec.  6     CBS pays $1.75 billion for rights to the NCAA Men's basketball
            tournament through the year 2002.

**1995**

Jan.  11    NHL owners end a lockout that threatened to cancel the entire
            season. The owners get more restrictions on free agency.

Jan.  26    President Bill Clinton threatens government intervention if major
            league owners cannot settle the baseball strike that canceled the 1994
            World Series.

Feb.  7     Students force the cancellation of a college basketball game at
            Rutgers University after President Francis Lawrence makes contro-
            versial racial remarks. Hundreds of students stage a sit-in at half-time
            of the game, refusing to leave the floor at the start of the second half.

Apr.  25    After 252 days, the baseball strike that canceled the World Series
            ends, but replacement umpires are used because the regular umpires
            are still on strike.

July  29    The NHL announces that its players will be allowed to participate in
            the 1998 Olympics.

July  31    Walt Disney Co. announces plans to acquire Capital Cities/ABC for
            $19 billion. The move gives Disney control of both ABC Sports and
            ESPN.

Aug.  7     Proving that you can go home again if you are paid enough money,
            Al Davis signs a sixteen-year deal to take the Raiders back to
            Oakland, California.

Oct.  12    The Wisconsin legislature approves $250 million in public funding
            for Miller Park, the new home of the Milwaukee Brewers. The move
            is representative of actions in many American cities in which public
            funds are spent to finance stadiums for millionaire owners and
            players.

Nov.  6     Cleveland Browns owner Ar Modell announces plans to move the
            club to Baltimore, Maryland. The Browns are regarded as one of the
            most stable franchises in the league and the move sends shock waves
            through the world of professional sports.

Dec.  12    NBC bids a record $2.3 billion for the right to broadcast the 2004 and
            2008 Summer Olympic Games and the 2006 Winter Games.

## 1996

Jan.   3    North Korea accepts an invitation to the Summer Olympic Games in
            Atlanta, Georgia. The acceptance means that for the first time in the
            history of the games all invited nations will attend.

Mar.  12    Mahmoud Abdul Rauf refuses to stand for the national anthem before
            an NBA game in Colorado because he says that the song celebrates
            a country that discriminates against Moslems.

Apr.   6    Major League Soccer begins play on the heels of the highly success-
            ful World Cup competition in the United States in 1994.

Apr.  30    The Houston Oilers announce that the franchise will move to
            Tennessee because the city of Houston will not build the team a new
            stadium.

May    5    Cincinnati Reds owner Marge Schott stuns baseball fans when she
            praises Adolph Hitler. Schott will be fined and eventually suspended
            by her fellow owners.

May   25    Christian Sanches impresses the world when she becomes the first
            woman to earn the rank of matador.

June  26    At Wimbledon, Mary Carilo, Billy Jean King, and Martina Navra-
            tolova become the first all-women broadcast team to cover a major
            sporting event.

Oct.  10    The US Department of Justice files suit against Ellerbe, Beckett, Inc.
            for designing stadiums that are inaccessible to handicapped persons.

## 1997

Feb.  20    Barry Bonds signs a two-year, $22.9 million deal with the San
            Francisco Giants. The deal is the richest in league history but will
            soon be dwarfed by other deals as salaries spiral upward.

Mar.  19    Displaying once again the fact that corporate America controls sports
            in the United States, Pepsi signs a five-year, $50 million deal to
            sponsor Major League Baseball.

May     6   The Hartford Whalers announce that the club will move to North
            Carolina. The move underscores the problem that small market teams
            have trying to survive in the big money era of professional sports.

June   18   High school basketball star Tracy McGrady signs a $12 million
            endorsement deal with Nike. It is another signal that sports is out of
            control in the United States.

June   21   The Women's National Basketball League debuts in New York City
            with the hometown Liberty defeating the Los Angeles Sparks, 67–57.

June   28   The dismal state of the world of boxing is exposed again when Mike
            Tyson is disqualified for twice biting the ears of Evander Holyfield
            during a bout.

June   30   Paul Allen, the billionaire co-founder of Microsoft, buys the Seattle
            Seahawks for $200 million. The record price reveals the inflated
            value of professional sports franchises.

Oct.    1   Kevin Garnett, a twenty-year-old forward for the NBA's Minnesota
            Timberwolves, signs a six-year, $125 million deal, the richest in the
            history of sports at the time.

**1998**

Jan.   11   Casey Martin uses a golf cart to win a Nike sponsored golf tourna-
            ment. Martin eventually sues the PGA and wins. He becomes the first
            disabled golfer to use a cart on the PGA tour.

Sep.   20   Cal Ripken's consecutive game streak ends at 2,632.

Sep.   27   Mark McGwire sets a new major league home run record with 70.

Oct.    1   The National Basketball Association suffers its first lockout in league
            history. It will cancel nearly half of the season.

Oct.   16   Venus Williams serves a tennis ball at 127 miles per hour; the fastest-
            ever serve in women's tennis.

**1999**

July   10   The United States defeats China, 1–0, to win the 1999 Women's
            World Cup of Soccer. The event is a watershed moment in women's
            sports history as the final game draws a record crowd of 90,185, as
            well as a huge television audience.

# Appendix 2

# Halls of Fame, Libraries, Museums, Periodicals, and Web Sites

## HALLS OF FAME, LIBRARIES, AND MUSEUMS

In his 1980 work, *Sports: A Reference Guide*, Jack Higgs includes detailed descriptions of various sports halls of fame and museums and libraries that house collections of sports artifacts. Over the last twenty years, there has not only been a proliferation of these repositories, but several good reference books that chronicle their addresses and contents have also appeared on the scene. The repositories are so numerous and the reference books so complete that it would be redundant for me to simply relist the material here. Thus, I have included only a short list of easily accessible reference works that contain the names and locations of nearly any resource area that a scholar might need to access.

For information on the hundreds of sports halls of fame that exist in the United States, one should consult Doug Gilbert's *Sports Halls of Fame: A Directory of Over 100 Sports Museums in the USA*, Paul Dickson's *The Volvo Guide to Halls of Fame: The Traveler's Handbook of North America's Most Inspiring and Entertaining Attractions*, or Victor Danilov's *Hall of Fame Museums: A Reference Guide*. For information on museums and libraries, one should consult Gretchen Ghent and Wayne Wilson's *North American Sport Library Network Sports Collection: A Selective Guide to Notable Resources in American and Canadian Libraries, Halls of Fame and Museums* or Matthew Rosenberger's *Sports Resource Directory*. Other important guides include Darren Smith's *Sports Phone Book USA: A National Directory of Professional, Intercollegiate, and Amateur Sports*, Edward Kobac's *The Comprehensive Directory of Sports Addresses III: The Global Sports Reference Guide for Everyone's Library*, and Mark Larson's *Complete Guide to Football, Basketball and Hockey Memorabilia*, a comprehensive book that includes many important addresses of relatively obscure places in North America in which sport memorabilia collections are located.

## PERIODICALS DEVOTED EXCLUSIVELY TO SPORT

*Aethlon: The Journal of Sport Literature* (Johnson City, TN)
*American Fitness* (Sydney, Australia)
*American Fitness Quarterly* (Dublin, OH)
*American Journal of Health Promotion* (Lawrence, KS)
*American Journal of Sports Medicine* (Waltham, MA)
*American Sports* (Rosemead, CA)
*Annals of Sports Medicine* (Hollywood, CA)
*Applied Research in Coaching and Athletics Annual* (Boston, MA)
*Athletic Business* (New York, NY)
*Athletics Administration* (Lexington, KY)
*Athletics Coach* (Peterborough, England)
*Athletics Weekly* (Peterborough, England)
*Australian Society for Sports History Bulletin* (Sydney, Australia)
*Baseball Research Journal* (Cleveland, OH)
*Biology of Sport* (Warsaw, Poland)
*Bowlers Journal International* (Chicago, IL)
*Brazilian International Journal of Adapted Physical Education Research* (Fort
    Worth, TX)
*British Journal of Physical Education* (London, England)
*British Journal of Sports Medicine* (Oxford, England)
*Bulletin D' Information Sportive* (Bruxelles, Belgium)
*China Sports* (Beijing, China)
*Chinese Journal of Sports Medicine* (Beijing, China)
*Chinese Sports Science and Technology* (Beijing, China)
*Clinical Journal of Sport Medicine* (Hagerstown, MD)
*Coaching and Sport Science Journal* (Rome, Italy)
*Contemporary Sport* (Amherst, MA)
*Cornerstones: A Fitness, Facility & Recreation Management Journal*
    (Mississauga, Ontario, Canada)
*Detroit College of Law Entertainment and Sports Law Forum* (Detroit, MI)
*Drugs in Sports* (Warkworth, Ontario, Canada)
*European Journal for Sport Management* (Groningen, The Netherlands)
*European Journal of Physical Education* (West Malling, England)
*European Physical Education Review* (Nafferton, England)
*Exercise & Society Journal of Sport Science* (Komotini, Greece)
*Exercise and Sport Sciences Review* (Baltimore, MD)
*Golf & Life* (Melbourne, Australia)
*Golf World* (London, England)
*Illinois Journal for Health, Physical Education, Recreation and Dance*
    (Champaign, IL)
*Inside Sports* (Evanston, IL)
*International Journal of the History of Sport* (Washington, D.C.)
*International Journal of Physical Education* (Schorndorf, Germany)

*International Journal of Sport Nutrition* (Champaign, IL)
*International Journal of Sports Psychology* (Rome, Italy)
*International Review for the Sociology of Sport* (London, England)
*International Sports Journal* (West Haven, CT)
*Interscholastic Athletic Administration* (Kansas City, MO)
*Journal of Applied Physiology* (Bethesda, MD)
*Journal of Applied Recreation Research* (Waterloo, ON)
*Journal of Applied Sport Science Research* (Champaign, IL)
*Journal of Applied Sports Psychology* (West Lafayette, IN)
*Journal of Athletic Training* (Dallas, TX)
*Journal of Interdisciplinary Research in Physical Education* (Dubuque, IA)
*Journal of Legal Aspects of Sports* (New York, NY)
*Journal of Leisure Research* (Ashburn, VA)
*Journal of Olympic History* (Oosterwolde, The Netherlands)
*Journal of Park and Recreation Administration* (Champaign, IL)
*Journal of Physical Education* (Reston, VA)
*Journal of Physical Education, Recreation and Dance* (Reston, VA)
*Journal of Physiology* (Cambridge, England)
*Journal of Sport & Exercise Psychology* (Champaign, IL)
*Journal of Sport and Social Issues* (Thousand Oaks, CA)
*Journal of Sport Behavior* (Mobile, AL)
*Journal of Sport History* (University Park, PA)
*Journal of Sport Rehabilitation* (Champaign, IL)
*Journal of Sports Management* (Champaign, IL)
*Journal of Sports Medicine and Physical Fitness* (Torino, Italy)
*Journal of Sports Philately* (La Grange, IL)
*Journal of Sports Sciences* (London, England)
*Journal of Strength and Conditioning Research* (Champaign, IL)
*Journal of Teaching and Physical Education* (Champaign, IL)
*Journal of the Philosophy of Sport* (Champaign, IL)
*Marquette Sports Law Journal* (Marquette, MI)
*Media Sports Business* (New York, NY)
*Modern Athlete and Coach* (Athlestone, Australia)
*NCAA News* (Overland, Park, KS)
*NCAA Sports Sciences Education Newsletter* (Overland Park, KS)
*New Zealand Journal of Sports Medicine* (Auckland, NZ)
*Nine: A Journal of Baseball History and Social Policy Perspectives* (Edmonton,
    Alberta, Canada)
*Peak Performance* (London, England)
*Pedagogy in Practice: Teaching and Coaching in Physical Education and Sports*
    (Plymouth, England)
*Physical Educator* (Indianapolis, IN)
*Physician and Sports Medicine* (New York, NY)
*The Physician and Sports Medicine* (Minneapolis, MN)
*Physiotherapy in Sport* (London, England)

*Research Quarterly for Exercise and Sport* (Reston, VA)
*Revue Olympique* (Lausanne, France)
*Ring* (Ambler, PA)
*Rugby World* (London, England)
*Runner's World* (Emmaus, PA)
*Running Research News* (Lansing, MI)
*SABR Bulletin* (Cleveland, OH)
*Sailing World* (Newport, RI)
*Scandinavian Journal of Medicine & Sciences in Sports* (Copenhagen, Denmark)
*Schole: A Journal of Leisure Studies and Recreation Education* (Ashburn, VA)
*Science & Sports* (Paris, France)
*Seton Hall Journal of Sport Law* (New York, NY)
*SGB: Sporting Goods Business* (San Francisco, CA)
*Ski Research News* (Eagle River, WI)
*Soccer Journal* (Mission, KS)
*Sociology of Sport Journal* (Champaign, IL)
*Sport* (New York, NY)
*Sport, Education and Society* (Abington, England)
*Sport Educator* (Canberra, Australia)
*Sport Health* (Pennant Hills, NSW, Australia)
*Sport History* (Leesburg, VA)
*Sport History Review* (Champaign, IL)
*Sport Science Review* (Champaign, IL)
*SportEurope* (Rome, Italy)
*Sporting Heritage* (Bickley, England)
*Sporting Traditions* (Bedford Park, Australia)
*Sports and the Courts* (Winston-Salem, NC)
*Sports Business* (Woodbridge, Ontario, Canada)
*Sports Historian* (London, England)
*Sports Illustrated* (New York, NY)
*Sports in Japan* (Tokyo, Japan)
*Sports inc.* (New York, NY)
*Sports Law Administration & Practice* (London, England)
*Sports Law & Finance* (London, England)
*The Sports Lawyer* (Miami, FL)
*Sports Marketing Quarterly* (Chicago, IL)
*Sports Medicine Digest* (Van Nuys, CA)
*Sports Medicine Update* (Birmingham, AL)
*Sports, Parks and Recreation Law Reporter* (Canton, OH)
*Sports Psychology* (Champaign, IL)
*SportsTech* (New York, NY)
*Spotlight on Youth Sports* (East Lansing, MI)
*Teaching Elementary Physical Education* (Champaign, IL)
*Teaching Secondary Physical Education* (Champaign, IL)
*University of Miami Entertainment and Sports Law Review* (Miami, FL)

*Villanova Sports and Entertainment Law Journal* (Villanova, PA)
*Women in Sport* (Adelaide, Australia)
*Women in Sport and Physical Activity Journal* (Fort Worth, TX)
*Women's Sport and Fitness* (Boulder, CO)
*World Badminton* (Cheltenham, England)
*World Leisure and Recreation* (Lethbridge, Alberta, Canada)
*World of Gymnastics* (Moutier, France)
*World Soccer* (London, England)
*World Weightlifting* (Budapest, Hungary)


## WEB SITES DEVOTED TO SPORT

The following sites were chosen for two reasons. First, they all represent important research areas within sport studies. Second, they are all "mega sites," sites that contain links to hundreds or even thousands of other related sites. For books that provide extensive information on doing sports research on the web, one should consult Terry Fain's *A Pocket Tour of Sports on the Internet* or Bob Temple's *Sports on the Net.*

| | |
|---|---|
| aafla.org | Web library for world sport |
| aahperd.org | American Alliance for Health, Physical Education, Recreation and Dance |
| aausports.org | Amateur Athletic Union |
| acsm.org | American College of Sports Medicine |
| allstarsites.com | Links to major sites for most sports |
| asama.com | American sports art museum archives |
| british-athletics.co.uk | Sports in Britain |
| clubsites.com | Sites for hundreds of sports clubs, both private and public, in North America |
| coachingstaff.com | Resources for coaches |
| crestcomm.com | Sports federations in North America |
| csi.ukns.com/sports | Sports in Australia |
| dmu.ac.uk | Sports philosophy sites |
| eas.ualberta.edu | Academy of Leisure Sciences |
| espn.com | Site of sport broadcasting giant ESPN |
| ets.uidaho.edu | History of sport philosophy |
| eurosport.com | Information on European sports media |
| exploratorium.edu/sports | Sports and science |
| fhw.gr/prjects/olympics | Olympic history |
| fiat.gslis.utexas.edu | Women's sports history |
| geocities.com/Colosseum | Sports media sites |
| hickoksports.com | Sports history sites for North American sports |
| iis-sports.com | Interactive sports sites |
| infohub.com | Recreational sports opportunities |
| ivanhoe.com/sportsmed | Sports medicine sites |

| | |
|---|---|
| justwright.com | World Wide Web Virtual Sports Library |
| megasports.com | Massive site for current sports news |
| mentalhelp.net | Sports psychology sites and information |
| nba.com | Official site of the National Basketball League |
| ncaa.org | Information on all intercollegiate sport activity |
| negroleaguebaseball.com | History of the Negro Leagues and black baseball |
| nfl.com | Official site of the National Football League |
| nhl.com | Official site of the National Hockey League |
| nsl.org | National Sports Library—horse and field sports |
| oldsport.com | Sports history sites |
| olympics.tufts.edu | Sites on the Ancient Olympics |
| olywa.net/jas/index.html | Women's writing on women's sport |
| parkland.cc.il.us | Sports psychology resources |
| pch.gc.ca | Information on sports in Canada |
| racegate.com | Track and field sites |
| runnersweb.com | Site for runners and outdoor athletes |
| sirc.ca | General sports information center with several links |
| sportcal.co.uk | International sports sites |
| sportingnews.com | Latest information on American sports |
| sportlink.com | Search engine for many sports sites |
| SPORTquest.com | Search engine for many sports sites |
| sportsdogs.com | Search engine for many sports sites |
| sportsearch.com | Search engine for many sports sites |
| sportsgateway.com | Search engine for many sports sites |
| sportsjones.com | Interactive site that features both popular and academic topics |
| sportsmedicine.com | Latest information on sports medicine |
| sportsplaces.com | Links to many sports sites |
| streetplay.com | History of street games in the United States |
| tc.umn.edu | Physical education resources |
| tns.Ics.mit.edu | World Wide Web of Sports |
| white.media.mit.edu | Latest information on sports technology from MIT |
| worldsport.com | Information center for sports around the world |
| yahoo.com (sports) | Exhaustive search engine for thousands of sports-related sites on many topics |

## REFERENCES

### Books

Danilov, Victor. *Hall of Fame Museums: A Reference Guide*. Westport, CT: Greenwood Press, 1997.

Dickson, Paul. *The Volvo Guide to Halls of Fame: The Traveler's Handbook of North America's Most Inspiring and Entertaining Attractions*. Washington, D.C.: Living Planet Press, 1995.

Faiu, Terry. *A Pocket Tour of Sports on the Internet*. San Francisco, CA: Sybex, 1995.

Ghent, Gretchen, and Wayne Wilson, eds. *North American Sports Library Network Sports Collections: A Selective Guide to Notable Resources in American and Canadian Libraries, Halls of Fame and Museums.* Calgary, AB: North American Sport Library Network, 1990.

Gilbert, Doug. *Sports Halls of Fame: A Directory of Over 100 Sports Museums in the USA.* Jefferson, NC: McFarland, 1992.

Kobac, Edward. *The Comprehensive Directory of Sports Addresses III: The Global Sports Reference Guide for Everyone's Library.* Santa Monica, CA: Global Sports Productions, 1987.

Larson, Mark. *Complete Guide to Football, Basketball and Hockey Memorabilia.* Iola, WI: Krause Publications, 1995.

Rosenberger, Matthew. *Sports Resource Directory.* Chicago: MGR Enterprises, 1993.

Smith, Darren. *Sports Phone Book USA: A National Directory of Professional, Intercollegiate, and Amateur Sports.* New York: Omnigraphics, 1998.

Temple, Bob. *Sports on the Net.* Indianapolis, IN: Que, 1995.

## Databases

SPORTSDiscus                    The only research database dedicated to sports

# Index

**About the Author**

DONALD L. DEARDORFF II is an English Professor at Cedarville College, Ohio.